CANADA:

A TASTE OF HOME / LES SAVEURS DE CHEZ SOI

GUERNICA WORLD EDITIONS 66

CANADA:

A TASTE OF HOME / LES SAVEURS DE CHEZ SOI

Edited by Ylenia De Luca
and Oriana Palusci

GUERNICA
World
EDITIONS

TORONTO—CHICAGO—BUFFALO—LANCASTER (U.K.)
2022

Guernica Editions Founder: Antonio D'Alfonso

Michael Mirolla, editor
Interior design: Jill Ronsley, suneditwrite.com
Cover design: Allen Jomoc Jr.

Guernica Editions Inc.
287 Templemead Drive, Hamilton (ON), Canada L8W 2W4
2250 Military Road, Tonawanda, N.Y. 14150-6000 U.S.A.
www.guernicaeditions.com

Distributors:
Independent Publishers Group (IPG)
600 North Pulaski Road, Chicago IL 60624
University of Toronto Press Distribution (UTP)
5201 Dufferin Street, Toronto (ON), Canada M3H 5T8
Gazelle Book Services, White Cross Mills
High Town, Lancaster LA1 4XS U.K.

First edition.
Printed in Canada.

Legal Deposit—Third Quarter
Library of Congress Catalog Card Number: 2022939987
Library and Archives Canada Cataloguing in Publication
Title: Canada : a taste of home = les saveurs de chez soi /
edited by Ylenia De Luca and Oriana Palusci.
Other titles: Canada (Guernica (Firm))
Names: De Luca, Ylenia, editor. | Palusci, Oriana, editor.
Series: Guernica world editions ; 66.
Description: Series statement: Guernica world editions ; 66 |
Text in English and French.
Identifiers: Canadiana (print) 20220258643E |
Canadiana (ebook) 20220258708E | ISBN 9781771838252 (softcover) |
ISBN 9781771838269 (EPUB)
Subjects: LCSH: International cooking. | LCSH: Ethnic food industry—
Canada. | LCSH: Cultural pluralism—Canada.
Classification: LCC TX725.A1 C36 2022 | DDC 641.59—dc23

TABLE OF CONTENTS

INTRODUCTION

A Taste of Home in Multiethnic Canada

CALIBAN: I must eat my dinner
(*The Tempest* I.ii.332).

She described the dish and I knew
instantly I had found a lost taste (Wah, 1996).

THE CONSUMPTION OF FOOD, TOGETHER with interconnected
human activities coming before and after ingestion (hunting, harvesting, fruit-picking, slaughtering and cooking; or packaging,
shopping, freezing, laying the table, up to the unpleasantness of
stomach pains, vomit, excretion, etc.), is one of the most crucial
events marking the life of the individuals and of a community.
Ethnic, local, imported foods compete on our table, are advertised,
compared, discussed and sometimes banned. Nutritional, medical,
psychological, socio-economical treatises lead the way towards the
more sophisticated and selective treatments of visual arts, creative
literature, movies. Literature has employed food or the symbolism
of food in many different environments, ranging from the celebration of good, healthy, sometimes divine, food to the horrible
fantasizing of cannibalistic rituals.

Usually connected to local, social and cultural dynamics, as
well as to production, distribution and consumption processes,
food is one of the most powerful means of communication. The
representation of food is embedded in cultural, symbolic and metaphoric webs located within imaginative spheres. In Canada, one of

1

the most multicultural countries in the world, where most people are connected to a range of cuisines from elsewhere, diverse food customs (both every day and festive ways of eating) multiply and intertwine, resulting in hybridity and fusion, appropriation and adaptation. Indeed, a certain culinary tradition, once on Canadian soil, may in some way 'resist' inside a family ethnic kitchen, but once outside in a restaurant, such a tradition is bound to be negotiated with local tastes, while being perceived as "ethnic".

Different food cultures and other hybrid procedures, from the Atlantic to the Pacific coast, testify to how foodstuff, identity, cultural belonging and terminology are deeply interconnected, reiterating the affective value of what one eats. As Mannur affirms, for diasporic peoples "food becomes both intellectual and emotional anchor" (2007: 11). Food fare is also at the centre of the performative production of gender and ethnic bodies, of power relations and of cultural practices as sites of resistance. Thus, food is to be seen as an open window onto different traditions, culinary skills, strange ingredients, tastes and flavors. Indigenous food and cultural discourses also articulate the projection of divergent ideologies and worldviews, from the act of supplying food to the relationship with the land and the body.

In a multiethnic and multicultural country such as Canada the choice and consumption of food have been the battlefield between ancient Indigenous traditions and the diverse tastes of the European conquerors, and later on a bone of contention among many different ethnic communities, migrating to Canada and bringing with them their national and regional culinary habits as well as family recipes.

In the history of literature, as Sandra M. Gilbert states in *The Culinary Imagination: from Myth to Modernity* (2014), narratives take their nourishment from food and, at the same time, the inclusion of food seems to nurture literary characters, suffice it to think of some of the iconic culinary episodes in fiction. Among the many books on literary Food Studies, a comprehensive overview, reflecting on its origins, developments, and applications is offered in *Food and Literature* (2018), edited by Gitanjali G. Shahani. Besides, the following journals have highlighted the importance of culinary research in contemporary societies: *Food, Culture and Society. An International Journal on Multidisciplinary Research* and, even more specifically, within Canadian cultures, *Canadian Food Studies / La Revue canadienne des études sur l'alimentation* and *CuiZine: The Journal of Canadian Food Cultures / Revue des cultures culinaires au Canada*. It is worth noticing that food and migration have been extensively investigated in the context of American literature and culture (Gabaccia 1998), and especially in the field of specific ethnic groups; for instance, on Asian diasporic cultures (Mannur 2009; Ji-Song Ku *et al.* 2013), or on Italian, Irish and Jewish migrants (Diner 2001). Surprisingly not enough has been published about the same issue in Canada.

The relevance of the discourse on food in Canadian cultures is underlined, among others, by Margaret Atwood. At the beginning of her long and rewarding career, she identifies Canada itself, adding a subversive touch, as a fat home-baked female body—and vice versa—to be chewed and swallowed (*The Edible Woman*, 1969). Without doubt, her novels and poems are replete with references to food, suffice here to mention her most recent "eustopian" novels, interwoven in the MaddAddam trilogy, in which the search and supply of edible goods has become terribly difficult, yet indispensable in order to survive in a highly contaminated world. Atwood's longstanding interest in the representation of literary food is recorded in her edited anthology *The Canlit Foodbook: From Pen to Palate—A Collection of Tasty Literary Fare* (1987), in which she extracts recipes from prose and poetry, putting together not a traditional cookbook, but setting 'imaginary' tables where characters select, taste, desire, reject dishes:

> Standard cookbooks put various foods in because they taste good, or are good for you, authors put them in because they reveal character, slimy as well as delectable, or provide metaphors or jumping-off points into the ineffable or to the inferno (Atwood 1987: 2).

Atwood envisages ethnic groups in Canadian kitchens, introducing the question of food, cultural practices and identity:

> A lot can be conveyed, too, about one ethnic group's views of another by the way they react to each other's treasured foodstuffs: as more than one author reminds us, one man's sea-squirt is another's *hors-d'oeuvre* (Atwood 1987: 2).

Ethnic cuisines in Canada do not reflect only a globalised trend to eat the food of 'the others', that is the lure of alien or exotic cooking, because the country is peopled by immigrants. As already mentioned, we must bear in mind that even in Food Studies one should consider that Canada has been a land of immigrants since the first French and English colonizers of the sixteenth century, and that today the annual immigration rate is still high, involving people coming not only from Europe, but also from other continents. Indeed, for most immigrants—new and old—what you eat defines your identity. As Hallorn aptly states in the introduction to *The Immigrant Kitchen: Food, Ethnicity, and Diaspora* (2016), referring to the United States, a book dealing especially with memoirs of immigrants from different countries and cultural contexts:

> Cooking and eating are two related activities that allow immigrants and their families to embody and perform their sense of national and/or cultural belonging both privately and publicly, thus concretely addressing the sense of emotional displacement occasioned by immigrants' decision to lay claim to a new homeland (Hallorn 2016: 7).

Can we speak of "emotional displacement" because of culinary dislocation?

The essays here collected survey 'the matter of food' from several points of view belonging to immigrants and their descendants without neglecting the Indigenous Peoples of Canada. They deal with literary, linguistic and cultural issues, without leaving totally aside a sociological approach. Nostalgia and the hybridity not only of languages, but also of savoring tongues, are the prevailing modes of representation and critical assessment, both in Anglophone and Francophone contexts, as deployed by Nathalie Cooke and Marco Modenesi, the opening keynote speakers at the International Conference *Sapori di casa / A Taste of Home / Les saveurs de chez soi*, held at the University of Bari on 14-16 November 2019 together with the Italian Association for Canadian Studies.

In *Reflecting on Home and Away—over a Canadian Literary Meal*, Cooke introduces us to a three-course meal common to many Canadian homes, which reflects three of the most important migrant groups of the twentieth century. Through the scrutiny of statistic data and literary texts of Canadian immigrant writers in English, she shows how each dish betrays "influences of home and away," negotiating ethnic identity and belonging and a form of adaptation to the new land. While Cooke takes into consideration different Canadian provinces, from British Columbia to Ontario, Marco Modenesi examines the gastronomic dimension in *Le Matou* by the French-Canadian novelist Yves Beauchemin, set in Montreal and published in 1981. Modenesi focuses on the small restaurant run by the ambitious Florent Boissonneault and on the implications between food and desire presented in a realistic, but also comic and grotesque way. The quotation in the title of his paper anticipates the comic turn of the story: "Un rigatoni jumbo spécial à la pepperoni mambo, ou quelque chose comme ça."

We remain at a Quebec table, this time in Little Italy and go back to the 1950's with "Repas de famille dans *Impala* de Carole David ou la déconstruction du stéréotype maternel". In her analysis of David's 1994 novel, Alessandra Ferraro examines how food is deeply entangled with the complex reconstruction of the life of a mother of Italian origin (Connie Ferragamo) and her daughter (Louisa). David revisits well-established stereotypes: Connie is not the traditional motherly nurturing figure, while domestic meals are associated with fighting.

Our travel in the field of literary food continues with papers interrogating stereotypical representations of food and ethnicity. Éva Zsizsmann's reading of "His Mother", a short story by Mavis Gallant and its film adaptation by Hungarian director Karoly Makk introduces the intriguing concept of food imagery as false memory, thus questioning the authenticity of immigration rituals, while Carmen Concilio undermines the myth of Canada as a world of plenty in "Fasting in Abundance in Canadian Literature", dealing in detail with *Cockroach* (2008) by Lebanese-Canadian writer Rawi Hage, a novel in which its lean protagonist, a Lebanese immigrant, is literally starving.

Shifting back to Quebec, in the following three essays, different critical approaches on French Quebec literature are discussed, all of them being in some way related to Italy. Angela Buono compares works by Hédi Bouraoui and Marco Micone, both immigrant writers, the former a Tunisian and the latter of Italian origin, showing how eating habits convey and at the same time deny identity, especially when they portray cultural stereotypes. Instead, in her investigation of a corpus of literary translations of Quebec authors into Italian Valeria Zotti chooses a linguistic perspective to pinpoint what happens to the culture-bound terms of traditional Quebec dishes. Another insight on culinary narratives, heritage, identity and migration is offered by Licia Canton, who introduces her memoir (or *foodoir*) on growing up in Montreal-North as the daughter of first-generation Italian immigrants in the 1970s and 1980s. Eating is indeed deeply connected to ethnic belonging, though intrinsically to the native tongue, as we have seen in the previous papers, through the use of specific culinary terms and expressions. Eva Gruber further explores the topic in texts by contemporary female writers of different ethnic descent, namely M. NourbeSe Philip (Tobago), Hiromi Ghoto (Japan) and Madeleine Thien (China), focusing on the strategies employed by the characters for the purpose of negotiating their respective cultural identity. Undeniably, Canadian culinary literature is imbued with the flavour and smells of immigrant dishes named in many different languages, changing the social texture of the urban environment.

In the following papers literature is left aside in order to tackle broader issues linked to foodfare. Thus public and private spaces, not only in fiction, reflect how transnational kitchens speak to the senses and hybridize each other. For instance, Ylenia De Luca deals with the Montreal phenomenon of first generation immigrants and their strong attachment to the dietary and culinary models from home, insisting on the fact that the new context produces an "art de vivre", which is deployed, among other things, through feelings and emotions linked to food, creating a social transcultural culinary space. Two essays focus on the Web and food lexicon. Silvia Domenica Zotto discusses Quebec culinary terminology on food forums from a metalinguistic viewpoint, while Roberta La Peruta questions and discusses the linguistic adaptations of Italian food-related terms in menus of eating venues in Toronto gathered online from *TripAdvisor*.

Turning back to culinary literature, Daniela Fargione selects speculative fiction to investigate crucial contingent aspects related to "economic greed, corporate power, dominating global capitalism and genetically modified food." Authentic food becomes a forbidden dream in the apocalyptic realms envisaged by writers Larissa Lai and Rita Wong. Yet in transcultural Canada authenticity is often juxtaposed with specific cuisines to attract consumers. Simona Stano introduces "translated sushi", considering the inevitable adaptation of the Japanese culinary code to local tastes in Canadian restaurants, to highlight, by borrowing Umberto Eco's book title on translation, the inevitable process of "eating almost the same thing."

During hundreds of years of colonial power and genocide, the culinary eating habits of the First Peoples have been depicted as utterly disgusting, and thus doomed to extinction. In this edited volume, we can follow cogent ongoing debates on Indigenous identity and food through a variety of sources, from novels to the media. Julia Siepak gives us an insight on the concept of food sovereignty linking it to the prominence of diet, restoration, wellbeing, and resistance in texts written by contemporary First Nations women writers such as Eden Robinson, Tracey Lindberg, Alicia Elliott. Instead, Kamelia Talebian Sedehi concentrates her attention on Basil H. Johnston's *Indian School Days*, published in 1988, to unravel the terrible experiences of the disgraceful Residential Schools, whose stories newspapers and reports *forgot* to mention, as Indigenous children were forced to suffer lack of food and when they did eat they had to swallow the oppressors' unsavory food. Leaving Johnston's previous shocking memoir aside, Anna Mongibello examines *Moosemeat & Marmalade*, a documentary food series aired on APTN (Aboriginal Peoples Television Network) through the lens of a Multimodal Critical Discourse Analysis in order to show "how food is transformed into a cultural trigger of Indigeneity and a vehicle of Indigenous storytelling."

After examining Indigenous culinary traditions in Canada, our journey in a *Taste of Home* continues dealing with the diasporic communities from the Indian subcontinent. Esterino Adami chooses the online and written work of Pakistani chef Niloufer Mavalvala to tackle the intricacies of Parsi food culture far from home and how the preparation of Parsi dishes functions as the site of ancient diasporic identity. On the other hand, Rita Calabrese explores the multivalent meaning of culinary practices in a corpus of Indian restaurant menus in the city of Mississauga on Lake Ontario to "restate/assert ethnic identity."

The last section of this collection on "a taste of home" in Canada returns once again to Quebec with questions on specific recipes and wines in the French speaking province. In "Pâté chinois, tourtières et autres délices de la cuisine québécoise," Marina Zito looks at the cultural origin of the popularity of certain 'traditional' dishes and on their elaborate preparation. Suffice it to mention pâté chinois, which is not, by the way, a Chinese delicacy. Zito ends up introducing among the tasty, but not particularly dietetic francophone specialties, the infamous *poutine*, on which Mirko Casagranda focuses his paper. Is poutine Canadian? Taking into account a selection of tweets collected in November 2019, he argues that poutine is discursively construed as a marker of identity in the definition of a 'cheap' nationalism. Leaving aside pâté chinois and poutine, very rich and fattening delicious food against the freezing winter climate, the volume winds up with a toast, with a glass of wine made in Canada. René Georges Maury speaks of the long history of the European 'transplant' of vineyards across the nation, on its increasing production, introducing wine tourism and especially Canadian wine in multicultural houses.

On a literary and cultural table so sumptuously prepared with recipes dearly carried from native homes near and far, full of strange ingredients, tastes, smells, colours, cultural practices, habits, Canada celebrates the triumph of a migrant country, whose life is rooted in the rich soil of far off cooking traditions and memories. Indeed, Canada is a culinary laboratory in which gastronomies showcase and confirm the ethnic diversity of its multicultural peoples.

—*Oriana Palusci*

Works Cited

Atwood, Margaret (1969). *The Edible Woman*. Toronto: McClelland and Stewart.

Atwood, Margaret (1987). *The Canlit Foodbook: From Pen to Palate—A Collection of Tasty Literary Fare*. Toronto: Totem.

Diner, Hasia R. (2001). *Hungering for America: Italian, Irish and Jewish Foodways in the Age of Migration*. Cambridge (MA): Harvard University Press.

Eco, Umberto (2003). *Dire quasi la stessa cosa. Esperienze di traduzione*. Milano: Bompiani.

Gabaccia, Donna R. (1998). *We Are What We Eat: Ethnic Food and the Making of the Americans*. Cambridge (MA): Harvard University Press.

Gilbert, M. Sandra (2014), *The Culinary Imagination: from Myth to Modernity*. London: WW Norton.

Halloran, Vivian Nun (2016). *The Immigrant Kitchen: Food, Ethnicity, and Diaspora*, Columbus: Ohio State University Press.

Ji-Song Ku, Robert, Manalansan, Martin F., Mannu, Anita eds. (2013). *Eating Asian America: A Food Studies Reader*. New York: New York University Press.

Mannur, Anita (2007). "Culinary Nostalgia: Authenticity, Nationalism and Diaspora". *MELUS* 32:4 (Winter).

Mannur, Anita (2009). *Culinary Fictions: Food in South Asian Diasporic Cultures*. Philadelphia: Temple University Press.

Shahani, Gitanjali G. ed. (2018). *Food and Literature*. Cambridge: Cambridge University Press.

Wah, Fred (1996). *Diamond Grill*. Edmonton: NeWest Press.

NATHALIE COOKE

Reflecting on Home and Away—
over a Canadian Literary Meal

Introduction

IF ONE WERE TO PREPARE a menu that speaks to Canadian literary fare, what *cries out* to be included?[1] How might one begin to choose representative foods from the many, many immigrant communities that have made Canada their home? I began by identifying the predominant immigrant communities. Because accurate statistical information is most available for the twentieth century, my colleague Colin Rier and I started there, finding six immigrant groups whose arrival during that time profoundly impacted Canada's population and cultural composition. Next, I sought to explore the engagement of those immigrant communities over time as they negotiated their relationship with home and away, figured first with Canada as the place of discovery and "home" as the place left behind, and later with Canada as home, and "away" as a place located in memory as much as in their present reality. Because two of the six communities migrated to Canada largely in the century's closing decades (those from India, and from the Philippines), the other four afforded more opportunity to explore the evolution of foodways over multiple generations.

---

1 This paper was first presented in Bari, Italy on 14 November 2019 for the Italian Association of Canadian Studies Conference. I am indebted to the invaluable research assistance of Colin Rier in preparing the original concept and presentation, and of Chelsea Woodhouse in preparing the final manuscript.

Finally, I set myself one last challenge: to *surprise* readers with new symbolic taste sensations, to bring to the fore significant yet largely unassuming foods and dishes that have largely been overlooked in favour of their outspoken counterparts. After all, how might a modest sweet compete with Canadian pastry inventions boasting dramatic and inventive names? Think of the shock value of a name like *"pets de soeur"*—cinnamon rolls marketing themselves as "nuns' farts." The entertainment value of "figgy duff," a raisin dessert cooked in a bag. Or the evocation of welcome and comfort implied by *"grands-pères à l'érable,"* a dough cooked in maple syrup, or by sharing a warm bowl of *"pouding chomeur,"* poor man's pudding, a basic cake with a sweet, syrup-based sauce. Instead, my choice for dessert is the small butter tart, which punches above its weight in terms of popularity, is heralded in odes and literary prose, and can trace a noble lineage to multiple venerable tarts originating from Britain and the United States. Rather than eat the sweet before the savoury courses, let us turn our attention now to the appetizer, and to Canadians of Italian heritage in particular.

Primi: Polenta

Joy Garnett (on Flickr), Attribution-ShareAlike 2.0 Generic (CC BY-SA 2.0) https://creativecommons.org/licenses/by-sa/4.0/

Prior to 1981, and especially around the First World War, Italian immigration to Canada was of notable significance. It is difficult to access information about the particular regions from which new Italians hailed, but records show that the majority of Italian migration came from the southern and central regions of Italy (Jansen, 1988). According to emigrant data collected by the Italian National Institute of Statistics from 1955–1980, 19% of Italian migrants to Canada were from the Northern regions, 13% from Central Italy and 68% from Southern Italy (59-60).

There are Italian-style dishes that are uniquely Canadian and would be unfamiliar to Italians, such as Montreal's slab pizza (Di Pasquale 2019). But for a dish that plays a starring role in meditations of home and away, polenta is perhaps the most appropriate to start our iconically Canadian meal. It contains no accompaniments—not even cold milk in which to place it, nor sauce to adorn it. Just plain polenta, for this meagre daily staple is metonymic in Canadian literature for what prompted many Italians to migrate to Canada.

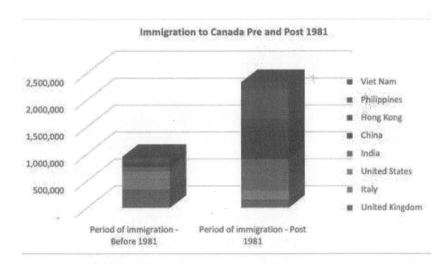

Immigration to Canada Pre and Post 1981[2]

---

2 Statistics, Canada 2017.

Anna Fornari's Italian father came from the Treviso area of the Veneto Region of Northern Italy in 1956. He told his new British wife about "how he missed his mother's cooking, his family and friends, his territory, his language. One of the things he mentioned often was *polenta*. So often that, once married, my [Fornari's] mother set about learning how to make it. She wanted to surprise him with what she understood to be his favourite dish." Fornari's father returned from work one evening to a dinner that was:

> … a nice steaming bowl of *polenta*, just *polenta*. He almost hit the roof. He had talked and talked about polenta, but not with fondness as his wife had supposed, but with horror at the memory of eating it for every meal during war time. He couldn't stand the sight of the bland, insipid concoction and definitely preferred bread, which back then was a rare luxury. To make matters worse, mom had served it without *"il tocio,"* stewed meat, not knowing that *polenta* is never served on its own (Fornari 2017: 99).

Giulia, a character in Frank Paci's *The Italians,* serves a feast with an overabundance of food. Alberto makes a quick and accurate assessment: "To judge from the meal's size, she still hadn't got over the years in the old country when they had been forced to eat *polenta* almost every day. They had scarcely seen meat then …" (Paci 1978: 74). Yet the Italian-Canadian style of polenta is typically inviting with generous helpings of accompaniments. For example, in the home of Valerie Mitchell, who lives and runs a small Italian restaurant in British Columbia, it is served with a rich sauce and sprinkled with Parmigiano or Romano cheese, a tradition inherited from her grandmother who came from the Abruzzi to Trail in British Columbia's interior (2003: 24). Mitchell's cooking stays faithful to tradition, but *polenta* in Canada is often served with an overabundance of toppings and flavourings. Might polenta with veal stew whet your appetite?

Even plain polenta in Canada is cooked and served in abundance! For example, did you know that Windsor, Ontario holds the Guinness World Record for producing the largest polenta? Many of the Italian-Canadians in Windsor hailed from Friuli in Italy's north, and the President of the local Fogolar Furlan club proudly acknowledges his members "eat a lot of polenta." Their first victory came in 2011, only to be out-produced by a group in Panello di Cagli in Italy, in 2012. Ever determined, they again set about the task two years later, eventually producing a polenta weighing 4.5 tonnes! (Pinto 2014).

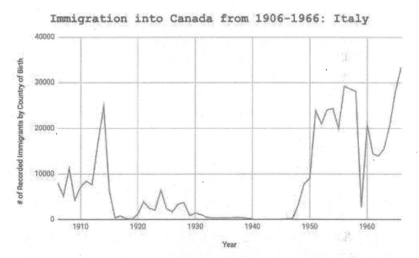

Immigration into Canada from 1906-1966: Italy[3]

Although Italians brought their foodways traditions to Canada, adjustments had to be made when they tried to duplicate their foodways from "home" or the "old country." For instance, Anna Pia DeLuca writes that the availability of ingredients in Canada

3 Statistics, Canada Historical Collection. *The Canada Statistics Yearbook* is an annual report published on a wide variety of quantitative data coming from the different ministries of the Canadian government. It began its publication in 1867, and its publication continued into 2012. *The Yearbook* included information on Immigration, Agriculture, Government spending & more. It is available via an online archive, as well as print copies in major university libraries across Canada.

bothered her mother: "Having to buy Canadian cornmeal, which was much too finely ground [and] thus mushy and tasteless when cooked, was a cultural shock to my mother who had visions of a coarse and consistent *polenta* that would retain its spherical shape when dropped onto a simple round wooden cutting board with oblong handles" (DeLuca 2013: 172).[4]

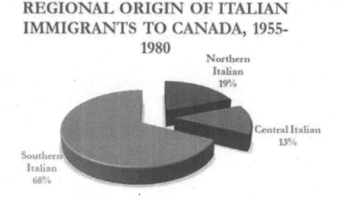

REGIONAL ORIGIN OF ITALIAN IMMIGRANTS TO CANADA, 1955-1980

Northern Italian 19%

Central Italian 13%

Southern Italian 68%

Regional Origin of Italian Immigrants to Canada, 1955-1980[5]

Glenn Carley, who married into an Italian Canadian family, describes his apprenticeship in the food traditions of his wife's family. He learns to make wine and rich tomato sauce, to roast peppers.

---

4   How is polenta made? One-part cornmeal to four parts liquid (water, milk, stock?), and if cooking on the stove top, prepare yourself for a good hour of cooking time. Corn, or maize, as it was then known, first made its way onto Italian soil during the 1490s following the expedition of Christopher Columbus. Due to the change in growing climate, it would take many years for the corn to truly take root in the Italian countryside in the sixteenth and seventeenth centuries. This was due to the importation of Southern American Alpine varieties of maize, which were naturally suited to the Alpine areas of Northern Italy (Brandolini 2009: 233–235). Before being produced with corn, polenta was made with chestnut flour (Davidson 2014).

5   Zucchi, Italian National Institute of Statistics found in "Italians in Canada" in the *Encyclopedia of Diasporas.*

His rite of passage comes when he is handed a wooden spoon to make the dish after which his book is named: *polenta*. "Here. Take this and stir," commands the woman of the house:

…passing over the stem of a very large wooden spoon, stuck in a beautiful yellow mixture.

Stirring *polenta* has nothing to do with the delicate turns of oil and vinegar. It is hard work and you have to keep your eyes on it. It is an enchanted food, however, because when it is ready, it is ready. Do not serve it if your guests are not reliable and are not already in your home. Here is what you do. Get a large pot and fill it half full with water. Heat it until just before it is going to boil; let it ride the edge of the tipping point. Add butter and salt. You may add the *polenta* now in slow, loving circles that spin up memories. Some may use the fine corn flour, but me, I prefer the coarse grain. Begin to stir now to infinity (Carley 2007: 188–189).

The book's back cover describes the way Carley spins the story of Italian foodways into one of magic and enchantment. "Come with me to Garibaldi's Court and I will tell you tales of gusto and enchantment. We will sing, dance, laugh, weep and eat polenta at midnight al fresco. I promise you homemade red wine and frittata. Have some more. For me! We will work hard and then we will rest." What is interesting, however, is that the food traditions preserved in Canada are ones that are faithful to memory, but not necessarily to Italy of the present day. When Carley's father-in-law eventually makes the trip back to Italy, he is disappointed to find trees laden with figs and vines "filled with beautiful clusters of yellow grapes" that the villagers are not bothering to gather. "It's the food," he says. "They grow it but they do not use it. It all goes to waste now … It was not like that when I left. You were lucky if there was any fruit left on the tree or the vine when they were ready" (2007: 191).

Polenta is linked even more explicitly with memory in an elegiac poem written by Fruili-born Dôre Michelut for her mother. The poem's narrator describes the way she purchases a rabbit from a local farmer. Eventually she brings herself to kill and skin it, an act which she does for the first time because it was a task previously undertaken by her mother or grandparents. She takes care to do it "properly: take a life and thank it at the same time." Then she meticulously prepares it for a dinner with friends.

> Overnight, I soaked the meat
> to drain the wild taste that rabbits
> sometimes have.
> Then I cooked it: first, I browned it well
> so it would dry; then, I added garlic,
> rosemary, salt, pepper and three full glasses
> of good white wine.
> I invited friends.
> As I made *polenta*, I told
> them the story of you and the rabbit.
> Then, we feasted. (Michelut 1990: 80)

Polenta is certainly not the *only* Italian dish that looms large in the Canadian literary imagination, though there are numerous examples of its very close association with memory and the mythic legacies of Italy from our literary landscape. When Mary di Michele writes a collection of poems conjuring Pier Paolo Pasolini, she feeds her characters cold polenta with salami and wine on the Monday morning following celebrations after the end of the Second World War (Di Michele 2013: 71). When Pasolini returns to his mother's house, he wakes to the "candid air I knew / so well, to the smells of fire, of polenta, / of the iron pot, my grandmother stirring it" (Di Michele 2013: 27).

Second-generation Italian-Canadian writers—that is, those born in Canada to parents who were first-generation immigrants—write of their childhood memories of trying to explain to classmates raised on TV dinners and peanut butter and jelly sandwiches what was in their lunch boxes. "Back then," poet Mary di Michele writes in 1986, the poem's speaker referring to her younger self:

"... you couldn't have imagined yourself
openly savouring a cappuccino,
you were too ashamed that your dinners
were in a language you couldn't share
with your friends: their pot roasts,
their turnips, their recipes for Kraft
dinners you glimpsed in TV commercials—
the mysteries of macaroni with marshmallows" (Di
Michele 1986: 45).

For the young Italian girl in a distinctly non-Italian community, food was a language needing translation, the glass of the TV screen exposing the mysteries of her friend's dinners to her, rather as the glass door of her own oven emphasized the "other-worldliness" of her own dinners. "*[M]elanzane* became eggplant," the "other-worldliness" of *melanzane alla parmigiana* "viewed as if / through a microscope / like photosynthesis in a leaf" (Di Michele 1986: 45). Notice di Michele's use of the second person here—"you" not "she"—could not have imagined the mysteries of *melanzane*, nor what it is like to have that exotic fare as everyday fare, what it is like to be Italian—from the inside out. Di Michele, the poet, is neither consumer of nor consumed by embarrassment; rather, as poet, she serves up this culinary fare as way of engaging her Canadian readers in an act of cultural negotiation that leads to community building.

As one Italian-Canadian writer, Antonio D'Alfonso, explains it, he "became an Italian" in 1977 when he discovered the work of Pier Giorgio de Cicco and others. For Canadian-born children of Italian-Canadian descent, he explains: "One is not born an Italian; one becomes an Italian" (D'Alfonso 1996: 24). How? Through sharing meals and stories, and through acts of writing and reading, for, as Priscilla Parkhurst Ferguson reminds us, "... literary connections enhance any cultural enterprise ..." (Ferguson 2004: 11).

And for the Main Course:

Kristie Warner (on Flickr), Attribution-NonCommercial-NoDerivs 2.0 Generic (CC BY-NC-ND 2.0)
https://creativecommons.org/licenses/by-nc-nd/2.0/

In her introduction to *Italian Canadians at Table*, Loretta Gatto-White writes: "The [Canadian] public's concept of sophisticated five-star cuisine was still solidly French with few exceptions, until the 1980s when Northern Italian cuisine, by little stretch of the culinary palate, became trendy with its focus on butter, cream, truffles, risotto, polenta and veal, and a notable absence of strong tastes and colours. Its soft and velvety textures were an easy segue from central France to Italy" (De Santis et al 2013: 2). Just as Italian Cuisine in Canada drew on different regional specialties post-1980, so too in the 1980s and thereafter, notably with an influx of Vietnamese immigrants, Asian restaurants in Canada became differentiated first by country of origin, and later by regional cuisines. Alan Nash, writing about the evolution of Montreal's ethnic restaurants based on evidence in the Yellow Pages, argues that as

of the 1970s the genre of the "Asian restaurant" is no longer understood as synonymous with Chinese cuisine, but rather begins
to reflect the diverse cuisines across the continent of Asia. In the
2001 Yellow Pages, for example, Nash notes restaurants listed according to such diverse Asian cuisines as Japanese, Vietnamese
and Thai (Nash 2009: 16).

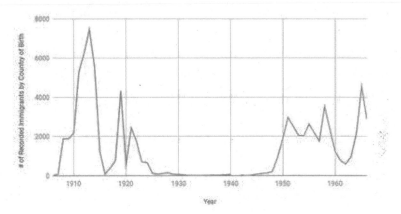

Immigration into Canada from 1906-1966: China[6]

Prior to the 1980s, however, "exotic" fare in Canada could be
readily identified as Chinese food, the food Canadians typically
did not cook at home, and food that was readily available at the
ubiquitous Chinese restaurants dotted across the country. After
completion of the railroad, Chinese workers found themselves
stranded in Canada with inadequate resources to fund their way
home. Because of the Head Tax imposed on the community,
stranded workers had few opportunities to send for their wives and
children to join them. In small towns, the Chinese restaurateur was
often the only Chinese resident, so his menu naturally catered to
palates unfamiliar with Chinese foodways.[7]

---

6   Statistics, Canada Historical Collection

7   "What is 'Restaurant Literature'?" Depictions of Chinese Restaurants in
Canadian Literature by Nathalie Cooke and Shelley Boyd; "Writing the Chinese
Restaurateur into the Canadian Literary Landscape." Studies in Canadian
Literature. 42.2 (2017). Released June 2018: 5–25.

A typical small-town Chinese restaurant would offer a hybrid menu—"Canadian" food, on the one hand and "Chinese" food on the other, though a visitor from China would have been hard pressed to find anything recognizable on that menu. What it offered more precisely was a cuisine born of the negotiation between available ingredients, the abilities of cooks and restaurateurs who had been trained by previous café operators and owners in Canada, and the (very limited) willingness of the Canadian public to venture to try new foods. In Canada, we call this "Chop Suey Chinese Cuisine," in part because of the inevitable presence of the catch-all dish Chop Suey on every menu and to signal its distinctly Canadian origin, since Chop Suey itself did not originate from China at all. When Ann Hui's father, who was skilled in authentic Chinese cuisine upon immigration, took over a Chinese restaurant in Abbotsford, British Columbia, he had to relearn how to cook—the Canadian way. "'The people here—they won't eat the food you cooked in Chinatown,'" former restaurant manager Mr. Cheung explains to him (Hui 2019: 188). "He showed him sweet and sour pork, one of the most popular items on the Chinese menu. Sure it was similar to *gu lou yuk,* a classic Cantonese dish, he explained but there were key differences. He showed Dad how to make the sauce out of sugar, vinegar and ketchup, then build a batter out of cornstarch, egg and flour …. 'This is Chinese?' Dad asked. Mr. Cheung nodded, grinning. 'Chop Suey Chinese'" (Hui 2019: 188).

What are the staples of Chop Suey Chinese food? Chop Suey itself certainly, with its primary ingredient being bean sprouts and anything else that was available, as well as General Tso chicken, and lemon chicken. Across the country, one encounters slight variations, adjusted to please local customers. For example, in Glendon, Alberta, a town with a Ukrainian population, Ann Hui found "Chinese pierogis" (Hui 2019: 101–102). In Thunder Bay, Ontario, she found "'Bon Bon ribs'—a made-in-Thunder-Bay invention of spareribs coated in allspice and MSG, then deep-fried quickly and spritzed with lemon. It was one of the dishes that helped make Mr. Lee so popular he was hired by a local cable TV station to host his own cooking show. Each week, he invited viewers into his kitchen to show them the secrets of cooking 'Chinese food'" (Hui 2019: 123).

Another staple of Chop Suey Chinese Food, found especially in Canada's prairie provinces, is Ginger Beef. The story goes that the idea originated at the Silver Inn Restaurant in Calgary, where Mr. Wong was testing recipes and having little success with a new Peking-style snack, reminiscent of jerky, that he was attempting to introduce rather unsuccessfully. Instead, he decided to offer his customers something more familiar to them: a fried dish, this time beef coated in a thin batter, then tossed in a "sweet chili-ginger-garlic mix" (Hui 79). Writes Hui, "It was, like all good chop suey dishes, the perfect combination of sweet, salty, tangy and crunchy. It had some of the 'exotic' Chinese flavours the customers were looking for, but blended with familiar 'Western' ideas" (Hui 2019: 79). That it became known as 'ginger' beef was a function of customers not fully recognizing the combination of seasonings and asking for "that beef with the ginger stuff" (Hui 2019: 80). In "The Process of Chop Suey," Caitlin Gordon-Walker explains that "Ginger beef is far from being representative of a discrete and static 'authentic' or 'traditional' Chinese culture, but rather emerged from interaction and mixture" (Gordon-Walker 2013: 34).

Cultural critic Lily Cho looks closely at how the "small town Chinese restaurant in Canadian literature ... reveals a construction of Chineseness in diaspora" (Cho 2010: 132). Cho devotes an entire chapter to the poetry of Fred Wah, with an emphasis on *The Diamond Grill*. In part this is because Wah's text, a collection of autobiographical poetry by an individual of mixed-race Chinese heritage about his family and the various Chinese restaurants in which they worked, including the titular Diamond Grill, is a sophisticated reflection on some of the same issues that preoccupy Cho. Both books pose two central questions: "How does a diasporic community," or community of immigrants from a wide variety of places, "understand itself as such?" (Cho, 2010: 131) and what is the relationship of the immigrant or "diasporic subject" to China and "Chineseness"? (Cho 2010: 139)

Wah's answer involves food choices, and his scrutiny falls in particular to ginger. As a mixed-race Canadian-born youngster, he winces at ginger, a central ingredient in his father's cooking (Wah 2006: 11). His father forces him to eat it, along with salt fish and seaweed, but he is spared having to eat wet rice (74). Only as an adult, does Wah understand the hurt he caused his father by turning away from ginger, hiding it under his plate.[8] Yet garlic, which he understands to be a "site of an implicit racial qualification" (11) becomes something that he loves, along with rice, for the rest of his life (39). When Fred Wah offers his readers a recipe with enough detail for them to follow, it is for tomato beef (44), one of the many Chop Suey Chinese dishes he cooks for himself. But he reserves for ginger beef a close scrutiny of its ingredients and the implications it had for his father, raised in China, and for his Canadian-born self:

> my father hurt-
> ing at the table
> sitting hurting
> at suppertime
> deep inside very
> far down inside
> because I can't stand the ginger
> in the beef and greens
> he cooked for us tonight
> and years later tonight
> that look on his face
> appears now on mine

8   Fred Wah (1985: 7) *Waiting for Saskatchewan.*

my children
my food
their food
my father
their father
me mine
the father
very far
very very far
inside (Wah 1985: 7)

With the exception of this very poignant small lyric by one of the most influential voices on the condition of racial hybridity in Canada, Ginger beef has no other poem dedicated to it in Canadian literature. But it so much a part of Chinese-Canadian foodways that it appears as an important and sometimes un-named backdrop in other pivotal scenes of racial qualification. For example, when Ming's Chinese parents move her to Toronto to begin medical school in a story entitled "How to Get into Medical School, Part II" by Vincent Lam, "they filled her freezer with white plastic containers of ginger beef, sesame chicken, and other favourites of Ming's" (2006: 58). Her white boyfriend, Fitzgerald, does not come to Toronto with Ming and her parents. In fact, they don't know of his existence and if they had, they would not have approved. Even at Ming's first meal with him, in Part 1 of this same story, as Fitzpatrick chokes on the hot sauce in a Thai restaurant, revealing his "Anglocentric intolerance to chili," it is clear this relationship is doomed. It will take Lam two stories to trace the gradual disintegration of a relationship between two like-minded individuals caught on different sides of a cultural divide (2006: 4).

In Wayson Choy's novel *All that Matters*, ginger beef is such a familiar home-cooked dish in a Chinese-Canadian home, that it is never even named. Poh-Poh, the "paper" grandmother of the

Chen family ("paper" relatives being those who can enter Canada by assumed names and claim close family ties to those already in Canada) prepares a feast for the neighbourhood ladies who have come to play Mah-jong. The feast's prelude is a "hot dish of beef and greens sprinkled with herbs, all steaming with flavours and glistening from the sesame oil ... and the three ladies rushed into the kitchen, exclaiming over the delicious smells" (Choy 2005: 92-93). If the appetizing descriptions of air smelling of "crushed ginger" that wafts from the dishes and makes everyone sigh "with delight"(93) cannot alone enchant the reader, then Choy teaches his readers about Chinese-Canadian table manners and good taste more pointedly. Says his young narrator, Poh-Poh "had taught me well ... so that I would survive in Gold Mountain among the barbarians who boiled greens into mush and blackened whole chunks of meat the size of a man's head, and carved the dead thing and ate whole slabs employing weapons at the table" (92). Gold Mountain here refers to Vancouver and the barbarians are Canadians with their methods of overcooking vegetables, a legacy of British immigrant foodways, and their preponderance of barbecuing large steaks and roasts, a proud food preparation technique of the Americas. The narrator here brings his reader into the community of the Chinese-Canadian table, where despite lack of material wealth, food is shared and appreciated, and ginger beef needs no introduction. "Clicking chopsticks rose and fell, and the clink of porcelain spoons in the large bowl made a happy chorus. Grandmother picked up choice pieces ... with her ivory chopsticks and generously put them into the rice bowls of her friends" (Choy 2005: 94).

Now, for our Sweet

Kaye Adams' Assessment of the Quality of Butter Tart Recipes
Annmarie Adams

Cake has long been linked to some of the most beloved Canadian texts. "Canada is the land of cakes," wrote Catharine Parr Traill in her 1855 classic, *The Female Emigrant's Guide*, astounded as she was by the variety of cakes and sweets on offer to European settlers to Ontario's backwoods. Lucy Maud Montgomery makes much of serving cakes. In *Anne of Green Gables*, she lingers over scenes of cakes being planned, debated, consumed and, occasionally, remembered with horror. The novel about Anne was written just after the fashion for cakes changed dramatically, beginning with what was called the "great uprearing" of food in France following the revolution, and subsequently in Victorian England after the spectacle of Queen Victoria's extraordinarily high sculpture that served as her wedding cake (Allen 2003: 460). The fashion for high cakes reached the colonies after some delay. But while the young Anne hopes for the high, fluffy cakes that are in fashion, her ever-sensible adoptive mother, Marilla, prefers the lower and more solid pound cakes. But the cake steals the show in *Anne of the Windy Poplars*, where Maud Montgomery tantalizes her readers. Just as Aunt Chatty finds it next to impossible to procure Miss Ellen's recipe for pound cake, finally obtaining a recipe that calls for thirty-six eggs no less (Montgomery 2013: 111–112), the reader has no such luck. The mystery has spawned intrigue over the years, including driving one reader to attempt a 36-egg pound cake in the style of the period (Bergstrom & Osada 2015).

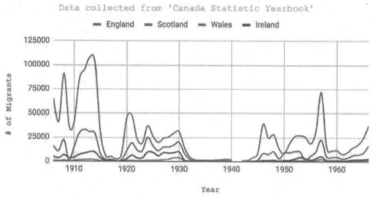

Figure 1.8 Immigration into Canada from 1906-1966: British Isles[9]

Colin Rier

But it would be a stretch to claim cake as a distinctly immigrant food tradition, and that has been so creolized as to become distinctly Canadian over time. Indeed, it is not a cake at all that has become iconically Canadian, but rather a very small, rather bland, and not terribly attractive little tart that is known simply as the "butter tart." Writes Alexia Moyer: "As of April 2019, the butter tart, as it would become known, has been immortalized in stamp

---

9 Statistics, Canada Historical Collection

form, issued by Canada Post. No doubt for the express purpose of sweetening your letters" (Moyer 2019). It made its first appearance in 1900, in a modest recipe entitled "filling for a tart," involving one cup of sugar, a half-cup butter, two eggs and a cup of currants.

By 1913, when included in the classic *Five Roses Cookbook* (a cookbook that could be found in half of Canadian homes just after 1915), it was linked to its forever name—at least in Canada. And around that modest little name and tart has grown a tourist industry—largely centred in Ontario—and a confidence that this is a distinctly, even iconic, Canadian dainty (Mosby 2007).

But of course, it's only Canadian because we have claimed it to be so—prepared it and served it up as such. Phillip Resnick argues that American and Canadian English are remarkably similar but acknowledges the existence of "distinctly Canadian terms" (2012: 37).[10] Among such terms, he says butter tart is a uniquely Canadian word, along with francophone, postal code, smoked meat and Nanaimo Bar (37). Sarah Bonisteel wrote recently in *The New York Times*: "The butter tart is Canada's gift to the dessert canon." She continues, tellingly assigning the task of naming to my countrymen: "*Canadians* will tell you that these diminutive treats hold an expanse of flavor and textures: flaky pastry, caramelized crust and a bracingly sweet filling" (Bonisteel, 2018).

Its forebears are multiple and include, according to Bonisteel, "The brown sugar pie, the Scottish border tart, Bakewell tarts and the Quebec sugar pie" (2018: 1), as well as variations coming north from the United States, incorporating treacle, molasses and pecans. In an extraordinarily comprehensive article on the tiny tart's origins, Gary Gillman (2019) offers other plausible forebears including Scotland's Ecclefechan tart (41), UK's Border tart (42) and British butter tart (42), all of which seem to have originated from the borderlands between England and Scotland (43). He distinguishes

---

10 For more on uniquely Canadian words, please see "Canadian English" by Laurel J. Brinton and Margery Fee in the The Cambridge History of the English Language, Vol. VI, English in North America, ed. John Algeo (Cambridge University Press 2001) 422–40, 434–38.

between the fruited tarts of German origin and the butterscotch tart, where the filling is cooked before being poured into the tart shell (53). He ultimately concludes that "The butter tart is deservedly Ontario's pet *snack* ..." (53) and that the multiple variations he can identify in the United States, United Kingdom and on the continent "appear episodic and isolated, never rising to the ubiquity or gastronomic reputation of the butter tart in Canada" (54).

Despite variations on the general principle of sugar, butter and egg—including additions of currants or nuts—what all our Canadian variations share is their unassuming appearance and size (small), shape (round), and taste (overly sweet). When they appear in Canadian fiction, they are typically devoured in multiples, as a guilty indulgence.

For instance, when Alice Munro's young semi-autobiographical protagonist, Rose, is sent to her room after a 'royal beating,' in a story of the same name, butter tarts are part of the ritual. Proud, sobbing alone in her room, she will eventually succumb to the tempting foods her stepmother puts outside the door. The verb tense here is instructive, as the narrator describes how the post-beating ritual that is a battle of wills shall inevitably unfold:

> "Later still a tray will appear. Flo will put it down without a word and go away. A large glass of chocolate milk on it, made with Vita-Malt from the store. Some rich streaks of Vita-Malt around the bottom of the glass. Little sandwiches, neat and appetizing. Canned salmon of the first quality and reddest color, plenty of mayonnaise. A couple of butter tarts from a bakery package, chocolate biscuits with a peppermint filling. Rose's favorites, in the sandwich, tart and cookie line. She will turn away, refuse to look, but left alone with these eatables will be miserably tempted...Soon in helpless corruption, she will eat them all. She will drink the chocolate milk, eat the tarts, eat the cookies" (Munro 1996: 23).

What prompts the royal beating in the first place is Flo's sense that her stepdaughter thinks she is better than her, superior to her (McGill 2002). The story collection is entitled: *Who Do You Think You Are?* The name was changed for publications outside North America, the story goes, because readers might not catch the implication of that title, one that tells readers this will be morality tales of individuals who are too big for their own boots, full of presumption: *Just* who do you think you are? All the more poignant, then, are the foods that tempt young Rose—*store-bought* tarts, the processed and branded sugar drink product Vita-Malt, and *canned* salmon.

The last story of Munro's collection is itself called "Who Do You Think You Are?" and focuses on the preposterously presumptuously named Milton Homer, and one other character who gains attention from mimicking him. Ironically, far from being a figure of epic proportions or aspirations, Milton Homer is learning delayed, a figure who some might understand to be the village idiot. One pivotal scene finds Milton seated in the corner at an event hosted by his two spinster sisters, where he steadily and greedily devours the pastries on offer at this very Canadian event in a way that affronts all the small-town citizens and their sense of moderation and propriety. "Some day it will just blow up in their faces," says Flo of the spinster sisters' self-righteousness (2006: 341). And indeed narrator Rose wonders if that's why the guests come each year, to see "Milton with his jowls and stomach swollen as if with bad intentions, ready to blow?" (341).

> After the slides, plates of sandwiches, cookies tarts were served. All were home-made and very good ... All [Milton] did was stuff himself at an unbelievable rate. It seemed as if he downed date squares, hermits (sic) Nanaimo bars and fruit drops, butter tarts and brownies, whole, the way a snake will swallow frogs (341).

Butter tarts—again in the plural—tempt another troubled soul in a young adult novel called *The Hunger*, written to warn and inform young readers about the dangers of anorexia nervosa. The teenage protagonist, Paula, is a perfectionist and anorexic with bulimic tendencies. After her doctor correctly diagnoses her and calls her out on her dangerously unhealthy food habits, she grabs forty dollars from the stash she knows is hidden in her house, and heads to scour the aisles of a local store. What does she first find? A dozen store-baked butter tarts for $4.99. She grabs them rationalizing that she would eat one and leave the rest for the family (Skrypuch 1999: 42), but then thinks "a tiny glass of rich chocolate would be good with a butter tart" (43). Then the food frenzy begins until she spends all the money available to her. Ashamed, Paula tells the bemused cashier, "it's a birthday party. Mom's got a carload of kids to feed" (43). But her readers fully understand all this food is not to assuage real hunger, and it will all be eaten by Paula, and all at once. "Her mouth filled with saliva at the sight of so much forbidden food" (44).

What happens when one does eat just one small butter tart by itself? Rather than a guilty indulgence, one small butter tart is just a snack, the stuff of everyday Canadian life. For example, in the opening of Dave Margoshes' story *The Gift*, the protagonist's eye is first caught by an exotic beauty in the cafeteria. She seems to Gerry at first "native or Asian of some sort, Chinese perhaps, or Filipino; at any rate breath-taking. Beautiful" (81). When he sees her again, she's walking to her friends carrying coffee and—yes—just one butter tart (81). It's then that Margoshes' readers realize she's not as other worldly and exotic as he assumed; rather, that the story's protagonist is unreliable, a flawed perceiver. Margoshes' reader interprets all this by assessing the character on her choice of food (the butter tart), and dining location (the cafeteria). And, indeed, the story is about just that—how the protagonist time and again gets it wrong, especially in interpreting the women around him.

However, precisely because butter tarts are just so reliable, so very predictably middle-of-the-road Canadian, our writers can shock us by transforming them into something else. Journalist Mark Thrice in *The Chivaree* tells a story about a modern-day enactment of an old Canadian tradition in which friends play tricks on a newly married couple on their wedding night. In this case, it's the author and his pals playing tricks on his newlywed sister, switching baking powder and corn starch, adding chicken chunks to the lemon drink mix, adding Tabasco to the corn syrup. It is as a result of this last trick that butter tarts enter stage left. The new bride spends a full day baking butter tarts, but when she tastes one her tongue burns, and she correctly guesses who the culprit must be. She phones her brother to announce: "I'm bringing over a batch of butter tarts and you're going to eat every one of them" (Thrice 2007: 33).

Two poets surprise us in a different way: rather than spicing up the mixture, they wax eloquent about the humble tart. Dennis Cooley adds it to his list of many round objects in a resonant, meditative and alliterative catalogue of lines, each one introduced by a colon, in a poem called "Moon Musings." "A butter tart," he muses as the line pauses, "full of raisins," and the line pauses again, "for whatever reasons ..." (Cooley 2007: 23). The line is nestled between others, some metaphysical ("a tear on the face of night"), others onomatopoeic and humorous ("a hub cap hubba hubba ding ding"), and still others haunting ("an eye of a cat open in sleep/death"), before the poem concludes with "glad tidings to all" (21–23).

Poet Barry Butson is even more effusive. "My mother wrote no poetry," his contained six-line ode to the butter tart—no, to *his mother's* butter tarts—begins. A poignant poem, it offers no hint of irony, just a bite of pure sweetness. "My mother wrote no poetry, / but baked the most epic butter tarts. / Pastry soft as ear lobes cradled / a circle of corn syrup and raisins, / crowned with a crust of golden bubbles." Like his mother's tarts, Butson's poem offers soft and sweet sibilance ("pastry soft as ear lobes," "full of "syrup and raisins") alongside the texture of its alliterative hard 'c' sounds (cradled, corn, crowned and crust). "Her poems came sonnet-sweet from the oven" (Butson 1998: 47). Such a small dainty the butter tart, but its literary and touristic footprint is formidable.

Conclusion:

In a mouth-wateringly delicious passage, Loretta Gatto-White writes, tongue firmly in cheek:

> "A bite of Canada's culinary minestra might taste like smoked salmon stuffed perogies, on a bed of curried lentil couscous layered with foie gras quenelle, garnished with a crackling of pemmican prosciutto and a dusting of dulse in a pool of ginger, lemon grass and sake reduction, followed by a molten butter tart a la mode; a feast to which every culture calling Canada home has contributed" (2013: 1).

The counter suggestion to this exotic and eclectic feast is a Canadian meal of everyday fare, modest cooking prepared to quell hunger pangs and offer familiar and comforting foods. It is not what Canadians like to advertise in glossy magazines showcasing the wonderful variety of indigenous foods, the best of local produce, the inventiveness of the best chefs as they benefit from the bounty of Canada's many cultural influences. But it is quintessentially Canadian—because it has been claimed, refined and defined by our home cooks over the generations—and steadily taken up its place first in the background and then in the foreground of our literature.

Works Cited

Allen, Emily. "Culinary Exhibition: Victorian Wedding Cakes and Royal Spectacle" *Victorian Studies*, 45, 3. (2003): 457–484.

Bergstrom, Jenne and Osada, Miko. "Miss Ellen Pringle's Pound Cake" (2015, Mar. 22), Retrieved from: https://36eggs.com/2015/03/22/miss-ellen-pringles-pound-cake/

Bonisteel, Sara. "Butter Tarts, Canada's Humble Favorite, Have Much to Love," *New York Times*,. (2018, Jan. 12) Retrieved from: https://www.nytimes.com/2018/01/12/dining/butter-tarts-canada.html

Brandolini, Andrea. "Maize, Introduction, Evolution and Diffusion in Italy," *Maydica*, 54, (2009):233–242.

Brinton, Laurel J and Fee, Margery (2001), "Canadian English," in John Algeo (ed.), *The Cambridge History of the English Language Vol. VI, English in North America*. Cambridge: Cambridge University Press, 422–440, 434–438.

Butson, Barry (1998), "Butter Tarts." in *East End Poems*, London: Moonstone Press, 47.

Charsley, Simon R. (1992), *Wedding Cakes and Cultural History*. London: Routledge.

Carley, Glenn (2007), *Polenta at Midnight: Tales of Gusto and Enchantment at North York*, Montréal: Véhicule Press.

Cho, Lily (2010), *Eating Chinese: Culture on the Menu in Small Town Canada*, Toronto: University of Toronto Press.

Choy, Wayson (2005), *All That Matters*, Toronto: Anchor Canada.

Cooke, Nathalie. "Writing the Chinese Restaurateur into the Canadian Literary Landscape," *Studies in Canadian Literature*, 42.2 (2017): 5–25.

Moyer, Alexia, "Butter Tarts" in *Canadian Literary Fare*. Cooke, Nathalie, Boyd, Shelley and Moyer, Alexia (2019). Unpublished Manuscript.

Cooley, Dennis (2007), *By Word of Mouth: The Poetry of Dennis Cooley*. Nicole Markotić (ed.), Waterloo: Wilfrid Laurier University Press, 2007.

Davidson, Alan (year), *Oxford Food Companion*, 3rd edition. ed. by T. Jaine. New York, NY: Oxford University Press. Retrieved April 17, 2020 https://www-oxfordreference-com.proxy3.library.mcgill.ca/view/10.1093/acref/9780199677337.001.0001/acref-9780199677337?btog=chap&hide=true&jumpTo=polenta&page=149&pageSize=20&skipEditions=true&sort=titlesort&source=%2F10.1093%2Facref%2F9780199677337.001.0001%2Facref-9780199677337

D'Alfonso, Antonio (1996), *In Italics: In Defense of Ethnicity*, Toronto: Guernica.

DeLuca, Anna Pia (2013), "Polenta and Frico," in Loretto Gatto-White & Delia De Santis (eds.), *Italian Canadians at Table*, Lancaster: Guernica, 172–175.

De Santis, Delia (2013), "Introduction," in Loretto Gatto-White & Delia De Santis (eds.), *Italian Canadians at Table: A Narrative Feast in Five Courses*, Lancaster: Guernica.

Di Michele, Mary (2011), "Dancing After the War," in *The Flower of Youth: Pier Paolo Pasolini Poems*, Toronto: ECW Press, 69–71.

Di Michele, Mary (1986), "Life Is Theatre, or, O to Be Italian in Toronto Drinking Cappuccino on Bloor Street at Bersani & Carlevale's," in *Immune to Gravity*, Toronto: McClelland & Stewart, 45–47.

Di Michele, Mary (2011), "The Return," in *The Flower of Youth: Pier Paolo Pasolini Poems*, Toronto: ECW Press, 27.

Di Pasquale, Casullo, "Montreal's Slab Pizza, La Slab Pizza Di Montreal, The City's Unique Taste of Home, Il Particolare 'Sapore Di Casa' Della Città," *Panoram Italia, Living Italian Style*, 14, 2. (2019):46–47.

Ferguson, Priscilla Parkhurst (2004), *Accounting for Taste: The Triumph of French Cuisine*. Chicago: University of Chicago Press.

Fornari, Anna (2013). "Roast Turkey and Polenta," in Loretta Gatto-White and Delia De Santis (eds.), *Italian Canadians at Table*, Lancaster: Guernica, 99–104.

Gillman, Gary. "Butter Tarts in North America," *Petits Propos Culinaires*, 114 (2019): 37–57.

Gordon-Walker, Caitlin (2013), "The Process of Chop Suey." Susan L. T. Ashley (ed.), *Diverse Spaces: Identity, Heritage and Community in Canadian Public Culture*, Newcastle upon Tyne: Cambridge Scholars Publishing: 16–38.

Hui, Ann (2019), *Chop Suey Nation: The Legion Cafe and Other Stories from Canada's Chinese Restaurants*. Madeira Park: British Columbia.

Jansen, Clifford (1988), *Italians in a Multicultural Canada*. Lewiston: The Edwin Mellen Press.

Lam, Vincent (2006), *Bloodletting & Miraculous Cures: Stories*. Toronto: Anchor Canada.

Margoshes, Dave. (2007), "The Gift" *Antigonish Review*, 151, 2007:81–137.

McGill, Robert. "Who Do You Think You Are?". *The Literary Encyclopedia: Exploring Literature, History and Culture*, 3, 1/3. (2002):1–3.

Michelut, Dôre (1990), "The Earth," *Ouroboros: The Book That Ate Me*, Laval: Éditions Trois: 79–80.

Mitchell, Valerie (2003), *Polenta on the Board, Italian Family Cooking Abruzzese Style*. Vancouver: Benwell-Atkins.

Montgomery, Lucy Maud (2014), *Anne of windy poplars (Anne of green gables novels, 4)*. Naperville: Sourcebooks Fire.

Mosby, Ian. "We are what we ate: Canada's history of cuisines". *The Globe and Mail*, (March 13, 2007): Retrieved from: https://www.theglobeandmail.com/news/national/canada-150/we-are-what-we-ate-canadas-history-incuisines/article34289538/.

Munro, Alice (1996), "Royal Beatings." Who Do You Think You Are?: Stories, Penguin, 1–27.

—. (2006), "Who do you think you are?", in *Who do you think you are? Stories*, Ontario: Penguin Canada [ereader version]. 327–356. Retrieved from: https://mcgill.overdrive.com/search?query=who+do+you+think+you+are

Nash, Alan. "From Spaghetti to Sushi." *Food, Culture & Society*, 12, 1. (2009): 5–24.

Paci, Frank Gilbert (1996), *The Italians*. Ottawa: Oberon Press.

Pinto, Jonathan. "5-Tonne, World-Record Polenta Made by Windsor Italian Club". *CBC*,. (2014, Sept. 11): Retrieved from: https://www.cbc.ca/news/canada/windsor/5-tonne-world-record-polenta-made-by-windsor-italian-club-1.2762117.

Resnick, Philip (2012), *The Labyrinth of North American Identities*. Toronto: University of Toronto Press.

Skrypuch, Marsha Forchuk (1999), *The Hunger*. Toronto: Dundurn Group.

Statistics Canada Historical Collection. *The Canada Year Book 1910 3c. Arrivals at inland and ocean ports in Canada in fiscal years 1906–1910*. https://www66.statcan.gc.ca/eng/1910/191004670411_Immigration.pdf: p. 411.

—. The Canada Year Book 1915 3c. *Arrivals at Inland and Ocean Ports in Canada in fiscal years 1910–1916.* https://www66.statcan.gc.ca/eng/1915/191501440112_p.%20112.pdf: p. 112.

—. The Canada Year Book 1921 3c. *Arrivals at Inland and Ocean Ports in Canada in Fiscal Years 1915–1922.* https://www66.statcan.gc.ca/eng/1921/192101630127_p.%20127.pdf: p. 127.

—. The Canada Year Book 1926 3c. *Immigrant Arrivals in Canada, by Nationalities and Races, fiscal years 1919–1926.* https://www66.statcan.gc.ca/eng/1926/192602120172_p.%20172.pdf: p. 172.

—. The Canada Year Book 1927–1928 3c. *Countries of Birth of Immigrations arriving via Ocean Ports and from the United States, fiscal years ended Mar. 31, 1926 and 1927.* https://www66.statcan.gc.ca/eng/1927-28/192702370195_p.%20195.pdf: p. 195.

—. The Canada Year Book 1929 3c. *Countries of Birth of Immigrants arriving via Ocean Ports and from the United States, fiscal years ended Mar. 31, 1927 and 1928.* https://www66.statcan.gc.ca/eng/1929/192902320190_p.%20190.pdf: p. 190.

—. The Canada Year Book 1931 3c. *Countries of Birth of Immigrants Arriving via Ocean Ports and from the United States, fiscal year ended Mar. 31, 1929 and 1930.* https://www66.statcan.gc.ca/eng/1931/193102190179_p.%20179.pdf: p. 179.

—. The Canada Year Book 1933 3c. *Countries of Birth of Immigrants, arriving via Ocean Ports from the United States, fiscal years ended Mar. 31, 1931 and 1932.* https://www66.statcan.gc.ca/eng/1933/193302360192_p.%20192.pdf: p. 192.

—. The Canada Year Book 1936 3c. *Countries of Birth of Immigrants, calendar years 1930 – 1934.* https://www66.statcan.gc.ca/eng/1936/193602510191_p.%20191.pdf: p. 191.

—. The Canada Year Book 1939 3c. *Countries of birth of Immigrants, calendar years 1931 – 1937.* https://www66.statcan.gc.ca/eng/1939/193902290163_p.%20163.pdf: p. 163.

—. The Canada Year Book 1941 3c. *Countries of Birth of Immigrants into Canada, calendar years 1936 – 1939.* https://www66.statcan.gc.ca/eng/1941/194101730115_p.%20115.pdf: p. 115.

—. The Canada Year Book 1942 3c. *Countries of Birth Immigrants into Canada, calendar years 1937 – 1940.* https://www66.statcan.gc.ca/eng/1942/194202190157_p.%20157.pdf: p. 157.

—. The Canada Year Book 1948 – 1949 3c. *Birthplace of Immigrant Arrivals, 1942 – 1947.*
https://www66.statcan.gc.ca/eng/1948-49/194802400178_p.%20178.pdf: p. 178.

—. The Canada Year Book 1950 3c. *Birthplaces of Immigrant Arrivals, 1946 – 1948.*
https://www66.statcan.gc.ca/eng/1950/195002440188_p.%20188.pdf: p. 188.

—. The Canada Year Book 1952 – 1953 3c. *Birthplaces of Immigrant Arrivals, 1949 – 1951.*
https://www66.statcan.gc.ca/eng/1952-53/195202200168_p.%20168.pdf: p. 168.

—. The Canada Year Book 1955 3c. *Birthplaces of Immigrant Arrivals, 1951 – 1953; Origins of Immigrant Arrivals, 1951 – 1953.* https://www66.statcan.gc.ca/eng/1955/195501960170_p.%20170.pdf: p. 170.

—. The Canada Year Book 1956 3c. *Birthplaces of Immigrant Arrivals 1954.* https://www66.statcan.gc.ca/eng/1956/195602150183_p.%20183.pdf: p. 183

—. The Canada Year Book 1959 3c. *Birthplaces of Immigrant Arrivals 1955 – 1957.* https://www66.statcan.gc.ca/eng/1959/195902070181_p.%20181.pdf: p. 181.

—. The Canada Year Book 1963 – 1964 3c. *Birthplaces of Immigrant Arrivals, 1960 – 1962.*
https://www66.statcan.gc.ca/eng/1963-64/196302250203_p.%20203.pdf: p. 203.

—. The Canada Year Book 1965 3c. *Birthplaces of Immigrant Arrivals, 1961 – 1963; Origins of Immigrant Arrivals, 1962 – 1963.* https://www66.statcan.gc.ca/eng/1965/196502400210_p.%20210.pdf: p. 210.

—. The Canada Year Book 1968 3c. *Immigrant Arrivals by Country of last Permanent Residence, 1964 – 1966; Immigrant Arrivals, by Country of Birth, 1964 – 1965.* https://www66.statcan.gc.ca/eng/1968/196802620234_p.%20234.pdf: p. 234.

Statistics Canada (2017), Immigration and Ethnocultural Diversity Highlight Tables. 2016 Census. Statistics Canada Catalogue no. 98-402-X2016007. Ottawa. Released October 25, 2017.

http://www12.statcan.gc.ca/census-recensement/2016/dp-pd/hlt-fst/imm/index-eng.cfm (accessed August 04, 2019).

Thrice, Mark (2007), "The Chivaree" in *Halfway to Crazy*, Morgan James Publisher.

Wah, Fred (2006), *Diamond Grill*. Edmonton: NeWest Press.

Wah, Fred (1985), *Waiting for Saskatchewan*. Winnipeg: Turnstone Press.

Zucchi, John (2005), "Italians in Canada," in Ember M., Ember C. R., Skiggard I. (eds.) *Encyclopedia of Diasporas*. Boston: Springer.

MARCO MODENESI

"Un rigatoni jumbo spécial à la pepperoni mambo, ou quelque chose comme ça". La dimension gastronomique dans Le Matou *d'Yves Beauchemin*

LE MATOU d'Yves Beauchemin (né le 26 juin 1941) voit le jour en mars 1981. Dans les mois qui suivent sa parution, il "est l'objet de nombreux comptes rendus, presque tous extrêmement élogieux" (Anonyme 2017: 766). Le succès du roman, à grand tirage, va bientôt rebondir en France et, à travers presque une vingtaine de traductions, dans le monde entier. Un film inspiré du roman de Beauchemin et réalisé par Jean Beaudin sort le 28 août 1985 et sera accompagné d'une mini-série de six épisodes.

Il est impossible de synthétiser l'intrigue narrative du *Matou*, "immense roman" (Cagnon 1983: 95) qui se déroule sur 700 pages dans l'édition de poche de la version de février 2007.

Par une remarquable maîtrise de l'art de conter, Yves Beauchemin, comme le relève Maurice Cagnon, "trame [...] un complot de surface composé d'aventures rocambolesques, de fausses pistes, de rebondissements loufoques, de revirements inattendus, de rencontres inopinées, le tout se multipliant à une allure effrénée et colorée par une ironie cruelle." (*Ibid.*: 97)

L'auteur, d'ailleurs, semble bien conscient de cet aspect de son roman, comme en témoigne la réaction de Maître Rodrigue Théorêt—à qui s'adressent, vers la fin du livre, Florent Boissonneault, sa femme et ses amis—face au récit de tout ce qu'il leur est arrivé dans les mois qui précèdent la rencontre avec l'avocat :

> L'histoire de son client lui apparaissait comme un tissu d'aventures abracadabrantes qui tenaient plus de la littérature fantastique que de la réalité et il en vint à se demander si ses trois interlocuteurs ne faisaient pas partie d'une espèce de secte pour détraqués légers qui n'osaient pas avouer leur appartenance. (Beauchemin 2017: 654)

Et ce qui s'avère encore plus étonnant, c'est que les sombres et inquiétantes aventures et, surtout, mésaventures que Florent et Élise, un jeune couple, doivent traverser pendant presque deux ans sont, après tout, le développement d'une modeste affaire : l'achat de La Binerie, un petit restaurant sur la rue Mont-Royal, dans la fiction narrative aussi bien que dans la réalité.

Dans les premières pages du roman, lorsque Florent va dîner à La Blanche Hermine, "une crêperie [de la rue Saint-Hubert] qu'il avait prise en affection", (*Ibid.*: 15), le narrateur relève qu'il "était une fine fourchette, et [qu'il] professait des théories fort élaborées sur la profession de restaurateur". (*Ibidem*)

Ce n'est donc pas par un simple hasard que Florent s'est lié, depuis longtemps, d'une solide amitié, à Aurélien Picquot, «un vieil original de cinquante-deux ans, arrivé de France après la guerre, qui dirigeait les cuisines du Château Frontenac" (*Ibid.*: 30) et avec qui il partage "une passion commune pour la bonne cuisine et la franchise" (*Ibid.*: 31).

Et comme le relève Egon Ratablavasky, après sa rencontre fortuite avec Florent, ce dernier rêve d'avoir un restaurant : "Vous aimez les restaurants. Vous avez le rêve … d'en posséder un. N'est-il pas vrai ?" (*Ibid.*: 19)

Et c'est justement grâce à celle que l'on croirait être l'inattendue et gratuite générosité de Ratablavasky que Florent, juste après leur première rencontre, peut en acheter un :

— Connaissez-vous un restaurant du nom de La
Binerie ? fit [Ratablavasky] doucement.
— Le restaurant de la rue Mont-Royal, près de Saint-
Denis ?
— Exactement. Eh bien, il est en vente. Et pour un prix
ridicule. Vous savez que la nourriture en est excellente ?
— Oui, bien sûr. On y sert de la cuisine québécoise.
C'est une sorte d'institution dans le coin.
— Institution, voilà qui est le vrai mot ! Trente-six ans
de bonne cuisine, il y a là un trésor inestimable que
personne ne peut vous voler, n'est-ce pas ? Vous avez
des économies ... 11780$, si ma mémoire dit vrai ...
(*Ibid.*: 20)

La Binerie (qui a été, en réalité fondée en 1938) est "un minus-
cule établissement coincé entre deux immeubles qui ne lui avaient
laissé que cinq mètres de façade, la forçant à s'allonger comme un
wagon-restaurant" où "chaque centimètre cube avait été judicieu-
sement exploité [...]. On ne pouvait y accommoder que dix-sept
clients à la fois, mais ces derniers se succédaient à une belle cadence,
car l'endroit était renommé pour sa bonne grosse nourriture pay-
sanne". (*Ibid.*: 26)
    Autrement dit, institution montréalaise, La Binerie est avant
tout un haut lieu de la cuisine populaire québécoise, comme,
d'abord, en témoigne discrètement, l'ancien cuisinier du restaurant dont nous faisons la connaissance lorsqu'il sort une "tarte aux
pommes" (*Ibid.*: 27) du four ou lorsqu'il prépare "un énorme pâté
chinois" (*Ibid.*: 37) quelques jours avant de quitter La Binerie pour
être remplacé, de la part de Florent, par Picquot.
    Loin de vouloir suggérer le peu d'espace que la cuisine québé-
coise semble occuper dans le tissu et dans l'imaginaire montréalais,
les dimensions limitées de l'établissement traduisent plutôt son statut de cuisine à mesure d'homme.
    La preuve en est que lorsque Florent découvre—après avoir
fait un marché de dupes avec son ancien associé Slipskin, qui lui

vole le restaurant—que l'anglophone vient d'acheter le magasin à côté de La Binerie, il s'exclame : "—Quoi ! il a acheté la bijouterie Lemieux ? Ah ! le cochon ! il est en train de virer ma Binerie en restaurant américain !" (*Ibid.*: 495)

En écho, Picquot n'avait pas hésité à écrire dans une lettre à Florent : "*La Binerie a été agrandie. Le menu est devenu bilingue, horreur et décadence !*" (*Ibid.*: 425)

La Binerie est une institution de la cuisine traditionnelle, à mesure d'homme, comme on vient de le relever, et notamment à mesure de québécois.

L'adjectif *américain*, d'ailleurs, n'est jamais employé avec une nuance positive lorsqu'on parle de cuisine et de nourriture dans *Le Matou*.

Lorsque Picquot avoue sa perte d'enthousiasme pour son travail au Château Frontenac, il s'exprime de manière fort significative à ce propos :

> J'en avais par-dessus la tête, vois-tu. Quel sens y a-t-il à s'échiner sur un faisan Souvaroff qu'une brute du Connecticut va mâchouiller en enfilant des rasades de Seven-Up ? C'est jeter des perles aux pourceaux. Voilà pourquoi je me suis dégoûté de la haute cuisine. Je n'y retoucherai plus jamais. Des amateurs de potages instantanés, voilà tout ce que l'on voit à présent. Dans vingt ans, il n'y aura plus que des Amerloques, d'ignobles Amerloques sur toute la planète. (*Ibid.*: 59)

Lorsqu'il aperçoit "sur une tablette des boîtes de purée de pommes de terre instantanée" (*Ibid.*: 91), Picquot, chef français, n'hésite pas à demander : "Qu'est-ce que c'est que toutes ces horreurs ? [...] Jetez-moi ces ordures américaines dans la rue : elles déshonorent la profession." (*Ibidem*)

Obligé d'abandonner son travail à La Binerie, Picquot cède, pour gagner de l'argent, au monde de la publicité, ce qui ne l'empêche de continuer à mépriser tout ce qui relève de la cuisine de masse des États-Unis :

De cuisinier, je suis devenu prostitué ! J'aide les Américains à répandre leur nourriture infecte à travers le monde. C'est la fin de tout. Mieux vaut mendier. Hier, je suis tombé sur un échantillon qu'on venait de recevoir des U.S.A. : des amandes, tenez-vous bien … à saveur de Bar-B-Q ! oui, je dis bien des amandes, ces princesses de la confiserie, comme les appelait Brillat-Savarin, qui a écrit sur elles des pages sublimes ! J'en suis resté gaga tout l'après-midi. (*Ibid.*: 477)

On m'a chargé de faire des présentations ragoûtantes pour ces ignobles préparations industrielles que l'Amérique bouffe depuis trente ans avec l'impression de fréquenter les sommets de la haute cuisine. Je ne ménage pas les colorants, les vernis, les bouts de fil de fer, la gélatine et la fécule de maïs, et, ma foi, les résultats ne sont pas trop mauvais. Et ils me payent un salaire fou, ces idiots. (*Ibid.*: 234)

Si, comme le relèvent Marie-Noëlle Aubertin et Genevière Sicotte, en parlant de la réalité québécoise, "notre patrimoine alimentaire a longtemps été dans l'ombre de ceux de la France ou de la Grande Bretagne" (Aubertin, Sicotte 2013), il est temps de s'interroger sur la manière dont il en est rendu témoignage dans *Le Matou*, par La Binerie, d'abord, et, ensuite, par *Chez Florent*, le restaurant que le héros du *Matou* ouvre vers la fin du roman, à son tour petit "*par vocation*" (Beauchemin 2017 : 677) et qui sera situé juste en face de La Binerie, otage, depuis de longs mois, de Slipskin.

D'abord, nul doute sur la haute considération que l'on réserve à cette cuisine *populaire* c'est-à-dire relevant de la tradition d'un peuple.

Lassé des cuisines du Château Frontenac, où il ne trouve plus d'inspiration pour se consacrer au "filet de bœuf Richelieu", "à la chartreuse de perdreaux", au "caneton aux navets", aux "fricadelles de veau Smitane" ou à "la tarte Bordaloue" (appétissants exemples du patrimoine gastronomique de la France), Picquot accepte de devenir le nouveau chef de La Binerie de Florent.

En vue de son nouveau rôle, il avoue alors s'être mis à l'étude avec une remarquable application pour acquérir dignement, ce qui est pour lui un nouveau savoir :

> — À Saint-Sauveur, jeune homme ! Je viens de passer deux semaines dans un chalet à Saint-Sauveur afin d'acquérir ma nouvelle science. J'ai rassemblé tous les manuels de cuisine traditionnelle québécoise qui se trouvaient sous nos cieux et je m'en suis nourri, en quelque sorte. Soit dit en passant, je te conseille la méditation d'un recueil de recettes publié en 1879 par la révérende mère Caron, des Sœurs de la Charité de la Providence. Tu verras que l'odeur de sainteté et les arômes de la bonne cuisine forment un mariage délicieux. (*Ibid.*: 87)

Le bilan de l'activité de La Binerie pour ce qu'on pourrait appeler le patrimoine gastronomique québécois est particulièrement éloquent :

> La Binerie servait une moyenne de 300 repas par jour. En un mois, les clients avaient engouffré 2000 litres de soupe, 122 pains, 80 douzaines d'œufs, 150 kilos de bœuf aux légumes, 77 cœurs de veau, 125 kilos de pâté chinois, autant de ragoût de boulettes, 897 kilos de fèves au lard, 168 tourtières, 150 tartes au sucre, 2200 litres de café et 28 bassines de pouding chômeur. La force du restaurant résidait dans la qualité de sa nourriture, la rapidité du service et la modicité relative des prix, rendue possible par l'économie d'entretien d'un local tellement exigu qu'on se demandait comment il pouvait servir de passage à une telle avalanche de nourriture. À moins d'un malheur, le restaurant pourrait donc se payer plus vite que prévu. (*Ibid.*: 84)

Dans une énumération qui témoigne du grand succès de l'établissement et qui fait chavirer l'esprit du lecteur qui perd le nord avec tous ces chiffres, on reconnaît les plats qui composent normalement le menu de La Binerie : au-delà des soupes, on retrouve le bœuf aux légumes, le cœur de veau (probablement au vin rouge), le pâté chinois, les fèves au lard, les tourtières, le ragoût de boulettes, la tarte au sucre et le pouding chômeur. Une véritable apothéose de la cuisine traditionnelle du Québec.

S'il est vrai que "le patrimoine advient lorsqu'une collectivité identifie un objet pour lequel elle manifeste un goût particulier et décide d'en faire un emblème qui sera reconnu par tous, c'est-à-dire par ses membres (actuels et idéalement futurs) et par les autres nations, puisqu'il s'agit d'une sorte de preuve d'identité" (Aubertin, Sicotte), la cuisine traditionnelle du Québec qui est l'essence du menu de La Binerie—restaurant populaire au succès ahurissant où "les clients continuaient d'affluer [...] [où l]es chaudrons de soupe, de fèves et de ragoût se vid[ent] aussitôt remplis, les pointes de tourtière grésillantes, fleurant la sarriette et le laurier, s'envol[ent] dans les assiettes"—(Beauchemin 2017: 123) est incontestablement l'expression de l'existence d'un patrimoine gastronomique québécois.

D'ailleurs, celui-ci apparaît aussi, mais avec une fréquence sensiblement plus discrète, au-dehors du cadre de La Binerie : Ange-Albert, ami fraternel de Florent et d'Élise dévore "une tourtière et demie" (*Ibid.*: 37); Gustave Bleau entre en scène "avec une bassine de fèves au lard, toutes luisantes de graisse" (*Ibid.*: 78); Picquot montre à monsieur Émile comment préparer "une cipâte au lièvre" (*Ibid.* : 153); Madame Boissonneault, dans un goût un peu plus raffiné, prépare pour son fils Florent et sa femme Élise «une magnifique jardinière en gelée sertie dans une couronne de champignons farcis à la chair de crabe" (*Ibid.*: 143), "un poulet à la mode de l'île d'Orléans" (*Ibidem*) et «un pâté aux framboises" (*Ibid.*: 146); un petit garçon assis sur le perron d'une boulangerie mord "dans un chômeur encore tout chaud, gonflé de confiture de fraises" (*Ibid.*: 504).

Cependant, la cuisine traditionnelle de La Binerie ne s'avère pas conservatrice et impénétrable. Pour assurer une petite nouveauté à la cuisine qu'il prépare pour La Binerie, Picquot propose le lance-ment d'une recette savoyarde :

> — [...] Nous allons lancer une vieille recette savoyarde qui fera fureur : les *crics* !
> — Qu'est-ce que c'est que ça ?
> — Un plat merveilleux à base de rien du tout. Pomme de terre râpée, œuf, poivre et lait, mélangez le tout et faites poêler sous forme de petites crêpes. [...]
> — Les *crics*, ce sera notre marque de commerce, la signature de La Binerie. On les sert avec n'importe quoi : ragoût, tourtière, viandes froides ou rôti, ou même toutes seules, à la place d'une omelette.
> — *Crics*, ça fait ... étranger, remarqua Slipskin. *We need another word.*
> Un long moment de réflexion suspendit la conversation.
> — Des *grands-mères*, suggéra Florent, hésitant. Picquot le bras vers lui, galvanisé :
> — Un trait de génie, déclara-t-il [...]

> Deux jours plus tard, Rosario Gladu pondait un ar-ticle dithyrambique au sujet d'une ancienne recette québécoise que La Binerie venait de tirer d'un oubli immérité. (*Ibid.*: 110-111)

La *cric* ou plutôt *crique* selon l'orthographe la plus répandue, est un plat français qui s'insère, de manière harmonieuse, dans le menu de cuisine rigoureusement traditionnelle de La Binerie. Pour ce faire, la crique fait quand même peau neuve du point de vue linguis-tique et devient une *grand-mère* (fort probablement par analogie avec les grands-pères au sirop d'érable). En tant que telle, selon le journaliste Gladu, dont le rôle est d'assurer une bonne publicité au restaurant, elle se fait québécoise.

Au-delà de la petite supercherie linguistique, l'assimilation de la recette savoyarde à la cuisine traditionnelle québécoise témoigne d'une opération de métissage culturel et culinaire qui enrichit l'identité profonde de la cuisine québécoise tout en lui ôtant un tout petit peu de son statut d'authenticité. (cf. Brind'Amour 2005: 246)

Le menu que propose le nouveau restaurant de Florent, *Chez Florent*, inauguré vers la fin du roman, reprend en écho celui de La Binerie pour le modifier légèrement mais significativement:

Le menu [de *Chez Florent*] s'appuyait pour l'essentiel sur la cuisine traditionnelle québécoise, mais une cuisine discrètement affinée, complétée en sourdine par quelques spécialités françaises ou européennes. Les crêpes au sirop d'érable, la tourtière, la cipâte, les fèves au lard et le pâté chinois voisinaient avec le coq au vin et le sauté de veau Marengo, sans oublier les fameuses grands-mères qu'avait popularisées Picquot à La Binerie. Mais comme l'on s'adressait à une clientèle populaire, facile à effaroucher, Élise avait suggéré de rebaptiser les plats européens pour leur donner un petit air de chez nous. La crème de brocoli, la crème de carottes, le potage Parmentier et le velouté Aurore se retrouvèrent sous la rubrique des BONNES SOUPES DE MA TANTE DÉLIMA avec la soupe aux pois et la soupe aux choux. Le coq au vin se présentait comme un "fricot de poulet à la mode du Bas-du-Fleuve". Le sauté de veau, méprisant les hauts cris des manuels culinaires, portait le nom de "fricassée de veau de Saint-Félicien". Le tout se complétait de quelques plats vite faits : foie de porc et foie de bœuf poêlés, steak haché, saucisses et les indispensables sandwiches.

La section des desserts affirmait clairement sa double allégeance québécoise et française, car l'amour des douceurs, c'est bien connu, donne de l'audace au dîneur le plus peureux. On y trouvait les tartes à la farlouche et au sirop d'érable, les beignes et les galettes à la mélasse, mais aussi la crème caramel, les mokas et même les diplomates. (Beauchemin 2017: 677-678)

La cuisine traditionnelle est donc affinée par quelques plats qui viennent de France et d'Europe où l'on peut déceler la contribution, encore une fois, du chef français.

Afin de ne pas heurter une clientèle populaire et qui pourrait se montrer méfiante face à ce qu'elle ne connaît pas, sur le modèle des *grands-mères*, les noms des plats étrangers sont modifiés afin qu'ils puissent s'intégrer sans difficulté au niveau de la cuisine traditionnelle.

La cuisine traditionnelle québécoise—pour des raisons économiques et pour témoigner sa reconnaissance vis-à-vis de la dévotion de Picquot—renonce en partie à son authenticité d'origine, et choisit ainsi d'être davantage métissée et timidement multiculturelle. Elle est encore plus ouverte pour ce qui est des desserts, car elle est disponible à accueillir explicitement l'autre à côté d'elle sans ressentir le besoin, dans ce cas spécifique, d'atténuer l'impact que pourrait impliquer sa diversité.

Dans ce sens, la cuisine de La Binerie ou de son avatar, celle de *Chez Florent* véhiculent et focalisent, sans aucun doute, un imaginaire collectif québécois, mais elles annoncent, en même temps, le début d'un parcours qui se fait sous le signe du multiculturalisme à travers un mécanisme d'hybridation.

Par ailleurs, la cuisine, les mets ont même une fonction de repère identitaire individuelle et non seulement collective, ils parviennent à raviver des liens émotifs avec la culture du berceau, ils se révèlent être une sorte de témoignage d'appartenance.

Madame Jeunehomme, la tante de Florent qui habite depuis des années à Key West, en Floride, surprend son neveu et sa femme alors que son cuisinier leur sert une tourtière, suivie d'un "pouding aux framboises" (typiquement québécois) :

> Le cuisinier apparut de nouveau. Mademoiselle Lydie, l'œil courroucé, lui fit signe d'aller vitement changer son tablier taché de sauce. Il obéit, penaud, et revint avec un plateau où grésillait une belle tourtière.
> — C'est ma façon à moi de soigner le mal du pays, fit madame Jeunehomme. (*Ibid.*: 348)

Picquot, pendant l'un des nombreux moments de détresse qu'il connaît au fur et à mesure que le temps passe, se galvanise à la proposition que lui fait Florent de se rendre au Saint-Malo :

> — En attendant, que diriez-vous d'aller au Saint-Malo ? proposa Florent. On y sert des filtres.
> — À la bonne heure, s'exclama Picquot. Nous autres, Français, quand nous sommes à l'étranger, il nous faut toujours un petit morceau de pays à suçoter pour être dans notre assiette. (*Ibid.*: 236)

De même, la nourriture privilégiée par un personnage met souvent en évidence un trait de sa personnalité.

C'est le cas de monsieur Émile, enfant alcoolique, livré à lui-même, qui semble vivre plus dans les rues avec son matou (nommé Déjeuner) que chez sa mère dont les nombreux amants absorbent tout le temps et toute l'attention. Les bouteilles de bière et d'alcool accompagnent systématiquement l'enfant dans le quotidien. Le désordre de son existence perce à travers sa faim atavique et la manière qu'il a de la soulager: "[…] Je fouille dans le frigidaire, puis je mange des Mae West, des beurrées de beurre de pinotte, toute sorte d'affaire." (*Ibid.*: 106)

Qui plus est, pour évoquer la démesure qui caractérisait son frère Antoine, Rosario Gladu, journaliste du petit journal du quartier, rappelle ce qui s'est révélé être son dernier repas:

> — Un soir, reprit [Gladu], la voix toute changée, aux alentours de minuit, l'idée lui prend de se faire livrer un rigatoni jumbo spécial à la pepperoni mambo, ou quelque chose comme ça. (*Ibid.*: 167)

Dans le cas de Gladu, cela semble être une marque de famille, vu que, plus tard dans le roman, on le retrouvera dans un restaurant où "il s'attaqu[e] à une pizza pepperoni-olives-anchois au restaurant La Feuille d'Érable, rue Mont-Royal, qu'il fréquentait depuis deux semaines." (*Ibid.*: 257)

Mais le cas le plus flagrant, à ce propos, est celui de l'abbé Octavien Jeunehomme, le cousin de Florent, qui montre un penchant immodéré pour la pâtisserie, québécoise mais aussi bien française, ce qui pourrait suggérer une forme de compensation pour d'autres plaisirs de la chair auxquels son statut de religieux l'empêche de goûter:

> L'abbé y avait disposé une série d'assiettes chargées d'un amoncellement incroyable de pâtisseries recouvertes d'une feuille de cellophane. Des madeleines, des langues de chats, des doigts de dame, des millefeuilles voisinaient avec des clafoutis, des barquettes, des petits fours, des babas, des polonaises. (*Ibid.*: 69-70)

Par ailleurs, seule sa passion pour la littérature (il n'hésite pas à signer de son nom suivi de *amans litterarum*), presque maniaque, dépasse celle pour la pâtisserie, et elle se manifeste aussi dans le domaine de la gastronomie. C'est ainsi que l'abbé organise de temps à autre des repas littéraires pour célébrer la mémoire d'un écrivain. Outre un dîner Zola dont le menu est transcrit en détail dans le roman (cf. *Ibid.*: 244), l'évocation du souper qu'il organise pour célébrer la mémoire de Philippe Aubert de Gaspé ne peut que frapper le lecteur:

> En octobre, [l'abbé Jeunehomme] eut une idée fort heureuse pour célébrer la mémoire de Philippe Aubert de Gaspé, l'auteur des *Anciens Canadiens* : la tenue d'un banquet dans un décor seigneurial québécois du XVIIIe siècle, reconstitué pour l'occasion. Il s'appuya pour l'élaboration du menu sur le sixième chapitre du roman : "Un souper chez un seigneur canadien". Pendant une semaine tout le monde potassa le vieux roman afin d'être en mesure de soutenir une conversation distinguée, puis on se rendit à la boutique de Jean-Denis Beaumont, transformée par celui-ci en salle à manger

seigneuriale. […] Le cuisinier du Quinquet avait préparé un pâté de Pâques : dinde, poulets, perdrix, lièvres et pigeons, le tout recouvert de bardes de lard gras, emprisonné dans une croûte épaisse et reposant sur un godiveau de viandes hachées relevé d'oignons et d'épices fines. Le plat fit parler de lui pendant longtemps. (*Ibid.*: 760)

La rigueur philologique dont témoigne l'abbé ne se limite pas à insérer dans *Le Matou* le témoignage d'un des premiers romans qui favorisent "la valorisation des usages gastronomiques" (Sicotte) de la période de la Conquête mais elle suggère aussi, de manière presque métanarrative, le rapport profond qui peut s'instaurer entre la nourriture et la littérature.

Les représentations littéraires de l'alimentation dans *Le Matou* ne se limitent pas à exercer une simple fonction réaliste et descriptive mais elles s'avèrent systématiquement porteuses de sens.

Les habitudes alimentaires des personnages du *Matou* parlent d'une partie de leur âme, témoignent de quelques traits de leur personnalité, expriment aussi un lien avec le territoire auquel ils appartiennent.

D'ailleurs cela dépasse la dimension individuelle comme en témoigne le succès de masse que sa clientèle attribue à La Binerie dont le menu (comme celui qu'offre *Chez Florent*) parvient à composer et à consacrer une sorte de paradigme de la cuisine traditionnelle du Québec.

Dans ce sens, le roman de Beauchemin montre bien que "l'alimentation […] est inextricablement liée aux processus identitaires et fait partie des lieux communs dans l'imaginaire collectif des sociétés." (Marcotte)

Un imaginaire qui, dans *Le Matou,* se fait même expression de la spécificité de la tradition *québécoise* sans pour cela pencher vers une attitude de défense particulièrement étanche de cette spécificité.

En effet, on a pu relever, à ce propos, que les plats qu'offrent les deux restaurants du *Matou* renoncent par degrés à une authenticité traditionnelle intégrale (par l'introduction des plats français avec et sans déguisement linguistique), ce qui dénote une ouverture discrète mais incontestable à la cuisine d'un autre lieu, d'après une attitude qui témoigne, quoique de manière encore modeste, de l'apparition d'une ouverture à la diversité (une diversité certes mitigée : la cuisine de France), l'annonce d'un trait du multiculturalisme qui, après le milieu des années 1970 (époque des événements du *Matou*), se fera de plus en plus évident dans la société québécoise.

La dimension alimentaire du *Matou* s'avère ainsi être un témoignage littérairement fascinant et culturellement révélateur du fait que le patrimoine alimentaire du Québec existe et qu'il est déjà, au début des années 1980, dans le sillon du métissage et indiscutablement en évolution.

Et le cas des *grands-mères* de La Binerie est alors exemplaire de l'incontestable réussite de ce multiculturalisme prometteur en devenir :

> Les grands-mères reçurent un accueil d'abord surpris, puis affectueux ; finalement une certaine vogue commença à s'emparer de la trouvaille d'Aurélien Picquot. La gloire leur vint peu après grâce à un long commentaire de Maurice Côté, le célèbre potineur du *Journal de Montréal*, qui s'amena lui-même à La Binerie pour en déguster une demi-douzaine sous les éclairs de la caméra. (Beauchemin 2017: 111)

Works Cited

Anonyme (2017), *Yves Beauchemin et "Le Matou"* in Beauchemin, Yves, *Le Matou*, Montréal: Québec Amérique, collection "Nomades", pp. 764-768.

Aubertin, Marie-Noëlle, Sicotte, Geneviève, *Gastronomie québécoise et patrimoine*, Québec: Presses de l'Université du Québec, 2013 (édition électronique).

Beauchemin, Yves (2017), *Le Matou*, Montréal: Québec Amérique, collection "Nomades".

Brind'Amour, Lucie (2005) *La Binerie, espace paradoxal dans "Le Matou" d'Yves Beauchemin* in Russo, Adelaide, Harel, Simon, *Lieux propices*, Laval: Les Presses de l'Université Laval: 241-254.

Cagnon, Maurice, "*Le Matou* d'Yves Beauchemin: une lecture idéologique". *L'Esprit créateur*, 23, 3. (Fall 1983): 95-104.

Marcotte, Sophie, 2013 *Le rituel du repas familial dans le roman québécois du XXe siècle* in Aubertin, Marie-Noëlle, Sicotte, Geneviève, *Gastronomie québécoise et patrimoine*, Québec: Presses de l'Université du Québec (édition électronique).

Sicotte, Geneviève, *L'aliment dans la littérature du XIXe siècle québécois* in Aubertin, Marie-Noëlle, Sicotte, Geneviève, 2013 *Gastronomie québécoise et patrimoine*, Québec: Presses de l'Université du Québec (édition électronique).

ALESSANDRA FERRARO

Repas de famille dans Impala *de Carole David ou la déconstruction du stéréotype maternel*

LE PRESTIGIEUX GRAND PRIX DU livre de Montréal attribué à Carole David en 2019 pour le recueil de poèmes *Comment nous sommes nés* clôt une longue liste de prix couronnant une œuvre que composent plusieurs volumes de poésie (*Terroristes d'amour suivi de Journal d'une fiction*, 1986; *Feu vers l'est*, 1992; *Abandons*, 1996; *La Maison d'Ophélie*, 1998; *Terra vecchia*, 2005; *Manuel de poétique à l'intention des jeunes filles*, 2010; *L'année de ma disparition*, 2015; *Comment nous sommes nés*, 2018); des textes pour la jeunesse (*Averses et réglisses noires*, 2003; *Poèmes 1*, 2011); de deux récits (*Impala*, 1994; *Hollandia*, 2011) et deux recueils de nouvelles (*L'Endroit où se trouve ton âme*, 1991; *Histoires saintes*, 2001).

Dans ses textes, hybrides et polymorphes, narration et poésie fusionnent, produisant un métissage générique original. L'écriture de Carole David est néanmoins marquée par une profonde unité de ton et de thèmes: à travers des instantanés, elle parvient à saisir le quotidien des personnages—des perdants, des victimes ou des marginaux—et à mettre à nu d'une manière réaliste, à travers un style essentiel et coupant, leur détresse, leur désarroi ou leur condition intime. C'est souvent à travers l'interrogation de la figure maternelle que Carole David parcourt son itinéraire de recherche généalogique tout au long de sa production. Comme le constate Catherine Parent à propos de son œuvre, en commentant l'avant-dernier recueil de poèmes, *Comment nous sommes nés*: "Ces livres adressent la question de notre provenance, de ce qui nous constitue et de ce que nous deviendrons, trois lignes de force qui composent l'ossature d'une œuvre sensible" (Parent 2019). Déjà dans les premiers poèmes de *Terroristes d'amour*, David déconstruisait les stéréotypes de la figure maternelle à travers la mise en scène d'une mère-prostituée et inaugurait ainsi, pour ces femmes qui sont rarement représentées en littérature, un espace d'énonciation qu'elle explorera par la suite.

Un autre fil rouge qui traverse son écriture à partir des nouvelles "Le Rialto sans elle" et "Le roman de Lina" (David 1991: 57-59; 60-61) est constitué par le thème de l'italianité, décliné au sein de rapports familiaux tendus, dans le contexte d'une Amérique peu hospitalière qui déçoit les rêves des immigrants. L'intérêt de Carole David pour des sujets liés à l'immigration italienne en Amérique du Nord tient en partie à des raisons autobiographiques puisque, malgré un nom et prénom québécois, l'auteure, née à Montréal, a une ascendance italienne de la part de sa mère, originaire de la région méridionale du Molise. Ces origines ne sont dévoilées qu'au moment de la publication de son premier texte littéraire "Misères et beautés de Lula" (Caccia et D'Alfonso 1983: 241-247), mouture d'un ouvrage de fiction en cours. On remarquera que ce texte paraît dans *Quêtes. Textes d'auteurs italo-québécois*, anthologie qui marque le début de la littérature migrante au Québec. Les éditeurs, Fulvio Caccia et Antonio D'Alfonso, qui réunissent pour la première fois au Québec des textes d'écrivains d'origine italienne, soulignent les liens de l'auteure avec l'Italie, en écrivant qu'"après avoir parcouru l'Italie du nord au sud à plusieurs reprises, elle se propose de retracer ses origines" (Caccia et D'Alfonso 1983: 242). Il y est question d'une fille qui recherche sa mère Lula, une chanteuse des années Cinquante; celle-ci l'a abandonnée ne laissant d'elle que des vêtements et des photos de son époque d'or:

De Lula, je ne sais pas grand-chose. On m'a dit que c'était le nom de ma mère, son nom d'artiste. Elle m'a abandonnée, comment savoir, peut-être que la réalité est beaucoup plus simple. Tout ce qu'elle m'a laissé se résume à ce cahier bleu, *Le Journal d'une jeune fille perdue*, et je sais que c'est là le seul lien qui peut encore me rappeler à cette femme. (Caccia et D'Alfonso: 243)

On dirait que, dans le cas de Carole Fioramore David, la prise de conscience de ses origines a permis l'éclosion de l'écriture fictionnelle. En effet, cette intellectuelle, déjà connue dans le milieu de l'édition québécoise par son nom de famille, David, ajoute à son patronyme, pour son baptême littéraire en 1983, le nom de famille de sa mère, Fioramore. Elle a voulu ainsi souligner ses origines italiennes. En 2005, enfin, avec le recueil poétique *Terra vecchia*, qui porte les traces d'un voyage autobiographique vers le Molise, son italianité sera thématisée aussi dans le titre.

On retrouvera ce même thème, élaboré et développé, d'une fille à la recherche de sa mère au centre d'*Impala*, fiction narrative parue en 1994, sur laquelle nous concentrerons notre attention. Louisa mène sa propre enquête généalogique à travers un récit fragmentaire qui multiplie les points de vue—tout en gardant l'énonciation à la première personne du singulier, l'histoire est racontée par la narratrice du point de vue, tour à tour, des trois autres personnages de la famille—les analepses et les prolepses qui perturbent la linéarité du récit et, encore, le recours à des genres différents (lettre, carnet, journal intime). La jeune femme, en effet, essaie de reconstruire sa vie en s'interrogeant sur la figure de son père Roberto, un boxeur affilié à la mafia, qui a disparu quand elle était petite, mais surtout sur sa mère Connie, chanteuse de night-club morte en prison après avoir avoué un meurtre commis par son mari. La toile de fond est constituée par la 'Petite Italie' de Montréal, ersatz de la vraie Italie que les personnages n'ont pas connue, où se conjuguent les stéréotypes d'une italianité d'opérette et la société américaine des années Cinquante, représentée par l'Impala du titre, un modèle de Chevrolet chérie des parvenus. Le succès poursuivi par Connie et Roberto en pratiquant des métiers—elle est soubrette, lui boxeur—qui doivent leur apporter de l'argent et une réussite facile, est un moyen pour fuir leurs origines de migrants et de réaliser leur rêve américain. C'est dans la perte définitive de la mère—l'annonce de sa mort ouvre le récit—que celui-ci a son origine; le décès de Connie, en réalité, ne fait que réactiver le sentiment d'abandon que Louisa a éprouvé enfant et qui la marque d'une manière ineffaçable. Cette privation du corps maternel, corps nourricier par excellence, constitue une amputation originaire qui aura de graves conséquences pour Louisa.

Si les sujets de l'italianité et de la filiation dans *Impala* ont déjà été soulignés par la critique (Nardout-Lafarge 2006, Ferraro 2007, Kuhn 2019), il nous paraît intéressant ici de les reprendre en focalisant sur la relation mère-fille, relation que l'écriture littéraire a souvent abordée et que la critique considère comme l'un des thèmes privilégiés de la littérature féminine (Hirsch 1989, Giorgio 2002, Rye et al., Saigal 2018). Cette perspective apparaît d'autant plus pertinente si l'on se réfère à l'itinéraire intellectuel de Carole David, proche de ce courant méta-féministe qui, au cours des années 90, a pris la place d'un féminisme militant au Québec (Boisclair et Dussault Frenette). L'auteure a d'ailleurs toujours revendiqué la volonté de se rapprocher de la réflexion féministe, ce que la critique a également mis en évidence:

> Le féminisme de Carole David, tel qu'exprimé dans son œuvre, est une lutte acharnée contre ce qui la réduit en miettes, l'abandonne, mutile sa psyché. C'est à la fois un mémorandum des violences faites aux femmes et un rappel constant de l'influence qu'a eue l'œuvre féministe décapante de Josée Yvon dans sa vie. (Laverdure 2016)

L'imaginaire de l'écrivaine s'en est nourri, ce qui apparaît de manière évidente dans sa thèse de doctorat en création, qui coïncide avec l'écriture du roman *Impala*, dont le sous-titre est *Les filles d'Électre: le lien entre la littérature et la maternité. Essai et fiction* (David 1994a). C'est, en effet, en représentant le lien ambigu entre Louisa et Connie que David aborde la question de la maternité et de la filiation dans *Impala*. L'histoire se construit alors par rapport à la figure maternelle, à laquelle la narratrice essaie de donner corps.

Dans ce contexte, il nous a paru intéressant de saisir cette relation à la mère—qui est aussi une relation physique passant par le corps et le *care*—, à travers les occurrences liées à la nourriture, autre topos de l'écriture des femmes. Si, comme le remarquent De Salvo et Giunta dans leur introduction à une anthologie qui réunit des textes d'auteures italo-américaines autour de ce thème, il est "impossible to talk about food without also talking about gender and culture" (De Salvo et Giunta 2013: "Introduction"), il est vrai aussi que l'alimentation structure le rapport mère-fille. De plus, cette figure triangulaire mère-fille-nourriture acquiert une valeur ajoutée dans un contexte lié à l'émigration, où la mère, à travers la nourriture, joue un rôle fondamental dans la transmission transculturelle de la mémoire (Goolcharan-Kumeta 2003, Serafin et Marcato 2010, Pascual Soler et Abarca 2013).

La focalisation sur la représentation des occasions dans lesquelles la famille se retrouve autour d'une table nous permettra de cerner le rapport de Louisa avec sa mère Connie, sur lequel se greffent celui avec Angelina, la grand-tante maternelle qui a élevé l'enfant après l'abandon de ses parents et, enfin, bien des années plus tard, la relation avec son père Roberto qui a changé d'identité et de statut social et se fait appeler Angelo Bisanti. La figure maternelle, présente dans les deux premières scènes analysées, sera également centrale, *in absentia*, dans les deux autres repas, auxquels elle ne prendra pas part parce qu'elle est en prison et, puis, morte. L'ombre de Connie comme celle d'un fantôme, plane sur toute la narration.

Il s'agira de parcourir ce réseau de la filiation, principalement axée sur la lignée maternelle, à travers les représentations de quatre scènes fondamentales qui ont lieu lors d'un repas familial. Nous nous focaliserons d'abord sur Connie lors de rares moments où on la voit attablée; ensuite sur la seule occasion où toute la famille est réunie pour l'anniversaire de Louisa et, bien des années plus tard, sur un repas d'adieu entre Louisa et Angelina dans un restaurant du centre-ville. Il sera question, enfin, des dîners que Louisa et Roberto consommeront en face à face avant le dénouement tragique de l'histoire.

Connie: scampis et cocktail de crevettes

Aux yeux de Louisa, Connie n'apparaît en aucun moment comme une mère traditionnelle, une mère nourricière; jamais elle ne sera représentée en train de cuisiner ou attablée devant un repas à la maison. La narratrice, d'ailleurs, ne la désigne jamais en l'appelant "maman" ou "ma mère", mais par son nom d'art, Connie. Costantina, tout en ayant refusé le rôle féminin d'infériorité auquel la condamnait traditionnellement la culture italienne de l'émigration dans les années Cinquante, et ayant adopté un pseudonyme anglophone pour fuir ses origines en devenant chanteuse, a été happée dans un autre univers, basé sur le faux mythe du succès facile et du luxe, qui, finalement, s'avèrera pour elle non moins marginalisant que l'autre.

D'ailleurs, souvent partie en tournée avec son Impala, elle vit rarement dans la maison de la rue Drolet; dans sa loge ou dans des chambres d'hôtel, elle est entourée d'objets *kitsch*, de vêtements voyants en tissus synthétiques; si elle avale quelque chose, c'est des somnifères ou de l'alcool, du whisky ou bien du champagne, selon les occasions. Quand Louisa rapportera le récit que fait sa mère de la période qui a précédé son emprisonnement (David 1994b: 67-85), on la verra manger en vitesse un sandwich sur la route, noyer son malaise dans l'alcool à des tables de bar ou, encore, partager avec son mari Roberto et son chef, le mafioso M. Cobetto, des plats des grandes occasions, des scampis arrosés au rhum (David 1994b: 84) et un cocktail de crevettes géantes (David 1994b: 85), dans un Holiday Inn en Floride. C'est pendant ce repas qu'elle apprend qu'elle doit avouer un meurtre à la place de Roberto (David 1994b: 85). Ces "fruits de mer" qui donnent le titre au chapitre final du récit de Connie, constituent les seuls plats évoqués; ils incarnent son rêve d'une vie facile et luxueuse où bonheur rime avec richesse. Cependant, Connie n'aura pas droit au reste du banquet et s'arrêtera au hors d'œuvre, puisque ces fruits de mer ne seront pas suivis d'un repas somptueux, réservé aux mafiosi celui-ci, mais qu'ils constituent le prélude aux repas de la cantine de la prison où Connie passera le reste de sa vie. Les fruits de mer, ces amuse-gueules qui ne nourrissent pas, s'avèreront des fruits interdits pour la jeune prolétaire fille d'immigrés qui a voulu s'approprier le rêve américain. Seulement pour y avoir goûté elle sera destinée à sa perte: ils deviendront donc le symbole des illusions déjouées et de sa vie ratée dont les répercussions atteindront sa fille Louisa.

Louisa: la fête d'anniversaire et les sandwichs colorés

Dès sa naissance, la petite Louisa suit sa mère dans ses voyages dans le continent américain et vit une enfance précaire, ne voyant son père que de temps en temps. Avant sa disparition définitive, Roberto lui apporte des "friandises" (David 1994b: 20) espérant lui faire oublier son absence. Les friandises, les bonbons et les gâteaux évoqués dans le récit, tous des avatars de la vraie nourriture, représentent le superflu et artificiel qui prend la place des repas de famille; il s'agit d'un substitut de l'affection et des soins dont les parents ne savent pas entourer leur enfant. Parmi les souvenirs de la jeune adulte, il y en a un qui nous paraît à cet égard significatif. C'est celui de la fête de son cinquième anniversaire, une fête sans enfants, pendant laquelle sont offerts des mets élaborés, prévus moins à l'attention de Louisa que des adultes.

> Je regardais les adultes danser quand je n'aidais pas Angelina, que j'appelais ma tante, à préparer les plats de sandwichs roses, blancs et verts que ma mère avait commandés dans une pâtisserie de la rue Saint-Denis. [...] Ma tante n'avait jamais vu du pain coloré et ne

voulait à aucun prix en manger. Elle disait que ce n'était
pas naturel (David 1994b: 21).

Ces amuse-gueules raffinés, bariolés, achetés dans une pâtisserie
du centre-ville, répondent à l'idée que Connie se fait du bonheur,
qu'on peut atteindre si l'on s'entoure d'objets inusuels et artificiels,
prétendument chic, mais en réalité seulement prétentieux. Elle
les achète pour l'anniversaire de sa fille sans comprendre qu'ils ne
peuvent pas être appréciés par la petite qui ne désire que l'attention
de ses parents; de plus, cette nourriture artificielle est refusée par
Angelina, la seule figure familiale qui remplit le rôle parental, trop
attachée à des valeurs conventionnelles pour en manger. Angelina,
née en Italie au début du siècle, est la gardienne d'une tradition
qu'elle n'abandonne pas en Amérique, continuant à s'habiller en
noir, à cultiver son jardin avec des herbes aromatiques et à vivre
avec parcimonie.

Les sandwichs colorés deviennent dans le récit un objet symbolique; leur refus de la part de sa grand-tante fait prendre conscience
à l'enfant de son malheur: "J'avais décidé de mourir cette journée-là.
Ma tante ne voulait pas partager avec moi les sandwichs multico-
lores et ma mère m'ignorait totalement" (David 1994b: 22). Car
cette fête d'anniversaire est conçue selon le code d'un train de vie
basé sur le paraître et le tape-à-l'œil, où l'enfance de Louisa est
ignorée, tout autant que les coutumes d'Angelina.

Angelina: la salle à manger du transatlantique

Restée sous la tutelle de la vieille femme, pendant que sa mère suit
Roberto et son propre rêve de réussite, Louisa doit se confronter au
silence d'Angelina, silence qui n'est même pas rompu pendant les
repas qu'elles prennent seules l'une en face de l'autre, séparées par
un non-partage de la langue, Angelina ne parlant pas le français
et Louisa n'ayant pas appris l'italien (David 1994b: 44, 50). C'est
d'un silence impénétrable qu'Angelina entourera par la suite la

disparition de Connie que l'enfant croit morte, mais qui se trouve, en réalité, en prison dans la même ville. Séparée de sa propre mère, ignorant le destin de son père, partageant la vie d'une vieille personne réticente, Louisa vit flottant dans un vide intolérable que vient interrompre la découverte de la dernière des centaines de lettres de Connie qu'Angelina a oublié de renvoyer à l'expéditeur, comme pour les autres. Il s'agit sans doute, le récit ne le dit pas, d'une punition d'Angelina qui prive ainsi Connie de sa fille pour avoir suivi Roberto; il s'agit également pour elle de préserver l'enfant de l'influence maternelle, sans comprendre les dégâts que cela cause chez Louisa.

Pour réagir à la découverte de cette omission cruelle sur le destin de sa mère, Louisa décide de quitter la maison familiale et choisit, pour le communiquer à sa tante, le restaurant des grandes occasions, la salle à manger des grands magasins Eaton sur la rue Sainte-Catherine, au centre ville. Le chapitre 15, "Une grande salle à manger dans un bateau", décrit la rencontre. Cette salle se superpose pour la vieille femme à l'image du salon du transatlantique qui l'a emmenée en Amérique, dont le luxe suscitait des rêves de bonheur et d'opulence chez l'Angelina adolescente, l'éloignant de la réalité qu'elle partageait avec les passagers de troisième classe dont les cadavres étaient jetés à la mer. Tout en ayant survécu, la femme n'atteindra jamais cette vie faite d'aisance et d'insouciance qu'incarne le salon du bateau, prélude du rêve américain dont, comme la plupart des immigrants, elle sera exclue.

C'est alors qu'on comprendra que le silence d'Angelina renvoie à des raisons plus profondes qui prennent leurs racines dans son histoire personnelle de fille illégitime que son père a voulu envoyer en Amérique pour effacer la honte. Cette souffrance non exprimée, que cache le silence dans lequel la vieille femme vit emmurée, se propage comme une malédiction d'une génération à l'autre, tel un héritage dont on ne saurait se délester (Nardout-Lafarge 2006). Angelina séparera sa nièce Connie de sa fille Louisa tout comme elle avait été séparée de sa propre mère et, plus tard, de son fils, né d'une liaison illégitime. Incapable de sortir du destin tragique auquel est destinée toute sa lignée, Angelina en deviendra son principal instrument.

L'annonce de Louisa qu'elle va quitter la maison familiale déclenchera la folie chez la vieille femme (David 1994b: 51). Incapable de communiquer avec les vivants, elle entretiendra dès lors un dialogue perpétuel et incompréhensible avec ses propres morts (David 1994b: 36, 51).

Roberto/Angelo: combats de boxe autour d'une table de restaurant

Dans la troisième partie du récit, qui a lieu après le suicide de Connie en prison et l'enfermement dans un hospice d'Angelina, Louisa raconte ses retrouvailles avec Roberto; celui-ci a changé d'activité et vit dans l'Ouest de Montréal sous le nom d'Angelo Bisanti, entrepreneur dans le secteur du bâtiment. Il a une nouvelle famille. Il veut cependant renouer avec sa fille, moins pour assouvir son sens de culpabilité que pour retrouver son moi d'antan, quand il s'appelait encore Roberto.

Les rencontres entre père et fille se font autour d'une table de restaurant, et peu à peu, devant l'histoire racontée à partir du point de vue de son père, Louisa comprend le charme que sa mère avait dû subir puisqu'elle en est aussi la victime. Cependant, Louisa y échappe et, reconnaissant les mensonges de Roberto, prend, peu à peu, la décision de mettre fin à son jeu: "Comment se faisait-il que je me retrouvais devant celui qui nous avait abandonnées, ma mère et moi, et que je n'avais rien à lui cracher à la figure?" (David 1994b: 95). Pendant neuf fois ils se rencontrent dans des restaurants aux noms évocateurs *TicTac*, *Toit rouge*, *Rieno*, des endroits aux décorations vieillottes et tape-à-l'œil, datant des années 50, où l'on pratique des activités illicites (David 1994b: 97). Ce sont des décors qui renvoient à l'époque de l'histoire de la rencontre entre Connie et Roberto, époque que Louisa porte en elle comme une "tare" (David 1994b: 97). Elle ne peut s'empêcher, cependant, de continuer d'écouter avidement son père dans l'espoir d'en savoir plus sur ses origines. Celui-ci veut la convaincre, malgré toute évidence, de la vérité de sa propre version des faits, qui le blanchit et le déculpabilise: "Sa dernière mise en scène était celle d'un amant éploré retrouvant sa fille qu'il a à peine connue sur la tombe de son ex-bien-aimée" (David 1994b: 115).

C'est ainsi qu'autour de ces tables de restaurants, entre le père qui raconte son histoire d'ancien boxeur et mafioso, mais amoureux de Connie et attaché à Louisa, et la fille, prête à y détecter tous ses mensonges, se joue une lutte mortelle: "le dernier combat qu'il livrait, c'était avec sa propre fille et il le savait. Nous nous enfermions dans ces restaurants qui nous servaient d'arènes sans que l'on sache trop pourquoi" (David 1994b: 99).

Louisa comprend que Roberto est lui aussi la victime d'un mythe personnel dont le modèle lui est fourni par son père et dont il est incapable de sortir: "il s'était abandonné à cette vision réconfortante selon laquelle l'homme fort peut maîtriser non seulement son destin, mais aussi celui des autres. Le Nouveau Monde devait lui appartenir avec ses richesses, ses femmes et ses bonheurs illicites" (David 1994b: 106). Cette prise de conscience de la part de Louisa ne comporte cependant pas de compréhension envers son père et surtout pas de justification pour son comportement avec Connie car elle l'estime coupable de la mort de celle-ci.

Tiraillée entre la fascination qu'exerce Roberto, son désir d'apprendre la vérité et l'envie de se venger, Louisa le rencontre une dernière fois au restaurant habituel de la rue Sherbrooke avant qu'il n'aille la voir chez elle; le repas constitue encore une fois le moment de la révélation et de l'affrontement: "J'attendais qu'il se mette à table, qu'il me livre son secret; la vérité semblait toujours remise à plus tard" (David 1994b: 121).

C'est alors que Louisa, pour ne pas permettre à Roberto par ses mensonges de lui voler la mémoire de sa mère et pour ne pas voir se répéter le destin de la lignée féminine de sa famille, écrasée par un malheur que couvre un silence assourdissant, tire sur lui et le tue. En assassinant Roberto, Louisa venge ainsi sa mère. Si le récit de son histoire familiale, qu'elle fait dans le texte que nous sommes en train de lire, parvient à briser le silence qui l'a entourée depuis son enfance, on ne doit pas oublier cependant qu'il est fait à partir d'une prison.

Conclusions

Dans un pareil cadre, les repas de famille, au lieu de constituer des moments de partage, de rencontre et d'échange, se transforment en des huis clos, des occasions pour régler les comptes, où domine le silence ou bien dans lesquels les nœuds conflictuels émergent, s'amplifient et s'exacerbent. La métaphore filée de la boxe, utilisée par la narratrice, révèle que la table est assimilée à un ring où chaque participant mène un combat au cours duquel aucun coup bas n'est exclu. L'issue ne pourra qu'être tragique: la prison attend Connie après son dîner aux fruits de mer avec les mafiosi; Angelina tombe dans la folie après le rendez-vous avec Louisa dans la salle à manger d'Eaton; ce sera la mort pour Roberto et la cellule d'une prison pour Louisa à la suite de leurs rencontres devant une table de restaurant. Le suicide, la folie, la mort et la prison marqueront alors leurs destins tragiques.

L'absence de toute référence à la cuisine est d'autant plus surprenante dans un texte qui s'inscrit dans le contexte de l'émigration italienne, où l'évocation de la nourriture constitue une topique sur le plan social, anthropologique, historique et littéraire (cf. Cinotto 2018, Dottolo et Dottolo 2018). Si dans ce cadre, comme le soulignent De Salvo et Giunta (2013: "Introduction"), le récit canonique de la nourriture, imbu de nostalgie et de sentimentalisme, se fonde sur le couple classique femme /nourriture, il est évident qu'*Impala* subvertit ce cliché en ignorant la dimension liée aux mets italiens typiques. En cela, le récit suit le choix de Connie de renoncer au rôle traditionnel qui, par son statut social et ethnique, lui était destiné, celui de femme à la maison. En suivant son rêve américain de carton-pâte, elle n'a donc pas rempli son rôle de mère traditionnelle et, en cuisine, elle n'a pas permis la circulation des modèles alimentaires qui assurent, sur le plan symbolique, la continuation d'une mémoire familiale et communautaire; cette privation va de pair avec la décision de ne pas apprendre à Louisa l'italien, langue que, pourtant, elle parle couramment avec Angelina. C'est surtout Connie qui a court-circuité cette chaîne de transmission de la mémoire familiale représentée par la nourriture. Sur le plan pratique, ne faisant pas la cuisine pour sa fille, elle l'a exclue du processus affectif qui passe par les gestes de la préparation des mets qui est le propre d'une mère nourricière: c'est de cela que la petite fille souffre inconsciemment lors de la fête pour son cinquième anniversaire. De plus, le non-apprentissage de l'italien empêche Louisa de communiquer avec Angelina, seule figure familiale qui lui reste après l'abandon de la part de ses parents, ce qui contribue à jeter la jeune fille dans un vide existentiel dont elle sera incapable de sortir. En s'amputant de la cuisine et de la langue, domaines qui s'inscrivent sous le signe du "maternel" (Chodorow 1978), Connie a renoncé à nouer un lien intime essentiel dans une relation fille-mère et a privé Louisa d'instruments fondamentaux pour affronter sa disparition.

L'analyse de ce récit, à travers les notions de filiation et de nourriture, nous aura permis de montrer que Carole David a mis en scène, par le biais du personnage de Connie, l'envers du stéréotype de la mère italienne conventionnelle en contournant d'abord et en détournant ensuite, l'un des topoï liés à l'imaginaire italo-américain basé sur le couple femme/nourriture. Malgré son changement de nom—de Costantina à Constance à Connie (David 1994b: 13, 41, 94), prénoms qui marquent les différentes étapes de sa volonté de s'intégrer dans le *mainstream* américain et, en même temps, sa tentative de s'échapper du rôle traditionnel de femme à la maison pour devenir chanteuse—ce personnage féminin tragique et attachant sera rattrapé par un destin dont la prison est l'emblème le plus éloquent.

Notre étude aura montré, en outre, qu'*Impala*, récit lacunaire, fragmenté, traversé par le silence, dont la reconstitution est impossible, pourrait bien être intégré dans ce filon que constitue le récit contemporain de la filiation marqué par la mélancolie, la perte, le vide (Viart, Demanze), un récit où le généalogique n'est pas conçu comme un modèle pour restaurer un ordre perdu, pour retrouver un sens et une unité. À l'intérieur de ce filon, Carole David trouverait alors sa place parmi ces femmes écrivaines de la nouvelle génération qui se distinguent de leurs devancières pour ne plus devoir, comme elles, rompre les ponts avec le passé, mais, au contraire, l'interroger pour repenser l'histoire familiale d'une manière différente. Comme Annie Ernaux, Nancy Huston, Louise Dupré, en réactivant des topoï propres de l'écriture féminine et en mettant en scène une interrogation filiale selon la lignée maternelle, Carole David aura contribué à faire émerger ce qui questionne "l'altérité, voire […]; l'étrangement, également présente dans les écrits théoriques et critiques du féminisme de la troisième vague" (Ledoux-Beaugrand 2013: "Introduction. Génération héritière").

Works Cited

Boisclair, Isabelle et Dussault Frenette, Catherine. "Mosaïque: l'écriture des femmes au Québec (1980-2010)". *Recherches féministes*, 27, 2. (2014): 39-61.

Caccia, Fulvio et Antonio D'Alfonso (eds) (1983), *Quêtes. Textes d'auteurs italo-québécois*. Montréal: Guernica.

Chodorow, Nancy (1978), *The Reproduction of Mothering: Psychoanalysis and the Sociology of Gender*, Berkeley-Los Angeles-Londres: University of California Press.

Cinotto, Simone (2013), *The Italian American Table: Food, Family, and Community in New York City*, Champaign: University of Illinois Press.

David, Carole (1986), *Terroristes d'amour suivi de Journal d'une fiction*, Montréal: VLB.

David, Carole (1991), *L'endroit où se trouve ton âme*, Montréal: Les Herbes rouges.

David, Carole (1994), *Impala. Les filles d'Électre: le lien entre la littérature et la maternité. Essai et fiction*, Giguère R. dir., Thèse Ph.D., Lettres et littérature, Faculté des lettres et sciences humaines, Université de Sherbrooke.

David, Carole (1994b), *Impala*, Montreal: Le Herbes rouges.

David, Carole (2005), *Terra vecchia*, Montréal: Les Herbes rouges (Poésie).

Dottolo, Andrea L. et Dottolo, Carol (2018), *Italian American Women, Food, and Identity. Stories at the Table*, London-New York: Palgrave Macmillan.

Demanze, Laurent (2008), *Encres orphelines. Pierre Bergounioux, Gérard Macé, Pierre Michon*, Paris: Corti.

De Salvo, Louise A., Giunta, Edvige (2003), *The Milk of Almonds: Italian American Women Writers on Food and Culture*, New York: Feminist Press at CUNY.

Ferraro, Alessandra (2007), "Passaggi americani. Dall'Italia al Québec", in Ciani Sforza D. (ed.), *Quale America? Soglie e culture di un continente*, II, Venise: Mazzanti, 179-188.

Giorgio, Adalgisa (ed.) 2002, *Writing Mothers and Daughters. Renegotiating the Mother in Western Narratives by Women*, New York-Oxford: Berghahn Books.

Goolcharan-Kumeta, Wendy (2003), *My Mother, My Country: Reconstructing the Female Self in Guadeloupean Women's Writing*, Oxford: Peter Lang.

Hirsch, Marianne (1989), *The Mother / Daughter Plot: Narrative, Psychoanalysis Feminism*, Bloomingtont et Indianapolis: Indiana University Press.

Kuhn, Marion (2019), "Saisir le passé dans le présent. Mémoires familiales dans les fictions contemporaines québécoises (Barbeau-Lavalette, David, Quinn)", in Auger M. et Kühn M. (eds), "Expériences contemporaines du temps dans les fictions québécoises", *Voix et Images*, 44, 2 (131), (hiver 2019), 25–37.

Laverdure, Bertrand (2016), *La femme qui s'indigne. Le féminisme de guérilla de Carole David*. https://www.uneq.qc.ca/2016/08/31/la-femme-qui-sindigne/ (consulté le 15 février 2020).

Ledoux-Beaugrand, Évelyne (2013), *Imaginaires de la filiation. Héritage et mélancolie dans la littérature contemporaine des femmes*, Montréal: Éditions XYZ (Théorie et Littérature).

Nardout-Lafarge, Élisabeth (2006), "La malédiction de l'italianité dans *Impala* de Carole David", in Ferraro A., De Luca A.P. (eds), *Parcours migrants au Québec. L'italianité de Marco Micone à Philippe Poloni*, Udine: Forum, 55-65.

Parent, Catherine, "Carole David". *Portraits*, 3. (2019) https://www. blogues.cstip.ulaval.ca/portraits/carole-david (consulté le 2 février 2020).

Pascual Soler, Nieves, Abarca, Meredith E. (2013), *Rethinking Chicana/o Literature through Food: Postnational Appetites*, New York: Palgrave Macmillan US.

Rye, Gill, Browne, Victoria, Giorgio, Adalgisa, Jeremiah, Emily, Lee Six, Abigail (2018), *Motherhood in Literature and Culture: Interdisciplinary Perspectives from Europe*, New York-Londres: Routledge.

Saigal, Monique (2000), *L'Écriture: lien de mère a fille chez Jeanne Hyvrard, Chantal Chauvaf et Annie Ernaux*, Amsterdam-Atlanta: Rodopi.

Saint-Martin Lori et Gibeau Ariane (eds), "Filiations du féminin". *Les Cahiers de l'IREF*, 6 (Agora). (2014).

Santoro, Miléna (2002), *Mothers of Invention. Feminist Authors and Experimental Fiction in France and Quebec*, Montréal-Kingston: McGill-Queen's University Press,.

Serafin, Silvana et Marcato Carla (eds), "L'alimentazione come patrimonio culturale dell'emigrazione nelle Americhe". *Oltreoceano*, 4. (2010).

Smart, Patricia (1988), *Écrire dans la maison du père. L'émergence du féminin dans la tradition littéraire du Québec*, Montréal: Québec/ Amérique.

Viart, Dominique (1999), "Filiations littéraires", in Baetens J., Viart D. (eds), *Écritures contemporaines*, 2, Paris-Caen, Minard-Lettres modernes.

ÉVA ZSIZSMANN

Bits and Pieces of Home.
Food Imagery as False Memory

Introduction

As Linda Civitello states in the introduction to her book *Cuisine and Culture*, food is closely connected to social, religious and ethnic identity. We give food meaning far beyond its survival function (Civitello 2008: xiii, xiv). The place and the circumstances of food consumption carry special significance. Rituals connected to immigrant life and references to food items within these rituals mark the framework of my investigation.

The purpose of the present paper is to address the issue of food and ceremony, rituals conjuring up the image of home within the context of immigration and interpersonal relations between representatives of different generations in Mavis Gallant's short story, *His Mother* (1973) and its film adaptation, a Hungarian-Canadian coproduction directed by Károly Makk.

I will trace references to food as part of the émigré ritual and examine food imagery deployed as a means of creating false memory. I will focus on the difference between pre- and post-war generations in the short story (pride, dignity, "quality" versus the "stony generation") as well as the perpetuation of false memory, with mother and migrant son sharing in self-deceit. The son's letters, "praising her remembered skill with pies and cakes" is just one example of arbitrarily altering the past to keep up appearances.

Starting from the idea of food as a powerful means of communication, I propose to highlight references to food and the art of cooking in the exchange of letters between mother and son. I will also focus on the "émigré" ritual at Gerbeaud Café in Budapest: the meeting point of mothers whose sons had left the home country, and a café that was "a sign of caste and the mark of a generation." I will approach the film adaptation in question as story re-telling and cast light on representations of diasporic food (iconic scenes such as eating smoked pork head or the golden walnut dumpling recipe read over the phone) as a marker of social class besides ethnicity.

Bearing in mind Gallant's particular cultural situation—an expatriate Canadian in Paris, immersed in French culture, writing in English—perhaps it does not come as a surprise that many of her "stories are set in Europe. French, Italian, Swiss, German, the characters are variously survivors, exiles, émigrés, border-crossers, visitors, and prisoners-of-war." (New 1980: 154).

As W. H. New points out in *The Art of Haunting Ghosts*, the stories in the collection *From the Fifteenth District* display "Gallant's sardonic asperity and the precision of her social conscience" (1980: 154). Moreover, they draw attention to "our human compulsion to visit ourselves upon the past, in order to secure a significance we fear we might otherwise be unable to possess." Indeed, the ghosts of the past haunt the present; memory holds the individual hostage: "Having no reliable counter-event to put in its place, she let the memory stand," as the narrator of *The Moslem Wife* says.

"There are some strongly filmic moments in Gallant's stories," as Neil Besner remarks (2007: 155). Gallant herself often makes reference to films or images rising in memory. To give just one example, the narrator in *His Mother* "parted without pain from a soft, troubled memory, from an old grey film about porters wheeling steamer trunks, white fur wraps, bunches of violets, champagne. It was gone: it had never been" (Gallant 1973: 30). The "old grey film" conjures up the image of a pre-Second World War world, and marks a moment of epiphany, the realization that the age of "golden dust" belonged to a previous generation. Besner claims that Gallant's stories perform their distinctive versions of revisiting the past, considering all temporal layerings, discontinuities and ruptures that attend former places. In other words, Gallant's fiction has engaged in "the true rediscovery of time," as George Woodcock remarked, which is always subject to memory's interruptions, clarifications and corrections.

The "émigré" ritual: the pre- and post-war generation

Gallant spent a few years in Budapest, and her short story most probably originates in a recalled image of the Vörösmarty Café (Gerbeaud) in the Old City:

> At Gerbeaud's, the pastries are still the best in Europe [...] and so are the prices. There are five or six little rooms, little marble tables, comfortable chairs [...]. In summer one can sit on the pavement. There is enough space between the plane trees and the ladies with their elegant hats are not in too much danger from the sparrows [...] most of the customers, yes, most, belong to the magic circle of mothers whose children have gone away. (Gallant 1973: 33)

The short story makes us aware of the inadequacy of the mother-son relationship, one that partly originates in the contrasting nature of their respective generations: the metaphor of golden dust, carelessness and suppleness are attributes of the pre-war generation, whereas the son growing up in the post-war period is "a stone out of a stony generation." The everyday breakfast ritual sheds light on the insurmountable distance between them: he seldom looks up at her, waiting for her to cut bread and put it on his plate, while the mother smokes the finest smuggled Virginia cigarettes, drinks strong coffee and pesters him with questions to start a conversation.

The image of "a stately, careless widow with unbrushed red hair, wearing an old fur coat over her nightgown" changes as she becomes the mother of an émigré son. With the money sent by her son from

Glasgow, she buys a white blouse, combs with which to pin her hair and a blue kimono. It is not only her appearance that is suddenly altered: the perpetuation of false memories, the use of euphemisms in the letters exchanged by mother and son are all part of the game of deception. "She remembered long, tender conversations they had had together," while previously we learn that "talking to him was like lifting a stone out of water," the metaphor of an immense effort.

The ritual at the Gerbeaud Café is the central image of the short story: as with all rituals, there is a given time and place for it, participants, their roles and gestures well-defined. On Saturday afternoons, the circle of émigrés' mothers meet to exchange news and pictures, sharing the content of over-stamped letters received. There were strict rules governing the ritual, encompassing three distinct ranks an émigré mother could achieve, marked by letters, gifts and a visit abroad.

> Gerbeaud was a sign of caste and the mark of a generation, too. [...] A social order prevailed, as it does everywhere. The aristocrats were those whose children had never left Europe; the poorest of the poor were not likely to see their sons again, for they had gone to Chile and South Africa. Switzerland was superior to California. A city earned more points than a town. There was no mistaking her precedence here; she was a grand duchess. (28)

Glasgow, the city her son flew to with a soccer team, qualifies as a desirable target: "If Glasgow was unfamiliar, the very sound of it somehow rang with merit." Significantly, it is changed into Toronto, Canada in the film adaptation.

The list of tenants inhabiting the mother's house after her son leaves provides us with a nuanced picture, a social canopy: an uncouth forestry student, the widow of a poet, young librarians and, finally, the installed tenants from the communist period: "brokenly poor" but "endowed with dark, important connections." (29)

Status and identity are shown as volatile, moving, changing constructs: they shift according to the reference point (the circle of émigré mothers, the immigrant son's new family or the prevailing social-political order). In the circle of émigré mothers, she ranks as a grand duchess on account of the letters and gifts received from her son as well as her ability to read three foreign languages. The installed tenants have other considerations; in their terms she is "at the foot of the ladder."

Otherness appears in terms of language and religion in a passage rendering the mother's thoughts through free indirect discourse: the in-laws from Scotland send Christmas greetings with stern biblical messages "as if they judged her [...] for being frivolous, without a proper God." (30) An ironic comment on long-distance calls shows the process of adjusting to otherness, of measuring ourselves to others: "At least they knew now that she spoke correct English; on the other hand, perhaps they were simple souls unable to imagine that anything but English could ever be." (30)

Given the importance of keeping up appearances, holding onto an image, an illusion is an intrinsic feature of the mother's generation that values pride, dignity, "quality" above all. An unposed picture shows her son on top of a ladder, pasting sheets of plastic tiles onto a kitchen wall; he looks unappealing, and the mother is perplexed to see him working in his own home like a common labourer. "In response to the ladder picture she employed a photographer [...] to take a fiercely lighted portrait of her sitting on her divan-bed with a volume of Impressionist reproductions opened on her lap. She wore a string of garnets and turned her head proudly ..." (30). The reference to the Impressionists emphasizes the creation of illusion, just like the narrator's remark that "She had a long back-slanting hand she had once been told was the hand of a liar." Carefully selected props are also part of creating an image: she hangs a framed parchment to the back wall as proof of her nobility.

The letters exchanged between mother and son are vehicles of keeping up appearances. The son's letters "praising her remembered skill with pies and cakes" are a telling example of arbitrarily altering the past, making it more convenient than the bare truth that "she had never been any sort of a cook" (28). The image of the poppy-seed cake baked by the mother is an instance of creating false memory, just like the fantasy of delicious soups superposed on and erasing the distant memory of simple tomato soups. In the film adaptation of the short story, Mike—John's gypsy friend—contradicts him, rectifying a deliberately false memory.

Family jewellery, family photographs and homemade food (especially cakes) are among the immutable presents taken to family members living abroad. The narrator is slightly ironic when commenting on the ritual of transporting cakes to faraway places: "The cake was a bother to carry, for the traveller usually had one of her own, but who could say no? They all knew the cake's true value. Look at the way her own son claimed his share of nourishment from a mother whose cooking has always been a joke" (28). However, the immigrant ritual of mother and son remains forever incomplete. The mother's dream of visiting the absent son is thwarted.

At the end of the short story, the narrator's voice and the mother's voice in the letter overlap: the minute, photographic description of Vörösmarty Square and its environs turns into a piece of emotional geography: "There are plane trees full of sparrows, and there are bus stops, and even a little Métro, the oldest in Europe [...]—it goes to the Zoo, the Fine Arts Museum, the Museum of Decorative Arts, the Academy of Music and the Opera" (33).

The obsession with the voice, the missing voice and silence as a metaphor of distance, strangeness and camouflage runs through the story: "She began to wonder what his voice had been like. She could see him, she dreamed of him often, but her dreams and memories were like films with the soundtrack removed" (29).

The painful inadequacy of the mother-son relationship, the distance that has always spanned between them and has only become more tangible with actual physical distance, is a recurrent motif, connected to the image of the lost coin: "He was between the dead and the living, a voice on the telephone, an affectionate letter full of English words, a coin rolled and lying somewhere in secret. And she, she was the revered and respected mother of a generous, an attentive, a camouflaged stranger" (33).

Food imagery in the film adaptation

The film adaptation features two parallel stories, marked by alternating images of Budapest (iconic images such as the Chain Bridge, narrow downtown streets and condominiums) and Toronto with its high rises, office buildings, street front shops and a two-storey family house. While the short story is focalized through the mother's consciousness, the son only appearing as part of her narrative, the film develops two storylines where the main characters, Margit (the mother) and John (her son) share in deception while minor characters round out the narrative about self-deception. The mother (Klári Tolnay) paints dolls' heads for a living and keeps a tenant, while the son, John Feheregyházi (Gordon Pinsent) has worked as a draftsman in an engineering office since he emigrated to Canada twenty years hence, leaving behind his fiancée. He is about to turn forty and going through an identity crisis. The letters between mother and son, both longing for a romantic past that never existed, are communicated through a voiceover so they complement the visual action and setting. Despite the simple storyline, the film is masterful on account of the acting and the cutting. Director Károly Makk was mostly interested in the private lives of individuals, psychological aspects; critics often refer to his films in the 1970s as essayistic chamber plays.

Cultural markers, culture-specific objects and cultural stereotypes play an important role in the film. The best penknife ever craved by John's son is a point in question. The smoked pork head eaten by John's friend, Mike, another Hungarian immigrant, to the great horror of Mona, John's wife's colleague, underlines the near-impossibility of overcoming cultural differences. This latter results in huge tension within John's family as well. His mother-in-law, Mrs.

Fraser, is the embodiment of xenophobia: she calls John's room a "foreign country." The iconic scene of eating smoked pork head and drinking Hungarian wine is a representation of diasporic food as a marker of social class besides ethnicity.

The episode when John's mother sends a photograph of herself in folk dress against the background of the skin of the dog as a proof of nobility is utterly hilarious and tragic at the same time. The wish to impress is thwarted, as John's English wife and her mother find the picture repelling and the grandson inadvertently spurts out that she looks like a clown. Another fissure in the family develops when John's wife would like to change her Hungarian family name, as she finds it an obstacle in climbing the hierarchical ladder in the bank where she works.

The émigré mothers' meeting at Gerbeaud Café is a recurrent scene in the film. The social hierarchy displayed rests on the same principles as in the short story: letters and gifts received from the sons, and finally, a visit to the faraway place. When Mike's mother announces that she is going to move to Canada, Margit—John's mother—acts out a lie to save her reputation. She pretends to travel to Zürich to meet her son, while in fact she takes refuge at her brother's house, in the suburbs. Ironically, John decides to visit Budapest at the same time and therefore misses her.

Besides the scene of eating smoked pork head, there is reference to another culture-specific food item: the golden walnut dumpling. We see here another scene of shared deception. John praises his mother's food and asks for the recipe of this special Hungarian delicacy. The mother pretends to reel it off by heart while dictating the ingredients prompted by her tenant, Aranka, as she herself has no idea about it.

The world of illusions created by mother and son together is shattered from time to time. There are three characters in the film who spell out the truth and dispel illusions. The mother's brother, Béla (played by Antal Páger) sees through her, and does not hesitate to say so. When she sighs melodramatically, saying how she misses her son, he reminds her that she used to have lovers and could hardly wait to send her son away to the countryside. Secondly, John's former fiancée, Klári, asks her the most unpleasant question: "Why does he not invite you to Canada, if he loves you so much?" The sharpness of the remark hurts all the more as she has always shown contempt towards her daughter-in-law. Finally, it is Mike, John's friend, who tends to rectify his false memories about his mother's cooking skills.

In the final scene, the snapshots John takes of himself on his return to Budapest overlap with a distorted image of his mother, marking the consummation of the ceremony of deception. The mother is angry and revolted, not because of the failed encounter with her long-lost son, but on account of the realization that his visit marks the end of illusions, breaking the convention of lies. She reproaches him for coming home:

> "Why did you have to come back? Those twenty years were amazing. Whether I lied? Well of course I did! Have you not lied? Until you returned, I had a generous and unfaltering son. And you had a dear mother. Now we are both alone. What will become of us, my dear son?"

The film is masterful in creating atmosphere by showing objects in close-up: clocks, radios, chests of drawers, interiors with pieces of period furniture and photographs. The recurrent image of over-stamped letters and handwriting accompanied by nostalgic piano music provides a narrative frame, while the glass surface of Canadian skyscrapers refracting distorted images of the surrounding buildings is an epitome of the game of deception. The photo of the young man, John's friend who committed suicide, is crossed out.

The cast includes famous Hungarian actors (Klári Tolnay as the mother, Mari Törőcsik, the abandoned fiancée, Nóra Tábori as the tenant, Antal Páger as the gruff, outspoken but loving brother). John is played by a Canadian actor (Gordon Pinsent), just like the other characters in the Canadian scenes, so their parts had to be synchronized for the Hungarian TV production (1980). Canadian writer Suzanne Grossman wrote the Canadian segment and Gyorgy Kardos wrote the Hungarian portion, which has been dubbed into English for the Canadian version (1978). As a reviewer in the *Ottawa Journal* remarks, subtitles would have been more successful as the lip-synch is annoying and distracts from the drama.

Conclusion

Both the short story and the film catch a sense of the immigrant experience and the deliberate creation of a self-deceiving, illusory world. Gallant's story emphasizes the pre- and post-world war generational difference, while the film has no explicit time reference, though the locations, props and characters belong to the 1970s.

Food imagery is an important part of the ritual of conjuring up the image of home within the context of immigration. References to food and the art of cooking in the exchange of letters between mother and son creates a shared intimacy that was always missing while they lived together. The film adaptation features iconic scenes of diasporic food consumption.

By way of conclusion, we might say that the short story and the film adaptation is "full of nuance and personality and compellingly evocative detail. It draws us slowly into the vortices of human behaviour." (New 1980: 155).

Works Cited

Besner, Neil (2007), "Reading Linnet Muir, Netta Asher, and Carol Frazier: Three Gallant Characters in Postcolonial Time," in: Dvorak, Marta and New W. H. (eds.), *Tropes and Territories*. Montreal: McGill-Queen's UP, 155–163

CBC–Hungarian TV cooperate on His Mother, The Ottawa Journal, February 1, 1978, 13 https://www.newspapers.com/newspage/50103735

Civitello, Linda (2008), *Cuisine and Culture. A History of Food and People*, New Jersey: John Wiley & Sons.

Drága kisfiam! dir. Károly Makk, 1975, https://nava.hu/id/1985482/# M1, 1980-04-20; M3, 2014-10-08 CBC, International Cinemedia Center Ltd (Montreal) and Magyar Televízió

Gallant, Mavis. "His Mother," *The New Yorker*, August 13 (1973):28–33.

Gallant, Mavis (1979), *From the Fifteenth District*, Toronto: Macmillan.

Metcalf, John (1982), *Making It New: Contemporary Canadian Stories*, Toronto: Methuen.

New, W. H. "The Art of Haunting Ghosts," *Canadian Literature*, 85, Summer (1980):154.

Woodcock, George. "Memory, Imagination, Artifice: The Late Short Fiction of Mavis Gallant," *Canadian Fiction Magazine*, 28 (1978): 92–114.

CARMEN CONCILIO

Fasting in Abundance in Canadian Literature

> Today in Cosmopolitan Dublin, you can choose to eat an Indian curry, a Mexican burrito or an Irish breakfast. With an increasingly global food trade, a single meal can originate from ten locations across the planet. In the eagerness to minimize the distance our food travels and connect flavours to places, we may risk over-simplifying the complex systems that comprise our food systems. But whether one grows local or eats global, food will always be inextricably linked to place; and places are in constant flux. (Centre for Genomic Gastronomy 2012).

THIS IS AN EPIGRAPH TO the volume *Global Appetites*, scrutinizing the relationship between food and agriculture in American literature, but it could well be the description of what happens in any city of the world. After all, "talking about food systems means talking about cities. The city understood as a metropolitan region," writes Giacomo Pettenati (2015: 2).

Part of the flour we consume in Italy arrives from Canada and has been the cause of heated debate due to its potential or presumed danger within the CETA Agreements. Italy has long imported durum wheat from Canada—a key ingredient in pasta— but this incoming flow was stopped because of ongoing consumer concerns about the use of a popular weed-killer: glyphosate.

Although this herbicide has been declared safe in Canada if present within accepted limits, it has been rejected in Italy. In spite of Canadian studies claiming no harm for human health is detectable, Italian authorities tend to adhere to the concern raised by the World Health Organization, hinting at the possibility that glyphosate may be carcinogenic (https://ipolitics.ca/2018/04/03/pasta-spats-canadian-wheat-exports-to-italy-slump/).

Disputes and debates like this, having to do with both human and environmental health, will become more and more relevant in the future, for intercontinental trade will keep growing as the demographic boom continues to expand, and countless people will migrate from one continent to another, particularly to big cities, which are "the main drivers of the global food system" (Pettenati 2015: 2).

With this type of scenario at the back of one's mind, reading Rawi Hage's novel *Cockroach* (2008) becomes both a hilarious and a terribly dramatic experience, for we read about the entangled relations of migrants and food in the city of Montreal, Canada:

> Lately I find the city is being invaded by whining Parisians like Matild, who chant the "Marseillaise" every chance they get. They come to this Québécois American North and occupy every *boulangerie*, conquer every French restaurant and *croissanterie* with their air of indifference and their scent of fermented cheese—although, truly, one must admire their inherited knowledge of wine and culture. […] the Parisians are highly sought after and desired by the Quebec government. […] The Québécois, with their extremely low birth rate, think they can increase their own breed by attracting the Parisians, or at least for a while balance the number of their own kind against the herd of brownies and darkies coming from every old French colony, on the run from dictators and crumbling cities (Hage 2008: 28).

This passage brilliantly and ironically shows the inextricable interrelations between food, language, culture, ethnicity and migration; it shows how Western countries are afflicted by a stagnant birth rate and how migration from Asian and African countries is seen as an undesired countering principle to demographic degrowth, while ethnic and autochthonous food become rivals on the market. It is hilarious to think of how the Québécois *patisseries* become symbol of whiteness and Frenchness, fighting back the wave of "brownies" (both people and a type of sweet) and "darkies" from the French colonies, bringing in their own ethnic food and restaurants. It is interesting to ask at this stage where and what is the mother country, France or Québéc, Paris or Montreal, and what and where is the colony: Canada or French Africa? Paris and Montreal are thus set into a relational space thanks to food. Thus, this novel immediately presents itself as extremely challenging, as far as food and migration are concerned. After all, it is true that:

> Literature is a vehicle attuned to the modern food system due to the capacity of imaginative texts to shuttle between social and interpersonal registers and between symbolic and embodied expressions of power [...] literature has a facility with shifting from macroscopic to intimate scales of representation that can provide an incisive lens on the interactions between local places and global markets that are so central to how communities and corporations produce, exchange, and make use of food in the modern period (Carruth 2013: 5).

Thus, it is just natural and even predictable that the protagonist of the novel, who defines himself as an "impoverished migrant," "hungry," "broke" and "lonely," ends up asking for a job in a Persian restaurant, The Star of Iran: "It was a fancy restaurant with all the ornament necessary to transport you to the East. It surrounded you with dunes, lanterns, and handmade carpets that matched the brown plates flying from the waiter's hands onto woven tablecloth" (Hage 2008: 65).

The place is mostly a den, where the protagonist and his musician friend, Reza, also snort drugs. No particular ethnic dishes are described, rather "the smell of food from the kitchen" makes the hero—a petty villain of modern times—abandon his fantasies about Scheherazade and brings him back to "the land of forests and snow" (Hage 2008: 67). Nevertheless, the hero, who fantasizes of himself as a cockroach—any resemblance to Kafka is "coincidental"—claims: "All I wished was to crawl under the swinging door and hide under the stove, licking the mildew, the dripping juice from the roast lamb, even the hardened yogurt drops on the side of the garbage bin. With my pointy teeth, I thought, I could scrape the white drips all the way under the floor" (Hage 2008: 67).

The protagonist and almost "the main antagonist" in the story (Dahab 2018: 216) is a migrant in Montreal, from what the reader understands to be Lebanon, although the country is never named. He attends psychiatric sessions for he attempted suicide once. Yet, he cannot stand "the shrink," for she does not understand that his psychological problems are not due to his childhood, or his oedipal relations; rather, they have to do with a profound sense of injustice with regard to power imbalances and social asymmetry. In her close reading of the novel, Elizabeth Dahab argues that: "Rawi Hage's portrayal of an Arab antihero in a post-9/11 text belonging to the Arab-Canadian literature is a move away from political correctness toward freedom of contestation, artistic liberation, and political satire" (Dahab 2018: 216).

Migrants are never offered equal opportunities; they are only left with the "crumbs" white and rich people let them have. For instance, the protagonist is refused a job as a waiter in a French restaurant because of his dark complexion: "*Tu es un peu trop cuit pour* ça (you are a little too well done for that)! *Le soleil t'a brûlé ta face un peu trop* (the sun has burned your face a bit too much). I knew what he meant" (Hage 2008: 29). Furthermore, "crumbs" are a constant reminder of his condition of both hunger and anger, and of semi-animal identification (Concilio 2020):

Talking about crumbs, a nice sandwich would do me fine, I thought. Perhaps I could go to a restaurant nearby, enter it, and sweep up the little pieces of bread and other leftovers on the tablecloth, and then follow the trail of crumbs to the counter next to the kitchen and help myself to some of the warmth released from the toaster. But I know how hard it is to steal food in restaurants (Hage 2008: 56).

In the abovementioned paragraph, the reference might be the Biblical parable of "The Rich Man and Lazarus":

There was a certain rich man, which was clothed in purple and fine linen, and fared sumptuously every day: 16:20 And there was a certain beggar named Lazarus, which was laid at his gate, full of sores, 16:21 And desiring to be fed with the crumbs which fell from the rich man's table: moreover the dogs came and licked his sores. 16:22 And it came to pass, that the beggar died, and was carried by the angels into Abraham's bosom: the rich man also died, and was buried; 16:23 And in hell he lift up his eyes, being in torments, and seeth Abraham afar off, and Lazarus in his bosom (Luke 16: 20–23).

Hage's protagonist, this novel Lazarus, never content with crumbs, has dreams of elaborate dishes, such as "stuffed duck à l'orange!" (Hage 2008: 57). Similarly, he dreams of a luxury car and of fashionable clothes:

What I really, really wanted was [...] maybe a big fat golden ring on my finger, my chest gleaming under a black shiny shirt, my car keys dangling from a gadget that could open doors and beep and warm the driver's seat despite the cold snow. I wanted a gold chain around my neck and a well-dressed woman with kohl under her eyes [...] (Hage 2008: 66).

Reality sees him "dressed like a bum" (Hage 2008: 69), and always starving. When his friend Reza accuses him of being "a deranged, psychotic, spaced-out case of a petty, unsuccessful thief" (Hage 2008: 69), he is not far from the truth. When looking for Reza, who owes him money, he ends up in his apartment, where he steals food and sweets from the fridge, to eat them at home. Next, we find him eating "basmati rice and those few vegetarian leftovers from Mary the Buddhist's party" (Hage 2008:19), a neighbour he visits—uninvited—during a vegetarian party. On another day, he chronicles how "Hungry, I walked to the kitchen and opened the cupboards. A miracle indeed! A forgotten can of tuna was floating at the back of the shelves. I captured it, opened it, watched it quiver against the stillness of the oil, waited for the rice to boil, and ate sitting at the window" (Hage 2008: 36).

Permanently hungry and moneyless, he has no choice but to steal. This time it is the turn of chocolate bars stolen from a Korean grocer's. He is so slim that his psychiatrist asks him if he was well nourished in his childhood and if he had always been so skinny. Therefore, as a form of retaliation, he breaks into his therapist's house, paying a good visit to her fridge while observing himself as if from the outside, in the third person:

> The stranger stood up and walked to the kitchen, opened the fridge; it was filled with food—French cheeses, ham, and eggs. He made himself some toast, pasted on some ham and tomato slices, dropped a few thin sheets of cheese on top, decorated it all with lettuce, and moved to the living room with a large plate in his hand (Hage 2008: 82).

Thus, in a novel which is and is not about food, and which is a consistent *j'accuse* on the part of a migrant who feels excluded from the feasting of an opulent society, who feels invisible to the community who unwillingly hosts him, food is nevertheless a central obsession. The man knows he belongs to a class of servants, of subalterns, and is well aware of how "A servant should be visible but undetectable, efficient but unnoticeable, nourishing but malnourished. A servant is to be seen, always, in black and white" (Hage 2008: 85).

The ghostly invisibility of the migrant is countered by his conspicuous presence. In a climactic episode, the protagonist, while leaning against a sports car, decides to stare at a couple who are eating in an Italian restaurant. Soon the police are called to check his documents and invite him to go away. The couple also stares at him from inside the restaurant, acknowledging his annoying presence in the street, as if from a TV screen. Well aware of his being affected by "food envy syndrome" (Hage 2008: 87), he also feels the need to retaliate and thus hides in the couple's expensive car, making his way into their apartment and stealing jewellery and clothes. To his cursing them as "Bourgeois filth! I thought. I want my share!", the woman answers: "St-Laurent Street is becoming too noisy and crowded with all kinds of people" (Hage 2008: 88), and the allusion here is certainly to immigrants like him. For "the dehumanization suffered by victims of racism makes them more uncanny to the racist than, say, a dog or a faceless robot" (Morton 2013: 131). All this happens while the news anchor on the TV speaks of "famine" (Hage 2008: 89).

Famine, too, is a topic in the novel as if it were inevitable to juxtapose "rhetorical assertions of American abundance to lived experiences of hunger within and outside the United States." (Carruth 2013: 10) The narrator refers to famine back in Lebanon:

> My grandmother told me about the famine days, when zillions of grasshoppers came and invaded the countryside and ate all the grain, all the fruit, all the vegetables. Her family survived only because they had a few chickens and they dug up roots. But the famine

took the lives of half the population, and then the Turkish army came and confiscated the stores of grain and food (Hage 2008: 209).

The real historical—almost Biblical—famine, due to specific climatic conditions in a specific ecosystem, accentuates the irony of a novel dealing with starving in Montreal nowadays.

The exchange of reciprocal gazes as if through a flawed mirror that makes it impossible for people of different ethnicities to look and recognize each other, or to acknowledge the presence of "the other" is typical of migrants' urban experience. Just as Frantz Fanon taught us, when he immortalized that boy pointing at him and shouting "Look, A negro! *Maman*, a negro!" (Fanon 2008: 93).

The scholar Sherry Simon stresses how in this novel, St-Laurent street is described as a divide along which racialism and classism run, where different languages are spoken. The name of the street is given in French not in English, while the dispossessed, impoverished immigrants of the Artista Café speak Algerian, Lebanese and Farsi, thus providing a different profile to the not-too-hospitable city of Montreal:

> St Laurent figures prominently as the centre of immigrant culture [...] The novel is strong in its evocation of a generation of newcomers scarred from war zones, troubled by past histories, longing to break through the layers of cold that isolate them from the life of the city. The narrator's impotent rage leads him to imagine himself as a giant cockroach, which breaks into people's houses and moves among their possessions, crawling along their walls and their drains. He is driven by his thirst of revenge, and a desire to wreak havoc on the favoured classes. The immigrant is an outsider, doomed to reliving his old stories of hatred, and without any cushion of solidarity. [...] The polyglot community of Iranians, Algerians and

Lebanese speak a mixture of French and English, Arabic and Farsi. The cruelty and rage of Hage's novel are reminders that the immigrant contact zones of Montreal have not always been treated as pure conviviality. (Sherry 2012: 146-147)

The next meal—a nice soup with delicious bread, salad and wine—is obtained by the protagonist at a friend's place, an Iranian homosexual, who escaped from the dictatorial regime and persecution, with a half story told over two bottles of wine and still "many scores to settle" (Hage 2008: 112) in his life. Another nice meal, although too hot and spicy, is provided by a Pakistani couple, living in the same building, who also give him some sugar for his tea whenever he knocks at their door. While that apartment building is a layer upon layer of ethnicities—a Russian woman married to a Greek in the basement, a Pakistani couple with children on the lower floor, the protagonist himself, a Middle-Easterner on a higher floor and a lonely old WASP woman even higher up—the city reproduces a similar patchy ethnic variety on a horizontal scale, with its numerous ethnic restaurants.

At the Iranian restaurant where the protagonist works, a little drama occurs over an ethnic meal, one which is simple and at the same time sophisticated. Only a few guests are present: a short, fat, bald man with his bodyguard, and at another table Shohreh and her friend Farhoud. The latter are eating "rice and saffron, lamb in pomegranate sauce, and mast-o-khiar" (Hage 2009: 215). Only Shohreh has a fit of vomit and she has to leave in a hurry.

As a contrasting location, on the day he gets his wages, the protagonist feels a compulsion to enter the bar called Greeny, which is dark enough to hide in:

I ordered a mug of beer, some fries, and a large, fat hamburger that came to me in a basket [...] I have ambivalent feelings about these places. To tell the truth, they kind of repulse me, but I always end up coming back to them. [...] I order, I drink, and I eat. [...] And at the first sip of beer, the first fries, I forget and forgive humanity for its stupidity, its foulness, its pride, its avarice and greed, envy, lust, gluttony, sloth, wrath, and anger. (Hage 2008: 226)

Immediately, the protagonist feels conspicuous once again under the gaze of the locals:

I realize how exposed I must look to all these creatures who arrived before me. [...] They must have seen my gluttony, my conspicuous tendencies, my aloofness. I feel X-rayed, as if every bite of the fries that went down my stomach was anticipated, watched, analyzed, and bet upon. It is then that I start rushing, frantically waving my skeleton-like index finger at the waitress, and with my clacking jaws insisting on the calculation of the bill ... (Hage 2008: 227).

Soon after his fast-food-like meal, his junk food is described as "my consumption of dead animals, alcohol, scratchy soggy lettuce, and tomatoes. And I was overwhelmed with the particular guilt of the impulsive poor who in a moment of grandiose self-delusion, self-indulgence, and greed, want to have it all" (Hage 2008: 228). Quite interestingly, the protagonist seems to explicitly refer to the so-called "food desert":

Variously defined according to the geographical context (mainly in UK and USA) and the field of research, a "food desert" can be defined as "areas of relative exclusion where people experience physical and economic barriers to accessing healthy food" (Reisig & Hobbiss 2000: 138), or "those areas of cities where cheap, nutritious food is virtually unobtainable" (Pettenati 2015: 7).

This particular episode shows the double feeling of attraction to—and repulsion for—the specific way of life that is typical of urban reality in big cities, for "cities are the main drivers of the global food system, defined as 'the chain of activities connecting food production, processing, distribution, consumption, and waste management, as well as all the associated regulatory institutions and activities' (Pothukuchi & Kaufman 2000: 113)" (Pettenati 2015: 2). The immigrant is attracted by these types of cliché-encroached, cheap and popular eating places, while at the same time hating them and knowing he does not belong there. On the contrary, he is hardly ever seen eating in the Iranian restaurant if not secretly, on the cook's own initiative.

However, the greediness of the poor is dictated and controlled but also contaminated by the West. Another friend, an Iranian taxi driver, claims: "You know, we come to these countries for refuge and to find better lives, but it is these countries that made us leave our homes in the first place" (Hage 2008: 223). The responsibility of colonial and imperial Western policy is clearly stated here. The taxi driver refers to "Us! Exiles!" (Hage 2008: 224) as to a group set apart from the rest of society, never totally integrated, never totally belonging, always on the other side of the border: us, against them, "the Anglos, for instance, all those McGill University graduates, dressed up like beggars, hoodlums, dangerous degenerate minorities" (Hage 2008: 228).

Thus, the city seems an agglomerate of tribes, divided up, partitioned, recognizable, each with its own code: the really poor and those who pretend to be poor but are in fact "very wealthy" (Hage 2008: 228). Montreal appears as a city still affected by self-interest. Only by doing away with self-interest is it possible to achieve a more intimate proximity to others. "The no-self view is not a faceless, dehumanized abstraction, but a radical encounter with intimacy. What best explains ecological awareness is a sense of intimacy, not a sense of belonging to something bigger: a sense of being close" (Morton 2013, 139). What Morton proposes as an antiracist ecology is an ethic of proximity, closeness and openness to others. And that is exactly what Hage aims at and wishes for his migrants, and that is where his message becomes political. For Dahab is right when she claims that "Hage's protagonist gives us a minority or marginal perspective on society" (Dahab 2018: 215).

To bring this essay full circle, while the very first quotation was about cosmopolitan Dublin with its choice of ethnic glocal restaurants, the description of Montreal's Chinatown restaurants yields yet more evidence of modern food systems and de-localized consumption: "grilled ducks that now hang in the steamy windows of restaurants with dirty floors, hot woks, and solemn, quiet faces slurping whatever is fished out of bowls with chopsticks" (Hage 2008: 230). On this occasion, too, as in the fast-food joint, the dead animals, unclean windows and shop floors all look unappetizing.

In a city that offers multiple culinary possibilities and experiences, according to the concept of "foodshed," that is to say, "the areas from which the food that arrives to a city comes from," (Pettenati 2013: 6)—and the novel mentions France, Italy, Iran and China—the protagonist struggles with his stolen sandwiches and his crumbs, while all around people are feasting after various fashions—mirroring "a fragmented networked archipelago of places stretching all over the world" (Pettenati 2013: 6)—which are neither ethically nor aesthetically palatable nor pleasurable. In a time when slow food and the Mediterranean diet have become both a philosophy and a way of life, both a theory and a practice, the protagonist of Hage's novel is fasting in abundance. "Cities are already a scale of political action, where policies and strategies directly and indirectly addressed to the food system are developed and practised" (Pettenati 2013: 3).

Works Cited

Carruth, Allison (2013), *Global Appetites. American Power and the Literature of Food.* Cambridge: Cambridge University Press. Print.

Concilio, Carmen (2020), "Praktiken intertextuellen Recyclings bei Achmat Dangor, Rawi Hage und Igoni Barrett," in David Assmann (ed.), *Narrative der Deponie. Kulturwissenschaftliche Analysen beseitigter Materialitäten*, Frankfurt: Springer, 185–204.

Dahab, Elizabeth F. (2018), "A Close Reading of *Cockroach*," in Giulia de Gasperi and Joseph Pivato (eds.), *Comparative Literature for the new Century*, Montreal: McGill University Press. Print.

Fanon, Frantz [1952], *Black Skin, White Masks*, English translation by Richard Philcox, New York: Grove Press, 2008.

Hage, Rawi (2009), *Cockroach*, Toronto: Anansi, 215–228. Print.

Morton, Timothy (2013), *Hyperobjects. Philosophy and Ecology after the End of the World*, Minneapolis: University of Minnesota Press.

Pettenati, Giacomo (2015), *The Atlas of Food. A space of representation, a place for policies, a methodology of territorial analysis.* http://www.fao.org/fileadmin/templates/ags/docs/MUFN/CALL_FILES_EXPERT_2015/CFP1-05_Full_Paper.pdf. Web.

Pothukuchi Kameshwari and Jerome L. Kaufman (2000), "The Food System. A Stranger to the Planning Field," *Journal of the American Planning Association*, 66:2, 113–124. https://www.tandfonline.com/doi/abs/10.1080/01944360008976093. Web.

Reisig, VMT, A. Hobbis (2000). "Food Deserts and How to Tackle Them: a Study of One City's Approach." *Health Education Journal*, 59, 137–149. https://journals.sagepub.com/doi/pdf/10.1177/001789690005900203. Web.

Sherry, Simon (2012). *Cities in Translation. Intersections of Language and Memory*, London: Routledge. Print.

The King James Bible [1989], Project Gutenberg, e-book, 22 March 2010. http://www.gutenberg.org/files/10/10-h/10-h.htm#The_Gospel_According_to_Saint_Luke. Web.

ANGELA BUONO

Pas et repas : parcours littéraires de la nourriture entre stéréotypes et appartenance identitaire

1. Du pas au repas : Hédi Bouraoui et le transculturalisme

CETTE ÉTUDE PORTE SUR DEUX ouvrages de la littérature dite "migrante", le roman *La femme d'entre les lignes* de Hédi Bouraoui, franco-ontarien d'origine tunisienne, poète, romancier et critique reconnu, et la pièce *Addolorata* de l'écrivain italo-québécois Marco Micone, deuxième volet d'une trilogie qui compte aussi les pièces *Gens du silence* et *Déjà l'agonie*.

Dans ces deux textes, l'Italie occupe une place centrale, en tant que décor de l'histoire de *La femme d'entre les lignes* et en tant qu'arrière-plan de la pièce de Marco Micone, qui explore l'univers migrant de la communauté italo-montréalaise.

Le point de départ de l'analyse est le "pas" introduisant le titre de cet article :

```
Pas.          Pas.          Pas.
Pas.    ASP          SPA
Pas.                              SAP …
```
J'écris avec mes pas, mes trous, mes manques
Mes pas
Et chaque pas élargit le trou, le pas

Le manque rayonne poreux concentrique
Grandissant ... crible et ratures langagières (Bouraoui
1986: 230)

Ces vers du poème *Imminente apparition*, tiré du recueil *Échosmos*
de Hédi Bouraoui, un écrivain qui poursuit sa réflexion sur l'écriture à l'intérieur même du texte poétique ou narratif, peuvent être
considérés comme un manifeste de sa poétique centrée autour de la
notion du transculturel. Né à Sfax et ayant émigré à Toronto après
ses études en France et aux États-Unis, Hédi Bouraoui incarne à
lui seul, par son héritage culturel multiple, l'idéal transculturel qu'il
a élaboré à partir de sa singulière démarche existentielle et qu'il
définit en ces termes : "[...] connaître sa culture et la transcender
en même temps pour s'ouvrir à d'autres, créer des ponts de tolé-
rance et des faits d'interchange, de manière à élaborer une nouvelle
esthétique" (Dotoli 2003: 55). Ainsi qu'il l'affirme, son identité
s'est donc bâtie "dans la relation entre plusieurs cultures, il faut que
chaque culture soit ouverte pour accueillir la différence, ainsi l'autre
transvase sa propre culture en moi et je transvase ma propre culture
vers l'autre; c'est cet échange qui se passe dans les interstices des
cultures" (Falcicchio 2004: 117).

C'est sur ces assises que repose l'originalité de sa réflexion sur
l'écriture, qu'il qualifie de "transpoétique"[1] et dont le pivot est

la notion de *béance*, c'est-à-dire l'ouverture et sa dis-
ponibilité, le chiasme entre deux, trois ou plusieurs
cultures. La béance emprunte alors les valeurs culturelles qui l'entourent et présente un espace de gestation
en perpétuel mouvement, comme dans toute poïé-
tique, comme dans toute vie. Ceci a donné naissance à
ma notion d'écriture interstitielle (Bouraoui 2000: 16).

---

1 "Par transpoétique, nous voulons surtout signaler le trans/vasement des
cultures qui se chevauchent, se croisent et s'entrecroisent, s'attirent et se re-
poussent dans un travail incessant qui crée un espace particulier du faire poétique" (Bouraoui 2005: 42-43).

En tant qu'espace interstitiel, la béance s'identifie au vide. Loin d'être un concept négatif, dans la poétique de Hédi Buoraoui "c'est ce vide du milieu qui donne naissance à la vie, à tout son dynamisme" (Bouraoui 2002: 9). Le rien, le vide créateur est un leitmotiv de l'œuvre dès son début. Qu'on relise dans son premier recueil *Musocktail* ces vers du poème *Cocktail Poétique* :

> La Poésie est partout
>   et Nulle part
> [...]
> Agencer des mots
> Ces trous inaccessibles (Bouraoui 1966: 2-3)

L'identification du "trou" avec la parole poétique revient dans le dernier poème du recueil *Échosmos* qu'on vient d'évoquer tout à l'heure. Dans ce poème, la parole poétique est associée au trou, au manque, au "pas". Le poète joue sur le double sens du mot "pas", appréhendé et en tant que négation et en tant qu'expression du mouvement. Par le biais de ce petit mot transpoétique—un *mot à béance*, d'après la terminologie de l'auteur—il présente en extrême synthèse les fondements de sa poétique—le "pas" contenant, d'un côté, la béance de la négation, le vide de la béance en tant qu'interstice transculturel et, de l'autre, la mouvance essentielle pour combler ce vide par les traversées des langages et des cultures.

Le "pas" peut donc être assumé comme l'une des catégories d'analyse d'une critique nouvelle que Hédi Bouraoui qualifie de "créativité-critique" :

> Si nous avions suggéré l'abolition des frontières entre créativité et critique, c'est que les textes de création du monde francophone, en plus d'être conscients de leur propre genre, reflètent une préoccupation théorique dans leurs propres paramètres d'écriture (Bouraoui 2005: 29).

Par conséquent, la valeur transpoétique du "repas" n'a certainement pas échappé au grand jongleur des mots qu'est Hédi Bouraoui,
et en tant qu'élément linguistique évoquant la répétition du "pas", et
dans son sens ordinaire de nourriture, pouvant se charger d'implications identitaires et culturelles.

C'est dans ce double sens que les repas acquièrent le rôle de
pivots narratifs dans *La femme d'entre les lignes*, un roman qui se veut
une réflexion sur la création littéraire, dramatisée à travers l'histoire
d'amour du narrateur poète avec une femme italienne qu'il appelle
Lisa et qu'il rencontre à l'occasion d'un voyage en Italie. Toutefois,
comme Jean-Max Tixier le remarque opportunément :

> [...] ce roman est un faux roman d'amour, et peut-être
> même un faux roman dans la mesure où il sert de pré-
> texte à la mise en espace d'une réflexion sur le langage
> et l'usage qu'en fait la littérature. Il souligne l'autono-
> mie du mouvement romanesque une fois lancé, lorsque
> les mots prennent l'initiative et s'enchaînent dans des
> directions non prévues par le scripteur (Tixier 2006:
> 369).

De même, ce récit de voyage n'en est pas un, puisque, comme le
souligne Giuseppina Igonetti, "il s'agit [...] d'un voyage immobile
qui s'ouvre sur la recherche d'un lieu qui permette à l'auteur d'arti-
culer tous les éléments de cohérence textuelle" (Igonetti 2006: 352).

Dans ce "voyage immobile", le mouvement se ferait entièrement au niveau de l'écriture du texte où, comme le remarque encore
Jean-Max Tixier, "Hédi Bouraoui opère un double transfert : du
réel au romanesque et du romanesque au jeu linguistique, pour retourner au romanesque, puis au réel" (Tixier 2006: 368).

La relation entre le narrateur et Lisa est tout d'abord celle entre
le poète et sa lectrice, envisagée comme une histoire d'amour qui se
déroule surtout dans et par les mots, *entre les lignes* du texte, ainsi
que le titre le suggère, et dont l'évolution est toutefois déclenchée

par des passages anecdotiques concernant, la plupart du temps, des repas traditionnels ou conviviaux. C'est au cours du premier déjeuner qu'ils prennent ensemble, dans "un petit restaurant, l'Antica Trattoria Don Peppino" (Bouraoui 2002: 23), que s'établissent la relation d'amour au niveau de la narration, la relation d'écoute et de lecture critique entre l'écrivain et sa lectrice, la relation linguistique entre l'histoire racontée et les stratégies stylistiques et lexicales, qui exploitent les sens multiples du vocabulaire de l'alimentation pour filer la métaphore de l'amour et de l'écriture :

> Je remplis nos deux verres de vin rouge. Je marque un court silence afin d'aiguiser son appétit de paroles. Et je pense en moi-même : "Mon Dieu, comment vais-je satisfaire cette femme si assoiffée de mots brûlants […] !" (Bouraoui 2002: 25)

La jalousie de la femme, qui s'éveille à cause d'un récital de poésie auquel le narrateur a participé et dont il lui fait le récit, se manifeste également par son attitude à table et sa façon de se nourrir :

> Elle aurait voulu que ce récital n'ait eu lieu que pour elle seule. […] On apporte le repas, je me mets à l'observer en train d'avaler littéralement sa nourriture comme si elle n'avait rien mangé depuis deux ou trois jours. Elle se gratifie ainsi en compensation terrestre, cache maladroitement sa nervosité. Mon repas refroidit, et elle exige plus de détails sur cette rencontre à laquelle elle regrette de n'avoir pu assister (Bouraoui 2002: 26).

S'il est vrai que, "alors qu'en maints endroits le narrateur ne fait pas mystère de ses exigences sexuelles, sa relation avec Lisa reste singulièrement désincarnée, voire platonique" (Tixier 2006: 369), ce n'est que pendant un repas convivial comparé à la lecture d'un texte littéraire que le rapport d'amour s'accomplit dans sa plénitude :

On décide d'aller dîner en groupe pour "célébrer mon passage en Italie" à la Trattoria Locanda Isetta, à Grancona. Trois couples de nationalités différentes s'installent autour d'une table ronde pour un festin qui se prolongera jusqu'au milieu de la nuit. La nourriture très bonne est accompagnée d'un vin rouge servi avec panache. Il suffit de voir le maître d'hôtel le décanter dans une carafe arrondie à la base et emmanchée d'un long cou, puis le verser en giclées splendides pour s'enivrer. La conversation tourne autour des mets dégustés ou ceux que l'on a déjà goûtés. Lisa suit la discussion sans dire un mot. Nos regards se croisent. Personne ne remarque nos silences. Nous sommes dans le royaume d'une commune tendresse tacite qu'aucun dialogue ne peut exprimer. Ainsi nous faisons l'amour en plein public sans que personne ne puisse en décoder le moindre signe, à la manière d'une dégustation de texte dans l'intimité de la lecture (Bouraoui 2002: 116).

L'amour des protagonistes se déploie donc sur de multiples niveaux : celui de la réalité de l'espace socio-culturel, constitué d'un restaurant typique qui existe bel et bien à Grancona en Vénétie, et d'un repas convivial qui se veut aussi une occasion d'échange transculturel par la présence de convives de nationalités différentes ; celui de la métaphore du texte, en tant qu'espace du récit dans le sens double de lieu de l'intrigue et lieu de l'énonciation ; et celui du langage qui relie ces plans en les ramenant tous dans le champ sémantique du goût, savamment choisi pour exprimer l'idée de partage, tour à tour convivial, amoureux, poétique et transculturel.

Le long passage que nous venons de citer se prête aussi à d'autres considérations. Hormis un cas que nous allons examiner plus loin, l'évocation des repas auxquels le protagoniste participe ne s'accompagne jamais de véritables descriptions des mets ou de l'ambiance. Cela confirme le caractère de faux récit de voyage du roman où Hédi Bouraoui, "[...] donne à lire à son destinataire l'espace qui lui convient, et sa narration est construite en accord avec le personnage qu'il crée autour de sa propre personne" (Igonetti 2006: 353), un personnage "qui se promène, un pied dans la vie, l'autre dans l'artifice, [...] dans les rues et les places italiennes, avec leurs fontaines, leurs somptueuses demeures et leurs statues, qui exhalent un certain art de vivre, un certain hédonisme, bref, une "certaine idée" de l'Italie" (Igonetti 2006: 344). Cette idée de l'Italie qui se dégage de la lecture du roman correspond le plus souvent à une idée stéréotypée qui, pour ce qui concerne les repas, les associe invariablement à la bonne chère arrosée de bon vin ou à l'hyperbole "d'un repas gargantuesque [...où] nous avions tous bien mangé, bien bu, bien chanté, bien caqueté à d'énormes décibels plus hauts que la norme [...]" (Bouraoui 2002: 84). Néanmoins, il ne faut surtout pas en conclure à une représentation superficielle : en plus de répondre à une précise stratégie de narration, comme l'a démontré Giuseppina Igonetti, il faut considérer, avec Jean-Louis Dufays, que "les stéréotypes sont, au même titre que les mots et les concepts, des aliments indispensables de la pensée et de l'expression" (Dufays 2006: 64), d'autant plus lorsqu'ils sont employés dans le contexte transculturel qui constitue le décor typique des romans de Hédi Bouraoui :

> La démarche interculturelle [...] semble avoir tout à gagner d'un va-et-vient constant entre la mobilisation des stéréotypes relatifs à l'étranger, qui nous permettra une première appropriation globale, certes sommaire, mais indispensable, de sa culture, et la mise à distance (par la comparaison, le jeu, la réécriture) de ces stéréotypes, qui nous permettra d'accéder à une connaissance à la fois plus diversifiée et plus complexe (Dufays 2006: 76).

Le rapprochement des cultures à des fins de connaissance réciproque constitue l'une des stratégies majeures de promotion de l'idéal transculturel dans le roman bouraouien. Le seul repas sur lequel le narrateur s'attarde pendant plusieurs pages est le banquet de la Pâque juive dont il décrit en détail tous les rituels, les aliments qu'on partage et leur signification symbolique, tandis que l'évocation de la tradition italienne de la fête des Pâques se borne "aux œufs en chocolat, à *l'agnello pascuale* (*sic*) qui réunit toute la famille cloîtrée dans un rituel de mangeaille bien installé dans toute l'Italie" (Bouraoui 2002: 55),—une description tout aussi sommaire et stéréotypée que celles des autres repas dont il est fait mention dans le roman.

En plus d'une fonction didactique qui n'est pas la moindre des intentions des textes bouraouiens, on peut avancer l'hypothèse que le repas traditionnel juif occupe beaucoup d'espace dans le roman parce qu'il recèle toutes les significations qu'implique le "pas" en tant que clé d'interprétation du texte bouraouien, à savoir le mouvement, l'ouverture de la béance, le jeu verbal :

> [...] le repas du *seder de Pesah* ("passage", en hébreu), de la Pâque juive, ou comme ils disent en anglais, de *Passover*. Une amie française ne cesse de me répéter que cette "passe au vert" devrait m'ouvrir les portes et les cadenas du sexe. Du fait même que je les célèbre, même si je ne suis pas de croyance juive. Mais ce passage au vert par la porte du paradis charnel n'empêchera pas ma vie de se terminer un jour (Bouraoui 2002: 56).

Qu'ils se déploient dans l'espace géographique ou scripturaire, le nomadisme, l'errance et l'aller vers l'Autre et l'Ailleurs constituent des leitmotive dans l'œuvre bouraouienne, et les traditions de la Pâque juive plus que toute autre gardent intactes toutes les implications contenues dans son étymon :

> Symbole de l'exode, ce festin n'est rien d'autre que la célébration de la fuite, dit-on, du joug du pharaon, de l'esclavage du peuple juif vers la liberté [...]. Libération incomplète jusqu'au moment où le peuple accueillera

le Messie. *Pesah* est donc la "Nuit de la vigile pascale".
On doit laisser la porte de chaque maison ouverte,
pour pouvoir accueillir le prophète ou tout passant af-
famé … (Bouraoui 2002: 57)

2. Du repas au pas: Marco Micone et la culture migrante

Dans la trilogie dramatique de Marco Micone—*Gens du silence*
(1982), *Addolorata* (1984)[2], *Déjà l'agonie* (1988)—c'est le stéréotype
dans son sens de modèle fixe qui s'impose et qui répond à l'intention de l'auteur de représenter l'immobilisme de la condition
migrante de la communauté italienne au Québec. Dans *Addolorata*
tout particulièrement, la stéréotypie affecte les repas et la nourriture
constituant de parfaites métaphores d'une identité qui en même
temps se fige en se repliant sur elle-même et s'effrite au contact avec
la communauté d'accueil.

   Dans *Addolorata*, où l'attention est centrée en particulier sur la
condition de la femme immigrée, le rêve de la protagoniste d'un
somptueux mariage marquant le début d'une vie heureuse est vite
démonté par son futur époux qui évoque en peu de mots la plati-
tude du banquet de noce traditionnel et en fait une transparente
métaphore de la vie conjugale des immigrés :

> Quel mariage! […] Des heures à être dégoûté de la
> petite olive ratatinée, du filet d'anchois pourri couché
> dans son cercueil de céleri et de la tranche de prosciutto
> mauve; des heures à attendre le bol de soupe que per-
> sonne a mangée, les pâtes trop molles et la viande trop
> dure, pendant que tout le monde disait du mal de la ma-
> riée, du marié, de leurs parents, de l'orchestre, du voisin,
> de la réception et… des *francesi* (Micone 1996: 94).

---

2 En 1996, Marco Micone a réuni ses trois pièces dans une *Trilogia*, en rédi-
geant par la même occasion une deuxième version d'*Addolorata* qui prolonge
l'action de la première et lui attribue un nouveau dénouement.

Le voyage de noces aussi ne se réduirait qu'à un passage de nourriture d'un côté à l'autre de l'océan :

> En voyage de noces? Une semaine dans ton village et une semaine dans le mien, [...] pour revenir ensuite avec dix chaînes en or autour du cou, des gallons d'huile d'olive et du fromage pecorino pour tes parents et les miens? Mes vêtements sentiraient encore le mouton. Ç'aurait été ça, notre voyage de noces (Micone 1996: 142).

Dans la pièce de Marco Micone, l'éclatement identitaire de l'immigré italo-québécois se reflète de façon saillante dans son babélisme mêlant l'anglais, le français et le patois italien dans un pâté linguistique où c'est encore au lexique de la nourriture de marquer l'appartenance italienne, par des mots figés qui s'incrustent dans le discours en pièces éparses, comme autant de fragments d'une identité révolue :

> Qu'est-ce qui te fait penser qu'on parle anglais, *christ*? [...] quand je dis à ma sœur : *"Hey, Carmelina (Il prononce Carmelina à l'anglaise) what's that?* Es-tu folle? *Me, I don't eat zucchini cù l'aglio."* [...] *Well, you can't say it's French; it's certainly not Italian; it's not even English.* C'est quoi, tu penses? [...] *Did you ever try naming all the objects around you, with the first word that comes to your mind?* Sans tricher là. *Fast, real fast, without thinking. Like this: table, chairs, stove, fridge, counter,* le toaster était pas là, *floor, ceiling, a salsa, u fiasco, i piatti. That's when I was in the kitchen.* [...] *Then I went into my father's garden: a cipolla* à gauche, *u lacce* à droite, la salade au centre, *i zucchini* plus loin, les tomates de l'autre côté, *and watchmacallit* dans des pots: *u basilico* (Micone 1996: 112-113).

Ainsi que l'affirme la protagoniste de la pièce, "chez nous, après la question de la langue, c'est la sauce tomate qui cause le plus de chicanes. [...] Il faut qu'elle soit ni trop sure ni trop sucrée; ni trop brune ni trop rouge; ni trop pimentée ni trop salée; ni trop épaisse ni trop liquide..." (Micone 1996: 103). La sauce tomate revient comme un leitmotiv dans la pièce en tant que symbole prégnant de la condition migrante. Elle marque tout d'abord la réitération immuable d'us et coutumes: "Je me demande qu'est-ce qu'on ferait sans sauce tomate"—s'exclame Lolita—"Depuis l'âge de douze ans que je fais ça tous les jeudis. Le dimanche matin, c'est au tour de ma mère" (Micone 1996: 103); la condition malheureuse de la femme immigrée clouée à son foyer est bien représentée par cette sauce qui bouille, toujours sur le point de coller au fond de la casserole chaque fois qu'une rêverie de liberté soustrait la protagoniste à son devoir, et son exclamation "Oh! ma sauce tomate!" (Micone 1996: 102, 109, 125) revient comme le refrain d'un rappel à l'ordre. D'ailleurs, c'est encore la sauce tomate qui se pose finalement aussi en symbole du rachat de l'immigrée, en signe du rejet de la soumission aux sacro-saintes traditions familiales et de l'enfermement dans une identité italienne aussi stéréotypée que nébuleuse :

> Maudite sauce tomate! Hum! Ça y est! Ça commence à sentir le brûlé! Continue, continue de brûler!
> De Montréal-Nord à Ville Émard, de Parc-Extension à Saint-Léonard, tous les jeudis, tous les dimanches cinquante mille Italiennes tiennent dans leurs mains cinquante mille cuillers en bois et brassent de gauche à droite, tournent de droite à gauche, deux fois par semaine, deux heures par jour. Mais à partir d'aujourd'hui, y en aura une de moins. Elle va se détacher du troupeau. Elle va prendre le large. [...] Brûle, brûle une fois pour toutes! (Micone 1996: 146)

Le repas brûlé, Addolorata peut accomplir le pas vers sa délivrance et vers l'évolution de la culture immigrée, un pas qui garde le sens double du "pas" bouraouien : dans sa valeur de négation, pour emprunter les mots à Pierre L'Hérault, il "[...] soulign[e] le paradoxe d'une culture qui se perpétue en disparaissant" (L'Hérault 2003: 193) ; dans sa valeur de mouvement, il exprime le caractère de transition que Marco Micone assigne à la culture immigrée :

> La culture immigrée est une culture de transition qui, à défaut de pouvoir survivre comme telle, pourra, dans un échange harmonieux, féconder la culture québécoise et ainsi se perpétuer (Micone 1998: 100).

En conclusion, s'il est vrai, comme l'affirme Jean-Max Tixier, qu'"en amont de l'écriture, il y a un manque, une blessure non cicatrisée [... et] écrire revient à la nier, à la dépasser, à chercher une compensation" (Tixier 2006: 371), écrire la nourriture se révèle bien l'une des plus riches stratégies de narration compensatoire.

Works Cited

Bouraoui, Hédi (1966), *Musocktail*, Chicago: Tower Publications.

Bouraoui, Hédi (1986), *Échosmos*, Toronto: Canadian Society for the Comparative Study of Civilizations and Mosaic Press.

Bouraoui, Hédi (2000), "Les enjeux esthétiques et idéologiques du transculturel en littérature", in Bélanger, Louis (ed.), *Métamorphoses et avatars littéraires dans la francophonie canadienne*, Ottawa: L'Interligne, 11-26.

Bouraoui, Hédi (2002), *La femme d'entre les lignes*, Toronto: Éditions du GREF.

Bouraoui, Hédi (2005), *Transpoétique*, Montréal: Mémoire d'encrier.

Dotoli, Giovanni (2003), "Entretien avec Hédi Bouraoui", in *Culture et littérature canadiennes de langue française*, Fasano, Italia: Schena Editore, 49-64.

Dufays, Jean-Louis (2006), "Stéréotypes, apprentissage, interculturalité : fondements théoriques et pistes didactiques", in Collès, Luc, Dufays, Jean-Louis and Thyrion, Francine (eds.), *Quelle didactique de l'interculturel dans les nouveaux contextes du FLE/S ?*, Louvain: E.M.E., 57-84.

Falcicchio, Adriana. "Entretien avec Hédi Bouraoui". *Rivista di Studi Canadesi*, 17. (2004): 117-137.

Igonetti, Giuseppina (2006), "L'écriture de l'errance dans *La Femme d'entre les lignes*", in Sabiston, Elizabeth and Crosta, Suzanne (eds.), *Perspectives critiques. L'œuvre d'Hédi Bouraoui*, Sudbury: Université Laurentienne, 343-355.

L'Hérault, Pierre (2003), "L'intervention italo-québécoise dans la reconfiguration de l'espace identitaire québécois", in Fratta, Carla and Nardout-Lafarge, Élisabeth (eds.), *Italies imaginaires du Québec*, Montréal: Fides, 179-202.

Micone, Marco (1996), *Addolorata*, in *Trilogia*, Montréal: VLB Éditeur, 78-161.

Micone, Marco (1998), *Le figuier enchanté*, Montréal: Boréal.

Tixier, Jean-Max (2006), "La fonction de transfert dans *La femme d'entre les lignes*", in Sabiston, Elizabeth and Crosta, Suzanne (eds.), *Perspectives critiques. L'œuvre d'Hédi Bouraoui*, Sudbury: Université Laurentienne, 365-371.

VALERIA ZOTTI

La cuisine du terroir dans la littérature québécoise traduite en Italie : les limites des corpus parallèles

> La cuisine d'une société est un langage dans lequel elle traduit inconsciemment sa structure, à moins que, sans le savoir davantage, elle ne se résigne à y dévoiler ses contradictions. (Cl. Lévi-Strauss 1968: 411)

Introduction: la source d'inspiration

L'IDÉE À L'ORIGINE DE CETTE contribution est née de la lecture d'un chapitre du roman *Les Anciens Canadiens* de Philippe Aubert de Gaspé, l'un des grands romans, voire le roman le plus important de la littérature québécoise du XIXe siècle, aux dires de plusieurs historiens et commentateurs (Boivin 2011: 15). Dans cet ouvrage, à la fois roman historique, roman de mœurs, roman d'aventures et roman témoignage à caractère autobiographique (Boivin 2011: 17), Aubert de Gaspé, dernier seigneur de Saint-Jean-Port-Joli, trace un portrait 'presque' idyllique de la société québécoise traditionnelle, sous le régime seigneurial. Dans le Chapitre Sixième notamment, intitulé *Un souper chez un seigneur canadien*, l'écrivain s'attarde longuement sur la description d'un souper chez le seigneur de Beaumont. Cette scène de mœurs, ainsi que tout le roman, constitue un document précieux sur les habitudes alimentaires des derniers seigneurs québécois au milieu du XIXe siècle[1].

On y découvre qu'à la table de ce seigneur canadien, on se délecte, en silence et de grand appétit, d'un excellent potage, d'un pâté froid, appelé pâté de Pâques, de poulets et de perdrix rôtis, recouverts de doubles bardes de lard, de pieds de cochon à la Sainte-Ménéhould (cf. Aubert de Gaspé 1863: 89-90). Pour le dessert, on déguste, accompagnés de vin blanc, deux tartes, un plat d'œufs à la neige, des gaufres. Dans le roman, il sera également fait référence aux pâtisseries, crèmes fouettées, blanc-mangers, qui régalaient ces seigneurs québécois. Un portrait des traditions culinaires de cette époque est ainsi dressé magistralement.

En nous inspirant de ce témoignage, nous nous proposons dans cette contribution de retracer les traditions du terroir québécois telles qu'elles sont décrites dans un corpus d'œuvres littéraires du XXe siècle, traduites en italien. Nous nous sommes demandé comment le Québec manifeste son existence en Italie. La culture québécoise est-elle convenablement représentée dans les textes d'arrivée ? L'image de la cuisine québécoise qui y est véhiculée est-elle folklorique ou moderne ?

Derrière ces questionnements, se cachent des questions à la fois d'ordre sociologique (Bourdieu 1998) et ethnologique (Lévi-Strauss 1968), mais surtout traductologique, respectivement sur la représentation de la culture et de l'identité québécoises en littérature, et sur les difficultés posées par la traduction des entités connotées culturellement (*realia*) tels que les plats du terroir. Partant de l'acquis que "la traduction représente un facteur nullement négligeable dans la question de la mondialisation de la culture et de la diversité culturelle, en particulier pour la francophonie" (Jolicoeur 2011: 394), l'enjeu de cette contribution est de savoir si les traducteurs italiens ont réussi à restituer, plus ou moins fidèlement, la spécificité

---

1   Nous tenons à remercier Myriam Vien, lectrice d'échange québécoise à l'Université de Bologne (CISQ), de nous avoir suggéré la lecture de cet ouvrage, ainsi que pour sa révision soignée de cette contribution.

culturelle des traditions culinaires du Québec. En parcourant des citations littéraires, accompagnées de leurs traductions, nous allons reconstruire l'histoire et l'évolution de la cuisine québécoise en tant que miroir et produit de l'histoire de la société québécoise. Nous examinerons de près les stratégies traductives adoptées consciemment ou inconsciemment par les traducteurs pour traduire le nom de certains mets traditionnels. Pour ce faire, nous présenterons une approche linguistique des phénomènes de traduction relevés, en nous appuyant sur les méthodes offertes par la linguistique de corpus (Baker 1993, Loock 2016) et en considérant, en particulier, le rôle joué par les corpus parallèles pour le travail des traducteurs professionnels et pour la recherche en traductologie.

1. Le corpus d'œuvres littéraires québécoises traduites en Italie

Dans cette première partie, nous nous arrêterons sur la présentation de notre corpus d'analyse. Le corpus littéraire que nous avons dépouillé dans le cadre de cette contribution est constitué d'une sélection d'ouvrages littéraires québécois du XXe siècle qui ont été traduits et publiés par des maisons d'édition italiennes à partir de 1924. Il s'agit de 10 ouvrages, dont 6 romans, 2 recueils de nouvelles, 1 recueil de poésie et 1 pièce de théâtre.

Bismuth, Nadine (1999), *Les gens fidèles ne font pas les nouvelles*, Montréal, Éd. du Boréal.
(2003), *La fedeltà non fa notizia*, [Trad. de Cristiano Felice], Rome, Voland.
Hébert, A. (1950), *Le torrent : nouvelles*, Paris, Éd. du Seuil.
(2005), *Il torrente*, [Trad. de A. Pasqualini], Roma, Sinnos.
Hébert, Anne (1970), *Kamouraska*, Paris, Éd. du Seuil.
(1972), *Dietro il gelo dei vetri*, [Trad. de S. Estense], Milan, Mondadori.

Hébert, Anne (1975), *Les enfants du sabbat*, Paris, Éd. du Seuil.

(2008), *I bambini del sabba*, [Trad. de V. Porro], Ferrare, Luciana Tufani Editrice.

Hébert, Anne (1982), *Les Fous de Bassan*, Paris, Éd. du Seuil. (2002), *L'ultimo giorno dell'estate*, [Trad. de V. Porro], Ferrare, Luciana Tufani Editrice.

Hémon, Louis (1916), *Maria Chapdelaine : récit du Canada français*, Montréal, J.-A. LeFebvre éditeur, 1916 [Paris, Grasset, 1921]

(1924). *Maria Chapdelaine. Racconto del Canadà francese*, [Trad. de Lorenzo Gigli], Torino, Paravia, coll. "Biblioteca Le Rose".

(1945). *Maria Chapdelaine*, [Traducteur anonyme], Milano, Gentile Editore.

(1954). *Lui non tornò più*, [Trad. de Melitta], Vicenza, Edizioni Paoline.

(1959). *Maria Chapdelaine*, [Trad. de Maria Luisa Cadeddu Fanciulli], Bologna, Edizioni Capitol, coll. "Flaminia".

(1986), *Maria Chapdelaine. Racconto del Canada francese*, [Trad. de U. Piscopo], Torino: SEI.

Miron, Gaston (1970), *L'homme rapaillé*, Montréal, Presses de l'Université de Montréal.

(1981), *L'uomo rappezzato* [Trad. de S. Zoppi], Rome, Bulzoni.

Poulin, Jacques (1984), *Volkswagen blues*, Montréal, Québec/ Amérique.

(2000), *Volkswagen blues*, [Trad. de M. R. Baldi], Rome, Hortus conclusus.

Thériault, Yves (1958), *Agaguk*, Québec, Institut littéraire du Québec/Paris, Bernard Grasset Éditeur.

(1993), *Agaguk. L'ombra del lupo*, [Trad. de O. Ceretti Borsini], Firenze, Giunti.

Tremblay, Michel (1968), *Les belles-sœurs*, Montréal, Holt Rinehart et Winston.

(1994), *Le cognate* [Trad. de J.-R. Lemoine et F. Moccagatta], dans *Il teatro del Québec*, Milan, Ubulibri.

Notre tour d'horizon sera donc partiel, car nous ne nous arrêterons que sur une sélection d'ouvrages ayant fait l'objet d'un dépouillement complet dans le cadre du projet de constitution d'une base de données de la littérature québécoise traduite en italien, mené à l'Université de Bologne par l'auteure de cette étude (projet Qu.It : www.quit.unibo.it, voir Zotti 2016). Pour la réalisation de cette base, qui n'est rien d'autre qu'un corpus parallèle enrichi de remarques métalinguistiques et traductologiques, nous sommes redevables au laboratoire de recherche du *Trésor de la Langue Française au Québec* (TLFQ) qui nous a fourni une partie des citations littéraires extraites de la base du *Fichier lexical* (http://www.tlfq.ulaval.ca/fichier/), ainsi qu'au travail accompli par De Vaucher et Gravili (2016) qui ont réalisé, au bout de plusieurs années de travail, une bibliographie, régulièrement mise à jour, des traductions italiennes d'ouvrages canadiens francophones.

Comme l'a remarqué Jolicoeur (2011: 397), "la littérature québécoise semble bien connue en Italie, du moins à en juger par le nombre impressionnant d'auteurs recensés". Dans notre corpus, le théâtre (Michel Tremblay), tout comme la poésie (Gaston Miron) sont représentés, bien que dans une moindre mesure, et, du côté du roman, nous trouvons aussi bien des écrivains classiques (Louis Hémon, Anne Hébert, Yves Thériault) que des auteurs plus contemporains (Jacques Poulin, Nadine Bismuth).

Il convient de souligner que les représentations identitaires des Québécois dans la littérature canadienne-française, devenue québécoise dans les années 1960, ont changé considérablement au fil du temps. Ainsi, si l'on prend comme point de départ les ouvrages de notre corpus, on observe que "la représentation de l'identité (idéal-typique) canadienne-française du début du XXe siècle dans *Maria Chapdelaine* [...] a peu en commun avec celle qui s'impose de l'identité québécoise après la Révolution tranquille" (Cordoba Serrano 2013: 233). En effet, cette identité, qui tourne autour de trois axes idéologiques, l'agriculturalisme, l'anti-étatisme et le messianisme (Thériault J.-Y. 1999: 125), est devenue moderne, 'américaine', urbaine et industrialisée depuis les années 1980. On en trouve une illustration dans les nouvelles de Bismuth où l'on assiste à "la représentation d'une identité québécoise plus hétérogène, multiple et ouverte à la diversité, une identité en accord avec le monde globalisé actuel" (Cordoba Serrano 2013 : 234).

Ce changement se reflète dans les traditions culinaires représentées dans les ouvrages que nous avons examinés. Si les origines autochtones de la cuisine typiquement canadienne-française sont présentes dans les romans du terroir (de Hémon par exemple) et dans les romans qui puisent dans l'imaginaire du Grand Nord (comme ceux de Thériault qui présentent le monde inuit), depuis 1980, apparaît la "nouvelle cuisine" (cf. Lebel 1996: 22), ainsi que la cuisine multiethnique ouverte à diverses influences internationales (américaine, italienne, grecque, etc.). Même la présence de québécismes employés pour décrire ce patrimoine culinaire est étroitement liée à la période de publication des ouvrages analysés. Dans le groupe d'ouvrages publiées dans les années 1970 ou avant, qui transmettent l'idée d'un Québec associé au monde rural, aux immenses forêts, aux bûcherons, etc., nous avons relevé un grand nombre de québécismes désignant des réalités propres, qui sont employées comme matières premières de la nourriture et dont la traduction n'est pas toujours aisée. En revanche, il n'est pas étonnant de constater, dans notre corpus, que la "spécificité québécoise" est peu représentée dans les ouvrages publiés plus tard, car, depuis les années 1980, les écrivains québécois ont pris progressivement leurs distances par rapport à la question linguistique qu'ils ou elles veulent transcender.

Nous nous consacrerons maintenant à parcourir les extraits littéraires qui décrivent le patrimoine culinaire du terroir québécois, dont nous commenterons simultanément les traductions. Par souci de brièveté, nous ne pourrons présenter que quelques extraits particulièrement significatifs[2]. Dans une perspective traductologique,

---

2   Dans la base Qu.It (www.quit.unibo.it), il sera possible de consulter l'intégralité des extraits littéraires étudiés ici, ainsi que d'autres ouvrages littéraires québécois qui font état du patrimoine culinaire québécois et que nous n'avons pu retenir dans le cadre de cette contribution, faute d'espace.

nous émettrons des hypothèses concernant le travail des traducteurs. Dans une perspective linguistique contrastive, nous nous
demanderons si la manière de procéder des traducteurs est moti-
vée par les caractéristiques divergentes des deux systèmes de signes
en contraste (la langue française et la langue italienne) et par l'in-
terférence de la variation topolectale du français québécois. Nous
tiendrons bien évidemment compte des facteurs socioculturels et
pragmatiques qui peuvent avoir orienté les choix des traducteurs,
ainsi que du fait que la traduction est un acte communicatif (cf.
Wecksteen 2007). Nous nous confronterons à des textes traduits
par des spécialistes de la culture et de la littérature québécoise (ex.
Sergio Zoppi, ancien professeur de littérature québécoise à l'Université de Turin), par des traducteurs professionnels (ex. Cristiano
Felice, Francesca Moccagatta), mais aussi par des traducteurs inconnus, probablement des amateurs (ex. Melitta). Cette variété de
profils et de compétences influence la qualité des traductions et jus-
tifie en quelque sorte l'hétérogénéité des procédés et des stratégies
adoptées.

2. La cuisine du terroir québécois et ses traductions

Qu'est-ce qui fait la spécificité de la cuisine québécoise ? La réponse
donnée par Michel Lambert, célèbre historien de la cuisine et auteur
de la série d'ouvrages *Histoire de la cuisine familiale du Québec*, est la
suivante : ce sont "ses diverses influences, naturelles et culturelles,
locales et étrangères" (Lambert 2011: 23).

2.1. L'influence autochtone

La première influence est certainement celle des cuisines autochtones. En décrivant les préférences alimentaires d'un groupe
d'autochtones qui a donné naissance aux nations de langue algonquienne du Québec, Lambert (2011: 23) nous apprend que, pendant

l'hiver, leurs préférences allaient principalement vers le gros gibier comme l'orignal, le caribou, le cerf de Virginie et le wapiti, et l'été, vers les gros poissons comme l'anguille, le saumon, l'esturgeon et le grand corégone. La disparition de ces groupes autochtones du territoire, entre la venue de Cartier et celle de Champlain, n'a cependant pas fait disparaître cette cuisine du Québec qui reste fortement empreinte de cet héritage (cf. Lambert 2011).

2.1.1. Les espèces zoologiques locales

Dans les extraits suivants de notre corpus, tirés de romans d'époques et de styles variés, on trouve par exemple un grand nombre de références à des espèces de poissons d'eau douce et d'eau salée indigènes qui sont à la base de la nourriture locale :

(1) *Iriook le vit entrer dans l'eau, patauger en cherchant à empoigner le poisson. Puis il ressortit, triomphant. Il tenait une **truite** aux flancs gras et rebondis qu'il avait réussi à saisir.* (Thériault Y. 1958: 211) Iriook lo vide entrare nell'acqua, muovere le mani in una rapida ricerca, afferrare un pesce. Poi egli riguadagnò la riva con aria trionfante, tenendo stretta la bella **trota** dai fianchi tondi che era riuscito a ghermire. (Ceretti Borsini 1993: 215).

(2) *Tout le village boit et mange dans les cuisines regorgeant d'**anguilles**, de volailles et de **caribou**.* (Hébert 1970: 84) Tutto il villaggio beve e mangia nelle cucine rigurgitanti di **anguille**, polli e **caribù**. (Selvatico Estense 1972: 90).

(3) *Joseph dit qu'il a pêché un **achigan** de deux livres et qu'il va le faire cuire pour moi.* (Hébert 1975: 75) Joseph dice che ha pescato una **trota di due libbre e che la farà cuocere per me.** (Nappi 2008: 78)

(4) *Jeanluidemandasi Normandluirapportaitplussouventdu saumon,
de la **perchaude**, de la **truite** ou de la **morue**.* (Bismuth 1999: 41)
Jean le domandò se Normand portava a casa più spesso **sal-
moni, persici, trote** o **merluzzi**. (Felice 2003: 27)

S'agissant, dans la plupart des citations, d'espèces de poissons
(*truites, anguilles, perchaudes, saumons*) qui sont aussi connus en
Europe et pour lesquelles des équivalents italiens existent, il sem-
blerait, au premier abord, que les traducteurs de ces ouvrages ne se
soient pas heurtés à de grandes difficultés pour traduire ces extraits,
proposant donc une traduction littérale. Nous soulignons bien 'au
premier abord', parce qu'une observation plus attentive nous amène
à croire que dans les extraits (1) et (4), le mot *truite*, qui a été traduit simplement par son équivalent lexical dans la langue d'arrivée,
"trota", ne corresponde pas exactement au Québec au poisson que
le même mot désigne en français de référence.

Il convient de souligner à ce propos que le lexique québécois
montre l'existence d'un français précolonial qui a intégré de nombreux éléments venant de diverses régions de France et qui serait
arrivé en Nouvelle-France à travers les pêcheurs, les marins et les
navigateurs dès le début du XVIe siècle (cf. Canac-Marquis et
Poirier 2005). Ainsi, il y aurait un bon nombre de mots empruntés
aux dialectes et langues parlées par les premiers colons (*orignal*,
du basque oregnac) ou à des peuples autochtones (*caribou*) ou encore utilisés pour désigner des réalités nouvelles (la *truite*, pour
l'omble).

En effet, en nous penchant sur les descriptions du mot *truite*
dans les principaux dictionnaires québécois, nous avons bientôt
pu constater que ce mot désigne en français québécois "un poisson salmonidé du genre Salvelinus, aussi appelé omble, qui diffère
de la truite (Salmo) par quelques traits anatomiques internes"
(*Dictionnaire du Français Plus*, DFP). Le *Dictionnaire Universel
Francophone* (DUF) précise qu'au Québec, *truite* est le nom courant de l'omble ("salmerino" en italien). Et le dictionnaire Usito

indique qu'"au Québec, dans la langue générale, le mot *truite* a une extension plus grande que dans la langue spécialisée", car il désigne aussi les poissons "qui présentent des taches claires (omble et touladi)".

En revanche, dans le cas du mot *achigan* (3), nom d'un "poisson d'eau douce originaire d'Amérique du Nord" (Usito), "plus connu en France sous les noms de black-bass et de perche noire" (TLFi)[3], la traductrice a choisi de le rendre par "trota" (*truite*), un nom vernaculaire ambigu désignant plusieurs espèces de poissons d'eau douce de la famille des salmonidés, comme nous venons de le voir, alors que, d'après la classification phylogénétique, l'*achigan* appartient à une autre famille de poissons, celle des centrarchidés. Il s'agirait ici d'une traduction par hyperonyme par laquelle seul l'essentiel de la dénotation du terme est traduit. En choisissant le nom d'un poisson d'eau douce très commun dans le monde entier, la couleur locale donnée par l'emploi du québécisme *achigan*, dérivé de l'algonquien, s'avère être complètement perdue dans la traduction italienne, ainsi que la valeur documentaire du roman en question en tant que témoignage de la diversité et de la richesse de la faune aquatique du Québec.

Par contre, cette perte ne se produit pas dans la traduction du mot *caribou* (2), utilisé en français de référence pour désigner le renne du Canada, autre espèce typique d'Amérique du Nord. Sur l'axe historique, *caribou*, tout comme *achigan*, est sans aucun doute un amérindianisme, lui aussi d'origine algonquienne (cf. DFP et *Grand Dictionnaire Terminologique*, GDT). La présence dans le lexique italien du mot "caribù" qui désigne le même animal, et qui a été, à l'évidence, emprunté à la langue française, a évité au traducteur de se retrouver dans une impasse pour traduire ce mot désignant une réalité nouvelle (*realia*), propre au Québec (cf. Leppihalme 2011, Zotti 2019).

---

3 "Pesce persico" en italien.

2.1.2. Les espèces botaniques locales

Les mots désignant des *realia* locales, c'est-à-dire des réalités culturo-spécifiques d'un territoire donné qui contribuent à la création de l'identité de ce territoire, abondent dans le corpus littéraire à l'analyse. Chaque *realia* suppose "la définition de frontières hors desquelles le référent du mot serait absent, et donc inconnu" (Farina 2011: 83). Outre les espèces zoologiques dont nous venons de voir quelques exemples, les premiers colons se sont trouvés face à la nécessité de nommer aussi des espèces botaniques qu'ils ont découvertes dans ce territoire inexploré. Le français du Québec présente en fait une production lexicale originale concernant en particulier les noms des baies et autres petits fruits sauvages d'Amérique du Nord (*atocas, bleuets, gadelles*, etc.). Il s'agit là d'une autre matière première très utilisée dans les cuisines des autochtones, qui les conservaient séchés ou en purées denses, ou pour qu'elles entrent dans la composition de plats très appréciés comme le célèbre pemmican (Lambert 2011: 23). Ces baies, initialement dédaignées par les colons nobles, qui préféraient faire planter des arbres fruitiers rapportés d'Europe, ont été par la suite adoptées par les colons pauvres, préoccupés avant tout d'assurer leur subsistance. Puis, progressivement, ces nouvelles habitudes alimentaires ont gagné les autres catégories sociales, si bien qu'au tournant du XVIIIe siècle, même les tables bourgeoises offraient à leurs convives ces petits fruits du pays (cf. Martin 2020).

Dans notre corpus littéraire, on trouve plusieurs traces de ces fruits sauvages. Le mot *bleuet*, un québécisme lexématique (Poirier 1995) qui désigne une "baie d'un bleu noirâtre, à saveur douce et acidulée" (Usito), très employée pour "faire des confitures ou les fameuses tartes qui sont le dessert national du Canada français" (Hémon 1916: 66), figure treize fois dans notre corpus, notamment dans Hémon (1916) et dans Hébert (1950). L'analyse des différentes traductions de ce mot dévoile clairement les atouts et les limites d'un corpus parallèle en tant que source d'inspiration pour un traducteur (cf. Loock 2006: 161). Regardons quelques exemples tirés du roman *Maria Chapdelaine* de Louis Hémon, qui a connu cinq différentes traductions italiennes, publiées entre 1924 et 1986.

(5)   *Les forêts du pays de Québec sont riches en baies sauvages; les atocas, les grenades, les raisins de cran, la salsepareille ont poussé librement dans le sillage des grands incendies ; mais le bleuet, qui est la luce ou myrtille de France, est la plus abondante de toutes les baies et la plus savoureuse.* (Hémon 1916: 65)

a)   Le foreste della regione di Québec sono ricche di frutti selvatici: le bacche, le melegranate, i ràfani, la salsapariglia si sono liberamente sparsi per i varchi aperti dai grandi incendi; ma le more, che corrispondono alle bacche del mirtillo di Francia, sono i frutti selvatici più abbondanti e più saporiti. (Gigli 1924: 48)

b)   Le foreste del paese di Québec sono ricche di bacche selvatiche; le atocas, le granate, l'uva di roccia, la salsapariglia son cresciute liberamente nel solco dei grandi incendi; ma il **mirtillo** è la più abbondante di tutte le bacche e la più gustosa. (Traducteur anonyme 1945: 66)

c)   Traduction de cet extrait absente. (Melitta 1954)

d)   Le foreste della regione di Québec sono ricche di frutti selvatici, bacche, melograne, uva spina, salsapariglia, che si sono sparse liberamente fra i varchi aperti dai grandi incendi; ma le more, che sono una specie di mirtillo di Francia, sono il frutto più abbondante e saporoso. (Cadeddu Fanciulli 1959: 68)

e)   I boschi del Québec abbondano di frutti selvatici: le bacche, le melagrane, l'uva selvatica, la salsapariglia si sono potute espandere liberamente negli spazi aperti dei grandi incendi; ma i **mirtilli** sono i frutti selvatici più abbondanti e saporiti. (Piscopo, 1986: 62).

(6) *Côte à côte il ramassèrent des **bleuets** quelque temps avec diligence, puis s'enfoncèrent ensemble dans le bois, enjambant les arbres tombés, cherchant du regard autour d'eux les tache violettes des baies mûres.* (Hémon 1916: 72)

   a) Per qualche tempo colsero insieme con attenzione i **frutti**, poi penetrarono nel bosco scavalcando i tronchi caduti e cercando di scoprire intorno le macchie violette delle bacche mature. (Gigli 1924: 62)

   b) Si misero a sgranare **bacche** con tale sveltezza che in breve i loro due secchi furono colmi. (Melitta 1954: 73)

D'une part, le corpus permet de découvrir qu'un même mot, dans différents textes, peut se traduire différemment, tout en montrant quelles sont les différentes stratégies de traduction possibles d'une *realia* en l'occurrence. Ici quatre équivalences lexicales sont attestées comme traductions de *bleuets* dans les différents extraits : "more", une **adaptation**[4], "mirtilli", un **équivalent lexical**, "frutti" et "bacche", des équivalents **hyperonymiques**.

D'autre part, le corpus dévoile que les erreurs de traduction existent et qu'on peut les retrouver dans ces bases de données. Le mot *bleuet* est rendu par le traducteur anonyme (1945) et par Piscopo (1986) par le mot "mirtillo", un équivalent lexical qui pourrait être pertinent sur le plan sémantique dans d'autres textes (dans des textes de vulgarisation de botanique par exemple ou dans d'autres romans), mais pas dans ce roman en particulier, car lorsque Hémon emploie pour la première fois ce mot dans son roman (extrait 5), il explique à ses lecteurs ce qu'est un *bleuet*, son but étant aussi de faire connaître cette culture 'exotique' à l'étranger, et, pour

---

4 On pourrait la considérer comme une adaptation culturelle visant à supprimer la distance culturelle entre le texte source et le texte cible, mais qui est mal réussie car, en proposant comme traduction un autre fruit, une baie commune dans l'univers du public cible, c'est-à-dire le fruit du roncier, la *mûre*, on perd complètement la référence à la spécificité de la flore québécoise, ainsi que le sens de la comparaison que Hémon a établi dans le texte source avec le régionalisme breton "luce", synonyme de "myrtille".

ce faire, il emploi le mot *myrtille*. Les traducteurs ont donc choisi d'omettre son explication (voir 5b et 5e) et, ce faisant, ils ont sans doute trahi le projet littéraire de Louis Hémon et appauvri le texte d'arrivée (cf. Acerenza 2011: 408).

Ailleurs dans notre corpus, notamment dans les traductions italiennes de deux ouvrages d'Anne Hébert, *Le Torrent* (1950) et *Les enfants du sabbat* (1975), on utilise le même équivalent traductionnel, "mirtillo", pour traduire respectivement le mot *bleuet* et le mot *atoca*, un autre québécisme lexématique désignant la baie appelée "canneberge" en français de référence.

(7) *Après le petit brûlé où chaque été je venais cueillir des **bleuets** avec ma mère, je me trouvai face à face avec la route.* (Hébert 1950: 23)
     Dopo il piccolo terreno bruciato, dove ogni estate andavo a raccogliere i **mirtilli** con mia madre, mi trovai proprio di fronte alla strada. (Pasqualini 2005: 26).

(8) *Elle réclame du blé d'Inde, des gadelles, du pimbina et de la gelée d'**atoca**; toutes sortes de nourritures qu'on ne trouve pas au couvent.* (Hébert 1975: 175)
     Reclama mais, grappoli di ribes, viburno e gelatina di **mirtillo** - tutti i più vari cibi, che non si trovano in convento. (Nappi 2008: 189).

On voit ainsi clairement l'un des risques dérivant de la consultation d'un corpus parallèle : le traducteur, ayant accès à des phrases isolées de leur contexte plus large, pourrait perdre de vue la cohésion du texte qu'il traduit et employer dans un texte le même équivalent pour deux lexies bien distinctes. Nous nous sommes arrêtés jusqu'ici sur les matières premières à la base de la cuisine autochtone offertes par le territoire canadien. Le dernier extrait (8), qui contient enfin le nom d'une préparation culinaire faite avec ces baies, la *gelée d'atoca*, ouvre la porte au paragraphe suivant où l'on montrera que la typicité culinaire naît de la rencontre de la nature et de la culture (cf. Lambert 2011: 24).

2.2. La rencontre de la nature et de la culture des ancêtres français

Il est clair que les garde-manger locaux ne peuvent être considérés comme les seuls garants de l'identité culinaire québécoise. Lorsque les ancêtres français sont arrivés au Québec avec leur bagage culturel général, un petit accent normand et qu'ils ont pris contact avec les Algonquiens installés à Québec, ils ont aussitôt adopté certains mets autochtones, comme la sagamité, plat à base de semoule de maïs, et ils ont également préparé les matières premières fournies par le territoire à la manière des cultures fondatrices françaises (cf. Lambert 2011).

2.2.1. Les produits de l'érable

Un exemple emblématique de cet échange mutuellement enrichissant est fourni par les produits de l'érable. Les Amérindiens furent les premiers à découvrir la sève d'érable et à la transformer en sirop ou en sucre. Ce sont eux qui ont transmis ce savoir-faire aux premiers colons français (cf. Auger 2020), lesquels ont, par la suite, à l'aide des instruments modernes et du savoir-faire artisanal, tiré avantage de l'érable en développant de nombreux produits vendus sur le marché : sucre mou et dur, gelée, suçons, bonbons, beurre, tire et cornets. À partir des années 1690, la production du sucre d'érable, utilisé comme accompagnement des desserts fruités et agent de conservation des fruits confits, sera ainsi généralisée.

Autour de l'érable, quantité de coutumes et de traditions se sont développées : avant l'arrivée des technologies modernes, la *cabane à sucre* était le lieu de rassemblement familial par excellence au Québec ; adultes et enfants aimaient célébrer le *temps des sucres* en faisant une promenade en calèche ou en traîneau, en trempant la palette dans le *sirop d'érable* ou en se délectant de la *tire d'érable* sur la neige. Les *oreilles de crisse* (friture de lard salé), les *œufs dans le sirop*, la *tire sur la neige* sont autant de traditions alimentaires qui perdurent (cf. Douville 2011: 34).

Tout cet univers qui fait partie de l'identité du Québec est bien représenté dans notre corpus d'analyse : si la traduction de *sirop d'érable* ne pose pas de problèmes de traduction, s'agissant d'un produit connu mondialement pour lequel une traduction consolidée existe ("sciroppo d'acero"), d'autres expressions comme *pain de sucre d'érable*, *tire d'érable* et *tire sur la neige* donnent du fil à retordre aux traducteurs.

(9) *Azalma lui servait une seconde tranche de lard ou tirait de l'armoire le **pain de sucre d'érable**.* (Hémon 1916: 19)

   a) Azalina allora gli serviva un secondo pezzo di lardo, o prendeva dall'armadio il **pan di zucchero di canna**. (Gigli 1924: 11)

   b) Azalma gli serviva una seconda fetta di lardo o cavava dall'armadio il **pan di zucchero d'acero**. (Traduttore anonimo 1945: 20-21)

   c) E Azalma premurosa e ridente tagliava il lardo, offriva una vecchia latta piena di **sciroppo di zucchero scuro**. (Melitta 1954: 25)

   d) Alzima gli allungava una seconda fetta di lardo, o andava all'armadio a prendere un **pan di zucchero**. (Cadeddu Fanciulli 1959: 21-22)

   e) Azalma, allora, gli serviva una seconda fetta di lardo o tirava fuori dal cassetto della dispensa un **pan di zucchero d'acero**. (Piscopo, 1986: 63)

Les différentes traductions donnent à penser que les traducteurs ne connaissaient pas le sucre d'érable préparé en forme de pain ou en morceaux. Gigli (9a) traduit *pain de sucre d'érable* par l'expression "pan di zucchero di canna" (pain de sucre de canne) "en déplaçant ainsi l'action du roman dans les îles des Caraïbes, car au Canada il n'y a pas de canne à sucre" (cf. Acerenza 2011 : 412). Melitta (9c) remplace dans sa traduction le pain d'érable par un référent différent, une latte pleine de sirop de sucre foncé. Les trois autres traductions proposées, "pan di zucchero (d'acero)" (9b, 9d, 9e), des **calques** ou **traductions littérales,** bien que correctement re-transcrites sur le plan morpho-sémantique, s'avèrent ambiguës aux yeux d'un lecteur italien qui ne comprend pas exactement à quoi ressemble cette sucrerie.

Concernant la traduction de *tire*, nous avons été obligées de reconstruire la cohérence textuelle d'un passage en assemblant différents extraits présents dans le corpus qui attestent l'emploi de ce mot. Dans ce long paragraphe qui couvre deux pages du roman, Hémon explique la signification de ce québécisme en donnant plusieurs détails sur les étapes suivies par la mère Chapdelaine pour préparer la "vraie" *tire*, par opposition à la *tire* sur la neige qu'on mentionne dans la première partie du même passage. Or, afin de bien traduire ce passage, il est nécessaire que le traducteur connaisse la différence entre la *tire (d'érable)*, ce que Hémon appelle la "vraie" *tire*, qui est une confiserie à base de sucre d'érable, traditionnellement confectionnée en étirant la préparation refroidie que l'on coupe ensuite en bouchées (cf. Usito) et la *tire sur la neige* que l'on obtient en versant sur de la neige tassée du sirop épaissi et bouillant, et que l'on déguste, à peine figé, à l'aide d'une spatule de bois ou d'un bâtonnet (cf. Usito).

(10) Le jour de l'an n'amena aucun visiteur. Vers le soir la mère Chapdelaine, un peu déçue, cacha sa mélancolie sous la guise d'une gaieté exagérée.—Quand même il ne viendrait personne, dit-elle, ce n'est pas une raison pour nous laisser pâtir. Nous allons faire de la tire. Les enfants poussèrent des cris de joie et suivirent des yeux les préparatifs avec un intérêt passionné. Du sirop de sucre et de la cassonade furent mélangés et mis à cuire ; quand la cuisson fut suffisamment avancée, Télesphore rapporta du dehors un grand plat d'étain rempli de belle neige blanche. Chacun fut servi à son tour, les grandes personnes imitant plaisamment l'avidité gourmande des petits ; mais la distribution fut arrêtée bientôt, afin de réserver un bon accueil

à la vraie **tire**, dont la confection ne faisait que commencer. Car il fallait parachever la cuisson, et, une fois la pâte prête, l'étirer longuement pendant qu'elle durcissait. Les fortes mains grasses de la mère Chapdelaine manièrent cinq minutes durant l'écheveau succulent qu'elles allongeaient et repliaient sans cesse ; puis une dernière fois la pâte fut étirée à la grosseur du doigt et coupée avec des ciseaux, à grand effort, car elle était déjà dure. La **tire** était faite. (Hémon 1916, p. 129-130)

a) «Quand'anche non venisse nessuno», disse, «non è una ragione per lasciarci andare. Ora faremo la *tire*». […] ma la distribuzione fu presto saggiamente sospesa, per riservare una buona accoglienza alla vera *tire*, la cui confezione era appena incominciata. […] La *tire* era fatta. (Traducteur anonyme 1945 : 121-122)

b) Allora la mamma per farli stare allegri dichiarò che avrebbe fatto il **«tira e molla»** una specie di caramella che si vede fare anche da noi nelle fiere di campagna. […] Si mette a cuocere lo **zucchero** finché diventa una **pasta elastica** che si allunga e si ripiega e poi si torna ad allungare finché se ne tagliano tanti **pezzetti** che diventano duri. Tutti volevano aiutare a fare e a mangiare. (Melitta 1954: 105)

c) «Anche se non è venuto nessuno» disse «non c'è ragione di rattristarsi. Dobbiamo stare allegri. Faremo lo **zucchero filato**». […] A un certo punto la distribuzione venne giudiziosamente interrotta in attesa di una seconda colata già in ebollizione sul fuoco. […] finché non divenne **pasta molle**; e allora stesala in fretta perché non si indurisse troppo, e ridotta all'altezza di un dito, venne tagliata a **pezzetti** con le forbici. (Cadeddu Fanciulli 1959: 124)

En observant les traductions proposées par les traducteurs de ce roman, il nous a semblé que la plupart d'entre eux ne se sont même pas posé la question de faire la distinction entre ces deux types de *tire*. Ils n'ont pas non plus tenu compte de la présence dans le texte source de l'explication pour la préparation de la "vraie" *tire*. Trois traducteurs (Gigli 1924, Cadeddu Fanciulli 1959 et Piscopo 1986) ont traduit ce québécisme par le syntagme "zucchero filato" (*barbe à papa* en français de référence), une sucrerie bien sûr mais de consistance bien différente et que l'on ne peut pas étirer longtemps pendant qu'elle durcit… Pourrait-on supposer qu'il s'agirait d'une traduction cibliste (Ladmiral 2014) ? Même si c'était intentionnellement le but de ces traducteurs (ce dont nous doutons), nous estimons que les textes d'arrivée ne sont pas lisibles et font entièrement le deuil du texte original. Seul le traducteur anonyme (1945) a maintenu dans la traduction italienne *tire* en français, la meilleure stratégie selon Acerenza (2011: 412) car elle "vise à ajouter la 'couleur locale' du texte original à la traduction et permet d'enrichir également la langue d'arrivée".

Nous considérons intéressante dans son genre la version de Melitta (1954)[5] qui, en donnant comme équivalent "tira e molla", propose une **adaptation** à la culture italienne, cohérente avec le reste de sa traduction, qui nous semble tout à fait pertinente, parce que Melitta montre, pour le moins, avoir parfaitement cerné le référent de la *tire d'érable*, la ressemblance avec la *tire* à la consistance solide étant évidente. Le "tira et molla" est une spécialité de Sassuolo, ville italienne de la région de Modène, d'où probablement la traductrice est originaire (le prénom Melita et sa variante Melitta étant très diffusés dans cette aire géographique), que l'on prépare avec des procédés très similaires à ceux employés pour la *tire*[6]. Il s'agit dans ce cas sans aucun doute d'une traduction cibliste qui fait

---

5   Comme Acerenza (2011: 408) l'a observé pour la version italienne de Melitta : "les lecteurs ne lisent pas une traduction en bonne et due forme, mais plutôt une adaptation du texte de Louis Hémon, une forme réduite de *Maria Chapdelaine*".

6   Il s'agit de bonbons préparés à l'occasion du Jeudi Saint avec un mélange de sucre et de miel liquéfiés qui, une fois durci, est fixé sur un crochet pour être tiré et étiré (d'où son nom). Quand la pâte est assez solide, on la tranche en petits morceaux. On peut voir une démonstration de sa préparation sur ce site-web : https://www.visitsassuolo.it/la-tradizione-dei-tiramolla/ [consulté le 19/07/2022].

volontairement disparaître toute référence à la culture québécoise. C'est pourquoi cette traduction a été considérée à juste titre comme une "réécriture".

En définitive, si le but de Hémon était aussi de faire connaître à ses lecteurs la culture québécoise, aucune des traductions italiennes proposées, mis à part celle du traducteur anonyme, n'a tenu compte de cette finalité. Dans un autre extrait du corpus, tiré de *Les enfants du sabbat* de A. Hébert, on trouve la *tire sur la neige,* mentionnée de manière explicite. La traductrice Nappi a, elle aussi, opté pour une **adaptation** pour traduire cette *realia* en visant un référent encore différent, le caramel, qui fait disparaître encore une fois la référence à une préparation culinaire de la tradition québécoise.

(11) *Les palettes de bois minces et grises, si utiles autrefois pour étendre la tire sur la neige.* (Hébert 1975: 85)
Spatole di legno sottili e grigie, un tempo così utili per stendere il **caramello.** (Nappi 2008: 93)

Il est donc naturel d'en déduire que la traduction la plus respectueuse serait sans doute celle, qui en gardant le québécisme *tire* en français, proposerait une périphrase dans le texte ou une explication dans une note de bas de page (Acerenza 2011: 411).

2.2.2. Les préparations à base de blé d'inde

Un autre produit de la terre, qui occupe une grande place dans l'alimentation des Québécois, figure dans plusieurs extraits. Il s'agit du maïs, appelé au Québec *blé d'inde* depuis l'arrivée des premiers explorateurs français qui pensaient avoir découvert la route des Indes lorsqu'ils sont arrivés la première fois en Amérique. On sait combien le maïs fait partie intégrante des fêtes traditionnelles de la Belle Province, comme l'épluchette de blé d'Inde, qui remonterait à l'époque de la Nouvelle-France, durant laquelle le maïs était cultivé comme céréale essentielle pour la subsistance des colons. Le maïs est aussi un des ingrédients fondamentaux du *pâté chinois*, une recette traditionnelle remaniée par les colons français en utilisant les produits offerts par le terroir québécois : maïs, viande et pommes de terre.

Dans les extraits suivants, nous remarquons encore des données intéressantes sur le plan traductologique.

(12) *Chapelets, dominos, cordes à sauter, scarlatine, première communion, coqueluche, otites, rosbif, puddings, **blé d'Inde**, blancs-mangers, manteau de lapin, mitaines fourrées.* (Hébert 1970: 19)
Rosari, domino, salto alla corda, scarlattina, prima comunione, pertosse, otiti, roast-beef, pudding, budini, dolci, pelliccette di coniglio, manopole imbottite. (Selvatico Estense 1972: 20)

(13) *Le **blé d'Inde** sucré bout à plein chaudron.* (Hébert 1975: 44)
Il **mais** dolce ribolle a fuoco vivo nel paiolo. (Nappi 2008: 47)

(14) *Mon oncle François nous a demandé si nous souhaitions nous inscrire à l'épluchette de **blé d'Inde**.* (Bismuth 1999: 74).
Zio François ha chiesto se volevamo iscriverci alla festa della **pannocchia**. (Felice 2003: 48)

(15) *- Une cuisse de poulet ! - Un **pâté chinois** ! - Un chop suey !* (Poulin 1984 : 155)
- Una coscia di pollo! - Un **paté cinese**! - Un chop suey! (Baldi 2000: 144)

Si dans (13) et (14) la traduction de *blé d'Inde* ne pose pas de problème, car Nappi et Felice l'ont traduit en italien respectivement par les lexies simples "maïs" et "pannocchia", la traduction de l'extrait (12) présente un exemple emblématique d'**omission**. La traductrice n'a pas rendu en italien le québécisme *blé d'Inde*, probablement parce qu'elle ne connaissait pas la signification de ce syntagme ou parce que, cette traduction étant assez lointaine (1972), elle ne disposait pas de ressources lexicographiques fiables à cette époque[7]. Les omissions des items lexicaux en traduction nuisent considérablement à la représentation de la culture québécoise dans le texte d'arrivée car ses traits culturels les plus significatifs y sont délibérément effacés. Dans l'exemple (15), la **traduction littérale** donne à penser qu'il s'agit véritablement d'un pâté de type chinois. (Jolicoeur 2010: 192). Force est de constater que le traducteur ne connaît pas ce plat de la tradition rurale, concocté dans le passé avec des restes de bœuf (Douville 2011: 34). Cette ignorance de la culture québécoise engendre une grave erreur qui ne permet absolument pas au lecteur italien de découvrir ce mets québécois. La mauvaise qualité des équivalents traductionnels proposés surprend encore.

2.3. Un métissage unique

Toutes les cuisines ethniques ou nationales sont constituées, d'une part, d'aliments naturels autochtones, d'aliments importés et transplantés dans le pays à l'aide de techniques agricoles, puis d'une collection de recettes créées sur place ou apportées d'un peu partout dans le monde par des immigrants, des résidents voyageurs ou des chefs de communauté influents (cf. Lambert 2011: 24). Cette fusion des influences s'est opérée concrètement au Québec tout au long de son histoire caractérisée par différentes dominations (française, anglaise), par le voisinage géographique avec les États-Unis et par les vagues d'immigrants venus du monde entier.

Jusqu'ici, nous avons relevé en général une méconnaissance des traducteurs concernant la variation de la langue française sur le sol québécois, ainsi que de la culture et de la société québécoises. Ce constat négatif se confirme dès lors que nous poursuivons l'analyse

---

7 Si le nombre de « mauvaises » traductions est plus élevé pour les ouvrages traduits entre 1924 et 1990, c'est probablement parce que jusqu'à l'avènement d'Internet, les traducteurs italiens ne disposaient pas facilement d'outils lexicographiques décrivant les particularismes du français du Québec.

des extraits de notre corpus qui portent sur la cuisine québécoise concoctée avec des aliments importés ou originaires d'autres pays. Nous nous arrêterons sur des extraits mentionnant des mets traditionnels désormais ancrés dans l'identité culturelle québécoise mais qui sont, en fait, d'origine américaine, anglosaxonne et italienne.

2.3.1. L'influence américaine

Les *fèves au lard* sont un plat issu de la rencontre entre un produit de la terre, le haricot, le savoir-faire des colons français et l'influence de la culture américaine. Par *fèves au lard*, que l'on appelle aussi dans les contextes familiers "bines au lard" (de *beans* en anglais), on désigne aujourd'hui au Québec un mets traditionnel de la cuisine québécoise, composé de haricots blancs secs cuits au four à feu modéré avec de la mélasse, de la moutarde sèche et du lard salé (cf. Usito). La co-existence dans l'usage courant du signifiant "bines" permet d'entrevoir les racines états-uniennes de ce mets. Comme Poirier (1988: 96-97) l'explique, les *fèves au lard* sont d'origine bostonnaise. Cette réalité alimentaire des plus modestes était déjà répandue dans les chantiers au XIXe siècle sous le nom de 'beans' (Poirier 1988: 96), anglicisme dont, à l'époque, l'orthographe et la prononciation n'avaient pas encore été francisées. Ensuite, dès le XIXe siècle, "le mot est étayé dans l'usage par *beanery* (ou binerie)", désignant au départ un petit restaurant où l'on pouvait manger des 'beans', puis tout restaurant de second ordre (Poirier 1988: 97). Toutefois, sur les menus des restaurants qui ne sont pas des bineries, l'on trouve encore plutôt l'appellation *fèves au lard*, "perçue comme appartenant au niveau soigné par tous les Québécois" (Poirier 1988: 97).

Ces précisions linguistiques nous permettent d'entrevoir le succès et la grande diffusion de ce mets, au point que vers 1900, on désignait sous le nom de "débits de fèves au lard" de petits établissements de restauration dans les quartiers défavorisés de la ville de Québec" (cf. Lebel 1996: 21). Anne Hébert évoque ce plat dans un passage de *Les enfants du sabbat* (1975). La traductrice Nappi n'a cependant pas reconnu ce particularisme du français du Québec et, dans (16), a traduit *fèves au lard* par le **calque** "fave alla pancetta", à savoir par la traduction littérale du mot *fève*. Autrement dit, elle ne s'est nullement rendu compte que le mot *fève* est un québécisme sémantique (cf. Poirier 1995), c'est-à-dire un mot qui existe en français de référence mais avec une signification différente. Étant donné que dans la recette des *fèves au lard*, il n'y a pas de fèves ("fave"), mais plutôt des haricots ("fagioli"), l'erreur s'avère plutôt grossière.

(16) *Les jarres de **fèves au lard** cuisent sur la braise enfouie dans la terre.* (Hébert 1975: 44)
   Le giare piene di **fave al lardo** cuociono sulla brace sepolta nella terra. (Nappi 2008: 47)

Si, d'une part, le procédé du calque, qui consiste dans la traduction littérale d'un mot simple ou composé, peut parfois s'avérer approprié pour la traduction de lexies désignant des *realia*, car le résultat du calque est un néologisme dans la langue-cible qui pourrait contribuer à son enrichissement (Leppihalme 2011: 129), dans ce cas, le calque est la cause d'une traduction fautive qui gomme toute référence aux traditions culinaires québécoises. La traduction italienne est en ce sens franco-centrique parce que le lecteur ne décodera que le sens du français de France.

2.3.2 L'influence anglo-saxonne

La cuisine des ancêtres français est fondée sur les cuisines celtique, romaine et germanique. Dans les siècles suivants, elle s'est enrichie de nouveaux légumes, grâce à Catherine de Médicis, et de chocolat, avec Marie-Thérèse d'Autriche. Au XVIIIe siècle, les Britanniques ont apporté d'autres aspects des patrimoines celtique, romain et germanique, comme les pâtes cuites dans un liquide (les grands-pères ou le gruau d'avoine), tout en partageant leurs nouvelles découvertes asiatiques comme le thé, le curry et le ketchup (cf. Lambert 2011: 24). Nous donnerons deux exemples de mets d'origine anglo-saxonne qui peuvent engendrer des traductions simplistes, voire erronées : *chips* et *bacon*.

(17) *(je vois ces lueurs pourpres de coke dans leur main*
       *J'entends ces craquements de **chips** entre leurs dents [...]* (Miron
       1970: 148)
       (vedo quei bagliori purpurei di coke nella loro mano
       sento i crepitii di **patate fritte** tra i loro denti [...] (Zoppi
       1981: 207)

(18) *Samedi matin, j' ai voulu aider maman à préparer les plats de*
       ***chips**, les cerises au **bacon**, les mini-hot-dogs, les boissons gazeuses,*
       les jus et tout le reste, [...]. (Bismuth 1999:162)
       Il sabato mattina volevo aiutare la mamma a preparare i piatti di
       patatine, le ciliegie alla **pancetta**, i mini hot dog, le bibite gasate,
       i succhi di frutta e tutto il resto, [...]. (Felice 2003: 106)

Ces deux extraits montrent que l'emploi d'un anglicisme peut engendrer des ambiguïtés concernant le décodage d'un mot de la part d'un traducteur. Qu'est-ce qu'on désigne par *chips* au Québec ? Alors que le terme anglais britannique et australien *chips* désigne en fait les frites (en italien : "patate fritte"), en français ce mot indique des pommes de terre coupées en tranches minces et frites, vendues en sac, sachet ou en boîte (en italien : "patatine"). La différence entre français de référence et français du Québec porte sur le fait qu'au Québec, cette réalité est désignée aussi par le terme *croustille*, d'emploi plus fréquent. Dans la traduction du poème de Miron, le traducteur Zoppi a choisi de rendre en italien le signifié anglais, probablement en se trompant comme le suggère le contexte ("le craquement des chips entre leurs dents"), alors que Felice a sans aucun doute cerné l'équivalent traductionnel le plus approprié.

Le deuxième exemple suggère encore une fois que le même mot, dans ce cas *bacon*, peut renvoyer à deux systèmes d'organisation conceptuelle différents (anisomorphisme structurel et sémantique des langues). Ici, on a affaire à un terme qui renvoie, dans deux horizons linguistiques, à deux découpes de viandes distinctes. Autrement dit, le bacon "américain" (poitrine) et le bacon "canadien" (dos) ne correspondent pas exactement au même référent : le premier est une tranche de poitrine de porc, plus ou moins fumée, alors que le deuxième désigne une "longe de porc salée et fumée, débarrassée du gras de surface" (cf. Usito). Si, dans la traduction d'un texte littéraire, la différence n'est pas flagrante, dans un texte gastronomique par exemple, elle pourrait l'être. Ici, le choix de l'équivalent italien dépendra du type de traduction envisagée : sourcière dans (19) ou cibliste dans (20) et aussi dans (18), étant donné que les Italiens ont une autre réalité plus ou moins correspondant au *bacon*, la "pancetta", une poitrine roulée et mise en salaison, qui peut servir comme équivalent dans une traduction qui vise à la transposition culturelle.

(19) *J'avale un autre café fort et brûlant. Le **bacon** se tortille dans la poêle, les œufs cuisent, je les aime brillants, ni trop cuits, ni trop liquides, parfaits.* (Hébert 1982: 67)
Butto giù un altro caffè forte e bollente. Il **bacon** si arriccia nella padella, le uova cuociono, mi piacciono fatte a puntino, né troppo morbide, né troppo cotte, perfette. (Porro, 2002: 51)

(20) J'me lève, pis j' prépare le déjeuner! Des toasts, du café, du **bacon**, des oeufs. (Tremblay 1972: 23)
Io mi alzo, preparo la colazione! Toast, caffè, **pancetta**, uova. (Moccagatta 1994: 4)

2.3.3 L'influence italienne

Nous terminerons notre tour d'horizon sur un exemple, à notre avis, très réussi d'adaptation culturelle que l'on trouve dans la traduction de la pièce *Les belles sœurs* de Michel Tremblay, une œuvre dont l'action se situe dans le Québec urbain de la fin des années 1970 et dans laquelle l'auteur a récréé le joual caractéristique du parler mon-tréalais. Il s'agit de la traduction du mot *baloney*, dont il existe aussi la variante *béloné*, attestée dans cet extrait. Ce mot est le synonyme non standard, parfois critiqué au Québec, de *saucisson de Bologne* ou *bologne*, une préparation de charcuterie que les nouveaux arrivants italiens du XXe siècle ont importé au Québec, enrichissant ainsi la cuisine locale.

(21) *Midi arrive sans que je le voye venir pis les enfants sont en maudit parce que j' ai rien préparé pour le dîner. J'leu fais des sandwichs au béloné.* (Tremblay 1972: 24)

Arriva mezzogiorno, non me ne accorgo nemmeno, i ragazzi sono incazzati perché non ho fatto da mangiare. Gli faccio i panini con la **mortadella**. (Moccagatta 1994: 4)

Bien que la forme marquée (registre familier) dans le texte source devienne non marquée dans le texte cible, comme cela arrive très fréquemment dans les traductions, dans ce cas, le procédé de l'adaptation ne nous semble pas réducteur. Bien au contraire, en uti-lisant l'équivalent "mortadella", le traducteur a réussi à restituer non seulement la signification, mais aussi tout le réseau de connotations et de résonances que ce mot véhicule aussi dans la langue italienne (après la Seconde Guerre mondiale, c'était en effet l'emblème de l'alimentation pauvre en Italie). L'absence d'une variété comparable au joual en italien, tant au niveau linguistique qu'au niveau socio-logique, empêchait un travail plus approfondi sur la langue utilisée par les personnages. Il faut tenir compte aussi du fait que dans la traduction d'une pièce théâtrale, le travail des actrices au niveau prosodique et accentuel permet de récupérer, du moins en partie, ce qui est perdu sur le plan segmental (cf. Regattin 2019: 212). Ainsi, ce dernier exemple fournit un exemple très intéressant de la richesse de propositions que, malgré les erreurs relevées ailleurs, un corpus parallèle peut fournir à un nouveau traducteur qui se pencherait sur la traduction d'une œuvre littéraire ou de tout texte écrit en français québécois.

Conclusions : la représentation du Québec en Italie et les limites des corpus parallèles

L'analyse de notre corpus a montré dans quelle mesure la littérature du Québec reflète des traditions culinaires qui relèvent de différentes influences culturelles, réinventées et en continuelle évolution. Le premier enjeu de cette étude était de savoir comment ce patrimoine culinaire est transféré en Italie à travers l'activité de traduction. Nous nous sommes demandé si la traduction pouvait contribuer à la diversité culturelle dans le monde d'aujourd'hui, ainsi qu'à une meilleure compréhension de la perception du Québec à l'étranger. La réponse est dans l'ensemble négative. Lors du passage de la littérature québécoise à sa traduction italienne, les traditions culinaires québécoises en ressortent quelque peu gommées. Les plats de la cuisine québécoise, chargés d'éléments matériels de la culture de la langue de départ (espèces autochtones, produits de la terre, etc.) et d'éléments immatériels (mœurs, traditions, fêtes, etc.) sont mal transposés, principalement à cause de deux facteurs : la différence naturelle des *realia* socio-ethnologiques d'un pays à un autre, et la méconnaissance de l'espace ethnographique de la culture source de la part des traducteurs. La plupart des traducteurs des ouvrages dans notre corpus semblent en effet ne pas connaître profondément le Québec, ni la langue française que l'on y parle, ni son univers référentiel et extralinguistique. Les deux conditions qui devraient être remplies pour pouvoir bien traduire un texte—"connaître la langue étrangère ainsi que la civilisation étrangère" (Mounin 1963 : 236)—ne sont donc pas satisfaites. Les textes analysés sont de la sorte soumis, au cours de la transposition culturelle, à de nombreuses pertes signifiantes. Le recours à certaines stratégies récurrentes utilisées pour la traduction des *realia*—le calque ou traduction littérale, la traduction par hyperonyme, l'omission et l'adaptation—fait en sorte que les lecteurs de la langue et de la culture cibles ne découvrent pas le contexte socioculturel évoqué dans le texte source. Les traductions italiennes de la littérature québécoise pèchent ainsi souvent par excès d'ethnocentrisme, si l'on tient aussi compte du fait que la visée même de la traduction—ouvrir dans l'écrit un certain rapport à l'Autre, féconder le propre par la médiation de l'étranger (Berman 1984 :16)—heurte de front la structure réductrice de toute culture.

En même temps, nous nous sommes intéressés dans cette étude à la façon dont les corpus parallèles peuvent être exploités dans le cadre de travaux de recherche en traductologie, afin d'analyser l'activité traduisante par le biais de l'observation de textes déjà traduits. Bien que la recherche en linguistique de corpus repose sur le concept de représentativité d'une langue dans des corpus bien plus larges, les données que nous avons sélectionnées, qui ne sont pas exhaustives évidemment, constituent un petit échantillon qui se voulait représentatif de l'emploi du français du Québec dans des œuvres littéraires. Nous ne pouvons donc pas affirmer que des généralisations peuvent être obtenues sur la base des choix effectués par le petit nombre de traducteurs pris en considération. Cependant, nous considérons que l'échantillon examiné révèle des données significatives sur la présence importante de "mauvaises traductions" dans un corpus parallèle, concernant tout particulièrement la traduction des *realia* culinaires. L'observation de ce corpus nous a permis de relever certains inconvénients dus à l'approche segmentée typique des corpus parallèles, comme le risque que court l'analyste/traducteur de considérer comme justes des propositions de traduction isolées de leur contexte plus large, en faisant abstraction de la cohésion générale du texte traduit. Cette analyse engendre ainsi une réflexion sur l'utilité effective des corpus parallèles pour la traduction des lexies culturellement chargées. Si la plupart des études en linguistique contrastive sur les corpus parallèles trouvent leur application au niveau morphologique et syntaxique ainsi que lexical, nous avons l'impression que pour la traduction de ce type de lexique, fortement dépendant du facteur socioculturel, cette méthodologie de travail n'est pas encore suffisamment fiable. Comme l'a suggéré Jolicoeur (2011: 402), la solution aux difficultés rencontrées ne peut venir que "d'une meilleure connaissance de la réalité culturelle et linguistique québécoise, ainsi que d'une multiplication des outils lexicographiques en ligne". Les traducteurs trouvent aujourd'hui dans le bon "vieux" dictionnaire de langue de plus en plus de descriptions approfondies qui s'avèrent incontournables pour comprendre la spécificité d'une culture. L'exemple du dictionnaire Usito, "le premier dictionnaire électronique à décrire le français standard en usage au Québec, tout en faisant le pont avec le reste de la francophonie", dont nous nous sommes amplement servis dans cette étude, est emblématique à cet égard.

Works Cited

Acerenza, Gerardo. "Les canadianismes, ces inconnus : les traductions italiennes de *Maria Chapdelaine* de Louis Hémon", *Études de Linguistique Appliquée*, 4/164 (2011):405-420.

Aubert de Gaspé, Philippe (2007), *Les Anciens Canadiens,* édition critique par Aurelien Boivin, Montréal : Les Presses de l'Université de Montréal.

Auger, Pierre. "L'acériculture", dans le dictionnaire en ligne Usito. Consulté le 17 avril 2020 (version 1586364412). https://usito.usherbrooke.ca/articles/thématiques/auger_pelletier_1

Baker, Mona (1993), "Corpus linguistics and translation studies: Implications and applications", dans M. Baker, G. Francis and E. Tognini Bonelli (eds.), *Text and Technology: In Honour of John Sinclair*, 233-250. Amsterdam: John Benjamins.

Berman, Antoine (1984), *L'épreuve de l'étranger*, Paris: Gallimard.

Boivin, Aurélien. "L'édition critique des *Anciens Canadiens* : une histoire (re)corrigée". *Port Acadie*, 20-21. (2011):15-28. https://doi.org/10.7202/1010321ar

Bourdieu, Pierre (1998). *Les règles de l'art. Genèse et structure du champ littéraire*, Paris : Seuil.

Canac-Marquis, Steve, et Poirier, Claude (2005), "Origine commune des français d'Amérique du Nord : le témoignage du lexique", in

Valdman, A. et al. (eds.), *Le français en Amérique du Nord. État présent*, Sainte-Foy : Les Presses de l'Université Laval, 517-538.

Córdoba Serrano, María Sierra (2013), *Le Québec traduit en Espagne : Analyse sociologique de l'exportation d'une culture périphérique*, Ottawa : Les Presses de l'Université d'Ottawa.

De Vaucher, Anne et Minelle, Cristina, *Traduzioni italiane di opere canadesi francophone*, 2003-2016. [En ligne] : http:// www. lilec.it/cisq/wp/wp-content/uploads/2012/04/Traduzioni-italiane-opere-quebecchesi_Aggiornemanto-otto bre-2016:pdf . Consulté le 9 avril 2020

Douville, Judith. "La mémoire passe à table". *Continuité*, 130 (2011): 32-35.

Farina, Annick. "Les 'realia francophones' dans les dictionnaires : le modèle d'une traduction exotisante", *Études de linguistique appliquée*, 4/164 (2011):465-477.

Jolicoeur, Louis. "Traduction littéraire et diffusion culturelle : entre esthétique et politique", *Cahiers franco-canadiens de l'Ouest*, 22/2 (2010:177-196). http://id.erudit.org/iderudit/1009122ar

Jolicoeur, Louis. "Traduction littéraire et enjeux nationaux : le cas de la littérature québécoise en Italie et dans le monde hispanophone", *Études de linguistique appliquée*, 4/164 (2011):393-403.

Martin, Paul Louis, "Les baies et les autres petits fruits du Québec", dans le dictionnaire en ligne *Usito*. Consulté le 14 avril 2020. https://usito.usherbrooke.ca/articles/thématiques/martin_1

Lambert, Michel. "Retour aux sources". *Continuité*, 130 (2011):23-25.

Ladmiral, Jean-René (2014), *Sourcier ou cibliste*, Paris : Les Belles Lettres.

Lebel, Jean-Marie. "Tables d'hier et d'aujourd'hui : deux siècles de restauration à Québec". *Cap-aux-Diamants*, 44 (1996): 18-23.

Leppihalme, Ritva (2011). "Realia", in Gambier, Y. et van Doorslaer, L. (eds), *Handbook of Translation Studies*, Amsterdam: John Benjamins, 126-130.

Lévi-Strauss, Claude (1968), *Mythologiques III. L'origine des manières de table*, Paris: Pion.

Loock, Rudy (2016), *La traductologie de corpus*, Villeneuve d'Ascq: Presses de l'Université de Lille.

Poirier, Claude. "Préférez-vous les 'beans', les bines ou les fèves au lard ?", *Québec Français*, 72 (1988): 96-97.

Poirier, Claude (1995), "Les variantes topolectales du lexique français : proposition de classement à partir d'exemples québécois", in Francard, M. et Latin, D. (eds), *Le régionalisme lexical*, Louvain-la-Neuve: Duculot, 13-56.

Regattin, Fabio (2019), "Révisions, retraductions ? Les mauvaises traductions du théâtre québécois en Italie, en creux", in Acerenza, G. (ed), *Qu'est-ce qu'une mauvaise traduction littéraire ? Sur la trahison et la traîtrise en traduction littéraire*, Trento : Dipartimento di Lettere e Filosofia - Università di Trento, 207-231.

Thériault, Joseph-Yvon (1999), "La nation francophone d'Amérique : Canadiens, Canadiens français, Québécois", in Andrew, C. (ed), *Dislocation et permanence : L'invention du Canada au quotidien*, Ottawa: Presses de l'Université d'Ottawa, 111-138.

Wecksteen, Corinne (2007), "Le corpus en traductologie : un moyen d'observation pour une approche réaliste de la traduction : application à quelques phénomènes connotatifs", in Ballard, M. et Pineira-Tresmontant, C. (eds), *Les corpus en linguistique et en traductologie*, Arras : Artois Presses Université, 261-282.

Zotti, Valeria. "QU.IT une plateforme électronique d'aide au travail des traducteurs littéraires". *Publif@rum*, 25. (2016):1-16. http://publifarum.farum.it/ezine_pdf.php?id=337

Zotti, Valeria. "Ressources numériques pour la traduction des mots désignant des 'realia'". *Etudes de linguistique appliquée*, 194/ 2. (2019):227-246.

Dictionnaires

DFP = Shiaty, A. E. (ed.) et Poirier, C. (rédacteur principal) (1988), *Dictionnaire du français plus: à l'usage des francophones d'Amérique*, Montréal: Centre Éducatif et Culturel.

DUF = Guillou, M. et Moingeon, M. (1997), *Dictionnaire universel francophone*, Paris: Hachette/Edicef.

GDT = *Grand Dictionnaire Terminologique*, OQLF. http://www.
granddictionnaire.com

TLFi = *Trésor de la Langue Française informatisé*, ATILF CNRS &
Université de Lorraine. http://atilf.atilf.fr

Usito = Dictionnaire en ligne *Usito*, Université de Sherbrooke.
https://usito.usherbrooke.ca/

LICIA CANTON

A Taste of Home: Growing Up Italian in Montreal-North

I MOSTLY WRITE SHORT STORIES and essays in English, a language I learned after French but before Italian. My fiction often includes scenes and dialogues revolving around food. In the story "Easter Morning" (in *Almond Wine and Fertility*), two colleagues (a man and a woman) are about to have an affair or perhaps fall in love. He conquers her heart with his mother's recipe, gnocchi and *rapini*, which he brings to work to share with her as they finish a project late into the night. He also brings long-stemmed wine glasses and red wine (a Rosso Piceno) to go with the gnocchi and *rapini*.

In another story, "Refuge in the Vineyard" (in *The Pink House and Other Stories*), a man and a woman are overwhelmed at dinnertime with their four little kids. They are eating pasta without cheese, either because there isn't any Parmigiano or someone forgot to grate it. There's wine in this scene: red wine that the twins spill all over the white tablecloth. It is possible that the frustrated and exhausted parents in "Refuge in the Vineyard" are the same man and woman who fell in love or had an affair in "Easter Morning." It is very likely since the characters and scenes were inspired by real people in my life.

"Can you get the water please?"
"L'acqua, l'acqua, manca l'acqua."
"Did anyone grate the cheese? Where's the cheese?"

"Il formaggio. Dov'è il formaggio."
"We don't have any more Parmigiano cheese."
"What, no cheese? It isn't pasta without cheese."
"Mangia la pasta che è calda."
"I don't want to eat pasta without cheese!"
"Well, get some mozzarella and grate that over the pasta."
"Where's the wine? You forgot the wine. Who's going to get the wine?"

This is a fictional scene in a short story ("Refuge in the Vineyard"), but it could have happened in my parents' home on Bruxelles Street in the 1970s. In fact, my parents' kitchen is front and centre in my memoir, a work-in-progress, tentatively titled *Growing Up Italian in Montreal-North.* These are sketches about food and heritage, inspired by my youth, mostly. In fact, at the conference in Bari, keynote speaker Nathalie Cooke asked if I would call my work-in-progress a *foodoir.* I was not familiar with the term until she mentioned it, but I would say that *Growing Up Italian in Montreal-North* is indeed a foodoir. I am writing the book in English, and I am self-translating each chapter into French. In the fall of 2019, I worked on the French text with Laure Morali, a French-language writer-in-residence at the St. Leonard library in Montreal.

In *Growing Up Italian in Montreal-North,* I remember some of the meals and recipes that I learned from my parents. They were farmers in Italy and butchers in Canada, until they retired when they reached their eighties. In the early years, they had a tiny basement butcher shop within walking distance from our home. In the late 1970s, they owned a wholesale meat packing on Cantin Street in Montreal-North's industrial sector.

In *Growing Up Italian in Montreal-North,* I revisit some of the sad moments after we left Italy in 1967, and adjusting to new ways and languages in Canada. The book is about love of food but also about a labour of love, that is, the act of writing. And labour *as* love: the tireless labour of first-generation immigrants as an act of love towards their children and their descendants.

Polenta and Radicchio

Few people know that I am a writer with a backup plan. I put myself
through school (all the way up to and including university) working
in my parents' butcher shop. I can handle several types of butchers'
knives. I can debone a pig's head and make a variety of cuts out of
a pork shoulder or a side of beef. I've always found solace knowing
that, if times were to get really tough and I wouldn't be able to pay
the bills by working with words, I could always seek employment
in the meat department of a supermarket. Of course, being raised
by parents who had left behind their hometown and everyone they
loved, there were expectations which I did not meet. My parents,
like others of their generation, did not leave their country so that
their children would pursue a career in writing. No, we were to
pursue careers that make money so as to justify having left one's
country. I should mention that my husband is also a writer, my oldest child is a spoken-word artist and my youngest wants to become
a writer. That leaves the middle child. Maybe he will become a law-
yer and meet his grandparents' expectations. But I digress.

I grew up in a Venetian-Canadian family. My parents' butcher
shop was at the corner of Sabrevois and Rome streets in Montreal-
North. That's where my sister and I went every day after (elementary)
school and during the summer holidays. In fact, the butcher shop
was just one block south of St. Alice School, and my home was
just one block north of the school. My first job in the butcher shop
was dusting and sweeping. By the age of eleven, I graduated to
the cash register. I was actually quite impressed that I had moved
up so quickly. But I was an A-student, and I was really good with
numbers, not so much with people because I was so shy. When my
younger sister moved up to the cash register, I was (in my mind)
demoted to slicing cold cuts.

We ate a lot of meat, all kinds of meat. Whatever was not sold
ended up in our plates at dinnertime. Fillet mignon was a rare treat.
We mostly ate pork chops, lamb chops, T-bone steak, minced meat,
sausage, liver. One late afternoon, I was in the shop with my father
on Saturday, February 14. I reminded him that it was Valentine's

Day and that he should do something special for his wife. So he made sausage with heart instead of liver as he always did. I think that's about the most romantic he ever got.

I got to slice the salami, the ham, capicollo, prosciutella and mortadella for customers but rarely got to eat the cold cuts. And I really liked them. I especially liked mortadella and artichoke sandwiches. My parents also sold a few types of canned items such as *giardiniera*, and small jars of mushrooms and artichokes in oil. And to this day the artichoke is my favourite vegetable.

We ate a lot of polenta and radicchio, staples in my parents' hometown. It was my responsibility to prepare dinner after school and lunch every second Sunday. I made the meat sauce for the pasta, what we called *el sugo*. (Sautéd onion and celery, minced or cubed meat, diced fresh or canned tomatoes, salt and pepper and let it simmer.) The sugo was reddish-brown, much different than the very tomatoey meatless red sauce I now make for my family. That's my Calabrian-Canadian husband's influence.

I was taught by my parents that every recipe takes a long time to make. Polenta, for instance, needed to be stirred nonstop. Years later, I found out that there is a shortcut to making polenta. Simply add salt to boiling water, add the cornmeal, put the lid on the pot and let the polenta cook by itself. No need to stir for 30 to 45 minutes. I could have gone outside to play while the polenta cooked had I known that the end product was the same. I am convinced that my parents taught me the long version because they wanted me to stay *inside* the house. Some nights, instead of having pasta or soup as a first course, we had *polenta e latte*. Once the polenta was ready, we added spoonfuls to a bowl of cold milk. The polenta warmed up the milk. It was like drinkable cornmeal.

At the end of the workday, my parents called to tell me to throw in the pasta because it needed to be ready just in time for their arrival. Summer evenings, I set the table and sliced the bread and grated the Parmigiano ahead of time. I set the pot of water on the burner, added salt then went out to play with the neighbours until the time came to turn on the burner and bring the water to a boil. Then I threw in the pasta and cooked the spaghetti. My father had taught me to toss a strand of pasta against the wall to test if it was cooked. Well, since I was cooking the pasta and also playing with my friends at intervals, one evening I decided to test the pasta on the boys who lived right next to us. I ran out, spaghetti in hand, and tried to catch one of the boys to see if the pasta would stick.

In our vegetable garden, we mostly grew radicchio—our staple vegetable year round. We ate fresh red radicchio until the snow came. (Early in the season we ate the tender baby leaves, then the bigger bitter greens.) It was a big deal when my parents had to *trapiantare il radicchio.* When it got cold, in the fall, my father covered the red radicchio with discarded window panes, thus creating a sort of greenhouse. That allowed us to eat the fresh radicchio longer. I remember walking through the snow in the backyard and pushing aside the windows to get the last few leaves of radicchio. By the time the short winter days came, we had cooked and strained the radicchio, shaped it into balls and frozen them. On dark and cold winter nights, the dark green balls were taken out of the freezer, diced and sautéd in onion. It was rather bitter, but we ate it with meat, polenta, *pasta al ragu* and wine. I only remembered recently that, back then, we did not have a spinner to dry the radicchio leaves. So I used "the swinger" method to dry the leaves. I placed the wet leaves in the centre of a clean dishtowel, bringing all four corners together and twisting the towel with all the leaves inside. With the ends gathered in one hand, I swung the towel back and forth or around like a lasso several times. Of course, it was my job to do this, and I had to do it outside. Summer wasn't a problem but when it started to get cold, I didn't like to be the one to have to step outside to dry the leaves.

Fresh Eggs and Polenta Chips

I have always felt the need to go back "home"—to retrieve the tastes and smells I left behind in my hometown of Cavarzere, in the province of Venice. I was only four years old when my family moved to a basement apartment in Montreal-North. I missed the sunny, rural setting that we left behind. We arrived in June of 1967. Summer ended too soon. Grey days quickly turned to snowy white. I cried a lot that first year.

I cried on my fifth birthday in February of 1968. There's a silent film of me in front of a big cake, a Canadian cake, a store-bought cake. My father is encouraging me to blow out the five candles, but all I can do is cry. Maybe it was the room full of people from our hometown, none of whom was related to me. Maybe I cried because the cake did not look like the one I had had on my fourth birthday in my grandmother's kitchen. Maybe I was just unhappy after having been uprooted and replanted (much like the radicchio) in a foreign land at an early age.

They say I was a talkative and adventurous child in Italy. But in Canada I missed my grandparents, aunts, uncles and cousins. I missed a whole town full of people who knew who I was and who escorted me back home whenever I ventured to the piazza on my Graziella, the little white and blue bicycle I still have 53 years later. That bicycle was the symbol of my freedom. I could go anywhere, and I was safe. In Montreal I was cooped up in a cold, tiny apartment. My parents wouldn't let me go out to play. Big cars went by fast, even on des Récollets Street where we lived. I couldn't play in the backyard because it was reserved for the owner of the duplex who lived upstairs.

I especially missed the foods that I was used to in Italy, those my mother couldn't replicate because the ingredients in Montreal just weren't the same as those in Cavarzere. The bananas purchased at Steinberg's did not taste like the bananas in Italy. They were big and odourless. The oranges felt like plastic. They didn't taste right either. Cherries were hard to come by or too expensive. My mother purchased red and green candied cherries one time. I still recall my frustration at the sight. That's not what I wanted. I did not say so because I was sure my mother had spent a pretty penny for them. She ended up making a cake with them.

Mostly, I missed my daily breakfast routine on my grandparents' farm. I fed myself because my mother was busy with my baby sister, three years my junior. Every morning I went into the warm, smelly chicken coop. The rickety door alerted the chickens, and they all scattered about when I walked in. I looked into every nest before choosing my egg. It was always a little dirty but very warm in my hand. *Tap, tap.* I cracked it open and drank it on the spot. Yes, there were eggs at Steinberg's and at the *dépanneur* at the corner of des Récollets and Prieur streets, just a short walk from our basement home. But they were cold and spotless. Not what I was used to. My mother often appeased me by making *sbattutino*. *Sbattutino* or *uovo sbattuto* is supposed to cure all ailments.

Sbattutino Is Love

"What's the most important ingredient in this meal?" I grew up with that question.

I did a lot of the cooking after school. I was taught that every meal is made slowly and caringly. Love is the main ingredient to every meal.

Of all the foods I learned to prepare, from my mother and father, the *sbattutino* is the one that I equate with love. My mother's love. My mother is the only one who has ever made *sbattutino* for me. It's quite simple to make really: simply beat an egg yolk with two tablespoons of sugar until it becomes a creamy white mixture and the grains of sugar are no longer distinguishable. Getting it just right involves constant beating for about fifteen minutes.

The *sbattutino* is comfort food: it tastes good and it's uplifting. I yearn for my mother's *sbattutino* when I am really down. A few years ago, when I was bedridden after a car accident, my mother asked if there was anything she could do for me.

"Can you make me a *sbattutino*?" I asked. "That's all I want."

Very early the next morning, she came over and made my childhood treat for breakfast.

The other day I visited my mother, now 84, in her Montreal-North home. She wanted to feed me, of course. She had leftover polenta and guinea hen. She had homemade *biscotti*.

"How about a *sbattutino*?" I asked.

Without hesitating she went over to the kitchen, took out the eggs and the sugar bowl.

We had some on bread—spreadable *sbattutino*. We had some with espresso and milk. And we also had some with Marsala.

Even today, when I am sad or disappointed I crave my mother's *sbattutino*. Of course, it is not the same colour as the *sbattutino* she made for me with eggs from the chicken coop. Over the years I've made *sbattutino* for my children, but it just doesn't taste the same as my mother's.

Literally *sbattutino* means "little beaten one." The word has its root in the verb *sbattere*—to beat, as in "to beat an egg." *Sbattuto* means beaten. And the suffix "ino" is the diminutive. Isn't it interesting that this drinkable or spreadable, uplifting treat has a name that means the opposite?

Cod Liver Oil for Breakfast

By the age of six, I had been in Canada for two years. I was obliged to drink a little homemade wine at dinner because it was good for me. It would make me stronger, my parents said. The same with garlic. I didn't like garlic and I wasn't crazy about wine as a child, either. But I disliked cod liver oil the most.

Every morning my mother put a spoonful of the slimy liquid into my mouth, followed by a teaspoon of sugar. That horrible taste of fish lasted all morning. It didn't matter how much more sugar I sneaked before going up the hill on Bruxelles Street to St. Alice School, I was still burping fish at recess time.

I was a good, obedient daughter and therefore could not refuse the cod liver oil. My mother was the one who administered the medicinal fluid right after breakfast, and she was the gentlest person I had ever known. I was convinced that it wasn't her idea. My father was the one who went on and on about how good cod liver oil was for kids.

Did he take it every morning before going to work? I don't know. I never asked. He was already at work by the time we had breakfast.

He didn't go to church every Sunday morning either. But his kids wouldn't get any Sunday lunch if he came home from work (yes, he worked Sunday mornings, too) and we couldn't say "yes!" to his "Did you go to church?" The times he did come to church (Christmas, Easter or a communion) he stood at the back. He never sat with us. I asked once why he did not sit with us. It would have been good for the regular churchgoers to know that I had a father. Standing was his way of doing penance, he said, for all the masses he had missed.

Eventually, I stopped taking cod liver oil, just as I stopped wearing the *canottiera* (the sleeveless undershirt I was forced to wear even after I began wearing a bra). My sister and I had to wear the *canottiera* (supplies of which we bought in Italy in the summer) all year round, even on the hottest summer days, because it was good for us!

I'd totally forgotten about cod liver oil by the time I had ditched the undershirt, but it came up again decades later, after I became a mother.

"Are you giving the children cod liver oil?" My father had pointed out that my kids looked a little pale. "You should give it to them every morning before they go to school. That's what made you strong, remember?"

I didn't like the thought of that at all. I remembered the fish taste in my mouth.

I was in the pharmacy one winter and stumbled upon the shelf with cod liver oil capsules. Either out of curiosity or sheer desire to stop my father's "Are you giving them cod liver oil?" I bought the capsules and took them home. I had read that cod liver oil enhances immunity. It also contains high levels of Omega 3 fatty acids and is a good source of Vitamin A and D.

I gave the capsules to the kids on a Saturday morning, not a school morning. Of course not.

Surprise! They didn't like cod liver oil, either. I tasted a capsule to see if it was better than what I used to get … It wasn't. It was the same oil even in capsules.

The next time my father asked if I had given my children cod liver oil, I quickly said yes.

Conclusion

Looking back, there were good times and some not-so-good, but there was always food. Good food. Wholesome food.

I learned to cook from my mother and father, who also taught me how to grow vegetables and how to prepare different kinds of meat. There were certainly challenges but also many comforts in being raised by first-generation immigrants. They clung to their rural heritage while slowly (ever so slowly) letting go of their children so that they could benefit from the opportunities of modern Canadian society. From my parents, I learned to appreciate the preparation and sharing of food and the importance of working towards all that is good. I also learned the art of negotiation and translation which children of immigrants had to develop and refine in order to function in often conflicting and tumultuous worlds. I remember the early years in Montreal as being quite sad and lonely. I cannot complain about my parents' decision to emigrate. It was the right decision for them. I have gotten over my sadness. And I am grateful that my childhood memories are so full.

Works Cited

Canton, Licia (2008), "Easter Morning" in *Almond Wine and Fertility*, Montreal: Longbridge Books.

Canton, Licia (2018), "Refuge in the Vineyard" in *The Pink House and Other Stories*. Montreal: Longbridge Books.

Le radicchio

Dans notre potager, nous cultivions du radicchio. Nous mangions du radicchio rouge frais jusqu'à ce que la neige arrive. Au début de la saison, nous mangions les jeunes feuilles tendres, puis les grosses feuilles amères. C'était un évènement quand mes parents devaient *trapiantare* le radicchio. Lorsqu'il faisait froid, à l'automne, mon père couvrait le radicchio rouge avec de vieilles fenêtres, créant ainsi une sorte de serre. Cela nous permettait de manger du radicchio frais plus longtemps. Je me revois marcher dans la neige dans la cour arrière et déplacer les fenêtres pour chercher les dernières feuilles de radicchio. Quand les courtes journées d'hiver arrivaient, nous avions déjà cuit et congelé le radicchio en boules. Pendant les nuits d'hiver sombres et froides, les boules vert foncé sortaient du congélateur, coupées en dés et sautées dans l'oignon et l'huile d'olives. C'était amer, mais nous le mangions avec de la viande, de la polenta, des pâtes au ragoût et du vin.

J'ai toujours ressenti le besoin de retourner "chez moi."—pour retrouver les goûts et les odeurs que j'ai laissés dans ma ville natale de Cavarzere, dans la province de Venise. Je n'avais que quatre ans lorsque ma famille a déménagé dans un appartement au sous-sol à Montréal-Nord. La campagne ensoleillée que nous avions laissée me manquait. Nous sommes arrivés en juin 1967. L'été est passé trop vite. Les journées grises se sont rapidement transformées en blanc de neige. J'ai beaucoup pleuré la première année.

J'ai pleuré le jour de mon cinquième anniversaire en février 1968. Il y a un film muet de moi devant un gros gâteau, un gâteau canadien, un gâteau acheté dans un magasin. Mon père m'encourage à souffler les cinq bougies, mais je ne peux que pleurer. C'était peut-être la salle remplie de gens de notre ville natale, dont aucun n'était de la parenté. Peut-être que je pleure parce que le gâteau ne ressemble pas à celui de mon quatrième anniversaire dans la cuisine de ma grand-mère. Peut-être que je suis simplement malheureuse après avoir été déracinée et replantée (un peu comme le radicchio) dans un pays étranger à un jeune âge.

EVA GRUBER

Eating, Speaking, Belonging:
Food and/as Communication in Canadian
Immigrant Fiction

THE MOUTH AND TONGUE ARE the organs by which we both in-gest and taste food and produce language. Both language and food convey information about ourselves to the world around us and connect our inside with the outside, and the individual with the group. And while "[e]ating and talking are universal human traits," both activities are also culturally determined: "There is nothing natural or inevitable about food preferences or syntactic structures" (Gerhardt 2013: 3). As Terry Eagleton succinctly summarizes:

> Food is cusped between nature and culture, and so too is language, which humans have as a dimension of their nature, but which is also as culturally variable as cuisine. Nobody will perish without Mars bars, just as nobody ever died of not reading *Paradise Lost*, but food and language of some sort are essential to our survival (1998: 205).

Consequently, as Roland Barthes shows, food, like other forms of cultural expression, can be analyzed semiotically as a "system of communication" (Barthes 2008 [1961]: 29). What we eat, how we prepare it, when and how we eat, in which settings, circumstances and company are all factors that transmit information, that "signify" (ibid.) intentionally or unintentionally. In turn, they are informed or even conditioned by our respective social environment. In this respect, food, due to its affective component, may be instrumental in establishing boundaries and hierarchies and mark inclusion or exclusion from particular groups (see Kalcik 1984: 47). Language, of course, is the foremost human communication system, and it is the juxtaposition or entanglement of food and language which I will focus on in the following essay. If both food or eating practices and language are used in literary texts to convey meaning—both between characters through some version of "dialogue" in the widest sense, and discursively between narrator and reader—do both systems signify in a similar way? Do they convey the same "messages" or even amplify each other? Or do they complement each other in that one expresses what the other fails to do? May they even deliver contradictory ideas?

These questions attain further complexity when the texts under analysis come from immigrant writers whose narrators and/or characters have a repertoire of more than one language and more than one food culture at their disposal. Which language is used or neglected, which food consumed or rejected and in which context? And what is the role of each in negotiating transcultural identities and questions of belonging? In the following pages, I will argue that food in the texts discussed conveys meaning where verbal expression and communication have broken down; that, at its most extreme, it can overcome an immigration-induced aphasia. It is both expressive of and can alleviate feelings of cultural dislocation and nostalgia, confusion, internalized racism or even trauma, and it is instrumental in establishing a more balanced existence: a transcultural identity.

To illustrate my point, I will discuss texts by Chinese-Canadian writer Madeleine Thien, Caribbean-Canadian writer M. NourbeSe Philip and Japanese-Canadian writer Hiromi Goto. I will partly rely on Annie Hauck-Lawson's (2004) concept of the "food voice," i.e. the idea that "[f]ood choices expose a group or a person's beliefs, passions, background knowledge, assumptions and personalities. [... They] *tell stories* of families, migrations, assimilation, resistance, changes over times, and personal as well as group identity" (Almerico 2014: 3, my italics). Yet, as I will show, they are more than just markers that allow for fuller characterization; they are semiotic units which characters or narrators consciously or unconsciously deploy to communicate, to coerce or to claim. Whether characters or narrators reflect on their culinary practices or not, "through cooking and eating, [... they] perform rituals of cultural belonging" (Fellner 2013: 242), positioning themselves in a transcultural context.

Madeleine Thien's short story "Simple Recipes" (2002) centres on the fate of a Malaysian-Chinese family. The parents and a son have immigrated to Canada, while the youngest child—a daughter, the story's first-person narrator—was born there. The controversies on the issue of the preservation of Malaysian-Chinese traditions vs. acculturation to Canadian culture and society, as is so often the case in immigrant fiction, run along generational lines. They are expressed not least in the characters' linguistic and culinary choices: the father, while speaking English to his children, preserves traditional food practices when cooking for his family.[1] For him, "eating is a daily reaffirmation of cultural identity" (Kittler, Sucher and Nelms 2012: 4)—an identity which he perceives to be threatened by the impact of immigration and assimilation (see Garzone 2017: 217). While the daughter, having been born in Vancouver, admires her father's skillful cooking as a child and is forgiven for not being able to speak her parents' language, the older son rejects his father's traditional food, and the father holds it against his son that he lost his ability to speak his first language (presumably Cantonese) upon immigration.

---

1 This is a typical pattern among immigrants, where food practices may be retained much longer than other cultural markers such as language, mostly because they take place within the private sphere of the home (see e.g. Almerico 2014: 5; Kalcik 1984: 37, Kittler, Sucher and Nelms 2012: 6).

Attempting to fit into his Canadian surroundings, the son distances himself as much as possible from his family. He spends all
his afternoons away from the family apartment, in which "the air
was heavy with [cooking grease]" (Thien 2002: 7), to return just before dinner. Only reluctantly does he join the family meal—"Why
do we have to eat fish?" (Thien 2002: 10-11)—and tensions come
to a head when, having refused to at least try the fish the father
prepared, he chokes on a piece of cauliflower, spitting it back onto
the plate:

> My father slams his chopsticks down on the table. In
> a single movement, he reaches across, grabbing my
> brother by the shoulder. "I have tried," he is saying. "I
> don't know what kind of son you are. To be so ungrate-
> ful." His other hand sweeps by me and bruises into my
> brother's face.
>
> My mother flinches. My brother's face is red and
> his mouth is open. His eyes are wet.
>
> Still coughing, he grabs a fork,[2] tines aimed at my
> father, and then in an unthinking moment, he heaves
> it at him. It strikes my father in the chest and drops.
>
> "I hate you! You're just an asshole, you're just a fuc-
> king asshole chink!" My brother holds his plate in his
> hands. He smashes it down and his food scatters across
> the table. He is coughing and spitting. "I wish you wer-
> en't my father! I wish you were dead" (Thien 2002: 14).

The son takes out the racism he himself is likely experiencing
on his father, making food the arena in which to conduct this battle.
Eating the Asian meals his father prepares epitomizes "being an
asshole chink," an identification he desperately wants to shed in
order to be acknowledged as "Canadian" by his soccer buddies. "The

---

2 Tellingly, while the parents use chopsticks, the children eat with cutlery,
underlining Asian vs. Western modes of consumption (cf. Fellner 2013: 256).

way we speak and what we eat is not based on individual choice only, but also on the society we live in and the place in society we occupy or wish to occupy," writes Gerhardt (2013: 4). The son's rejection of the "non-Canadian" food (in choice of ingredients and in modes of preparation and consumption), in combination with the rejection of his first language, signals his wish to occupy a position other than the immigrant. "Other,"[3] a wish to belong to the society he lives in rather than adopting his father's Malaysian-Chinese identification. For this, he is punished: After the incident at the dinner table, the enraged father wordlessly proceeds to severely beat his son with a bamboo pole, leaving his son's back bleeding and his daughter, who witnesses the abuse, deeply traumatized.

Tellingly, when the problems arising from the question of acculturation are discussed at all among the family members, they are addressed in Chinese in conversations between the parents that the narrator cannot understand. The father finds no (English) words of explanation or apology to offer to his son, a lack that is passed on across generations as the relationship between the narrator and her brother is marked by the same silence, leaving much of their experience unexpressed—hovering "on the edge of semantic availability," as Lily Cho (2014: 125) puts it. Instead, after the incident, the narrator awakes the next morning to the smell of French toast, which the father is preparing for breakfast. "Food is just as much materialised emotion as a love lyric," writes Terry Eagleton (1998: 204), so that the French toast can be read as the father's signal that he will make an effort to understand his son's skewed attempts to establish belonging in a country he himself seems not to have fully reached (see Fiamengo 2014: 213). Rather than verbal expression, the father resorts to North American food as a signifier to acknowledge the complexities his son faces in coming to terms with his Asian-Canadian identity; indeed, as the French toast seems to show here, there are no "simple recipes" to negotiate belonging.

---

3 As sociologist, Claude Fischler states, "[t]he way that any group eats helps it to assert its oneness and the otherness of whoever eats differently" (1988: 275).

While the story thus offers ample material for looking at the interplay of language and food on the content level, its narrative mediation proves just as interesting. The story's nameless first person narrator is a grown Asian-Canadian woman. Yet for the most part, the focalizer is her much younger self—a girl with limited comprehension who does not understand her parents' language when they communicate about complex issues, and who therefore relegates herself to reading culinary signs instead. Her intuitive, food-based mode of comprehension and interpretation in turn informs the narration: instead of describing emotions or offering explanations on the traumatizing impact that immigration can exert on several generations, the text uses food imagery to convey these issues, both in the violent incident the narrator recollects from her childhood and in metaphorical and symbolic references to the art of cooking rice and to a dying fish which frame this embedded narrative (and which both comment on the father's sense of displacement and the violence ensuing from it, see Fiamengo 2014: 213–215). The story's tenses moreover switch between present and past in both the embedded and the framed narrative, indicating the narrator's inability to distance herself from past events which still reverberate in the present, thus emphasizing the transgenerational impact of immigration-induced loss and trauma. As a grown woman, the narrator keeps her rice-cooker at the back of her cupboard and opens all the windows when cooking in an attempt to avoid recreating the atmosphere of her childhood home; at the same time, she nostalgically longs for that very atmosphere (see Fiamengo 2014, 214), illustrating the conflicting tendencies of affiliation and acculturation to a North American immigrant context.

In M. NourbeSe Philip's short story "Burn Sugar" (1987), traumatic events are also not discussed verbally but negotiated through food. Here, the historic experience of slavery and the middle passage as well as the contemporary experience of emigration and exile are communicated through the ritualized baking of a bitter-sweet black cake made with burned sugar (see also Miller

1999: 236)—the very crop Caribbean slaves were forced to grow and harvest—which a mother sends from the Caribbean to her immigrant daughter in New York for Christmas every year. The description of the cake's blackness, its ingredients and violent manner of preparation, as well as its change in smell after having been shipped across the ocean, all powerfully resonate with the historical trauma of slavery—without it ever being spelled out. As the daughter admits, "she had never spoken to the Mother about it—about what, if anything, the cake and the burn sugar might mean …" (Philip 1992: 159), and this insecurity about its interpretation infects the story's discourse. The text offers alternative formulations as if testing/tasting various registers (standard and creole), various timeframes (past and present), various versions of history and global capitalism (hegemonic and subaltern). To give an example, after receiving the cake,

> [t]he weeks them use to, would pass, passed—she eating the cake, would eat it—sometimes alone by sheself; sometimes she sharing, does share a slice with a friend. And then again—sometimes when she alone, is alone, she would, does cry as she eating—each black mouthful bringing up all kind of memory—then she would, does choke—the lump of food and memory blocking up, stick up in she throat—big and hard like a rock stone (Philip 1992: 155).

For much of the story, the narrator's allusive language and the food itself thus complement each other in mediating the protagonist's disorientation and sense of exile to readers. Towards the end of the story, the cake's meaning is tentatively explored in words when the daughter tries to explain her conclusions about its historical dimensions to her mother. Yet she meets with resistance as the mother refuses to translate her culinary practices into historical commentary: "Cake is for eating not thinking about—eat it and enjoy it—stop looking for meaning in everything" (Philip 1992: 161). She chooses food over language in working through and communicating about issues of rupture and uprooting, otherwise too painful to confront.

The most complex and most rewarding example for the topic at hand is Hiromi Goto's postmodern novel *A Chorus of Mushrooms* (1992). Like Thien's "Simple Recipes," the characters in the novel also position themselves with regard to their ideas of belonging both through the languages they speak or refuse to speak and through the food they eat or refuse to eat. Initially, the distribution of these traits seems to go strictly along generational lines within the Tonkatsu family (see also Harris 2008: 24): Grandmother Naoe, although having lived in Canada for two decades, speaks only Japanese and feasts on care packages of Japanese delicacies sent to her from Japan by her brother; her "culinary citizenship," as Anita Mannur (2007: 13) succinctly terms it, remains Japanese. The parent generation, Keiko/Kay and Shinji/Sam, speak English only and dine on roast and potatoes, having intentionally left behind their Japanese language and food practices upon their arrival in Canada in order to catalyze their daughter's integration. Their child Muriel, or Murasaki, as her grandmother calls her, speaks English only and eats her mother's cooking, yet finds both the conversations with her parents and the food her mother cooks bland and lacking, neither of them "nourishing" or "sustaining" her adolescent Japanese-Canadian identity. As Muriel explains, "the things we talked about would never have the power to linger. 'How was school?' and, 'Pass the gravy boat' were sad substitutes for my malnourished culture. But how to ask the questions if you don't have the vocabulary to express them?" (Goto 1992: 99). She finds what she subconsciously craves in secret nightly Japanese feasts with her *Obachan* (her grandmother), sharing dried squid and listening to the never-ending stream of Japanese coming from Naoe's mouth. Muriel cannot understand Japanese, yet they conduct entire conversations through food:

Smack, smack! (Obachan)
Smack, smack! (Me)
Smack, smack! (Obachan)
Smack, smack! (Me) (Goto 1992: 17)

Muriel "swallow[s] sound" (Goto 1992: 29) in what is alternately referred to as Naoe's "bed of feasts" and "bed of tales" (Goto 1992: 18), emphasizing the way food and words complement each other in providing missing pieces in the puzzle of Muriel's cultural identity.[4]

Grandmother Naoe did not have a say in her daughter's extreme all-in assimilation decision and feels estranged from Keiko, whom she calls

> [...] a child from my heart, a child from my body, but not from my mouth. The language she forms on her tongue is there for the wrong reasons. You cannot move to a foreign land and call that place home because you parrot the words around you. Find your home inside yourself first, I say. Let your home words grow out from the inside, not the outside in. [...] Keiko. My daughter who has forsaken identity. Forsaken! So biblical, but it suits her, my little convert. Converted from rice and *daikon* to weiners and beans. Endless evenings of tedious roast chicken and honey-smoked ham and overdone rump roast. My daughter, you were raised on fishcakes and pickled plums. This Western food has changed you and you've grown more opaque even as your heart has brittled (Goto 48, 13).

---

4 This reading is supported by part three of the book, which consists of only one page. It begins with the heading "An Immigrant Story With a Happy Ending," yet goes on to detail "Part three. Everything that is missing or lost or caught between memory and make believe or forgotten or hidden or sliced from the body like an unwanted tumor. [...] Part three. The missing part" (Goto 1992: 159); see also Colavincenzo 2005: 225.

Naoe most clearly understands that Keiko's new "Canadian" identity is marked by absence and self-loathing, contingent on the assessment of her white neighbours. Her linguistic and culinary display of full assimilation leaves her psyche malnourished, and her thinly veiled internalized racism erupts in a tragicomic incident in which Muriel threatens to increase the family's visibility as the Asian "Other." For Christmas, Keiko buys what are popularly referred to as "Jap oranges," based on the rationale that "if the Church could buy Christmas oranges, then she might make this one allowance and [Muriel] wouldn't be contaminated" (Goto 1992: 91). Muriel, however, overindulges and eats the entire box, causing her skin to take on a yellow taint. While Muriel feels "replete" for once and happily laughs at her skin colour, Keiko panics and violently tries to scrub the colour off her daughter's skin: "'Ow!' I screamed. 'Don't Mom! It's only the oranges! It's only the oranges!' 'Yellow,' she was muttering, not even hearing me. 'Yellow, she's turningyellow she'sturningyellow she's—'" (Goto 1992: 92). Ingesting the "wrong" food emphasizes Muriel's—and by implication also Keiko's—precarious belonging in Canada by associating her with the proverbial "yellow peril": the idea that Asian immigrants constitute a threat to Canada from within (see Latimer 2006). It blatantly expresses the otherness Keiko so desperately struggles to suppress (see Slapkauskaite 2006: 118–119) and thus literalizes Lorna Piatti-Farnell's observation that

> [...] the act of eating [...] serves as an important means through which social and ethnic exclusion or inclusion is perpetrated. [...] Eating the same food becomes symbolically important for cultural identification; choosing to eat certain foods rather than others represents human beings' acknowledgement of their belonging—or wish to belong—to a particular cultural faction (2011: 12).

Keiko, overly aware of the dangers of exclusion, strategically uses food to position herself and her family in the Canadian mainstream, testifying to Molly Schuchat's observation that "food style [...] becomes a means of self-identity as well as a group-membership card. In other words, people tend to eat as they would like to be perceived, so that it is as much a matter of 'you eat what you wish to be' as of 'you are what you eat'" (quoted in Kalcik 1984: 54). In her eagerness to establish belonging in their adopted country though, Keiko neglects the detrimental consequences of her rigorous denial of her Japanese heritage on her mental health.[5] Her decision's traumatic and damaging consequences come to light only when Naoe disappears. Once any trace of Japanese culture—in the form of food and language—is gone from the house, Keiko suffers a breakdown and severe depression. It falls to Muriel to nurse her mother back to health and, acting upon advice she telepathically receives from the missing Naoe, she does so by preparing Japanese food (see Goto 1992: 131).

Eschewing ideas of purity, authenticity or simply nostalgia, the novel breaks the aforementioned assignment of characters to either one cultural identity or the other through their eating habits and language. Naoe, as readers come to find out, learned English early on in Canada: She repeatedly cites Shakespeare and—as the above quote shows—even contemplates the connotations of words such as "forsaken." When she leaves her daughter's house for good, the food she takes is Western, including several bottles of beer which she will consume with the cowboy/scholar who gives her a ride along the way. What is more, as Muriel finds out, her apparently well-adapted father always keeps a stash of Japanese

---

5 In this context, see Koc and Welsh's observation: "Especially in the case of new immigrants who deal with tensions of adaptation or resistance to changes in life style, consumption patterns and forms of cultural expression would have consequences on their physical and mental health, their perceptions of self and relations with the others, and their potential for successful settlement and integration" (2010: 9).

seaweed paste, and his aphasia—his inability to speak a word of Japanese ever since entering Canada, turning him into a "voiceless man" (Goto 1992: 59)—does not include his ability to read the language; in fact, he keeps an extensive library of Japanese books in his office. Finally, after her grandmother's disappearance, Muriel also learns to speak—and cook—Japanese—and significantly, the Japanese food which Muriel first prepares is "Tonkatsu": "a type of breaded deep-fried pork cutlet" (Goto 1992: 137), which itself is not "authentically Japanese," but a hybrid creation of Western and Japanese elements both in regard to ingredients and linguistic designation (see also Beauregard 1995: 59 and Pich Ponce 2012: 76). As Sam explains to Muriel, "*tonkatsu* isn't really a purely Japanese word. *Ton*, meaning pork, is Japanese, but *katsu* is adopted from 'cutlet'" (Goto 1992: 209). Tonkatsu, of course, is also the family's surname, assumed upon arrival because it was the only word Sam could remember in Japanese. It is therefore no coincidence that the ingestion of this hybrid food which bears their name alters the family's view on their own identity as immigrants. The text's use of both language and food thus suggests that a strict separation into pre- and post-immigration identities is impossible to uphold and psychologically devastating. Instead, it showcases the possibilities of a transcultural, hybrid existence (see Beauregard 1995: 59).

Time and again, the text emphasizes the close interconnection between eating and speaking (or rather, not speaking): "We don't talk about it. Some things you don't talk about" (Goto 1992: 207), Sam tells his daughter in reference to his traumatic loss of culture and language. In turn, Muriel presumes her mother's absent stories to be "ugly things filled with bitterness and pain. The pain of never having told" (Goto 1992: 32). Indeed, at the level of verbal communication, the narrative seems to literally mute any explorations of loss or nostalgia and thus to endorse or at least rationalize the family's decision for exclusive assimilation. A subtext comprised of food, however, signifies this decision's emotional cost—and at the same time endows the characters with the agency to overcome the trauma of cultural displacement. Whereas before, Muriel's experiences were determined by her mother's choices—"She chose the great Canadian melting pot and I had to live with what she ladled" (Goto 1992: 175)—by introducing Japanese food practices into the family, she sparks a renegotiation, a food-based conversation of identity.[6] As Muriel explains: "There wasn't a sudden wellspring of words, as if everything we never said burst forth and we forgave each other for all our shortcomings. We sat and ate. No one saying a word, just the smack of lips and tongues" (Goto 153; see also Goto 190); neither does Keiko simply give up her Canadian cooking. But she does ask Muriel to continue cooking Japanese meals for the family, burying her paranoid fears of racial exclusion on culinary grounds and opening herself up to a kind of integration into Canadian society that does not require a total rejection of her former self.

Again, as with the aforementioned short stories, the novel's metaphoric use of language and food on the story level, i.e. in the communication between the characters, is intricately intertwined with its discursive properties. The cultural hybridity introduced through the tonkatsu meal at the story level is mirrored at the discursive level in terms of narrative situation, character constellation, setting and language.[7] The narrative situation, for instance, undulates between first and third person with both Naoe and Muriel taking turns as first-person narrators at different temporal levels, being at time intradiegetic narrators, at times narratees, at times characters in a narrative told by a heterodiegetic third-person

---

6 Cf. also Terry Eagleton's comments on the analogies between language and food, which connect the idea of eating together with conversation and communication: "Fast food is like cliché or computerese, an emotionless exchange of purely instrumental form of discourse; genuine eating combines pleasure, utility and sociality, and so differs from a take-away in much the same way that Proust differs from a bus ticket. Snatching a meal alone bears the same relation to eating in company as talking to yourself does to conversation" (1998: 205).

7 As Beauregard (1995) and Colavincenzo (2005) point out, it also affects the myths Goto integrates in revised, hybridized form.

narrator, to the extent that at times it becomes impossible to determine who is actually telling the story and whom it is addressed to, problematizing any notions of "authentic origin." Moreover, just as food serves as a system of communication which translates the characters' issues and emotions whenever language fails them, the novel plays with the idea of translation also between languages and between characters, conceptualizing both linguistic representation and identities as multiple and contingent. As Tengu asks, the cowboy/Japan scholar who offers Naoe (who now calls herself Purple) a ride:

> "So, who is Murasaki and who is Purple?"
> "The words are different, but in translation, they come together."
> "So you're a translation of Murasaki and Murasaki is a translation of you?" (Goto 1992: 174).

His question addresses the most prominent of the doppelgangers, grandmother and granddaughter, who increasingly blur into one (see also Condé 2001: 140–141[8]). Yet the novel also blurs the line between Tengu and Murasaki's unnamed lover, and the setting of Naoe's bed of feasts/tales almost seamlessly translates into a giant purple futon in which Muriel, eating Japanese food or pizza or Chinese takeout, tells her Japanese lover stories *about* herself and her grandmother, and into a hotel bed in which Naoe exchanges stories with Tengu after an opulent feast of Asian food in Calgary's Chinatown. Finally, the text blurs the line between the languages any of these characters speak. While initially we can be confident

---

8 For instance, Keiko/Kay mistakes Muriel for Naoe in the dark and Muriel responds in Japanese (which is Naoe's language, not hers), an incident which Muriel later describes as "[not so much a] taking over—more of a coming together" (Goto 1992:162) between her and the absent Naoe. What is more, when Muriel gets stuck in her narrative, Naoe offers: "Why don't I talk sometimes and you just move your lips and it will look like you're the one who's talking?" (Goto 1992: 127).

that we're reading an English language text with Romanized words in Japanese, duly marked in italics, or even some Japanese characters when Naoe delves deep into her memories (for instance Goto 1992: 50–51), this certainty is increasingly undermined as the novel proceeds. Both Naoe and Muriel are at one point alerted to the fact that what they—and we as readers—have considered a narrative in English has actually been told in "Japanese all along" (Goto 1992: 187, 197). "The reader," as Pich Ponce points out, "cannot be sure of the language that is actually being spoken nor of the identity of the different characters" (2012: 82).

The highly postmodern narrative thus self-reflexively and metafictionally folds back upon itself in successive layers. It comments on its own processes of creation and reception, and repeatedly questions its own authenticity and truth value,[9] while at the same increasingly straining the limits of realistic representation far towards the fantastical. This fluidity of both language and identity is complemented, however, by a reassertion of the centrality of materiality and experience,[10] not least the experience of culture through food. Naoe reflects:

> There are people who say that eating is only a super-
> ficial means of understanding a different culture. That
> eating at exotic restaurants and oohing and aahing
> over the food is not even worth the bill paid. You ha-
> ven't learned anything at all. I say that's a lie. What
> can be more basic than food itself? Food to begin to

---

9 Whereas Muriel begins the narrative by assuring her lover that "Here's a true story," (Goto 1992: 2, repeated 87), she later admits "I'm making up the truth as I go along," (Goto 1992: 12) and concedes: "It's funny how you can sift your memories, braid them with other stories. Come up with a single strand and call it truth" (Goto 1992: 93).

10 For instance, Muriel's lover complains: "Everything you think of, you have to interpret as story. I'm not just a story. You're not just a story. We feel and think and age and learn. If you hit me, it will hurt. If you leave me, I will cry" (Goto 1992: 185).

grow. Without it, you'd starve to death, even academics (Goto 1992: 201).[11]

Food, that is, may be as "endlessly interpretable" as language, as Terry Eagleton claims, pointing to the cup of tea as "[t]he ultimate floating signifier for the English" (1998: 204). But whereas language is forcefully confronted with the crisis of representation in this complex postmodern text, with endless deferral of meaning in the free play of signifiers, through its visceral and affective qualities, food anchors identity in a way language cannot, while at the same time not foreclosing aspects of choice, hybridity and plurality. Naoe's jibe at postmodern theorizing playfully showcases the novel's awareness of the impossibility of authenticity or "truth," while introducing food as a concrete, material counterpoint. After having refused Western food and having mumbled in Japanese in the corner of a Canadian farmhouse for two decades, Naoe eventually takes to the road and explores all of Canada as well as herself—and she can freely do so because, as she says, "I carry my home [...] in the small hollows of my mouth" (Goto 1992: 203).

Food and words are, as Eagleton has pointed out, "media of exchange" (1998: 207) and thus means of communication. In immigrant literature, as I hope to have shown with these examples, food is put to work in negotiating questions of identity and belonging in ways that on the one hand complement and permeate, while on the other transcend the purely linguistic aspects of literary texts. It creates meaning in combination with language and constitutes a language of its own, enabling both communication between characters and communication between text and reader. Beyond mere

---

11 See also Koc and Welsh (2002: 9–10): "Some dismiss the new cosmopolitan cuisine that is emerging in the global cities such as Toronto as a form of rhetorical folkloric multiculturalism with no positive structural impacts to our everyday realities. While there is an element of truth in this dismissal, we believe that such an approach underestimates the significance of cosmopolitan diets in introducing a symbolic awareness of diversity, in challenging ethnocentrism, and for many in creating a feeling of home away from home."

symbolical and metaphorical usage, beyond being a mere tool for characterization, it informs the very organization and discourse of these texts and is thus inseparably intertwined with language in the discursive formation of identity and belonging.

Works Cited

Almerico, Gina M. "Food and Identity: Food Studies, Cultural, and Personal Identity," *Journal of International Business and Cultural Studies*, 8. (2014):1–7.

Barthes, Roland (2008 [1961]), "Toward a Psychosociology of Contemporary Food Consumption," in Counihan, Carole (ed.) *Food and Culture: A Reader*. New York: Routledge, 28–35.

Beauregard, Guy. "Hiromi Goto's Chorus of Mushrooms and the Politics of Writing the Diaspora," *West Coast Line*, 29, 3. (1995):47–62.

Cho, Lily (2011), "Affecting Citizenship: The Materiality of Melancholia," in Fleischmann, Aloys N. M., Nancy Van Stvyendale, and Cody McCarroll (eds.), *Narratives of Citizenship: Indigenous and Diasporic Peoples Unsettle the Nation-State*. Edmonton: University of Alberta Press, 107–127.

Colavincenzo, Marc, "'Fables of the Reconstruction of the Fables': Multiculturalism, Postmodernism, and the Possibilities of Myth in Hiromi Goto's *Chorus of Mushrooms*," *Cross Cultures*, 79. (2005):223–230.

Eagleton, Terry (1998), "Edible écriture," in Griffiths, Sian and Jennifer Wallace (eds.), *Consuming Passions: Food on the Age of Anxiety*. Manchester: Mandolin, 203–208.

Fellner, Astrid M. (2013), "The Flavors of Multi-Ethnic North-American Literatures: Language, Ethnicity, and Culinary Nostalgia," in Gerhardt, Cornelia, Maximiliane Frobenius and Susanne Ley (eds.), *Culinary Linguistics*. Amsterdam: John Benjamins, 241–260.

Fiamengo, Janice. "Understanding a Father's Pain in Madeleine Thien's 'Simple Recipes'," In Beran, Carol L. (ed.), *Critical Insights: Contemporary Canadian Fiction*. Amenia, NY: Salem, 2014: 207–219.

Fischler, Claude. "Food, self and identity," *Social Science Information*, 27. (1988): 275–292.

Garzone Giuliana. "Food, Culture, Language and Translation,"*Journal of Multicultural Discourses* 12.3 (2017): 214–221.

Gerhardt, Cornelia. "Food and Language—Language and Food." In Gerhardt, Cornelia, Maximiliane Frobenius and Susanne Ley (eds.) *Culinary Linguistics*. Amsterdam: John Benjamins, 2013: 3–49.

Hauck-Lawson, Annie. "Introduction." *Food, Culture & Society*, 7, 1. (2004):24–25.

Kalcik, Susan (1984), "Ethnic Foodways in America: Symbol and the Performance of Identity," in Brown, Linda Keller (ed.), *Ethnic and Regional Foodways in the United States*. Knoxville: University of Tennessee Press, 37–65.

Kittler, Pamela Goyen, Kathryn P. Sucher and Marcia Nahikian-Nelms (2012), *Food and Culture*, 6th ed., Belmont: Wadsworth.

Koc, Mustafa and Jennifer Welsh (2002). "Food, Foodways and Immigrant Experience," Multiculturalism Program, Department of Canadian Heritage.

Latimer, Heather. "Eating, Abjection, Transformation in the Work of Hiromi Goto," *Thirdspace: Journal for Feminist Theory and Culture*, 5, 2. (2006):1–12.

Mannur, Anita. "Culinary Nostalgia: Authenticity, Nationalism, and Diaspora," *MELUS*, 32, 4. (2007):11–31.

Miller, Cristanne (1999), "Mixing It Up in M. Nourbese Philip's Poetic Recipes," in Brogan, Jacqueline Vaught and Cordelia Candelaria (eds.), *Women Poets of the Americas: Towards a Pan-American Gathering*. Notre Dame: University of Notre Dame Press, 233-253.

Philip, M. NourbeSe (1992 [1987]). "Burn Sugar," in Penelope, Julia and Sarah Valentine (eds.), *International Feminist Fiction*. Freedom, CA, The Crossing Press, 155–161.

Piatti-Farnell, Lorna (2011), *Food and Culture in Contemporary American Fiction*, New York: Routledge.

Pich Ponce, Eva. "Memory and Language in Hiromi Goto's Chorus of Mushrooms." *Language Value*, 4, 2. (2012):70–88.

YLENIA DE LUCA

L'alimentation en situation de minorité. L'apport des immigrants à la diversification de l'espace social alimentaire de Montréal

> Rien de plus original, rien de plus soi que de se
> nourrir des autres. Mais il faut les digérer. Le lion
> est fait de mouton assimilé. (Valéry 1960: 478)

LA NOURRITURE, ON LE SAIT, est le lieu par excellence où convergent les influences et les suggestions de l'imaginaire culturel et où la contamination avec le Divers se fait de façon immédiate et spontanée. On parle désormais d'*altérité alimentaire*, c'est-à-dire du sentiment de la différence dans la pratique alimentaire qui peut être vécu d'une façon positive, ou au contraire constituer un des éléments de dévalorisation de l'identité en crise[1]. Il est fort intéressant d'observer le cours de l'histoire culturelle à travers le cheminement des habitudes culinaires et gastronomiques et d'analyser la place qu'a eue la nourriture dans les changements de la société québécoise.

On sait que la nourriture a toujours eu une fonction très importante dans le processus de migration : les migrants s'identifient avec leur culture d'origine en consommant leur nourriture traditionnelle

---

1 Au contraire, la *xénophobie alimentaire* contribue à construire l'étrangeté alimentaire souvent déguisée sous des désignations nationales ou raciales, des quolibets divers qui ont, de tout temps, accompagné toute ségrégation et toute xénophobie.

de même qu'ils s'identifient avec leur pays d'adoption en adoptant sa cuisine. Le lien très intime entre nourriture et culture est confirmé par le fait que les migrants ont tendance à conserver leurs habitudes alimentaires plus longtemps que leur langue maternelle.

Si on laisse de côté les préjugés, il sera effectivement facile de remarquer combien la réalité vue de la table, et de ses assiettes pleines de nourriture, acquiert mille facettes, mille nuances différentes, exactement comme à travers un prisme. C'est le domaine des propriétés révélatrices de la sphère alimentaire, propriétés capables de donner un aperçu fascinant et un visage nouveau à l'évolution sociale et culturelle d'un pays et de son peuple. Pourtant, pour avoir la possibilité de "voir" ces propriétés, il est nécessaire d'aller au-delà de l'essence matérielle de l'alimentation, il faut découvrir le lien presque magique entre imaginaire et physiologie, corps et esprit, homme biologique et social.

C'est Savarin qui a écrit la phrase très célèbre "dis-moi ce que tu manges et je te dirai ce que tu es" (Brillat-Savarin 1967:13). Ces mots condensent évidemment les convictions de leur auteur à propos des propriétés révélatrices de la nourriture, grâce auxquelles l'alimentation d'un individu permettrait l'accès à beaucoup d'informations sur son identité : l'appartenance ethnique, le statut social, les habitudes, le style de vie, etc.

L'alimentation est une quotidienneté des groupes fortement soumise au passé individuel et collectif et liée aux systèmes de production/consommation/communication dans lesquels elle s'inscrit. Cela signifie que la pratique alimentaire est tributaire de la manière de penser, de sentir et d'agir des groupes ethniques. Elle possède de plus la capacité de mettre en relation les autres ensembles intéressant le comportement économique, social, culturel, etc. L'observation de la pratique alimentaire est susceptible de révéler, au sein de la société globale, des situations originales provoquées par la mise en contact de réalités socio-culturelles éloignées. L'alimentation des groupes est partie intégrante du processus de maintien et d'affirmation de l'identité, dans la mesure où elle peut être fortement liée à l'identité ethnique.

S'il est vrai que l'enquête sur les habitudes alimentaires d'un individu est en mesure de révéler sa personnalité et sa pensée, de la même manière l'étude de la représentation de la nourriture dans la littérature d'un pays devrait permettre de découvrir les détails qui caractérisent sa société, sa culture et ses valeurs. En outre, si l'on donne à cette étude une valeur chronologique, on aura une sorte d'histoire sociale sous un angle gastronomique. Au Québec, l'analyse de la perspective gastronomique nous apparaît très intéressante, car le contexte culturel est hybride : mi-européen, mi-américain, enrichi par les cultures, de plus en plus manifestes, des immigrés du monde entier. La thématique de la nourriture constitue un véritable fil conducteur dans la construction identitaire du Canada francophone.

Depuis que le Québec est devenu un pays d'immigration, les rues et les habitudes alimentaires ont changé: on retrouve des restaurants ethniques dans de nombreuses villes, surtout à Montréal, et pour beaucoup de Québécois, consommer de la nourriture ethnique constitue la rencontre préliminaire avec "L'Autre". Pour l'immigré, la nourriture peut être un lien tangible avec la culture de son pays, distant dans l'espace et dans le temps. Les principaux traits culturels de l'alimentation des immigrés appartiennent toujours à la société de départ et ce *continuum alimentaire* exprime le maintien spatial et temporel d'un fait culturel, pour une durée variable et indéterminée, après que le groupe a quitté le milieu d'origine.

La présence des immigrants (c'est-à-dire des personnes qui ne sont pas nées au Canada) dans la société québécoise ne cesse d'augmenter, particulièrement depuis le milieu des années 1990, et contribue à la diversification de la population et donc de ses habitudes alimentaires.

Donc, depuis plus de deux cents ans, les immigrants (surtout européens jusque dans les années 1990) n'ont cessé de contribuer à la diversification de l'espace social alimentaire de Montréal. D'abord par leur présence même, ensuite par leurs épiceries, leurs restaurants, leurs cafés, voire leurs jardins, ils participent à le structurer comme un espace transculturel. Transculturel au sens où les aliments, les produits alimentaires, les recettes, les techniques, les discours et les imaginaires circulent dans l'espace social alimentaire et que celui-ci se caractérise aussi par des espaces d'échange, d'adoption et d'influences réciproques, par des logiques de différenciation, mais aussi d'intégration donnant lieu à des phénomènes de transculturalité. Par exemple, on constate au quotidien l'adoption de certains plats ou aliments de la culture culinaire perçue comme majoritaire comme le pâté chinois, les macaronis au fromage, les sandwichs, le pain, la plupart du temps adaptés selon la culture culinaire et les principes des saveurs de la cuisinière ou du cuisinier. On observe aussi les emprunts d'une culture "minoritaire" à l'autre, comme l'adoption de la cuisson sautée et de certains autres traits de la cuisine asiatique assez populaires dans les populations migrantes. Enfin, la culture culinaire perçue comme majoritaire a adopté maints plats, recettes, aliments, épices et types de cuisson; ainsi les plats de pâtes, les couscous, les tajines, les caris, le bok choy, la tortilla, le kimchi et la cuisson au wok font maintenant partie du répertoire culinaire de nombreuses familles québécoises francophones.[2]

Dans le but de retrouver des aliments et des sensations connues, les immigrants se sont donné des moyens de pouvoir pour se procurer ces aliments (marchés, boutiques) ou de les consommer en groupe (restaurants, cafés, lieux communautaires) dans l'espace social et urbain dans lequel ils s'installent. Toutefois, même si les pratiques alimentaires et culinaires se transforment après la migration dans un autre espace social alimentaire, permanence et rupture sont ici concomitantes : certains éléments de la culture culinaire pré-migratoire subsistent ou même se renforcent, alors que d'autres sont délaissés. Mais surtout, il y a de fait une complexification des cultures alimentaires, et ce, autant en ce qui concerne les usages de

---

2 Kyla Wazana Tompkins affirme que ce n'est pas tant le *ce que* nous mangeons qui est important que le *où* «of where we eat and where food comes from ; the « when » of historically specific economic conditions and political pressures; the «how» of how food is made ; and the «who» of who makes and who gets to eat. Finally, and most important, it is the many «whys» of eating, the differing imperatives of hunger necessity, pleasure, nostalgia and protest, that most determine its meaning» (in Shahani 2018: 23).

la communauté perçue comme majoritaire que du côté des communautés immigrantes en situation minoritaire.

Afin de se procurer les aliments dont ils ont besoin pour cuisiner dans leur style alimentaire pré-migratoire, les immigrants ne peuvent se contenter des grandes chaînes ; ils doivent compter sur des commerces spécialisés dans les produits issus de leurs cultures alimentaires. Aujourd'hui, on assiste à Montréal à une véritable explosion non seulement en matière de variété issue de toutes les cultures alimentaires et les régions géographiques, mais également du point de vue de la diffusion et de l'accessibilité, puisqu'on retrouve ces commerces dans tous les quartiers de Montréal. Par exemple, on peut non seulement acheter des produits en provenance de l'Afrique, mais aussi tout ce qu'il faut pour préparer des spécialités congolaises, et ce. dans le quartier Hochelaga Maisonneuve, traditionnellement francophone et ouvrier.

Ainsi, les immigrants, en offrant ces aliments dans leurs commerces (car ils sont tenus, la plupart du temps. par des personnes issues de l'immigration), offrent à manger une partie d'eux-mêmes non seulement à leurs "compatriotes", mais aux habitants du quartier ou à ceux qui y viennent en visite.

Dans son article "Pour une psycho-sociologie de l'alimentation contemporaine", Barthes affirme que la nourriture, comme la langue, dépasse l'individu et n'a de sens qu'à partir de "l'imagination collective" (Barthes 1961: 1107). Lorsqu'on sait à quel point de nombreuses personnes aujourd'hui s'identifient par, et s'identifient à la nourriture qu'elles consomment, on constate que les réflexions barthésiennes à propos de "la conscience alimentaire" sont très actuelles. L'expression récente *tribus alimentaires* (*food tribes*), qui désigne les végétaliens, les *locavores*, les *freegans*, les *zéro-déchets*, les *paléos*, et ainsi de suite, illustre bien le principe grégaire et moral qui dirige certaines personnes dans leur pratique d'un régime alimentaire particulier.

L'alimentation est une des multiples pratiques de la vie quotidienne de tout groupe social. Elle est en effet un lieu de rencontre et de synthèse du biologique, de l'économique, du social et du culturel

vécus par le groupe. Peu d'éléments échappent en réalité à une observation globale de l'alimentation : du sensoriel au sémiologique,
du religieux au biologique, de l'économique à l'imaginaire, presque
tout vaut d'être observé. C'est pourquoi l'alimentation est un des
systèmes révélateurs de la participation différentielle des groupes à
la société globale et des membres au groupe ; elle met en évidence la
place et le lieu que la société leur concède. Cela est justement ce qui
arrive à Montréal, où 74% des immigrants décident de s'installer.
Sur une population montréalaise d'environ 2 millions de personnes,
la proportion de personnes qui ne sont pas nées au Canada est
d'environ 44%. Le but de la présentation de ces chiffres n'est pas
de les discuter, mais de montrer l'importance des populations immigrantes parmi les populations montréalaises et la masse critique
qu'elles représentent maintenant.

Encore un exemple : dans le quartier du "Petit Maghreb" à
Montréal, habitent seulement 11% de tous les Montréalais issus des
pays de Maghreb. Ce quartier où la présence maghrébine reste toutefois très visible, est un lieu de rassemblement important pour la
communauté maghrébine montréalaise. Le fait qu'il y ait plusieurs
cafés témoigne d'un trait spécifique de la sociabilité communautaire, car comme plusieurs musulmans ne boivent pas d'alcool, ils se
rencontrent entre hommes surtout dans des cafés plutôt que dans
des bars. Les commerces mettent aussi en valeur des pratiques alimentaires chargées de tradition, de souvenir et d'évocation.

En outre, ce commerce est aussi un espace transculturel puisque
certains produits sont très connus, voire iconiques comme les bakla-
vas, et que la clientèle est de plus en plus diversifiée.

Il est évident alors que la masse critique que constituent aujourd'hui les immigrants dans la ville de Montréal constitue un
terreau particulièrement fertile pour le développement d'offres
alimentaires multiples. Les commerces dits "ethniques" ne sont
plus concentrés dans certains quartiers centraux comme ce fut
le cas durant une longue période de l'histoire de l'immigration à
Montréal. Ils se développent certes selon des logiques de concen-
tration de populations, mais aussi en synergie mutuelle grâce à la

vitalité de certains quartiers. Ce développement génère des possibilités d'échanges culturels, il ouvre la porte à un transculturalisme culinaire, comme nous l'avons déjà dit. Des emprunts surviennent désormais entre les communautés des Québécois d'origine (où se retrouvent francophones, anglophones, immigrants de deuxième génération) et des communautés récemment arrivées, ainsi qu'entre les communautés récemment arrivées elles-mêmes. De plus, le phénomène du transculturalisme culinaire se produit dans l'espace public des marchés, des cafés, des restaurants, bref dans des lieux de rencontre organisés autour des produits usuels ou iconiques et de sociabilités spécifiques. Globalement, les immigrants récents et ceux qui sont à Montréal depuis plus d'une génération (et qui, à notre sens, ne sont plus des immigrants) participent activement à la structuration de l'espace social alimentaire de Montréal, faisant de celui-ci un espace transculturel dont les traces sont partout visibles tangibles et sensibles.

Les cafés, par exemple, qui accueillent la plupart du temps des exilés sont un espace de retrouvailles, d'échange mais aussi de connaissance de la terre d'accueil qui s'étend bien au-delà des limites de ce lieu clos. Le café est, en effet, un espace à la fois conventionnel et rituel, espace où chacun a ses habitudes ; le café se configure comme un entre-deux, un lieu intermédiaire : "Certes, il constitue comme un prolongement de l'espace domestique dans l'espace public [...], et dans l'autre sens, une anticipation du retour chez moi [...]. Mais il est aussi un lieu en soi, avec son décor et ses acteurs, avec son histoire". (comme le dit Marc Augé dans son étude de 2015 : 62) En outre, on retrouve le café comme espace romanesque "au sens où il propose à l'imagination des fragments d'histoire en train de vivre [...]" (Augé 2015 : 85-86).

À ce propos, il vaut la peine de rappeler le dernier ouvrage de Sandra Gilbert, *The Culinary Imagination*, où elle nous offre un nouveau terme: «*eating words of novelists and memoirists, poets and polemicists*". *Eating words* est un terme qui apparaît dans toute une série d'essais sur la nourriture. Elle affirme que lorsqu'on pense à la nourriture, force est de constater que les *eating words* peuplent de nombreux ouvrages, surtout ceux qui ne sont pas spécifiquement liés à la nourriture. Les *eating words* nous donnent l'opportunité de comprendre comment les «ingrédients» se mêlent dans la création d'un texte littéraire. Sandra Gilbert insiste sur l'impératif: «Add food and stir», spécifiant que «we stir readers when we add food because we remind them their place at the complicated buffet of self, family, culture» (Gilbert 2014 : 8). À l'intérieur d'un texte, donc, les *eating words* nous invitent «to taste the words with our eyes» (in Daniel 2006 : 2), comme le soutient Lynne Vallone, qui dit : «Food descriptions in fiction, like menus in restaurants and television cookery programs, produce visceral pleasure, a pleasure which notably involves both intellect and material body working in synaesthetic communication» in Daniel 2006 : 2).

En fait, dès les années soixante, les romans québécois regorgent de nourriture et de restaurants étrangers, qui apportent une extraordinaire richesse au niveau culturel. C'est le reflet du phénomène de l'immigration. Les mentions sont innombrables : dans *Le matou,* on cite une délicieuse "pizza peperoni-olives-anchois" Beauchemin1981: 351); dans *Les grandes marées*, où un écrivain se retire sur une île déserte pour trouver son inspiration, on prépare un "savoureux spaghetti italien" (Poulin 1986: 79); dans *Salut Galarneau!,* histoire d'un homme malheureux qui trouve le bonheur dans son kiosque de frites et de saucisses, le protagoniste offre à la femme qu'il aime un dîner au restaurant chinois, avec des plats succulents "à la sauce soja" (Godbout 1982 : 53); dans *Volkswagen blues*, qui met en scène un long voyage à travers le Canada de deux inconnus à la recherche de leur passé, les personnages commandent avec plaisir "deux cappuccini" (Poulin 1984 : 286) ; dans *Lettres chinoises,* les protagonistes chinois pensent avec nostalgie à la "glace aux haricots rouges" (Chen 1998 : 94-95) de leur pays ; dans *La Brûlerie,* les personnages déjeunent dans un restaurant vietnamien qui sert "une soupe tonkinoise mémorable" (Ollivier 2004 : 23), etc. Les exemples montrent que le Québec est un pays complètement renouvelé, prêt à accueillir les traces de la diversité, et qui désormais ne fait plus peur, car la conscience identitaire a laissé de côté sa fragilité, et a manifesté avec force ses propres idées.

Et le phénomène du transculturalisme se déploie non seulement dans les espaces publics comme les cafés mais aussi dans l'espace domestique, privé, où celui ou celle qui cuisine crée ou recrée des plats en puisant à sa culture culinaire ainsi qu'en empruntant des éléments aux diverses cultures. S'il est clair que des rencontres inter ou transculturelles peuvent se produire dans l'espace public, l'espace privé est donc aussi un lieu de croisements et d'enrichissements des répertoires, et l'existence d'établissements soutient ce métissage et ces nouveaux emprunts culturels et culinaires.

Comme le montre Ghassan Hange, il s'agit pour les immigrants de s'entourer et de trouver des objets, des odeurs, des sensations socialement et culturellement reconnaissables afin de développer un sentiment de familiarité, de sécurité, un abri pour soigner les crises, mais également une base pour se projeter dans la société et y envisager un avenir, une vie bonne.

On connaît bien maintenant les liens puissants que les populations immigrantes de première génération entretiennent avec leurs modèles alimentaires pré-migratoires et la persistance dans le temps de la socialisation alimentaire.

Dans une recherche menée de 2008 à 2013, portant sur divers groupes d'immigrants qui provenaient d'horizons socioculturels et géographiques très variés, il est apparu que les nourritures participent plutôt d'une sensorialité ou plus précisément d'un rapport au monde qui passe par une dimension sensorielle et sensuelle (dont celle du plaisir) médiatisée par les saveurs, les odeurs ainsi que les émotions, la mémoire et l'intimité, autant de variables qui sont structurantes dans la construction d'un *chez soi*, c'est-à-dire dans l'appropriation subjective de l'espace, d'une famille, du genre, des identités individuelles et collectives. C'est pourquoi l'attachement à la nourriture et aux pratiques culinaires est très fort, particulièrement dans un contexte de migration où les repères et la sociabilité sont à reconstruire.

Elspeth Probyn soutient que la nourriture est «the last bastion of authenticity in our lives» (Probyn 2000 : 12): dans l'ère post-moderne où les identités sont fragmentées et faibles, la nourriture devient l'unique signe d'individualité. Et on écrit sur la nourriture pour appréhender ces identités changeantes et pour retrouver nostalgiquement une trace de ce que nous avons perdu. Essentiellement, comme le souligne Sandra Gilbert, «we have food on the mind, everywhere» (Gilbert 2014 : 4) .

La nourriture participe donc d'expériences sensorielles, émotionnelles, symboliques, mémorielles, ludiques, rassasiantes, festives. Les modèles alimentaires qui leur donnent des formes concrètes et imaginaires laissent des traces profondes dans la socialisation des individus, entre autres parce que ces nourritures sont liées aux identités intimes et communautaires, qu'elles participent d'expériences sensorielles souvent agréables et rassurantes et qu'elles organisent le monde comme lieu habitable.

Réunies à Montréal, les diverses communautés d'immigrants participent à la mise en place d'un modèle alimentaire métissé où coexistent des emprunts à des cultures alimentaires plus massivement répandues (celles des groupes perçus comme majoritaires) ainsi qu'aux autres cultures minoritaires. Cependant, il faut insister sur le fait que les groupes perçus comme majoritaires sont, sur le plan alimentaire, de plus en plus diversifiés. De ce fait, on peut avancer l'hypothèse que la "majorité" se dissout assez rapidement dans un cosmopolitisme culinaire (qu'on peut critiquer de nombreuses manières, bien entendu) ou en tout cas, qu'elle consent de plus en plus largement à des expériences gustatives et culturelles qu'elle fait siennes.

On peut affirmer que Montréal change de visage et de goût, si tant est qu'une ville puisse avoir un goût, à tel point qu'il sera bientôt difficile de conserver la dichotomie ou le paradigme majorité-minorité pour ce qui est de la nourriture.

Donna Haraway affirme que "aucune communauté ne fonctionne sans nourriture, sans manger *ensemble*. Il ne s'agit pas d'un point moral, mais d'un point factuel, sémiotique, et matériel qui a des conséquences (2008 : 294-295). Comme le dit Derrida : "On ne mange jamais seul" [...] Peut-être que Dieu peut avoir un repas solitaire, mais pas les bestioles terrestres" (1992 : 297). Nous ne mangeons jamais seuls, donc. Nous partageons notre table avec nos proches, et souvent avec des personnes étrangères. Les autres nous contaminent avec leurs habitudes et leurs pratiques et cet apprentissage alimentaire informe notre devenir. Tout s'invite à table, des deux côtés de l'assiette, de la bouche, dans un grand jeu de commensalité. Engagé dans et avec la nourriture, plurielle et vivante, l'humain n'a pas à se sentir seul ou minoritaire.

Du reste, c'est Bakhtin qui affirme que la rencontre de l'homme avec le monde: "is one of the most ancient, and most important objects of human thought and imagery" (Bakhtin 1968 : 280).

Cela est évident à Montréal, où les emprunts culinaires réciproques suivent des trajectoires nouvelles qui invalident l'ancien paradigme où le seul parcours envisagé pour les minorités était de s'intégrer (ou pas) à la culture de la majorité.

Works Cited

Augé, Marc, Éloge du bistrot parisien, Paris, Payot & Rivages, 2015.

Bakhtin, Mikhail, Rabelais and His World, traduit par Helene Iswolsky, Cambridge, MA: MIT Press, 1968.

Barthes, Roland, «Pour une psycho-sociologie de l'alimentation contemporaine», dans Œuvres complètes I, Paris, Seuil, 1961.

Beauchemin, Yves, Le matou, Québec, Québec-Amérique, 1981.

Brillat-Savarin, Anthèlme, Physiologie du goût, Paris, Pierre Waleffe, 1967.

Chen, Ying, Lettres chinoises, Arles, Actes Sud, 1998.

Derrida, Jacques, "Il faut bien manger, ou le calcul du sujet" dans Points de suspension. Paris, Éd. Galilée, 1992, p. 297.

Daniel, Carolyn, Voracious Children: Who Eats Whom in Children's Literature, New York, Routledge, 2006.

Gilbert, Sandra, The Culinary Imagination: From Myth to Modernity, New York, Norton, 2014.

Godbout, Jacques, Galarneau!, Paris, Seuil, 1982.

Haraway, Donna, *When Species Meet*, Minneapolis, University of Minnesota Press, 2008.

Ollivier, Émile, *La Brûlerie*, Montréal, Boréal, 2004.

Poulin, Jacques, *Volkswagen blues*, Montréal, Québec-Amérique, 1984.

Poulin, Jacques, *Les grandes marées*, Montréal, Leméac, 1986.

Probyn, Elisabeth, *Carnal Appetites: FoodSexIdentities*, New York, Routledge, 2000.

Shahani, Gitanjali G. (ed.), "Introduction: Writing on Food and Literature". In *Food and Literature*, Cambridge: Cambridge University Press, 2018, 1-36.

Valéry, Paul, *Oeuvres, tome II*, Paris, Gallimard, La Pléiade, 1960.

SILVIA DOMENICA ZOLLO

Représentations métalinguistiques profanes autour du lexique culinaire québécois

1. Introduction

PARMI LES NOMBREUX SITES D'INFORMATION où se déroulent des discussions profanes sur la langue et la culture québécoises, il convient de noter l'augmentation depuis quelques années des forums en ligne. Consacrés à des réflexions métalinguistiques, ces dispositifs permettent à tous les participants de s'exprimer sur les particularités propres à cette variété géolinguistique, celle-ci étant envisagée à partir de plusieurs points de vue (phonétique, syntaxique, morphologique, lexical, etc.), en favorisant de manière évidente la valorisation de la prise de parole des intervenants qui, dans la plupart des cas, sont des non-linguistes.

Dans le champ de la linguistique populaire (Niedzielski & Preston 2000 ; Achard-Bayle & Paveau 2008) et plus récemment de la lexicographie profane (Murano 2014 ; Celotti 2016 ; Molinari 2017 ; Vincent 2017 ; Steffens 2017), plusieurs études se sont focalisées sur le rôle que peuvent jouer les espaces discursifs numériques et leurs usagers dans la construction des connaissances linguistiques. Bien que n'étant pas scientifiques, les savoirs ordinaires et spontanés produits par des non-linguistes peuvent résulter, dans certains cas, pertinents et efficaces, car issus de leur vécu personnel et, par conséquent, contribuer à la légitimation d'une variété linguistique. Dans la première partie de cette contribution, nous ferons un tour d'horizon de ces études, en présentant les problématiques principales : on notera que les travaux les plus récents sont prospectifs (l'Internet est-il en train de révolutionner la représentation des connaissances linguistiques dans le monde francophone ?) et que les recherches lexicales descriptives d'inspiration sociolinguistique sont de plus en plus nombreuses. Dans la deuxième partie, nous explorerons les caractéristiques du forum *Les Foodies, Kessé ça ? Mangez&Parlez au Québec* où les participants s'interrogent sur le lexique culinaire québécois, en faisant appel aussi bien aux dictionnaires traditionnels qu'à leurs connaissances individuelles. Après avoir présenté notre corpus, nous verrons comment se construit collectivement une discussion linguistique profane en ligne autour du lexique culinaire québécois, en nous attachant particulièrement à l'analyse des emprunts à l'anglais, à leurs équivalents autochtones ainsi qu'à leurs déformations phono-morphologiques en français québécois. Au-delà de cet objectif, il s'agira pour nous d'explorer l'hypothèse selon laquelle les forums de discussion, en tant que dispositifs communicationnels gérés par des non-linguistes, favoriseraient l'émergence de nouvelles représentations du lexique culinaire québécois, mais aussi de nouvelles modalités pour leur traitement lexicographique.

2. Cadre théorico-méthodologique et présentation du corpus

L'intérêt pour la linguistique dite "populaire" n'est pas récent. Ce domaine d'étude a été explicitement ouvert dans les années 1960 par Hœnigswald et Labov qui revendiquaient la prise en compte des savoirs spontanés dans la constitution de toute science. Toutefois, il faudra attendre les études de Niedzielski et Preston (2000) pour que la réflexion soit portée plus spécifiquement sur les *speech communities* et sur la façon dont les croyances construites par la société informent la perception qu'ont les locuteurs des usages langagiers. Que ce soit dans une perspective purement linguistique ou plus largement sociale, ces recherches ont apporté des éléments d'analyse à plusieurs domaines des sciences du langage : ethnolinguistique, psycholinguistique, sociolinguistique, linguistique générale, linguistique descriptive, linguistique variationniste et linguistique appliquée.

Dans le contexte français, les études relevant de la linguistique populaire sont connues sous l'étiquette "représentations métalinguistiques ordinaires" (Beacco 2004), qui déplace légèrement l'approche perceptive américaine. Cela ne signifie pas que la question des savoirs linguistiques spontanés est méconnue en France, mais elle est abordée selon d'autres orientations. Plus particulièrement, il existe trois perspectives qui prennent en considération les questions relevant de la linguistique populaire et que l'on peut ainsi diviser : a) la perspective sociolinguistique s'occupant des normes et des représentations linguistiques populaires (Beacco 2004 ; Gadet 1997) ; b) la perspective métalinguistique qu'il soit question de la linguistique systématique (Rey-Debove 1997), des théories énonciatives (Authier-Revuz 2012) et de la didactique de la langue (Beacco 2001) ; c) et, plus récemment, la perspective de la lexicographie profane qui se "situe entre la lexicographie science savante et les productions de la linguistique populaire, zone pour laquelle nous venons d'avancer l'appellation de para-lexicographie" (Margarito 2007 : 172). En particulier, le progrès technologique, la création de dictionnaires et d'espaces numériques dédiés à la réflexion métalinguistique, d'ailleurs disponibles gratuitement, ont contribué à l'augmentation des savoirs et à l'effacement des différences entre savoirs professionnels et savoirs profanes. Et les forums de discussion sont, nous semble-t-il, un des résultats de ce processus : grâce aux nouvelles technologies, ils sont en croissance constante sur Internet, tant au niveau du nombre que de leur développement interne, ce dernier basé essentiellement sur des interventions spontanées sur la langue. C'est précisément dans ce cadre théorique et méthodologique d'unification des pratiques linguistiques profanes, que nous voudrions nous situer avec cette étude.

Avant de nous focaliser sur les pratiques métalinguistiques profanes rencontrées dans le forum *Les Foodies, Kessé ça ?*

Mangez&Parlez au Québec (dorénavant *Les Foodies, Kessé ça ?*),
commençons par présenter ses caractéristiques et le profil de ses
intervenants. *Les Foodies, Kessé ça ?* est un forum de discussion non
modéré accessible en ligne qui a été ouvert le 21 mars 2014. Son nom
porte en lui-même un cadrage thématique et définit la pertinence
des discussions qui se concentrent essentiellement sur le lexique
culinaire québécois. Comme tout forum, il contient implicitement
un contrat communicationnel (Charaudeau 1991) portant à la fois
sur le programme thématique, le type d'échange, le type de discours
et le cadre participatif des discussions. Lorsqu'on se connecte au
site Web du forum, on arrive sur une page d'accueil qui propose
des liens hypertextuels avec des articles et des textes complémen-
taires organisés en dossiers. Dans la page consacrée aux dossiers, on
trouve les *threads* (Kerbrat-Orecchioni 1990 : 218) suivants : "les
repas", "les termes dans les magasins", "les noms de produits pour
les bouches sucrées", "les noms de produits pour les bouches salées",
"les cookines", etc., constitués d'un message principal et des réac-
tions, elles-mêmes organisées selon une hiérarchisation permettant
la visualisation des échanges.

Fréquenté par un large public de passionnés de cuisine québécoise, ce forum se distingue pour une certaine réticence aussi bien
sur le plan de l'expertise de ses auteurs que des sources mentionnées.
Pourtant, en raison de son style captivant et de son intelligibilité, il
représente un bon point de repère pour les internautes désireux d'ap-
profondir un aspect linguistique sur le lexique culinaire québécois.
Les informations sur les intervenants du forum sont très restreintes,
voire indisponibles à cause de l'anonymat. Il est donc difficile de savoir qui contribue aux discussions, mais on peut néanmoins supposer
que la majorité des intervenants est constituée de non-linguistes,
c'est-à-dire de locuteurs ordinaires "dont la culture et les pratiques
sociales ne comportent pas de savoirs particuliers sur la langue"
(Paveau 2008 : 148). Si certains d'entre eux ont une formation dans
le domaine de la gastronomie québécoise, aucun n'a de formation
en lexicographie et aucun n'est spécialiste du français québécois. Ce
qui est plutôt mis de l'avant par les interventions faites, c'est le fait

que certains participants sont québécois ou vivent au Québec et ont une passion pour la langue, ce qui semble être un élément clé de leur crédibilité pour décrire les termes en usage. On peut émettre l'hypothèse que les intervenants de ce forum, sont des "linguistes amateurs" (Paveau 2008), des "ludo-linguistes" (Meyer et Gurevych 2012), voire des "lexicographes non professionnels" (Murano 2014) ou des "usagers profanes" (Molinari 2017) qui élaborent des représentations ordinaires et profanes au sujet du lexique culinaire québécois, en se basant sur leurs connaissances personnelles.

3. Analyse du corpus : entre créativité lexicale et discours spontanés

Notre corpus se compose de dix discussions enregistrées entre mars 2018 et septembre 2019 portant sur les déformations phono-morphologiques des emprunts à l'anglais et leurs équivalents dans le lexique culinaire québécois. Les participants recourent au forum pour interroger le sens et l'origine des mots et pour poser des questions d'ordre sociolinguistique, en suggérant eux-mêmes des solutions. Commençons par quelques exemples relevant de la déformation phono-morphologique de lexèmes d'origine anglaise. La première discussion concerne l'usage du lexème *grill tchîze* :

> 20.03.2018
> Thème : *grill tchîze*
> P1 : Bonjour à toutes et à tous, hier j'ai trouvé le mot *grill tchîze* dans un blog de cuisine québécoise. C'est quoi ce mot ? Existe-il ?
> P2 : Tu connais pas le *grill tchîze* ?? C'est un plat parfaitement maîtrisé par les Américains (ben ouais, notre chat serait capable d'en faire…). Une tuerie fondante.
> P3 : Le *grill tchîze*, comme on dit au Québec, c'est un *sandwich au fromage fondu*. C'est le *croque-monsieur du pays de l'Oncle Sam* !

P4 : La graphie *grill tchîze* n'est pas correcte ! Allez voir dans la BDLP Québec, il y a *grilled-cheese* … !

Plusieurs solutions sont ici proposées : P2 décrit le *grill tchîze* comme un plat parfaitement maîtrisé par les Américains alors que P3 décrit ce lexème par l'équivalent français *sandwich au fromage fondu*, et par la paraphrase à caractère analogique *le croque-monsieur du pays de l'Oncle Sam* qui renvoie au croque-monsieur typiquement français et à l'Oncle Sam, un personnage emblématique des États-Unis. P4 fait remarquer que l'orthographe n'est pas correcte et exhorte les participants à consulter la section "Québec" de la BDLP. *Grill tchîze* est, en effet, une déformation phono-morphologique de l'emprunt intégral à l'anglais *grilled-cheese* ou *grilled cheese*, en usage au Québec depuis le milieu du XXe siècle et parfois critiqué comme synonyme non standard de *sandwich au fromage fondant, sandwich au fromage fondu* et *sandwich grillé au fromage*, trois variantes lexicales qui s'inscrivent dans la norme sociolinguistique du français au Québec. Une discussion similaire a lieu dans le forum, à propos du lexème *poudzigne* :

24.07.2018
Thème : *poudzigne*
P1 : Il faisait super froid à Montréal la semaine dernière. Moins 29°C ressenti le dernier jour. Ça piquait ! Mais c'était superbe de contempler toute cette neige. Je crois que je n'en avais jamais vu autant. Et je comprends en voyant le froid polaire pourquoi il est important de manger sucré. J'ai donc préparé un *poudzigne*, parce que du sucre, dans le *poudzigne*, il y en a ! Rien que de lire la recette, tu sens le diabète arriver.
P2 : Un *poudzigne* ? Mais qu'est-ce que c'est ? Cela ne vend pas franchement du rêve !
P1 : Le *poudzigne* si vous êtes québécois vous connaissez. Ou alors si vous vous intéressez à la nourriture. Ou encore si vous êtes passé au salon du blog culinaire il y a

quelques années. C'est en fait un gâteau imprégné d'un sirop réalisé avec de la cassonade et de l'eau (ou encore d'un mélange de sirop d'érable, cassonade et eau).
P3 : Poudzigne … quelle horreur !!! Tu veux dire *pouding* ?????

L'usage de la variante *poudzigne* semble déstabiliser P2 et P3 qui n'en ont jamais entendu parler. Comme le fait remarquer P3, ce lexème est une déformation phono-morphologique de *pouding*, à son tour dérivé de l'anglais *pudding* qui désigne une sorte de boudin réalisé avec du sirop d'érable, de la cassonade et de l'eau. Cette graphie est en effet déconseillée par la norme linguistique québécoise, contrairement à celle de *pouding* qui s'est bien implantée au Québec depuis quelques années.

Très intéressante est aussi la réflexion autour de l'adaptation phono-morphologique de l'anglicisme *shortcake* :

15.04.2019
Thème : *shôrrtkêike*
P1 : Bonjour. Est-ce que la graphie *shôrrtkêike* est en usage au Québec ?
P2 : *shôrrtkêike* ? Je suis choqué :O
P3 : Non. C'est *shortcake* et c'est accepté par les dicos. Voici la définition donnée de la BDLP Québec : http://www.bdlp.org/resultats.asp?base=QU
P4 : Je dirais tout simplement *gâteau sablé*. Stop aux mots anglais, svpppp.

L'orthographe *shôrrtkêike* n'est pas très utilisée dans le lexique culinaire québécois. P3 mentionne l'usage de l'anglicisme *short cake*, effectivement employé en français québécois depuis le début du XXe siècle et s'inscrivant dans la norme sociolinguistique de cette variété géolinguistique. Cependant, son emploi est désapprouvé par P4 qui propose l'équivalent *gâteau sablé*, ceci surtout employé dans le langage publicitaire.

Notre corpus présente aussi un emprunt au chinois cantonais qui s'est implanté au Québec par l'intermédiaire de l'anglais nord-américain. Il s'agit de *chop soui*, ainsi discuté :

20.05.2019
Thème : *chop soui*
P1 : Saluttt ! Qui connaît le mot *chop soui* ?
P2 : Oui, c'est un mot chinois au fait … un plat chinois à base de légumes, de haricots et de viande sautés qui est trop la rue.
P3 : Ohhhh j'adoooore ! Je dirais plutôt un *chopsuey* (du chinois *jaahp-seui*) qui connaît cette graphie ???

Chop soui est la graphie francisée de *chop suey* dérivée, selon P3, du chinois *jaahp-seui* et qui signifie "divers morceaux" (GDT). Comme l'indique P2, il s'agit d'un plat d'inspiration asiatique composé de légumes, de haricots et souvent de viande. Dans le dictionnaire collaboratif du blog *Je parle québécois*, on relève aussi les variantes graphiques *chopsuey* et *chopsoui*, écrites en un seul mot. Plus complexe est la discussion concernant la signification et la forme orthographique de *baloné* :

15.06.2019
Thème : *baloné*
P1 : C'est quoi le *baloné* dans la gastronomie québécoise ?
P2 : Le *baloné* est un saucisson américain qui s'achète en tranches et s'apparente à la mortadelle italienne.
P3 : On écrit *baloneyyyyyyy*, pas *baloné*. Et surtout ça n'a rien à voir avec la mortadelle de Bologne … c'est un saucisson à base de bœuf, de veau et de porc dont la pâte est cuite à l'eau et fumé appelé *saucisson de bologne*, regardez : "*Le saucisson de Bologne rappelle des souvenirs à beaucoup de Québécois. Cette charcuterie a été grillée dans la poêle, cuite dans des ragoûts et transportée dans les lunchs*

de bien des enfants. Avec le temps, la popularité du baloney s'est un peu estompée … mais pas autant qu'on pourrait le croire" (*La Presse plus, 2016*).

P2 fournit une définition très générale du lexème *baloné*, en établissant une analogie avec la mortadelle italienne alors que P3 invite son interlocuteur à utiliser la graphie correcte *baloney* et à ne pas confondre ce saucisson avec la mortadelle de Bologne, une spécialité italienne qui appartient à la charcuterie fine. Ensuite, il donne une définition très détaillée, un équivalent - *saucisson de Bologne* - et un contexte d'usage par lequel on peut comprendre que le mot *baloné* est effectivement connu dans la cuisine nord-américaine sous le nom populaire *baloney*, une déformation phonétique de Bologne.

Très significative est la réflexion autour de l'expression *pizza all-dressed* et sa variante *all dresse* :

12.06.2018
Thème : *pizza all dresse*
P1 : Bonjour. Vous dites une *pizza all dresse* ou *all-dressed* ? Moi je préfère *pizza all dresse* …
P2 : Il n'y a pas de différence entre les deux. *All dresse* dérive de l'anglais *all-dressed* … franchement, c'est un emprunt inutile à l'anglais … on peut tout simplement dire *pizza garnie* ou *avec de la garniture complète*.
P3 : on dit une *pizza toute garnie* aussi …
P2 : non, l'usage de l'adverbe *tout* est déconseillé par l'OQLF. Regarde : "L'adverbe *tout* en français a le sens de "entièrement, dans sa totalité", or dans le calque pizza toute garnie, il signifie que la pizza est constituée d'un ensemble de garnitures et non pas que sa surface est couverte dans sa totalité". http://gdt.oqlf.gouv.qc.ca/ficheOqlf.aspx?Id_Fiche=8361411

On constate que pour *pizza all dresse* aussi, la graphie est adaptée à la prononciation québécoise. Or, cette graphie n'est pas très usuelle au Québec et on choisit généralement la graphie anglaise *pizza all dressed*. On peut donc penser que P1 vise davantage la langue orale que la langue écrite et qu'il croit que les participants du forum vont entendre cet emploi. P2 considère l'emprunt à l'anglais complètement inutile et propose les traductions *pizza garnie* et *pizza avec de la garniture complète*. P3 suggère aussi la traduction *pizza toute garnie*, mais l'insertion de l'adverbe *toute* est contestée par P2 qui incite son interlocuteur à consulter l'avis de l'OQLF. Analysons aussi l'observation autour du lexème *cipaille* :

> 24.01.2019
> Thème : *cipaille ou cipâte ?*
> P1 : Ehhhh les québécoisss, faut-il dire *cipaille* ou *cipâte* ?
> P2 : Tu peux dire les deux …
> P3 : *Usito* signale aussi la variante *six-pâtes*.
> P4 : Moi, je dis *sea-pie* direct ahahah … c'est plus simple.

La réflexion est ici entamée par P1 qui se pose la question de savoir quelle est la dénomination correcte entre *cipaille* et *cipâte*, un plat d'origine québécoise composé d'un mélange de gibier et d'autres viandes. Très intéressante est la réponse de P4 qui propose la variante *six-pâtes*, en faisant référence au dictionnaire en ligne *Usito* de l'Université de Sherbrooke. Il s'agit, en effet, de trois québécismes employés sans aucune différence dans le lexique de la cuisine québécoise, issus de l'adaptation de l'emprunt à l'anglais *sea-pie*, indiqué par P4 qui le préfère aux variantes québécoises.

Dans la conversation suivante, la problématique se développe à propos de l'origine et de la fréquence d'usage du lexème *sundae* :

> 20.05.2019
> Thème : *sundae*
> P1 : Voilà une belle trouvaille : *sundae*. Même le Wikébec le cite … quelle est sa fréquence dans le français québécois standard ?

> P2 : ça fait une dizaine d'années que *sundae* est en usage au Québec … on dit souvent : "la cerise sur le sundae" lol … ça vient d'où effectivement ?
>
> P3 : J'entends aussi *coupe glacée* … Quant à son origine, je cite l'étymologie du Wiktionnaire : "du mot anglais Sunday "dimanche".

Deux dictionnaires participatifs sont cités dans les commentaires et un exemple d'usage est présenté par P2. La réponse de P3 est riche en informations métalinguistiques : l'auteur fait tout d'abord référence à son équivalent français *coupe glacée*, également présent dans le GDT et donne, ensuite, une explication sur son origine, en citant le dictionnaire collaboratif *Wiktionnaire*. Le mot *sundae* désigne un dessert de crème glacée servie dans une coupe (d'où son équivalent *coupe glacée*), généralement garnie de sirop, de crème fouettée et d'une cerise. Sa première attestation remonte en anglo-américain à la fin des années 1980 et il s'agit d'une altération morpho-phonologique du mot anglais *sunday* qui signifie "dimanche", très probablement parce qu'il est servi et vendu le dimanche. Bien que le terme *sundae*, en usage depuis le début du XXe siècle, soit légitimé dans le français québécois, la norme préconise l'emploi de *coupe glacée*, comme confirmé par P3.

La conversation suivante se focalise sur l'interchangeabilité des lexèmes *pastrami* et *smoked-meat* qui apparaissent associés sur une étiquette commerciale :

10.10.2018

Thème : *smoked-meat* ou *pastrami ?*

P1 : Par curiosité : vous associez les mots *pastrami* et *smoked meat* ? Hier j'ai trouvé les deux termes ensemble sur une étiquette commerciale. Sont-ils des synonymes?

P2 : Le *pastrami* est utilisé aux États-Unis (on dit aussi *pastrami sandwich*), alors que le *smoked meat* c'est chez nous à Montréal …

P3 : Les deux termes sont souvent interchangeables, c'est vrai, mais ils ont une signification différente. Lisez

cet article : https://www.seriouseats.com/2014/06/
difference-between-pastrami-smoked-meat-katzs-
schwartzs-mile-end.html

P2 fait remarquer que le mot *pastrami* (également dénommé *pastrami sandwich*) est utilisé surtout en américain alors qu'à Montréal on emploie la forme anglaise *smoked meat*. En effet, le terme *smoked meat* est un emprunt culturel à l'anglais qui désigne un sandwich composé de pain de seigle, moutarde et tranches de viande, introduit à Montréal par les immigrés d'Europe de l'Est. Cette spécialité montréalaise est souvent corrélée au *pastrami* new-yorkais. Toutefois, même si ces deux viandes passent par les mêmes phases de préparation, elles n'ont pas le même goût parce que les tranches de bœuf sont différentes et le *smoked meat* est moins épicé, plus gras et plus fumé que le *pastrami*. Par ailleurs, dans les années 1980, on a tenté de remplacer l'anglicisme *sandwich au smoked meat* par l'équivalent *sandwich au bœuf mariné* qui avait été officialisé par l'OQLF, mais ce terme ne s'est pas intégré dans le lexique culinaire québécois.

La dernière conversation révèle la volonté de la part des usagers de bannir les anglicismes dans les discours sur la gastronomie québécoise. Voici un extrait :

14.02.2019
Thème : *les anglicismes*
P1 : Bonjour, je m'aperçois de plus en plus qu'on utilise tellement de mots anglais dans la gastronomie québécoise qu'on s'en rend même pas compte ! Je vous laisse quelques traductions sur des mots anglais pour que tout le monde puisse les substituer dans les recettes ! Bannissez l'anglais de ce forum, svp !!
Banana split : banana royale
Pickles : marinades, cornichons marinés
Trifle : bagatelle
Beaver Tail : queue de castor
OKA : fromage de lait de vache

P2 : *banana royale* … lol ! personne ne l'utilise !
P3 : Saluttt ! Merci, je suis tout à fait d'accord avec toi
… mais attention ! *Beaver Tail* c'est le nom de marque,
tu peux pas le traduire !! *OKA* n'est pas un anglicisme.
C'est le nom d'une petite ville québécoise ! ;-) Je dirais
fromage OKA.

P1 propose la traduction de cinq emprunts à l'anglais qui ne se
sont pas encore intégrés au système linguistique français. Les autres
participants semblent partager l'avis de P1 et interviennent avec
deux observations très intéressantes : P2 fait noter que l'équivalent
banana royale n'est pas utilisé au Québec ; P3 souligne que *Beaver
Tail* est un nom commercial qui ne peut pas être traduit et que *OKA*
n'est pas un anglicisme. En effet, *queue de castor* est la traduction
littérale du nom déposé *Beaver Tail*, mais il est couramment utilisé
au Québec pour indiquer un dessert fait de pâte frite en forme de
queue de castor, d'où sa dénomination. En outre, à partir de l'année
2019, l'expression *queue de castor* est considérée comme terme pri-
vilégié au Québec. Quant au terme *OKA*, il s'agit d'un toponyme
québécois qui renvoie au lieu de production de ce fromage et qui
ne peut pas être traduit, d'où la suggestion de l'apposition *fromage
OKA* de la part de P3.

Conclusion

L'étude des représentations métalinguistiques profanes autour
du lexique culinaire québécois permet d'envisager plusieurs conclusions. En premier lieu, nous avons remarqué que les participants
exercent une activité métalinguistique très intense essentiellement
basée sur la sauvegarde du français québécois dans les discours culinaires en ligne. Les discussions linguistiques profanes rendent
compte d'un sentiment linguistique très fort qui se manifeste, d'un
côté, par la volonté de traduire les emprunts à l'anglais ; de l'autre,
par le désir de réfléchir sur les nouvelles tendances lexicales, dans la

plupart des cas collées sur la prononciation québécoise et atteignant parfois des niveaux d'illisibilité et de fantaisie extrêmes.

En deuxième lieu, nous avons constaté que la naissance d'espaces de réflexions métalinguistiques profanes, tel que le forum *Les Foodies, Kessé ça ?*, ouvre de nouvelles dimensions dans le traitement lexicographique du lexique culinaire. Et, en cela, le passage de compétences des spécialistes vers des non-spécialistes de la langue joue un rôle capital, dans la mesure où il pose non seulement des questions liées à la représentation de la langue et à la norme, mais aussi à la légitimation de la langue, dans ce cas le français québécois. Il serait intéressant de voir dans quelles mesures ces représentations pourraient avoir un impact sur le travail des lexicographes traditionnels et quel pourrait être l'apport de ce forum à la description lexicographique des nouvelles tendances dans le lexique culinaire québécois. Toutefois, examiner la question des discussions métalinguistiques profanes signifie changer de perspective et ajouter l'élément perceptif à l'approche normative (descriptive et prescriptive). Comme signalé plusieurs fois par Paveau (2007) les paradigmes de la lexicographie profane, et plus en général de la linguistique populaire, doivent être pensés en termes perceptifs et non seulement systématiques, "ce qui implique également de substituer à une autre opposition binaire, savant vs populaire, un continuum qui tienne compte à la fois des objets examinés et du coefficient d'information social et culturel des savoirs produits" (Paveau 2007 : 107).

Works Cited

Achard-Bayle, Guy et Paveau, Marie-Anne (eds) (2008), "La linguistique 'hors du temple'?", *Pratiques*, 139-140, Metz : Centre de recherche sur les médiations, 3-16, http://pratiques.revues.org/1171.

Altmanova, Jana (2014), "L'industrie langagière dans l'espace francophone du Québec : réflexion sur la traduction-localisation des noms de marques", *Testi e linguaggi*, 8, 89-96.

Auroux, Sylvain (1989), *Histoire des idées linguistiques*, Bruxelles : Mardaga.

Authier-Revuz, Jacqueline (2012), *Ces mots qui ne vont pas de soi. Boucles réflexives et non coïncidences du dire*, Limoges : Lambert-Lucas.

Base de données lexicographiques panfrancophones, http://www.bdlp.org.

Beacco, Jean-Claude (2001), "Les savoirs linguistiques "ordinaires" en didactique des langues : des idiotismes" in Beacco, Jean-Claude et Porquier, Rémy (eds), *Grammaires d'enseignants et grammaires d'apprenants de langue étrangère – Langue française*, 131, 89-105.

Beacco, Jean-Claude (ed) (2004), *Représentations métalinguistiques ordinaires et discours – Langages*, 154 Paris : Larousse.

Brunner, Pascale et al. (eds) (2018), *Les métadiscours des non-linguistes. Les Carnets du Cediscor*, 14.

Celotti, Nadine (2016), "Voies novatrices du 'Dictionnaire de la Zone, tout l'argot des banlieues' en ligne : à l'écoute des voix sur la toile", *Publif@rum*, 26 : Genova : Università di Genova, 1-8, http://publifarum.farum.it/ezine_articles.php ?id=375.

Charaudeau, Patrick (1991), "Contrat de communication et ritualisation des débats télévisés", in Charaudeau Patrick (ed.), *La télévision. Les débats culturels "Apostrophes"*, Paris : Didier, 11-35.

De Luca, Ylenia (2018), "Dérives identitaires au Canada francophone : peut-on vivre ensemble ?", *Inverbis*, 179-190.

Dictionnaire Usito, https://usito.usherbrooke.ca.

Gadet, Françoise, *Le français populaire*, Paris : PUF.

Hœnigswald, Henry (1966), "A Proposal for the Study of Folk-linguistics", in *Sociolinguistics : Proceedings of the UCLA Sociolinguistic Conference 1964*, The Hague : Mouton, 16-26.

Je parle québécois, https://www.je-parle-quebecois.com/lexique/.

Kerbrat-Orecchioni, Catherine (1990), *Les interactions verbales*, 1, Paris : Armand Colin.

Le Grand Dictionnaire Terminologique, http://gdt.oqlf.gouv.qc.ca/index.aspx.

Marcoccia, Michel (2016), *Analyser la communication numérique écrite*, Paris : Armand Colin.

Margarito, Mariagrazia (2007), "Entre rigueur et agrément : de quelques microstructures de dictionnaires contemporains", in Galazzi, Enrica et Molinari, Chiara (eds), *Les français en émergence*, Berne : Peter Lang, 171-182.

Meyer, Christian et Gurevych, Iryna (2012), "Wikitionary : a new rival for expert-built lexicons ? Exploring the possibilities of collaborative lexicography", in Granger, Sylviane et Paquot, Magali (eds), *Electronic Lexicography*, Oxford : Oxford University Press, 259-291.

Molinari, Chiara (2017), "Nouvelle lexicographie vs anciennes représentations", *Repères - Dorif, Dictionnaires, culture numérique et décentralisation de la norme dans l'espace francophone*, 14, Rome : Dorif Università, http://www.dorif.it/ezine/ezine_printarticle.php?id=381.

Murano, Michela (2014), "La lexicographie 2.0 : nous sommes tous lexicographes ?", in Druetta, Ruggero et Falbo, Caterina (eds), *Cahiers de recherche de l'école doctorale en linguistique française*, 8, Trieste : EUT, 147-162.

Murano, Michela (2019) "La néologie dans les dictionnaires collaboratifs", in Altmanova, Jana et Zollo, Silvia Domenica (eds), *La néologie à l'ère de l'informatique et de la révolution numérique - Neologica. Revue internationale de néologie*, Paris : Classiques Garnier, 143-162.

Niedzielski, Nancy et Preston, Dennis (2000), *Folk Linguistics*, Berlin/ New York : De Gruyter.

Paveau, Marie-Anne (2007), "Les normes perceptives de la linguistique populaire", *Langage et société*, 1, 93-109.

Paveau, Marie-Anne (2008), "Le parler des classes sociales dominantes, objet linguistiquement incorrect ? Dialectologie perceptive et linguistique populaire", *Études de linguistique appliquée*, 2, Paris : Klincksieck, 137-156.

Rey-Debove, Josette (1997), *Le métalangage*, Paris : Armand Colin.

Steffens, Marie (2017), "Lexicographie collaborative, variation et norme : le projet 10-nous", *Repères - Dorif, Dictionnaires, culture* numérique et décentralisation de la norme dans l'espace francophone, 14, Rome : Dorif Università, http://www.dorif.it/ezine/ezine_printarticle.php?id=393.

Vicari, Stefano (2016), *Pour une approche de la linguistique populaire en France. Attitudes, prédiscours, questions de confiance*, Roma : Aracne.

Vincent, Nadine (2017), "Présence et description d'emplois québécois dans des dictionnaires disponibles gratuitement en ligne", *Repères - Dorif, Dictionnaires, culture numérique et décentralisation de la norme dans l'espace francophone*, 14, Rome : Dorif Università, http://www.dorif.it/ezine/ezine_articles.php?art_id=379.

Wikébec, dictionnaire participatif du Français Québécois, https://www.wikebec.org.

Wiktionnaire, https://fr.wiktionary.org.

ROBERTA LA PERUTA

Selling a taste of Italy on TripAdvisor: Italian Culinary Terms in Toronto's Little Italy Menus

1. Introduction

JUST AS SHAKESPEARE'S JULIET WONDERED "what's in a name?" this study addresses the issue of what's in a suffix. The suffix -ness (IPA: /nəs/, /nəs/) originated from Old English *-nes(s)*, which in turn derived from Proto-Germanic *in-assu-*. It appears at the end of past participles and adjectives to form nouns referring to an abstract quality or characteristic (e.g. restless + ness = restlessness, the state or quality of being restless; aware + ness = awareness, the state or quality of being aware of something). Therefore, Italianness is the uncountable quality of being Italian. In this paper, the construction of Italianness and the employment of Italian culinary terms in Little Italy, Toronto (Ontario, Canada), is explored through a usage-based analysis of the language adopted in several food establishment menus found on TripAdvisor, leaving aside its political and national connotation and taking into consideration the cultural domain of food-related terms as metaphorical icon of Italianicity.

Toronto's Little Italy, also known as College Street West, is a well-known district full of Italian-Canadian food joints and shops. In the early 1900s, thousands of Italians arrived in Canada, especially from rural areas of Central and Southern Italy, and first settled in a nearby area called The Ward. Later on, College Street became home to the many newcomers from the *bel paese*, and as early as the 1960s, Italians made up for more than 30% of the inhabitants of Little Italy. In the process of their integration in a completely new and different culture, Italian immigrants packed up their dialects and brought them to the New World, where a mingling of types of Italian and Canadian English led to the emergence of *Italiese*. In fact, the pluri-cultural Toronto is home to this peculiar dialect, which is spoken and practiced by first- and second-generation immigrants. Nowadays, Italians are one of the largest minority groups in Toronto (in 2016, 1.5 million people declared Italian origin). However, Little Italy currently accommodates a demographic mixture of peoples, and other communities are represented in this area as well, such as Latin-Americans. Nonetheless, Italian family-owned and run restaurants, trattorias, bars, social clubs and many other businesses are still found on both sides of the street, and still offer passers-by an Italian-flavoured atmosphere.

The aim of this study is to take stock of the usage, adaptation and translation of food-related Italianisms in a transnational context, looking into the notion of menu engineering and the construction of Italian (or Italian wannabe) cultural identity conveyed by the language of food. The methodological approach used to carry out this endeavour is illustrated in the figure below. On one hand, the concept of Italianness is addressed through a usage-based corpus linguistic and cultural analysis of the data, where lexical choices are examined with reference to their frequency of use and adaptation level. On the other hand, the multimodal nature of the menu design and layout is explored as a carrier of non-verbal but essential information about the visual model of what is thought to look Italian. Frequency, distribution of different constructions and the analysis of translation mistakes lead to the classification of the Italianisms in the corpus and a discussion of their strategic employment as a way to "cook up" and sell a taste of Italy.

Figure 1. Analysis of Italianness

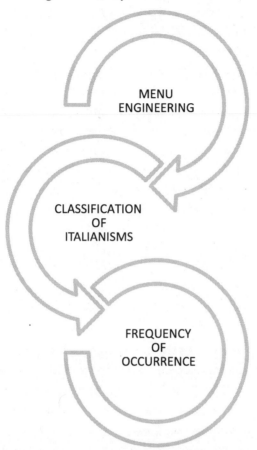

MENU
ENGINEERING

CLASSIFICATION
OF
ITALIANISMS

FREQUENCY
OF
OCCURRENCE

1.1 Theoretical framework and state of the art

The usage-based approach has emerged over the last few decades as a theory of language that rejects the idea of a fixed language, suggesting that it is in fact recursively shaped by its users during speech production (Barlow & Kemmer 2000). Thus, as usage can greatly affect and change language, it can also cause the rise of new linguistic structures (see Bybee 2006). Central publications containing detailed information on usage-based theories are Langacker 1987, Hopper 1987 and Goldberg 2006. In investigating language in actual use, usage-based procedures are directly concerned with establishing the role of frequency in language change and variation and providing methodologically sound perspectives that can be applied to a wide variety of linguistic branches, such as corpus, socio- and cognitive linguistics. According to Backus (2012), usage-based approaches have been widely used to investigate language-contact phenomena such as lexical borrowing, which directly addresses the entrenchment of linguistic units in a speech community, solidifying "the links between contact linguistics and cognitive linguistics" (Backus 2012: 1). Previous research shows that the degree of entrenchment of a linguistic unit, which is determined by its frequency of use, automates production (Bybee 2001, 2006; Leiven & Tomasello 2008; De Smet 2015), given that entrenchment is a gradual process by which "with repeated use, a novel structure becomes progressively entrenched, to the point of becoming a unit" (Langacker 1987: 59). Consequently, an entrenched linguistic unit refers to "an automated, routinized chunk of language that is stored and activated by the language user as a whole, rather than 'creatively' assembled on the spot" (De Smet & Cuyckens 2007: 188). However, it should be noted that methods for measuring the precise entrenchment level of a linguistic unit have not yet been developed. Nevertheless, in the present study, frequency of use will be taken as a measure of cognitive entrenchment, and thus adapted to the culinary terms taken into consideration in the speech community examined.

Loanwords are words that are transferred from a donor language to a recipient language through a process of modification, viz. their phonetic, grammatical and semantic integration in the target language. The process of borrowing is motivated by the necessity to fill the lexical gap of a corresponding word in the host langue or by pragmatic factors, such as the prestige value carried by the borrowed word, and is subject to typological rules. In fact, previous studies in the field of typology have highlighted the existence of a typological hierarchy in the acquisition of loanwords. To be more precise, words that belong to the noun category are more easily borrowed than items from a different word class, since they "extend the referential potential of a language" (Van Hout & Muysken 1994:42) to a greater degree than function words, and are easier to acquire than adjective-noun or verb-object collocations. Furthermore, high-frequency lexical items belonging to the core vocabulary of a language are resistant to borrowing (e.g. words for basic concepts such as *sleep, home, family*, etc.), whereas words that designate new objects or concepts—also known as cultural borrowings—are more easily introduced in a language as a consequence of language contact. Loanword adaptation can occur during speech production when bilingual speakers introduce words from one of their native languages into the other, or when monolingual speakers of a language borrow a foreign word to fill a lexical gap in their L1 (Calabrese 2009), in "the attempted reproduction in one language of patterns previously found in another" (Haugen 1972: 81). In recent years, the acquisition and integration of English loanwords in different L2s have received much critical attention in the literature (i.e. Jespersen 1922; Weinreich 1953; Campbell 1986; Varga 2011; and Cook 2018). For instance, Rando (1970) describes patterns of assimilation of English loans into Italian at the morphological, phonological, orthographical and semantic levels, systematically describing the stepwise transition that lexical borrowing has to undergo in order to be incorporated into the lexicon of the target language. However, the study of the same language-contact phenomenon from a foreign L1 to English has been somewhat neglected. To fill this gap, this paper aims to investigate how Italian culinary borrowings are used as a means of identity construction and commercialization of Italian food culture in Canada.

The language of food, along with the language of food menus as a text type of their own, is full of captivating qualifying adjectives and engaging terms, aimed at drawing customers' attention and arousing their appetite. As a consequence of migration, tourism and globalization, the use of a foreign language is often a key factor in the food service industry, insofar as it helps to establish a restaurant's (genuine) ethnic personality. For this reason, foreignisms not only have a certain impact on customer's perception of the authenticity of the products they are buying/eating, but they also bring a certain social value and prestige. For instance, top-end restaurants tend to mention the origin of the food they serve 15 times more than low-end establishments (Jurafsky 2014). In this respect, language is a mighty marketing tool that conveys emotional connotations and favours intercultural connections between the customers and the culture they are "trying." The frequent cross-pollination between languages in the culinary scene makes use of languaging (Swain 1985) as a discursive strategy to communicate and negotiate one's cultural identity, as well as to add local colour (Boyer & Viallon 1994) in the promotion of a specific culture or business.

2. Data and methods: using TripAdvisor as a source for linguistic analysis

The present research examines an opportunistic corpus of Italian culinary terms gathered from online menus of Italian food establishments in Little Italy as published on their TripAdvisor page.

TripAdvisor is a well-known American research website that offers free online information, bookings and reviews on travel experiences, hotels and restaurants around the world. With an estimated annual revenue of around $1.56 billion, it has changed the travel, hospitality and food service industry over the course of the last twenty years. Originally one of many travel company sites, it is now a multilingual social media website accessed worldwide by millions of users who choose how and especially where to spend their money based on the constantly updated reviews written by other users on this sort of guestbook platform.

The dynamic and ever so internetholic consumer society in which we live takes the digital space into great consideration, where the reputation economy and link popularity can inflate or reduce business profits. As life in cyberspace can actually influence the real world, new ways of making things appealing and sellable are starting to rise. From the 1980s onward, the food service industry has been using the interdisciplinary field of menu engineering (or menu psychology) to amplify profitability by strategically luring customers and food consumers to order or buy certain foods. Through textual psychological manipulations, menu engineering shapes customer perception, and consequently the degree of appreciation of a certain dish, using words that appeal to emotions, catching the reader's attention with an intriguing graphic design, or simply arranging items and categories in a memorable fashion. For instance, the word "specialty" (of the house) gives the idea of something unique and seems to justify a higher price, whereas dishes that are placed at the beginning and at the end of a menu seem to be those that customers remember the most. Therefore, according to the theory of menu engineering, restaurant owners who wish to boost profits would do well to put their best dishes in those sweet spots. Hence, there are a number of variables in a menu's visual presentation that can greatly affect sales, one of these being the language in which the dishes are written. Dealing with the representation of Italianness through online food menus, the use of Italian to name foods and food categories will be considered when discussing the results of this study.

Previous studies using TripAdvisor as a source for linguistic analysis have addressed the discourse analysis of online reviews from a contrastive perspective (Cenni & Goethals 2017; Zhu et al. 2017), focused on the pragmatic aspect of reviews as part of the language of tourism (Compagnone & Fiorentino 2018), or on the intelligibility of Thai restaurants' menus written in English (*Duangsaeng & Chanyoo 2017*). However, to the author's knowledge, no previous research has yet been conducted on the use of Italian in Little Italy's food menus.

2.1 Data: food menus on TripAdvisor

An initial search for food establishments serving Italian, Central Italian or Southern Italian cuisine in the area of Toronto produced as many as 415 entries, 268 of which did not have an online menu. At an estimated rate of 700/800 words per menu, the corpus size for the remaining 147 menus would have been too big to be analyzed manually, therefore only establishments in the area of Little Italy were selected. Of the 16 restaurants in that area, the following eight had a menu that was publicly accessible via TripAdvisor and thus satisfied the research criteria. As Table 1 shows, the dataset includes four restaurants, two trattorias, one pizzeria and one wine and pasta bar serving Italian food, most of which have checked at least another box in their TripAdvisor's "establishment type" and "cuisine offered" category (for instance, "restaurant," "bar," "pizzeria" or "trattoria" and "Italian," "pizza" or "vegetarian friendly," respectively). All businesses presented below have a good ranking, a popularity index ranging from 3.5 to 4.5, a medium to high price range and they mostly serve lunch and dinner or are exclusively open for evening meals. The information contained in the table was retrieved either from the establishments' own TripAdvisor page, when available, or from their websites or Facebook page.

2.2 Methods: data annotation and filtering

The eight menus composing the data for this study are mainly written in English, except for the names of some Italian dishes, foods and food categories, manually classified into different classes: adaptations (*antipasto, salami, prosciutto,* and *provolone* in example 1), loanwords (*Bomba* and *Nutella* in 2), regionalisms (e.g., *Panzanella* in 3), clumsy translations (*Agile e Olio* in 4) and innovations (such as *TIRAMISUPER* in 5).

1. *Antipasto Della Casa Salami, prosciutto, sundried tomato, provolone, olives & vegetables (Regina Pizzeria)*

2. *Pastries – New Bomba With Gelato Chantilly Cream or Nutella (Cafe Diplomatico)*

3. *Agile e Olio Spaghetti, extra virgin olive oil, peperoncino, anchovy, toasted bread crumbs & garlic (Il Gatto Nero)*

4. *Panzanella Salad Tomato, cucumber, Spanish red onion, avocado, croutons (Cafe Diplomatico)*

5. *TIRAMISUPER Marsala espresso soaked ladyfingers, ricotta–espresso custard (Trattoria Giancarlo)*

Table 1. Food establishments

ESTABLISH-MENT NAME	ESTABLISH-MENT TYPE	CUISINE OFFERED	ONLINE RANKING	PRICE RANGE	TYPE OF SERVICE
Bella Vista Trattoria & Wine Bar	Trattoria and wine bar	Italian	4	$$	Dinner
Café Diplomatico	Restaurant, pizzeria, café	Italian, Coffee, Pizza	3.5	$$–$$$	Breakfast specials, lunches, dinners, late-night menu, catering, delivery
Il Gatto Nero	Restaurant and bar	Italian, Pizza, Vegetarian Friendly	4	$$–$$$	Lunch, dinner
Marinella Simply Italian	Restaurant	Italian, Pizza	4.5	$$–$$$	Dinner
Regina Pizzeria	Pizzeria e trattoria	Italian, Pizza, Vegetarian Friendly	4	$$–$$$	Lunch, dinner
Sotto Voce Wine and Pasta Bar	Wine and pasta bar	Wine Bar, Italian, Vegetarian Friendly	4.5	$$–$$$	Lunch, dinner
Trattoria Giancarlo	Trattoria	Italian	3.5	$$$$	Dinner
Vivoli	Restaurant	Italian, Pizza, Mediterra-nean	3.5	$$–$$$	Lunch, dinner

In order to distinguish between adaptations, loanwords and regionalisms, the online versions of the Collins Dictionary, the Merriam Webster Dictionary, the Oxford Learner's Dictionary and the WordReference Dictionary were consulted (The Collins Canadian Dictionary was not included in the list because it did not appear to contain pertinent Italian loanwords). These dictionaries were chosen as a source for the present analysis due to their prestige, size and/or etymological information. In fact, when considered necessary, the origin of a word was also looked into. For instance, the word *café*, which is sometimes associated with Italian culture (e.g. *Cafe Diplomatico*) is actually of French origin (from Turkish *kahve*, source: Merriam-Webster Dictionary) and was thus not included in the analysis. Similarly, (*extra virgin*) *olive oil* is a widely used oil in all Mediterranean countries and its instances were discarded, since it is not exclusive to the Italian culinary tradition. In the adaptation process, words usually adapt their spelling and pronunciation, and sometimes they lose their original meaning or acquire a new one. When implanted in new sociocultural contexts, Italianisms are "continually resemiotised, taking on new meanings over time and across geographical and cultural boundaries. At the same time the culinary traditions and identities linked to them are refashioned" (Romaine 198: 2019). For instance, *pepperoni* is a widespread North American pizza topping consisting of a fine-grained spicy cured sausage, much like a Calabrian *soppressata*. In Nova Scotia, Canada, most pubs fry and serve this kind of *pepperoni* with a sweet mustard sauce, which is an example of cultural appropriation of both a food term and practice. Likewise, *prosciutto* is used differently than in Italy, insofar as it has come to indicate a particular kind of dried cured ham called *prosciutto crudo* in Italian, while the term *frittata* used in Anglophone contexts has the meaning of *frittata ripiena* (lit. stuffed omelet). As for the *caffè corretto*, there is more than a thread online discussing why Italians named a specialty coffee in such a way, where the word *corretto*, which in this case corresponds to the expression "with a splash," is obviously mistaken for English "right, correct." Alternative or metaphorical meanings of the terms that have undergone semantic change over time (e.g. *macaroni, linguini, spaghetti, salame*) were not found in the data, since menus are clearly concerned with the actual rather than metaphorical meaning of these items. The following examples show instances of semantically mutated adaptations drawn from the Oxford English Dictionary.

> (6) a. These days the word *salame* is also used to refer to an idiot with less brains than a sack of potatoes!
> b. One in military uniform, the other an octogenarian *macaroni* with his walking stick.
> c. In part two: *Pasta* Blaster ... Swindon's four-goal warning to Oxford for the Anglo-Italian Cup.

After manual extraction and annotation of the corpus data, including all forms of Italian culinary terms, an analysis of token frequency was conducted on the corpus, which includes 7,047 words of Italian food-related terms and compounds inserted in texts that are mainly written in English. Furthermore, a word list was generated using Laurence Anthony's AntConc software for corpus analysis, to rank and classify Italianisms in the data by classification type. The factors looked into and which will further be addressed in the results section are listed below:

- Establishment name: refers to the name of the food establishments taken into consideration.

- Item: or the culinary term in question.

- Menu section and course: each item was classified according to the menu section stated on each menu (e.g. *Amaro*, burgers, extra ingredients, Martinis, *per accompagnare*, etc.) and course to which it belongs (appetizer, beverage, dessert, etc.) as described in Table 1. Terms such as *pizza* and *panini* were classified as main course, despite the fact that tablemates can also share them as appetizers.

Table 2. Courses and classifications

COURSES	CLASSIFICATION
Appetizer	*antipasto/i, antipasto e stuzzichini,* appetizer/s, *salumi, spuntini*
Beverages	Amaro, beer, bevande, beverages, biera, cocktails, coffee & tea, digestive, draught beer, grappa, imported beer, liqueurs/liquors, Martinis, specialty coffee/& tea, vino, wine
Breakfast/brunch	breakfast, brunch, *colazione*
Dessert	dessert/s, *dolci, formaggio e dolce,* sweets
Entrée	Entrées
Main course	burgers, daily specials, fresh *pasta, pasta ai frutti di mare,* handmade *pasta, panini, panini*/sandwiches, *pasta/s, pizza/s, pasta alla crema, pasta della casa, pasta vegetariana,* signature dish, *risotto*
Salad	*insalate*/salads, salads
Second main course	*carni e pesce, dalla griglia, grigliata, secondi, vitello e pollo*
Side dish	extra ingredients, *per accompagnare,* side plates, *supplementi*/side orders, toppings
Soup	soups, *zuppe*/soup

- Frequency: or the frequency of occurrence of each item.
- Classification: each item was tagged as belonging to one of the following classes.
  - Adaptations, or words that have fully entered the English lexicon *(parmigiana, risotto)*.
  - Loanwords, *ad hoc* borrowings that do not belong to the English lexicon *(pacchetti, zuppe)*.
  - Regionalisms, regional terms referring to regional dishes *(fettunta, panzanella)*.
  - Clumsy translations, misspelled, semantic or morphologically bizarre words or compounds.
  - Innovations, words that do not belong to any of the former categories and can be considered as semantic innovations.

- Type: exclusively applied to the clumsy translations category, its levels are presented in Figure 3.

3. Results: the Torontonian vocabulary of Italian food

Italian food export and sale is beyond doubt one of the pillars of the Italian economy, along with manufacturing and tourism. In 2019, Italian food had a turnover of around 916 million euros in Canada, with an increase of 6.8% compared to 2018, providing Canadian customers with much-loved traditional high quality and affordable ethnic food. According to the Italian Trade Agency (ITA), despite the undeniable impact of coronavirus on the food service indus-try, among others, Italian food businesses are still going strong in 2020 and most Canadian distributors plan to keep buying Italian products. This result is partially due to the *Comprehensive Economic and Trade Agreement (CETA), which removed 98% of customs du-ties between Italy and Canada and assigned the label of* Protected Geographical Indication (PGI) to *41 Italian products.*

There are 7,530 restaurants on TripAdvisor situated in Toronto, and more than 400 are Italian. Although cooking and eating are everyday rituals that are common to the life of all humans, food-stuffs have a clear ethnic connotation and are central to the Italian culture. This paper explores the intersection of language and food practices as ways of communication to see how the musicality of the Italian language, perceivable even in its orthography, is used as a marketing strategy to appeal to customers' collective imagination and to further commodify Italian culture and food through the in-sertion of Italianisms in food menus published online. Making a menu freely accessible on the web is obviously an attempt to reach a wider clientele while affirming the cultural identity of a business. Therefore, this analysis focuses on the frequency of occurrence of the words that are thought to represent Italian culinary culture, the distribution of adaptations, loanwords, regionalisms, innovation and clumsy translations in the data, as well as on the translation mistakes and their linguistic classification.

3.1 Menu engineering and food advertising

Before turning to the actual analysis of the data, it might be of scientific interest to have a look at how these businesses are described on their official webpages.

According to its TripAdvisor page, the *Bella Vista Trattoria & Wine Bar* is a "family owned-and-operated" trattoria with a comfortable patio dining area, where customers find "traditions and authenticity of Italian cuisine, in a contemporary, yet relaxed dining atmosphere." Welcoming staff and a friendly environment, along with homemade pasta, fresh scallops and an exclusive wine selection, complete the description of this establishment, which has been serving Italian food for over 40 years. Opened in 1968 by Rocco Mastrangelo Sr., and now directed by Rocco Jr. and his wife Connie, *Cafe Diplomatico* (or the "Dip") is a popular spot in Little Italy where customers can indulge in "breakfast specials, delicious pizzas, panzerottos, calzones, pastas as well as [...] create-your-own menu items." This "classic spin on North American Italian food" is often used as a set for movies shot in Little Italy and features a large outdoor space where sport lovers can cozily watch their favourite teams play and offers special happy hour discounts on Sundays to Thursdays night, granting a "traditional Italian family experience." *Il Gatto Nero* (or the "Cat"), on the other hand, has been open since 1960, when Carmine and Michael Raviele decided to start a father-and-son business that soon became "an institution of Toronto, most especially Little Italy on College Street." The intimate and familiar atmosphere provided by the attentive dedication of its owners is almost palpable through their description: "no matter who you are or where you're from, you will feel yourself part of the family once you cross our threshold." On the other hand, customers at *Marinella Simply Italian* can enjoy "lovingly prepared Italian classics" in their "sun-drenched patio" or "beautiful dining room." Managed by John, a second-generation Italian whose mother makes homemade fresh pasta, *Marinella*'s authentic cuisine offers "traditional thin crust pizza, delicious pasta dishes, hearty risottos, tender mouthwatering steaks, and [...] exquisite homemade desserts" in a warm and casual environment. The other restaurants selected did not include any information on TripAdvisor. However, the "about us" section of *Regina Pizzeria & Trattoria*'s website states that it is a family-owned food establishment opened in 1967. Its staff take pride in providing their customers with authentic "great meals [...] great wine selection [...] great Italian food," ensuring "a wonderful Italian experience," in the hope "that every guest has a feel of what Southern Italian food really tastes like." *Sotto Voce Wine & Pasta Bar* (or "the Voce") is a twenty-year-old restaurant situated at the cornerstones of College Street and serving "traditional Italian comfort food and numerous wines by the glass in a style and atmosphere that is cool and relaxed to the hip and stylish." According to the web, *Trattoria Giancarlo* has been serving its customers "with fantastic and authentic Italian food" for over thirty years. *Carpaccio, prosciutto, ravioli, risotto, gnocchi* and homemade pasta *al dente* are among the many specialties and "truly special Italian meals" prepared by Chef Jason Barato and his mother Eugenia. "Classy yet intimate, sophisticated yet rustic," it serves "typical dishes" that have "personality, like Toronto [...] in a creative and unique way." Lastly, *Vivoli* Italian restaurant is specialized in "a variety of classic Italian food as well as authentic Italian pizzas," wine, martinis and sangria, served on their rooftop and street patios in trendy Toronto style. Originally opened in 2005 and recently purchased by new management, it now offers take-out and online ordering options.

In a nutshell, words such as "Italian," "homemade," "traditional/authentic" and "family/familiar" are very common in the online self-description of these establishments, which have given their menus a mostly Italian-looking layout, as shown in the table below. All establishments dedicated an entire section of their menus to starters/*antipasti*, *pasta* or *pizza* (in the case of pizzerias), but only *Il Gatto Nero, Sotto Voce Wine and Pasta Bar* and *Trattoria Giancarlo* used Italian both to introduce entire food categories (ex. *antipasti, dalla griglia, digestive, dolci*) and to name their dishes and most typical Italian ingredients. Interestingly, *Sotto Voce Wine and Pasta Bar* and *Trattoria Giancarlo* are among the newest restaurants on the list, and whether their Italianness is an artificially construed marketing strategy or a way to mark and reinforce the authenticity of their origin through the use of the Italian language is open for debate. On the contrary, the use of mixed language by other establishments possibly conveys the Canadian Italianness of their owners.

Table 3. Menu layout

ESTABLISHMENT	OPENED	MENU LAYOUT
Bella Vista Trattoria & Wine Bar	Over 40 years ago	Mixed: Italian and English
Cafe Diplomatico	1968	Mixed: Italian and English
Il Gatto Nero	1960	Italian
Marinella Simply Italian	1995 (?)	Mixed: Italian and English
Regina Pizzeria & Trattoria	1967	Mixed: Italian and English
Sotto Voce Wine and Pasta Bar	20 years ago	Italian
Trattoria Giancarlo	Over 30 years ago	Italian
Vivoli	2005	Mixed: Italian and English

3.2 Results discussion: Mirror, mirror on the wall, who is the Italiannest of them all?

The process of (loan)word acquisition and adaptation presents dynamic interaction between two distinct linguistic as well as cultural systems. The present section points out salient research findings, summarized by means of tables and figures.

The table below reports overall percentages for the whole data, where Italian terms account for 16% of the total, as well as establishment-specific frequency rates. The information in the table reveals that all of these food establishments show some Italian food-related lexicon in their menus, which is a clear indication that its use is a deliberate communicative strategy to provide their client with an extra touch of Italianness. However, the overall percentage in not strikingly high. As a matter of fact, *Il Gatto Nero* is the only restaurant that used words that have a "taste of home" more than one-third of the time, whereas *Cafe Diplomatico*, which is allegedly a rendezvous point for Italians in Toronto and a must for those who want to try North American Italian food, is second to last on the chart. This might also be due to the kind of clientele that the restaurants aim to attract: the more readable the menu, the more clients will feel comfortable reading it, on the understanding that exotic words from "home" are an essential element in their customers' dining experience.

Table 4. Overall percentages

CORPUS SIZE	ITALIANISMS
7047 words – 100%	1130 words – 16%
ESTABLISHMENT	**PERCENTAGE OF ITALIANISMS**
Il Gatto Nero	33%
Marinella Simply Italian	23%
Regina Pizzeria	19%
Vivoli	19%
Trattoria Giancarlo	18%
Sotto Voce Wine and Pasta Bar	17%
Cafe Diplomatico	12%
Bella Vista Trattoria	10%

Table 4 shows the overall frequency of Italianisms by course, indicating a higher degree of employment in the **Main course** (with a number of 521 out of 1,130 total items), **Beverages** (217) and **Appetizer** (174) sections of the menus considered. On the contrary, the food categories that trigger the use Italian the least are the **Entrée** and **Soup** classes, which were present in only two of the eight menus examined, followed by **Side dishes, Desserts,**

Breakfasts/brunches, Second/Main Courses and **Salads**. This figure highlights how Italian culture is more easily associated with a plate of pasta, pizza, savory starters and a glass of red wine rather than with brunch, soups and salads, which are indeed less typical Italian courses.

Table 5. Overall frequency by course

COURSES	OVERALL FREQUENCY
Appetizer	174–15%
Beverages	217–19%
Breakfast/brunch	41–4%
Dessert	34–3%
Entrée	12–1%
Main course	521–46%
Salad	43–4%
Second main course	43–4%
Side dish	30–3%
Soup	15–1%

To account for the distribution of adaptations, loanwords, regionalisms, clumsy translations and innovations in the data, the frequency of occurrence of each item in the corpus was calculated based on its repetitions, while compound units were either split or counted individually. For instance, to calculate the percentage of occurrence of *penne*, the clumsy translation *penne arrabbiate* (lit. angry pens) was split and each component was summed up to other instances of the same term, respectively *penne* (21 total occurrences) and *arrabbiate* (frequency of occurrence: 1). In this way, clumsy compound translations were discarded in the calculation of the overall data (while one-word translation mistakes were retained), in order to avoid counting their components twice. On the other hand, while calculating the total number of translation mistakes, compounds were added to one-word expressions, thus *penne arrabbiate* or *fettuccini salmone* were considered as items having the frequency of occurrence of one token, as exemplified in six. Following this procedure, 82 clumsy translations were identified and classified as in Figure 3, although only 39 translation mistakes were identified in the overall data.

> 6) *Fettuccini salmone* = *fettuccini* (plur. fem. noun, Anglicized adaptation from Italian *fettuccine*) + *salmone* (sing. masc. noun, loanword)
> Classification = clumsy translation, frequency = 1
>
> Components: *fettuccini*, adaptation, frequency = 6; *salmone*, loanword, frequency = 3
> Correct form = *fettuccini* (plur. fem. noun, adaptation) + *al* (prepositional article) + *salmone* (sing. masc. noun, loanword), frequency = 0

Figure 2. Distribution by construction

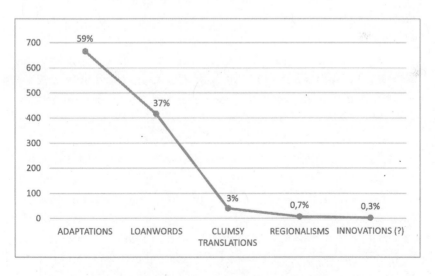

The figure above shows the distribution of tokens by construction. Adaptations amount to 59% of the Italian data and are often found in adapted term + postmodifying Italian or English noun/ phrase (i.e. *bruschetta Bella Vista*, *bocconcini* cheese, *pesto* cream sauce) and premodifier + adapted Italianism type of constructions (beef *carpaccio*, stuffed *calamari*, mussels *marinara*). Some are unmodified Italian words (*risotto*, *ravioli*, *ricotta*), while others are Anglicized terms (*pepperoni*, *salami*, *scallopini*). In order to be classified as an adaptation, each term had to be found in at least one of the dictionaries consulted. The words *peperoncino* and *spiedini* were only present in the Merriam-Webster, while *scamorza* and *peperonata* appear in the WordReference but not elsewhere. In such cases, a quick search on the internet solves any doubts: these terms can indeed be considered adaptations but have not stably entered the English lexicon yet, and thus do not appear in every dictionary. Notably, the Collins Dictionary reports the word *panzerotto* as a Canadian adaptation from Italian *panza* (belly), which is indeed a popular fast food in Canada.

Loanwords make up 37% of the Italianisms in the corpus, including proper nouns (i.e. *Bella Vista*, *Gatto Nero*), common nouns (*cozze*, *macedonia*, *insalata*), toponyms (*Napoli*, *Roma*), premodifying Italian proper nouns + English (*Bella Vista* anchovy dressing, *Regina* special), food brands (*Moretti*, *Nutella*, *San Benedetto*, *Yoga*), adjectives (*fritti*, *grigliato*, *vegetariano*) or names of specific dishes (*aglio e olio*, *(…) ai funghi*). Regionalisms are very rare and appear at a rate of 0.7% out of the total number of Italianisms. The term *fettunta*, for instance, is a kind of Tuscan bruschetta, while *ciambotta* is a southern Italian vegetable stew, *panzanella* is a central Italian salad made with stale bread and *matriciana* is another way in which people from Lazio refer to their beloved *amatriciana*.

Clumsy translations such as *fettuccini salmone*, *penne famosa*, *margarita*, and *bruschetta pomodoro* are found 3% of the time. Misspelled, semantic or morphologically bizarre words or compounds were further analyzed and divided by type, as in Figure 3. It is unclear whether clumsy translations highlight a lack of knowledge of Italian morphology and proper lexicon, or whether they are purposely featured in the menu to increase linguistic clarity and write something more understandable and recognizable to Anglophone eyes.

Innovations are extremely rare (0.3%) in the menus examined. The classification of the words *spinelli* and *Tiramisuper* was not straightforward, in that the first usually refers to cannabis cigarettes, while the second is a variation of the famous *tiramisu*. Although *spinelli* could be a regional term for *panini* (in fact, the *spinelli* proposed in the menu of *Il Gatto Nero* are long loaves of bread, which recall the shape of a joint), no information regarding its origin was found on the internet. As for *Tiramisuper*, giving a new name to the more traditional *tiramisù* is probably a marketing choice, insofar as the word "super" (which is usually used as an affix rather than a suffix) refers to something excellent, something extra, implanting the idea of a top-quality energizing coffee-based dessert in the customers mind. For these reasons, they were considered as innovations.

The tables below display five frequency lists divided by classification, where each item is ranked based on the number of repetitions found in the corpus. Given that the adapted terms were the most frequent in the data, the adaptation table is the longest, showing words that easily recall Italian culture and make Italian food lovers' mouths water just at the sight of them: *mozzarella, pasta, pizza, parmigiano* and *penne* nimbly take customers on an emotional journey through the sound of words that taste Italian. As for loanwords, the term with the highest distribution was *pomodoro*, with a token frequency equal to that of the fifth item in the adaptation word list, while the terms that follow it are certainly less frequent but serve the purpose of giving an exotic touch to the menus through an orthographic picture of Italy. Clumsy translations are further discussed in Table 7 and Figure 3, while the only regionalisms and possible innovations individuated are reported below. Overall, Table 6 is a list of the words that are thought to represent Italian culinary culture abroad, which were mindfully incorporated in the data to exploit the mental representation of flavours: a powerful weapon in the hands of detail-oriented owners and management staff who are willing to use marketing techniques put forward by menu engineering.

Table 6. Frequency by classification

ADAPTATIONS		
#	Frequency	Item
1	50	mozzarella
2	49	pasta
3	30	pizza
4	23	parmigiano
5	21	penne
6	18	calamari
7	18	prosciutto
8	18	spaghetti
9	15	parmigiana
10	14	bruschetta
11	13	espresso
12	13	pesto
13	12	gnocchi, gorgonzola, portobello, salami, risotto
14	11	caprese, linguine/i, pepperoni, zucchini
15	10	antipasto, Campari, crostini, pancetta
16	9	Martini
17	8	fettuccine/i, Prosecco, ravioli
18	7	Amaretto, Grappa, ricotta (cheese), rigatoni
19	6	Pinot Grigio, panino/i, provolone
20	5	bocconcini (cheese), latte, Vermouth

LOANWORDS		
#	Frequency	Item
1	21	pomodoro
2	14	Amaro
3	13	fior di latte
4	9	insalata
5	8	Poli

6	7	Aperol (Spritz), Nonino
7	6	capicollo, funghi, insalata, pesce
8	5	(…) alla Vodka, olio
9	4	bufala, Montenegro, prosciuttino, salumi
10	3	(…) della casa, (…) di pesce, (…) fritti, formaggio, Fra Diavolo, Frangelico, giardiniera, Pasqua, Peroni, pescatore, pesce, uova, Veneto

CLUMSY TRANSLATIONS		
#	Frequency	Item
1	5	bocconcino (cheese)
2	3	padano (cheese), tubetini
3	1	arrabiata, bufala caprese, linguini pescatore, penne primavera, Quattro Staggioni, spaghetti carbonara, spaghetti pomodoro, sugo pomodoro

REGIONALISMS			
#	Frequency	Item	Origin
1	3	fettunta	Tuscany
2	2	ciambotta	southern Italy
3	1	matriciana	Lazio
4	1	panzanella	central Italy

INNOVATIONS			
#	Frequency	Item	Establishment
1	1	Spinelli	Il Gatto Nero
2	1	Tiramisuper	Trattoria Giancarlo

As far as translation mistakes are concerned, there are as many as 82 clumsy translations in the corpus. According to the present analysis, the establishment that shows the shakiest mastery of Italian is *Marinella Simply Italian*, while the management at *Trattoria Giancarlo* and *Vivoli* seems to have paid close attention to the Italianization of their menu. Big and little slip-ups were sorted out as follows, according to the classification of the words of which they are made up.

Table 7. Translation mistakes by establishment

ESTABLISHMENT	#	%	% on full data
Cafe Diplomatico	19	23%	6%
Regina Pizzeria	17	21%	8%
Il Gatto Nero	13	16%	9%
Marinella Simply Italian	12	15%	12%
Bella Vista	7	8%	10%
Vivoli	7	8%	5%
Trattoria Giancarlo	4	5%	5%
Sotto Voce Wine and Pasta Bar	3	4%	6%
TOTAL	82	100%	7%

Figure 3. Translation mistakes by type

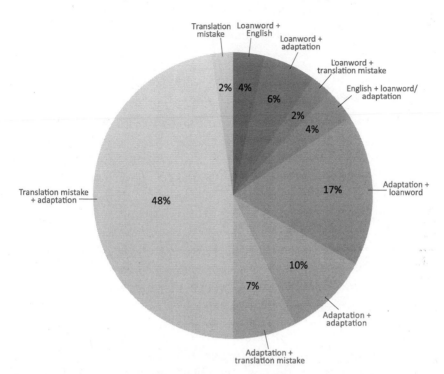

Figure 3 presents the different subcategories in which translation mistakes were sorted:

1. Loanword + English: *padano* cheese, frequency of occurrence = 3. These items show an Italian loan postmodified by an English word. The problem with this translation choice is that *padano* is part of the compound *grana padano* and does not function as a one-word expression.

2. Loanword + adaptation: *cotoletta milanese*, *bufala caprese*, *bufala mozzarella*, *limone granita*, frequency of occurrence = 5. The lack of articled preposition and/or inversion is a mistake in the translation of the names of these dishes.

3. Loanword + translation mistake: *quattro stagione*, *gamberoni a la puttanesca*, frequency of occurrence = 2, where the issue is the use of a singular word for a plural one

(*stagione* for *stagioni*) and the splitting of the preposition *alla* into *a* and *la*.

4.   English + loanword/adaptation: seafood *Marinella*, shrimp *Marinella*, seafood *fettuccine*, frequency of occurrence = 3. The naming of these dishes draws from English instead of Italian morphology.

5.   Adaptation + loanword: *fettuccini salmone, penne famosa, gnocchi/linguine genovese, bruschetta/spaghetti/risotto/sugo pomodoro, pappardelle Giovanni, spaghetti bolognese, spaghetti polpette, rigatoni contadina*, frequency of occurrence = 14. Essentially, these expressions look and sound unnatural because of the lack of combined prepositions *al/alla/alle*.

6.   Adaptation + adaptation: *penne primavera, ragù, spaghetti carbonara/pesto, gnocchi gorgonzola, rigatoni bolognese*, frequency of occurrence = 8. Once more, the omission of the combined preposition is improper.

7.   Adaptation + translation mistake: *penne arrabbiata/e, linguini/risotto pescatore, grana padana*, frequency of occurrence = 6. The postmodifying word is orthographically similar to the correct one but has a different meaning.

8.   Translation mistake: *bruscetta, margarita, zabajone, suco, mochacino, n'djua, bocconcino, tubetini, caci e pepe, Stregga, al arancia/lemone, caserecce, agile, rucula, arrabiata, stracietella, mare monti, quattro formaggio/staggioni, reggiano parmigiano, biera, aglio olio, cioccolat, Sambucca, Lemoncello*, frequency of occurrence = 39. Further subdivided into:

9.   Orthographic imprecisions (*biera, bruscetta, cioccolat, caserecce, lemone, Lemoncello, margarita, stracietella, rucula, zabajone*);

10. Pluralized Italian loanwords (*bevandes* for *bevande*);

11. undoubled double-consonant words (*arrabiata, suco, mochacino, tubetini* for *arrabbiata, succo, mochaccino* and *tubettini*)

and vice versa (*Quattro Staggioni* for *Quattro Stagioni*, *Sambucca* for *Sambuca* and *Stregga* for *Strega*);

12. Singular for plural *(bocconcino* cheese for *bocconcini*, *Quattro Formaggio* for *Quattro Formaggi*) and vice versa (*caci e pepe* for *cacio e pepe*);

13. Orthographically similar but semantically different words (*agile e olio* for *aglio e olio*);

14. Undoubled double-consonant combined preposition (*al arancia, al lemone*);

15. Lack of conjunction (*aglio olio, mare monti*) or preposition (*aceto Modena*);

16. Inversion (*reggiano parmigiano*)

17. Translation mistake + adaptation (*paisnella salami, tubetini pasta*), frequency of occurrence = 2. These are other examples of orthographic mistakes and undoubled double-consonant words.

To sum up, it appears that the language of menus pays close attention to linguistic economy, perhaps due to space limitations, and therefore embraces the deletion of function words such as prepositions and articles, which may be perceived as more opaque in the target language than noun + noun constructions. In addition, hybrid constructions such as adaptation + loanword (*antipasto* + *della casa, calamari* + *fritti, espresso* + *corretto, prosciutto* + *cotto*) are often used to name Italian dishes. In *calamari fritti*, for example, the term *calamari* is a long-adapted loanword first appearing in 1826 (source: Oxford English Dictionary), while *fritti* is an *ad hoc* momentary loan that avoids the use of the English adjective 'fried', serving the purpose of emphasizing the Italianness of the dish in question.

4. Conclusions

The present study set out to investigate the underexplored area of borrowed Italian culinary terms in the menus of several food establishments in Little Italy, Toronto, as an element of symbolic construction of the Italian identity. Gathering its data from TripAdvisor, an online platform where clients leave comments and reviews about hotels, places and restaurants they visit, this research addressed translation and adaptation choices in Italian food menus, put online by a number of restaurants, pizzerias and pubs located in Canada's megacity. The presence of Italianisms in the data was investigated through the calculation of their frequency of use, their adaptation status and the classification of translation mistakes found in the texts. Overall, the Italianisms found most commonly belong to the adapted terms and loanword categories, with a few exceptions of regional terms and two possible innovations. Translation mistakes amounted to only 7% of the data and perhaps need to be reconsidered and labeled as grammatical adaptations or linguistic hybridizations. In fact, the emergence of new linguistic constructions is an indication of the expansion of Italian culinary culture itself and of the shared nature of food practices across countries and continents. Using Italian terms instead of their English counterpart might as well be linked to the alleged sophisticated and traditional value that the Italian cuisine embodies so well, especially abroad. Food establishments in Little Italy (rightfully?) take advantage of one of the languages that are most associated with a prestigious culinary tradition to achieve symbolic and economic success in a pluri-cultural setting, where competition is quite high. In fact, besides the few culture-bound terms that are absent in the English language, the indexical prestige connected to this choice recalls the notion of the gastronomic register used as a means "to deal with socioeconomic scalar work within gentrification" (Järlehed et al. 2018). In this data, Italian was mainly used to name dishes or ingredients, as if the reading of Italian words anticipated their flavour, making a dish taste more like home. Perhaps Juliet was wrong to think that a rose, called by any other name, would smell just as sweetly.

Works Cited

Backus, Ad (2012), "A usage-based approach to borrowability," Tilburg Papers in Culture Studies; No. 27.

Backus, Ad. "Codeswitching and language change: One thing leads to another?" *International Journal of Bilingualism* 9 (3/4) (2015): 307–40.

Balirano, Giuseppe and Guzzo, Siria (eds.) (2019), *Food Across Cultures: Linguistic Insights in Transcultural Tastes*, Cham (Switzerland): Palgrave Macmillan.

Barlow, Suzanne and Kemmer, Michael (eds.) (2000). *Usage-based models of language*. Stanford, CA: CSLI Publications.

Boyer, Marc and Viallon, Philippe (1994). *La comunicazione turistica*. Rome: Armando.

Broselow, Epenthesis. 2000. "Stress, epenthesis, and segment transformation in Selayarese loans," in S. Chang, L. Liaw and J. Ruppenhofer (eds.) *Proceedings of the Twenty-fifth Annual Meeting of the Berkeley Linguistics Society*. Berkeley, CA: Berkeley Linguistics Society, 311–325.

Bybee, Joan (2000). "Lexicalization of sound change and alternating environments," in M. Broe and J. Pierrehumbert (eds.) *Laboratory phonology V: Acquisition and the lexicon*. Cambridge: Cambridge University Press, 250–268.

Bybee, Joan and Eddington, David. 2006. "A usage-based approach to Spanish verbs of 'becoming'," *Language* 82(2). (2006): 323–355.

Bybee, Joan and Hopper, Paul (2001), "Introduction to frequency and the emergence of linguistic structure," in Bybee, J. and P. Hopper (eds.) *Frequency and the emergence of linguistic* structure. Amsterdam: John Benjamins, 1–24.

Calabrese, Andrea. "Perception, production and acoustic inputs in loanword phonology," in Calabrese, A. and Wetzels, Leo W., *Loan Phonology.* (2009): 59–114.

Campbell, Lyle. (1986). "Cautions about loan words and sound correspondences," in D. Kastovsky and A. Szwedek (eds.) *Linguistics across historical and geographical boundaries: in honor of Jacek Fisiak on the occasion of his fiftieth birthday, Vol. 1: Linguistic theory and historical linguistics.* Berlin: Mouton, 221–225.

Cenni, Irene and Goethals, Patrick, "Negative hotel reviews on TripAdvisor: A cross-linguistic analysis," *Discourse, Context & Media,* 16. (2017): 22–30.

Collins English Dictionary [13th edition], collins.co.uk, HarperCollins. October 2019.

Compagnone, Maria Rosaria and Fiorentino, Giuliana, (2018). "Tripadvisor and Tourism: The Linguistic Behaviour of Consumers in the Tourism Industry 2.0," in Held Gudrun (ed.), *Strategies of Adaptation in Tourist Communication: Linguistic insights.* Leiden: Brull, 270–294.

Cook, Angela (2018). "A typology of lexical borrowing in Modern Standard Chinese," *Lingua Sinica.* 4: 6.

De Smet, Hendrik & Hubert Cuyckens (2007) "Diachronic aspects of complementation: Constructions, entrenchment, and the matching problem," in: Christopher Cain & Geoffrey Russom (eds.), *Shaking the tree: Fresh perspectives on the genealogy of English.* Berlin: Mouton de Gruyter, pp. 187–213.

De Smet, Hendrik (2015), "Entrenchment effects in language change," In: Schmid H. (ed.), *Entrenchment, memory and automaticity: The psychology of linguistic knowledge and language learning.* Washington: American Psychology Association.

Girarfelli, Davide. (2004), "Commodified identities: The myth of Italian food in the United States," *Journal of Communication Inquiry* 28, 4. (2004): 307–324.

Goldberg, Adele (2006), *Constructions at work: The nature of generalization in language.* Oxford: Oxford Univ. Press.

Haugen, Einar (1972), "The Analysis of Linguistic Borrowing," in Anwar S. Dil (eds.), *The Ecology of Language: Essays by Haugen.* Stanford: Stanford UP, 79–109.

Haugen, Einar. "The analysis of linguistic borrowing," *Language* 26. (1950) 210–231.

Hopper, P. 1987. Emergent grammar. In *Proceedings of the Thirteenth Annual Meeting of the Berkeley Linguistics Society.* Edited by Jon Aske, Natasha Beery, Laura Michaelis and Hana Filip, 139–157. Berkeley, CA: Berkeley Linguistics Society

Italian Trade Agency, ice.it. May 2020

Järlehed, Johan, Nielsen, Helle Lykke and Rosendal, Tove. "Language, food and gentrification: signs of socioeconomic mobility in two Gothenburg neighbourhoods," *Multilingual Margins,* 5, 1. (2018): 40–65.

Jespersen, Otto. (1922). *Language: Its Nature, Development, and Origin.* London: Allen and Unwin.

Jurafsky, Dan (2014). *The Language of Food: A Linguist Reads the Menu.* New York: W. W. *Norton* & Company.

Langacker, Ronald Wayne (1987). *Foundations of cognitive grammar. Vol. I: Theoretical prerequisites.* Stanford, CA: Stanford University Press.

Langacker, Ronald Wayne (1999a). *Grammar and Conceptualization.* Berlin and New York: Mouton de Gruyter.

Lieven, Elena and Tomasello, Michael (2008). "Children's first language acquisition from a usage-based perspective," in P. Robinson & N. C. Ellis (eds.), *Handbook of cognitive linguistics and second language acquisition.* Routledge/Taylor & Francis Group, 168–196.

Merriam-Webster Online, Merriam-Webster.com. October 2019.

OED Online. Oxford University Press, December 2015. Web. October 2019.

Oxford Learner's Dictionary, oxfordlearnersdictionaries.com. October 2019.

Rando, G. 1970. "The Assimilation of English Loan-Words in Italian," *Italica* 47: 129–142.

Romaine, Suzanne. "*Pizza Chiena* Between Two Worlds," in Balirano, G. and Guzzo, S. (ed.) *Food Across Cultures: Linguistic Insights in Transcultural Tastes*, Cham (Switzerland): Palgrave Macmillan., 169–203.

Swain, Merill (1985). "Communicative Competence: Some roles of Comprehensible Input and Comprehensible Output in its Development," in S. Gass & C. Madden (eds.), *Input in second language acquisition*. Rowley, MA: Newbury House, 235–253.

Van Hout, Roeland & Pieter Muysken (1994). "Modeling lexical borrowing," *Language Variation and Change* 6: 39–62.

Varga, Dražen and Orešković Dvorski, Lidija, "English Loanwords in French and Italian Daily Newspapers," *SRAZ LVI.* (2011*)*: 71–84.

Warangrut, Duangsaeng and Natthapong, Chanyoo. "Intelligibility of Thai English Restaurant Menus as Perceived by Thai and Non-Thai Speakers," *Journal of Language Teaching and Research* Vol 8, No 6. (2017): 1081–1089.

Weinreich, Uriel (1953), *Languages in Contact, Findings and Problems.* New York: Publications of the Linguistic Circle of NY.

WordReference, WordReference.com. October 2019.

Zhu, Dong Hong, Ye, Zhen Qui and Chang, Ya Ping, "Understanding the textual content of online customer reviews in B2C websites: A cross-cultural comparison between the U.S. and China," *Computers in Human Behavior*, 76. (2017): 483–493.

DANIELA FARGIONE

"vulture capital hovers over our dinner tables":
Larissa Lai, Rita Wong and
Ecological Transcultural Alliances

IN "SITES OF ARTICULATION," AN interview with Asian Canadian writer Larissa Lai, Robyn Morris affirms that Lai's fiction is the perfect arena to interrogate "racialized, sexualized and gendered borders" (Morris 2004: 21). Morris also reports that when she started publishing, mainstream Canadian culture defined her as "an outsider and from the outside, at the level of skin" (ibid.). One's appearance, Lai explains, is "loaded with all kinds of culturally and historically constructed expectations" that her writings are a reaction to. But "to react," she adds, "is to reproduce. [...] To keep stereotypes in play, critically, is the best way I can imagine to undo them." As a consequence, writing is "action situated in time," namely, "the making of a narrative mythological landscape for *people like myself*, so we have something to hang our hats on when we come into the world, a better place than Suzy Wong or Madame Butterfly to hang their hats on"[1] (ibid. 22, my italics). This process of homemaking—which involves writing, foods and odours—requires little moments of intervention capable of establishing what she calls "politics of contingency." Rather than

---

1 By "people like myself," Lai means "people who come from histories of travel and migration, people who are caught in various, often contradictory, positions in regards to the politics of race, class, gender, sexuality, the body, etc., people who are somehow marked as 'other,' as different" (Lai 2004: 171).

looking for fixed universal formulas to solve open ethical issues, Lai aims to explore new scenarios where her female characters, far from being powerful heroines, challenge a "colonialist technology-based Euro/phallocentric discourse" (ibid. 26) and offer narratives of transformation for Asian feminine subjectivities and an alternative model of diasporic community. This re-Action, however, is not a mere celebration of transgression; rather, Larissa Lai insists on the perspective of reproduction or rebirth that speculative fiction seems to grant her.

Especially after Margaret Atwood's international skyrocketing popularity—further enhanced by recent TV series and internet experimentations—this literary genre seems to have acquired more and more influence in contemporary culture, finally occupying a unique position for social critique. Nalo Hopkinson contends that "speculative fiction has reinvented itself repeatedly at the hands of the new wave, feminist, cyberpunk and queer writers" (quoted in Martín-Lucas 2014), while Patterson and Troeung recognize its wider spread among Asian diasporic writers and argue that such novelists have represented post-racial futures not as promises of neoliberal multiculturalism but rather as the result of non-normative queer politics and feminist solidarity (Patterson and Troeung 2016). To use the words of Madhu Dubey, by building on anti-realist subgenres (including science fiction, gothic, horror, ghost stories, fantasy and magic realism), speculative fictions can continue discourses of anti-racism as they "overtly situate themselves against history"[2] (Dubey 2010: 784), eventually sponsoring the imagination of multiracial coalitions.

---

2 In *Political Animals and the Body of History*, Larissa Lai wonders: "How do we diasporized types make a homespace for ourselves given all the disjunctures and discontinuities of our histories, and for that matter, the co-temporalities of some of them?" (1999: 149). Also *When Fox Is a Thousand* (1995), Lai's first novel, spins a poly-vocal narrative where the fox—the main character and a trickster—lives in the world of the dead as well as in the world of the living, can inhabit women's bodies across time, eventually becoming immortal when she turns one thousand, finally exploring the fabrication of a non-patriarchal home and the normalization of women's desires as based on what she defines "artificial history."

So, even when post-apocalyptic or dystopian in tone and atmosphere, speculative fiction is, after all, a genre of hope, and its cautionary tales foresee and eventually prevent catastrophic futures while at the same time foreshadowing future possibilities. In *Salt Fish Girl*, Larissa Lai's second novel, these materialize in alternative forms of communalism. In this sense, her speculative fiction becomes "an ideal site for experimenting with the contours of this radically contingent politics" (Lousley 2014: 152), where food, taste and odour function as driving forces. In "Future Asians," Lai explains that while writing *Salt Fish Girl*, she was "trying to think and narrate through a contemporary moment"; the novel, in fact, refracts 1990s headlines: "Dolly the sheep, maritime smuggling of Chinese migrants, Monsanto's lawsuit against a farmer whose crop picked up genetically altered DNA, the patenting of modified basmati rice by a Texas corporation, and Disney's construction of Celebration, a fully planned ur-American town" (Lai 2004: 172). All these events are yoked to past and future through myths, fairy tales, history and science fiction, eventually resulting in a hybrid corrosive narrative that features two female figures: the snake goddess Nu Wa of Chinese mythology and the transgenic human Miranda Ching, whose alternate separate stories traverse time (from pre-history to mid-twenty-first century) to finally merge in the final pages of the novel where we find out that they are indeed the same character: Miranda is the shape-shifting Nu Wa, reborn and reembodied in a different time period. These multiple fusions work as trans-feminist revisions of crystallized racial expectations and re-Orient the reader toward the acquisition of what Roy Miki calls "Asiancy" (Miki 1998): a process of racialized empowerment to act that encompasses female communal alliances and practices.

In the first pages of Lai's novel, Nu Wa is described on the banks of the Yellow River in prehistoric time during the pre-Shang dynasty: "In the beginning there was me, the river and a rotten egg smell. I don't know where the smell came from, dank and sulphurous, but there it was, the stink of beginnings and endings, not for the faint of heart" (Lai 2002: 2). Noxious smell and spoiled food pervade the book from the very first scene, where the goddess is depicted while fashioning humans by moulding mud as a mitigation to her loneliness. Half snake (or fish), half human, this well-respected goddess with a tail who is marked by doubleness and also her creation of humankind is in fact double.

According to Chinese mythology, people created by Nu Wa's hands out of yellow clay later became prosperous nobles. However, because this process was too time and energy consuming, she mass-produced the rest of mankind by dragging cords in the mud; these hybrids, instead, were the ancestors of the commoners (Lewis 1999: 202). Nu Wa's doubleness elucidates the social divide between people in China, but in Lai's novel dualities also stand for the social divide between locals and immigrants in Canada, homemade and industrial food, original creativity and artificial cloning. In the novel, when Nu Wa's irreverent creature mocks her, she splits her tail thus providing her with legs and with a wound between them. She keeps moulding her human experiments to whom she teaches how to build houses, to fish, to plant rice and cultivate riverside plants; in return, she is offered ritual food tributes such as roasted pork and steamed chickens.

Thus in the beginning, food is depicted as nourishment and Nu-Wa's teachings are the expression of care and concern for her own creatures. In her hybridization of Chinese myths with Genesis, *The Little Mermaid*, *Frankenstein* and *Blade Runner*, Nu Wa envies her own experimental creatures. She decides to become human herself and is eventually granted immortality. But with the unfolding of the story, the Asian goddess loses interest in humankind, and food ends up representing an arena of transgenic experimentation. Only at the very end does it become an expression of intergenerational solidarity and an effective form of resistance to neoliberal capitalism.

On the other hand, there is Miranda, who lives in the gated community of Serendipity (the ultra-capitalistic "paradise") from the year 2044 to 2062. Outside, there is the Unregulated Zone, a dirty and foul-smelling area later identified as Vancouver, where the Sonias—genetically identical clones made out of human biomaterial and selected freshwater carp genes—are manufactured to work for corporations such as Pallas Shoes.

But Miranda has a problem: she stinks. Her body indelibly reeks of durian, a genetically modified tropical fruit, "spiky" and "leather-hard" (14) with a very pungent odour which stands for the concepts of fertility and the resistance of nature against Serendipity's attempts to control women. Technocratic manipulation aimed at using women's bodies for various spare parts (Birns 2006: 4) calls for "the earth's revenge" (Lai 2002: 259). Although the presence of durian in British Columbia is the result of global warming and climate change—"The world has warmed up since we were young" (ibid. 209)—in Miranda's story, it becomes a mark of historical memory written on her body; more specifically, the memory of her own conception that she tags as "immaculate," considering that her mother was "a good eight years past menopause" (ibid. 15). That day, she states,

> there was a scent in the air [...] the reek of cat pee tinged with the smell of hot peppers that have not been dried and are on the verge of going off [...] something vaguely familiar in a subtropical kitchen sort of way [...] the smell of something forbidden smuggled on board in a battered suitcase, and mingled with the smell of unwashed underwear (Lai 2002: 13).

The forbidden fruit that Stewart, Miranda's father, smuggles into Serendipity from the Unregulated Zone penetrates her parents' flesh while they are having sex: the durian "tumbles between them, its green spikes biting greedily [...]" (ibid. 15) and from this moment it becomes a domineering trope in the novel.

A sort of spiky womb itself, the durian is an irregular seed containing other reproductive seeds. Largely cultivated in Southeast

Asia, it is a large evergreen tree whose pulpy, ovoid fruits have sweet edible arils used for propagation: animals are attracted by them and disperse the undigested seeds in their waste (Doijode 2009: 113). In Lai's novel, these seeds perpetuate Nu Wa's existence throughout the centuries and provide the DNA for a subversive queer trans-species community that by incorporating a sordid past can generate a hopeful future. Miranda, in fact, is one of "the new children of earth":

> Once we stepped out of mud, now we step out of moist earth, out of DNA both new and old, an imprint of what has gone before, but also a variation. By our difference we mark how ancient the alphabet of our bodies. By our strangeness we write our bodies into the future (Lai 2002: 259).

Due to its penetrating odour, the durian also epitomizes impurity, and for Miranda it becomes a stigma for racialized filth. As Robert Lee reminds us: "[...] analysis of the Oriental as a racial category must begin with the concept of the alien as a polluted body" (quoted in Lousley 153), thus perpetuating the stereotype of the immigrant as a person in need of hygiene to finally be transformed into a sanitized Other: not surprisingly, illegal migrants are forced to enter the house of Canada through "the back door" (Wong 2004: 111). Moreover, the unavoidable stink also pervades the immediate vicinity, seeping into the skin (Lai 2002: 17) of whoever is around Miranda, thus articulating a discourse on penetration. Skin, in fact, is a porous barrier: it separates an outside from an inside, but it cannot avoid mutual exchange. Cheryl Lousley contends that "both racism and disease are shown to be material-semiotic boundary constructions" (Lousley 2014: 155): when Miranda's symptoms are identified by some "medical experts" (Lai 2002: 71) as pertaining to the dreaming disease, her father pushes her to participate in a drug trial that supposedly would treat her odorous condition. "Suddenly and for the first time," Miranda says, "I felt dirty" (ibid).

But suddenly we also associate Miranda's condition with the food cycle that Stewart mentions in the very first pages of the book, when he resentfully regrets the moment he smuggled the evil fruit from the Unregulated Zone. Genetic manipulation and industrial modification have made the food risky to eat:

> I should have never bought you that evil fruit [...] Only barbarians eat those kinds of things. You know if it doesn't have a Saturna sticker it isn't safe. Everything has been affected by these modified pollens. If it grows wild in the Unregulated Zone you have no idea what kinds of mutations have occurred (Lai 2002: 32).

Larissa Lai's emphasis on the materiality of human and non-human relations is further articulated along the lines of the racist exclusion that Miranda experiences at school. The physical distance from the other children reflects the ostracism that immigrant kids are often subjected to. Repulsive odours are associated with unfamiliar foods that mark the alien, exotic origin of the child who eats them instead of the more popular peanut butter and jelly. Lai problematizes Miranda's case by imposing a double marginalization and vulnerability: not only is she the only Asian girl in her class but she also has a cat odour that pins her down to the equation of non-human "animality" (or even "ferality") to which moral categories are attached. The other children call her "Kitty Litter" and "Pissy Pussy," clearly evoking female genitalia and sexual exploitation, a condition that reminds us of Oryx, the young Asian girl depicted in Margaret Atwood's *Oryx and Crake* (2003), the post-apocalyptic story of a near future where biotechnology triumphs and base capitalist appetites result in genetically engineered hybrid critter.

Stephanie Oliver suggests that Larissa Lai innovatively uses smell and food as indicators of "politics of representation, regimes of racialization, the power of the gaze, and the dynamics of visibility and invisibility that are key to processes of social marginalization" in the diasporic experience (Oliver 2011: 208). By doing so, Larissa

Lai repeatedly criticizes the implicit celebration of post-racial discourses on Canada's neoliberal multiculturalism, a formula that "celebrates diversity while distracting from racial prejudices that help maintain income inequality and immigrant vulnerability" (Patterson and Troeung 2016: 77).

In order to elude "the postcolonial exotic" (Huggan 2002) and amend the exoticization of Asian diaspora that both capitalism and Canada's official multiculturalism support, *Salt Fish Girl* implements a strategy of storytelling hybridization that develops a non-linear lesbian genealogy and a female communality: a commitment, in other words, to democratic politics and future possibilities. This takes place through Miranda's alliance with the cyborg Sonias, the product of the Diverse Genome Project, focused on "the peoples of the so-called Third World, Aboriginal peoples, and peoples in danger of extinction" (Lai 2002: 160). They form a homogenized class of exploited "workers": "brown eyes and black hair, every single one" (ibid.).

By investing in these labourers (mostly illegal immigrants), corporations can easily bypass wage regulations and nurture transnational capitalism, but some of them are lucky enough to escape and establish some sort of enlarged family community based on solidarity and queer reproduction. This is an alternative that, again, relies on durians. These genetically modified fruits are in fact integrated into their sex acts to guarantee procreation without heterosexual copulation. Among these representatives of Dr. Flower's "patented new fucking life form" (158), Evie Xin—the perfect product of bioengineering and the Salt Fish Girl of the title—becomes "a primal creation, a new Eve" (Birns 2016: 7) that assumes different forms according to the different times in history. Besides, her fishy odour marks her as a feminized and exploitable commodity, another exotic Oryx ready to satisfy male illicit desires. And yet her smell of salty fish also symbolizes same-sex desire that indeed "erupts through the olfactory sense" (Paul Lai 2008: 171).

Evie, a reincarnation of the past salt fish girl to whom Nu Wa was once attracted, is recognized by Miranda by "a whiff of a familiar fragrance, briny and sweet" (Lai 2002: 104) that reconnects her to the past. "I'm not human…I'm a new life form" (ibid. 158), she states of herself, thus incarnating Donna Haraway's concept of "companion species." This figure, which substitutes the cyborg used in Haraway's first *Manifesto* (1985) to interrogate biotechnology and illustrate natural and cultural intertwinings, blurs the boundaries between the human and the nonhuman. Quite interestingly, also the philosopher's expression is associated with food: "companion," in fact, comes from the Latin *cum panis*, "with bread" (Haraway 2003: 100): Evie's genetic hybridity eventually guarantees that the human and the nonhuman do sit at the same table of life.

Living "at the west entrance of a haunted house called Canada" (Wong 2003/4: 109), Rita Wong shares with Larissa Lai the same ecological concerns—what she calls "my recurrent obsessions" (Wong 2008)—both as a poet and an activist.[3] Weaving together environmental and social justice, labour, decolonization and gender issues, Wong's poetry is the result of an observation of those *things* that fall through the net of everyday life and are inextricably woven into our existence. One example, she claims in an interview, is pollution: "an experience and concept that is not merely something out there (smog, huge amounts of plastic trash floating in the ocean) but also something that is *inside* each and every one of us, human and nonhuman, spread by our shared experience of air, water and food" (Aurelea 2011, italics in the text).

In *forage*, a collection of poems published in 2007 and recipient of the Canada Reads Poetry award, Wong engages with the challenge of making Asian Canadian literature a creative site to build transcultural alliances as an ecological re-Action to current depredatory capitalistic systems where food plays a special role.

3 Rita Wong's adamant commitment to the defense of environmental and social justice brought her to jail last August 2019. Her 28 days incarceration was the consequence of her participation to a pacific protest against a pipeline expansion on behalf of missing and murdered Indigenous women. More details at the following link: <https://pencanada.ca/news/vancouver-poet-rita-wong-incarcerated-for-4-weeks-for-peaceful-anti-pipeline-protest/> (Last accessed May 10, 2020).

With its deep symbolism and its trans-corporeal power, food has always functioned as a fundamental link between the human body and the environment, but it was only in the late 1970s that scholars from all over the world started to analyze the multiple relations of agro-industrial systems, unhealthy practices (monocultures, the use of pesticides, unsustainable agricultural policies, transgenic food, biotechnologies, etc.) and their effects on wellbeing. Since then, the profusion of books, fiction, documentaries and films on the subject has revealed the links between the production of food and environmental damage. Wong can certainly be included in this scholarly network, but in her poetry she further problematizes this "toxic discourse" (Buell 1998) by focusing on particularly vulnerable individuals of Chinese and Indigenous origins.

According to Roy Miki, Wong's poetry builds upon a "poetics of the apprehensive" (Miki 2011), which evokes the same sense of "doubleness" that we have seen in Larissa Lai's *Salt Fish Girl*. Her double concern rests on a personal disquiet and on the ability to grasp the essence of a situation:

> [...] a binary zone in which the nervous condition arising from insecurities that exceed control and threaten the well-being of the body exists alongside the vital capacity in the human organism to manage its conditions, including those conditions that might otherwise overwhelm its will to exist (Miki 2011: 184).

Wong's sense of anxiety that emerges from her observations of the material world and of its tangled coexistence with humans is often mitigated by a suffused sense of trust in new relational configurations of human beings with objects (Zantingh 2013) and with Indigenous people (women in particular) as an ethical practice to imagine possible futures of collective participation (Wong 2009). While Miki's reading of Wong's poetry builds upon a "poetics of the apprehensive," Christine Kim's analysis based on a "poetics of social justice" (Kim 2007) seems to be a perfect integration with it: capitalism, globalization and multiple articulations of current colonialism are exposed here in their violent forms as the result of national power systems: Wong's poetry, Kim argues, "explicitly work[s] to further a larger political project of decolonizing language and promoting social equality" (Kim 2009: 166). The exploitation of human and nonhuman forms—people, animals, the environment, objects—for profit is particularly visible in her food poems, starting with "the girl who ate rice almost every day."

The poem, which has a distinctive layout on the page, is divided into two vertical columns, each of which hosts a specific narrative. On the left, Wong's prose poem is a retelling of Little Red Riding Hood in the tradition of Angela Carter's and Marianne Moore's feminist re-readings.[4] In Wong's rewriting of Perrault's fairy-tale, however, Little Red Riding Hood's real name is "slow" and her journey through the forest does not contemplate her grandmother's food supply but rather the purchase of brown rice. Once at the supermarket, slow is appalled by the plumpness of the beets she finds there: "what big beets you have [...] all the better to tempt you with my dear, he [the manager of the supermarket] replied" (Wong 2007: 16). The beets' size makes her wonder whether these beets have been crossed with cabbages: "not cabbages, but cows, replied the manager, with a drosophilic glint in his melanophore eyes" (ibid.).

As for most of Wong's food poems, genetically modified food is under scrutiny here as its poisonous effects are not limited to those who eat it but to the whole food cycle. The entanglements between the human and the nonhuman is well expressed by the "drosophilic glint" that slow catches in the eyes of her personal "wolf." Drosophila, also known as "the small fruit fly," is an insect normally found around very ripe or rotten fruit: its image thus evokes a sense of impending death which is reiterated in

---

4 Cf. Angela Carter's *The Bloody Chamber* (1979) and Anne Sexton, *Transformations* (1971).

the following two paragraphs: she realizes that eating those beets would be tantamount to becoming an extinct animal herself, while "the oysters in the chiu chow congee yielded a small, imperfect pearl on her tongue" (Wong 2007, 17). According to a Chinese death ritual, a pearl is placed in the deceased's mouth to protect the dead's passage to the other world: a condition that the Chinese goddess Nu Wa in Larissa Lai's *Salt Fish Girl* experiences when she is transformed into a human creature and her body starts to be split in two: "The pearl will keep you alive forever [...] but you will never be without pain" (Lai 2002: 8).

Both Wong and Lai restate the need to yoke the past to the future in an effort to build new female alliances, to deceive their famished wolves and dismantle their supposed naïveté. Also consumers, Wong seems to suggest, should prove to be more informed when buying food from unscrupulous wolves. Not by surprise, Yeo insists that in less traditional funerals, pearls are substituted with a grain of rice to make sure that the dead person's stomach, before she embarks on her journey, is full and not hungry (Yeo 2019). Eventually, slow realizes that "she had been eating imported rice from china (white) and the united states of amnesia (brown) for most of her life" (Wong 2007, 18), and so decides to grow her own food in the sewers of her city, i.e. Vancouver.

The right column of the poem, written in italics and in scientific language, complicates Wong's toxic discourse and anti-GMO resistance by asking her readers to gain more awareness. By logging on the US government database, in fact, they can find the exact number—"current as of January 2007" (16)—of patented food "invention[s]" exposed in the very language of capitalistic corporations and thus underlining the insurmountable differences of the two narratives.

Two more poems, "nervous organism" and "canola queasy," illustrate how neoliberalism hovers like a haunting figure over our tables. In an interview, Rita Wong explains that *forage*—the title of her collection—"refers to the process of looking for what one needs to survive for the long term—be that food, philosophy, information, values ..." (Aurelea 2011). Information, however, can be tricky: wrong or excessive news, in fact, may be as harmful as no information at all, so much that during our current global health emergency of Covid-19, one neologism, "infodemia", has entered our vocabulary to refer to the parallel information pandemic, i.e. a huge amount of unchecked and unmonitored news rapidly spreading among people, mostly through non official channels (Grandi and Piovan 2020). Readers might easily apply defensive strategies to avoid this contagion, such as double-checking sources and finding official proof of truth. "nervous organism" displays a whole variety of food information—mainly of transgenic food—that are here listed by using a formal strategy reminding us of Walt Whitman's poetry: the catalogue.

The density of the text, which builds on a long list of risks and threats that we are exposed to, is presented in a non-stop flow of words that amplifies the gamut of possibilities: "jellyfish potato/ jellypo fishtato/ glow in the pork toys [...]" (Wong 2007: 20). Moreover, by leveraging on anxiety, the ideal readers are here positioned as (unacceptably) unaware consumers who need a wake-up call and are eventually encouraged to be more careful in their shopping behaviour. The typographical structure of the poem contributes to the visualization of this "whack": a rectangular bordered block of words vaguely reminiscent of a food label, the "Nutritional Facts" table that appears on the commercialized products with the list of ingredients. However, what we do not see listed here is of course what really matters. To say it in the words of Michael Mikulak: "What for most of human history was quite evident is now often inscrutable [...] who can fathom the mystery of the immortal Twinkie?" (Mikulak 2013: 3).

Also "canola queasy," a poignant prose poem first published in a slightly different form in *The Massachusetts Review* in 2004, delves into inscrutability: global agricultural food systems, origins, modes of production; economic, human, and ecological costs—everything is a mystery, especially the "twenty-year monopoly culled the patent regime" (3–4) while asking "how to converse with the wilfully profitable stuck in their monetary monologue" (7–8), namely an agriculture system built on mono-cropping or monoculture that starting from World War II has become standardized in the West. What's more, its capability to silently penetrate our lives also exposes the way neoliberalism has invaded both our food and our bodies. In *Biopiracy*, Vandana Shiva claims that "the seed and women's bodies as sites of regenerative power are, in the eyes of capitalist patriarchy, among the last colonies (Shiva 1997: 45) and highlights the social costs of big agribusiness's investment in monocultures, particularly the patenting of genetically modified organisms: the ownership of life forms makes farmers vulnerable and represents a serious threat to indigenous cultures who are subject to that "slow violence" that Rob Nixon exhibited in his ground-breaking volume. Not by chance, "canola queasy" is dedicated to Percy Schmeister, the Canadian farmer sued by Monsanto because genetically engineered canola seeds blew into his fields.

In conclusion, a few words about the frame written by hand and surrounding Wong's poems. "nervous organism" is bordered by a quotation from Canadian critic Northrop Frye, while "canola queasy" by a quotation from biologist and critic of GMOs, Mae-Wan Ho. In this way, Wong connects her poem and her poetic reaction to a lineage of anti-racist protest in North America. This embedded intertextuality is another attempt at providing transnational alliances and ties of kinship. Quoting indigenous Canadian poet Kateri Akiwenzie-Damm, Wong reminds us of the need to construct an eco-cosmopolitan ethic where diasporic subjects are involved in a process of fertile composting: "we find meaning and purpose as human beings, as anishnaabek, as people of good intentions, in connectedness, in community. we are supported and sustained within a web of relationships. and it begins with the land" (Wong 2009).

Works Cited

Aurelea, 2011, "Rita Wong. In Dialogue," <https://capliterature. wordpress.com/2011/04/02/rita-wong-in-dialogue/> (Last accessed: May 10, 2020).

Birns, Nicholas, "'The Earth's Revenge': Nature, Diaspora and Transfeminism in Larissa Lai's *Salt Fish Girl*" *ACRAWSA* (Australian Critical Race and Whiteness Studies Association), 2 (2006): 1–15.

Buell, Lawrence, "Toxic Discourse" *Critical Inquiry* 24.3 (1998): 639–665.

Doijode, S.D., (2009), *Seed Storage of Horticultural Crops*. Boca Raton, London, New York CRC Press.

Dubey, Madhu, "Speculative Fictions of Slavery." *American Literature.* 82.4 (2010): 779–805.

Grandi and Piovan, *Micromega* 26 March 2020, <http://temi.repubblica. it/micromega-online/i-pericoli-dell%E2%80%99infodemia-la-comunicazione-ai-tempi-del-coronavirus/>

Haraway, Donna, (2003), *The Companion Species Manifesto: Dogs, People, and Significant Otherness.* Chicago, IL: Prickly Paradigm Press.

Huggan, Graham, (2002), *The Postcolonial Exotic. Marketing the Margins*. New York and London: Routledge.

Kim, Christine, "Rita Wong's *monkeypuzzle* and the Poetics of Social Justice." *SCL* 32.3 (2007): 59–74.

Kim, Christine, "Resuscitations in Rita Wong's *forage*: Globalization, Ecologies and Value Chains," *Open Letter* 13.9 (2009): 166–73.

Lai, Larissa, "Political Animals and the Body of History," *Canadian Literature* No. 163, Winter 1999.

Lai, Larissa, (2002), *Salt Fish Girl*. Toronto: Thomas Allen Publishers.

Lai, Larissa, "Future Asians: Migrant Speculations, Repressed History & Cyborg Hope," *Larissa Lai. West Coast Line* No. 38 (Special Issue on Larissa Lai), 2004: 168–175.

Lai, Paul, "Stinky Bodies: Mythological Futures and the Olfactory Sense in Larissa Lai's *Salt Fish Girl*," *MELUS*, 33: 4, Alien/Asian (Winter, 2008): 167–187.

Lewis, Mark Edward, (1999), *Writing and Authority in Early China*. New York: State University of New York Press.

Lousley, Cheryl, (2014), "Ecocriticism in the Unregulated Zone" in S. Kamboureli and C. Verduyn (eds.), *Critical Collaborations: Indigeneity, Diaspora, and Ecology in Canadian Literary Studies*. Waterloo: Wilfrid Laurier University Press, 141–160.

Martín-Lucas, Belén, (2014), "Dystopic Urbanities. Civilian Cyborgs in TransCanadian Speculative Fictions" in A.M. Fraile-Marcos (ed.), *Literature and the Glocal City: Reshaping the English Canadian Imaginary*. New York, London: Routledge, 69–78.

Miki, Roy, (1998), *Broken Entries: Race, Subjectivity, Writing*, Toronto: Mercury Press.

Miki, Roy, (2011), "Are You Restless Too? Not to Worry, So is Rita Wong: Towards a Poetics of the Apprehensive," in Kamboureli S. (ed.), *In Flux: Transnational Shifts in Asian Canadian Writing*, Edmonton: NeWest, 177–205.

Mikulak, Michael, (2013), *The Politics of the Pantry. Stories, Food, and Social Change*. Montreal: McGill-Queen's University Press.

Morris, Robyn L., "'sites of articulation'—an interview with Larissa Lai," *West Coast Line*, Fall 2004, 38, 2: 21–30.

Nixon, Rob, 2011, *Slow Violence and the Environmentalism of the Poor*. Cambridge, MA: Harvard University Press.

Oliver, Stephanie, "Diffuse Connections: Smell and Diasporic Subjectivity in Larissa Lai's *Salt Fish Girl*," *Canadian Literature* 208, (Spring 2011): 85–107.

Patterson, Christopher B. and Y-Dang Troeung, "The Psyche of Neoliberal Multiculturalism: Queering Memory and Reproduction in Larissa Lai's *Salt Fish Girl* and Chang-rae Lee's *On Such a Full Sea*", *Concentric: Literary and Cultural Studies* 42.1, (March 2016): 73-98.

Shiva, Vandana, (1997), *Biopiracy. The Plunder of Nature and Knowledge*. Boston: South End Press.

Wong, Rita, (1998), *monkeypuzzle*. Vancouver: Press Gang Publishers.

Wong, Rita, "Troubling Domestic Limits: Reading Border Fictions Alongside Larissa Lai's Salt Fish Girl", *BC STUDIES*, 140. (Winter 2003/04):109–124.

Wong, Rita, (2007), *forage*. Gibson, BC: Nightwood Editions.

Wong, Rita, (2008), "12 or 20 questions: with Rita Wong", 5 January 2008. http://12or20questions.blogspot.com/2008/01/12-or-20-questions-with-rita-wong.html (Last accessed, 10 May 2020).

Wong, Rita, (2009), "seeds, streams, see/pages," *Open Letter* 13.9: 21–27.

Yeo, Teresa Rebecca, "Chinese death rituals", *Singapore Infopedia*, 2019, <https://eresources.nlb.gov.sg/infopedia/articles/SIP_2015-11-30_175737.html#:~:text=A%20pearl%2C%20believed%20to%20have,placed%20in%20the%20left%20hand>   (Last accessed 9 May 2020).

Zantingh, Matthew, "When Things Act Up: Thing Theory, Actor-Network Theory and Toxic Discourse in Rita Wong's Poetry". *ISLE* 3 (Summer 2013): 622–646.

SIMONA STANO

Eating almost the Same Thing: Japanese Cuisine in Canada[1]

Les animaux se repaissent,
l'homme mange,
l'homme d'esprit seul sait manger
—Jean-Anthelme Brillat-Savarin

1. Eating almost the same thing: translation, language and food

"Every sensible and rigorous theory of language shows that a perfect translation is an impossible dream" (Eco 2001: ix). With these words, in his introduction to *Experiences in Translation*, Umberto Eco alludes to the impossibility of existence of *equivalence* in meaning, describing translation as an operation consisting in "saying *almost* the same thing," namely a form of *similarity* in meaning. The Italian semiotician conceives translation as a special case of interpretation, thus insisting on the fact that it does not simply concern a comparison between two languages, but rather the interpretation of two texts in two different languages, that is

1 This project received funding from the European Union's Horizon 2020 research and innovation programme under the Marie Sklodowska-Curie grant agreement No. 795025. It reflects only the author's view, and the Research Executive Agency is not responsible for any use that may be made of the information it contains.

to say, a "negotiation" or "act of communication" (Nergaard 1995) between two cultures.

Although specifically referred to verbal language, Eco's reflections are also crucial to the understanding of the processes of translation of other codes—including food. As we illustrated in Stano 2015a and 2015b, in fact, food can be considered a "language" through and through. Just like language, food preferences and taboos, by revealing our taste, allow us to express our values, beliefs, morals, etc.—that is to say, our "cultural identity." Moreover, food is a powerful means of communication with other people, and in this sense it represents perhaps the most immediate way by which we can come into contact with other cultures:

> In order to be meaningful, every food system should be "ours" and not "theirs": we cook and eat this way, at this time, in this order, with these ingredients and without those others—because this is the polite way, the right recipe, and because this food is tasty, while others are disgusting. These oppositions can exist within one society—for instance underlining class, age, or clan distinctions. Or they can mark the boundaries between different societies, different structured layers (for instance, religious) of a society, and different cultures (Volli 2015: xiv).

Such a plurality of "languages" inevitably entails a process of translation: what happens when different food systems, or "foodspheres" (Stano 2015b), bump into each other? How does the passage of elements across such spheres take place? Evidently, the idea of a perfect translation is an impossible dream in this case too. Rather, an attempt to "eat almost the same thing" can be made.

Drawing on these considerations, the following paragraphs aim to explore how translation takes place in the food realm and with what effects of meaning, combining the observation of relevant case studies[2] with more theoretical reflections.

2. Canada: multiculturalism and food hybridization

Migrations, travel and communications incessantly expose local food identities to food alterities, activating processes of transformation that continuously reshape and redefine such identities and alterities with major consequences. In this sense, Canada is particularly relevant: since 2001, immigration has evidently increased and it still represents the main driver of the country's population growth, with an increase of 321,065 new immigrants in 2018 (Statistics Canada 2018). This entails great diversity and multiculturalism, with relevant effects on the gastronomic level. In fact, Canada has been said to have "a cuisine of cuisines" (Clark in Pandi 2008), with hybridization being elected as its main peculiarity. This is particularly evident in Toronto, the city with the highest proportion of immigrants (46.1% of the total population according to the 2016 census) in Ontario, which in turn is the Canadian province with the biggest immigrated population (29% of the total population, compared with 28% in British Columbia, 21% in Alberta and 14% in Quebec). With over 70 ethnic groups from the Pacific Rim, Asia, the Middle East, Britain and the Mediterranean, the city represents Canada's gastronomic and cultural hub, whose cuisine ranges from classic European fare to Latin American, from Asian to Caribbean flavours, and so on and so forth.

Within such a varied "melting pot," Japanese cuisine is of particular interest. Although having changed considerably over time, as a result of processes of translation and "fusion," hybridizing with

---

2 More specifically, we draw on an ethno-semiotic research carried out in 2013 in Toronto, Canada, whose main results were published in Stano 2015b and 2016. Relevant findings are used here, further discussing and elaborating them in view of the paper's objectives.

elements typical of other culinary cultures, it is considered one of the most "traditional"[3] cuisines of the world. The Japanese have a specific term, *washoku*, to refer to their traditional dietary cultures, in opposition to *yōshoku* (literally "Western food"), which spread in the country after the end of its isolationist foreign policy known as *sakoku*. Added to the UNESCO World Heritage List in December 2013, washoku is celebrated worldwide for its centuries-old cooking techniques and recipes. And even before the United Nations' acknowledgement, the intention to "protect" Japan's traditional cuisine brought to the establishment of a government-supported seal of "authenticity" for Japanese restaurants abroad.

Washoku is very rich in variety, both in terms of ingredients and culinary techniques. The usual format of its meals is known as *ichijū-sansai* ("one soup, three sides"): a bowl of soup (*ju*) containing vegetables or tofu, a bowl of plain steamed rice, a small plate of *konomono* (pickled seasonal vegetables), and *sai* (fish, tofu, meat or vegetables). Often overlooking such a variety, most Japanese restaurants abroad offer menus basically centred on sushi—which is certainly emblematic of the Japanese foodsphere but is not its only constituent. Despite its consistent Japanese community, gastronomic services in Toronto have also mainly served sushi to their customers, at least until the last decade: while Vancouver, being on the Pacific Rim, opened up to other specialties (such as *ramen*, *soba*, *udon*, *yakitori*, *tonkatsu*, *okonomiyaki*, etc.) before, "Toronto wasn't ready" (Matsumoto in Mintz 2020). Sushi is therefore crucial to the understanding of the processes of translation of the Japanese culinary code and the effects of meaning deriving from them. Based on this consideration, the following paragraphs provide a semiotic analysis of "traditional" sushi, then taking into consideration some emblematic cases of "translation" served in Toronto.

---

3 Although mainly referred to an "original" and crystallized status, "tradition" is a dynamic process involving continuous transformations and changes—in a sense, a series of "translations" which unceasingly redefine it (cf. Hobsbawm & Ranger 1983; Marrone 2016; Stano 2014, 2015b).

2.1. Traditional sushi

There is no evidence of the actual origins of sushi, but it is thought that it was introduced in Japan in the ninth century (Mouritsen 2009: 15). Originally, it represented a culinary technique for long-term preservation, namely a process of fermentation of fish stimulated by wrapping it in soured fermenting rice, so that the fermenting rice and fish resulted in a sour taste—which explains the name *sushi*, literally meaning "sour-tasting". Traditionally, when the fermented fish was taken out of the rice, only the former was eaten, while the latter was discarded (Itou *et al.* 2006). The reduction—almost elimination—of such a process of fermentation[4] (cf. Zschock 2005) and the new techniques of preparation and practices of consumption of sushi have profoundly changed it, leading to a great variety of fillings, toppings, condiments and shapes.

Building on existing literature describing the main varieties of sushi,[5] we introduced their semiotic analysis in Stano 2015b. On the level of *configuration* (cf. Greimas 1973), we classified the main components of sushi into humid ingredients (fresh vegetables, such as avocado, cucumber or carrots, raw or cooked fish, roe and condiments) *vs.* dry elements (dehydrated *nori*, dried seeds), with rice occupying an intermediate position between these two poles. In fact, the liquids (water and soy vinegar) used during the process of boiling permeate the previously dried grains (i.e. "natural"

---

4 Long fermentation still characterizes a few forms of sushi, which are not very common. An example is *narezushi*, in which skinned and gutted fish are stuffed with salt, placed in a wooden container, immersed in salt again and finally weighed down with a heavy pickling stone. After six months, during which the water seeping out should be constantly removed, the sushi may be eaten, remaining edible for another six months or more.

5 See in particular Detrick 1981; Hosking 1995; Ashkenazi and Jacob 2000; Barber 2002; Dekura, Treloar and Yoshii 2004; Lowry 2005; Mouritsen 2009; Zschock 2005; a synthesis can be found in Stano 2015b.

rice,[6] in Lévi-Strauss's 1964 terms), thus making "culturalized" rice move toward the humid end of the spectrum. On the other hand, the particular practices of preparation of sushi rice and the use of sugar and salt ensure a certain degree of cohesion among the cooked grains, which are not used and eaten separately but pressed together to form wider units, where they tend not to be clearly discernible nor too easily separable from each other. Therefore, from a semantic point of view, the grains of rice lose importance *per se*, moving the focus of attention to the solidity of the whole piece they become part of—which, compared to the fish and other ingredients such as fresh vegetables or roe, cannot be considered humid but should be rather placed on the continuum between the two poles. Furthermore, "culturalized" rice shares another important characteristic with one of the main dry ingredients of sushi: nori. While the latter allows consumers to hold makizushi between chopsticks (or temaki between their fingers), preventing their breakage or decomposition (*functional* level), the former has the same function in nigirizushi, whose rice grains are glued to each other because of sugar and other substances used in or resulting from the process of boiling (e.g. the starch, partially eliminated by the common practice of washing rice before cooking it, yet still present), thus forming small compact pieces that diners may pick up using chopsticks or their own hands.

Moreover, as regards the structure of sushi, we identified other crucial factors that make it possible to distinguish its ingredients: *external* elements *wrap* the *internal* ones, which are on the contrary *wrapped* by the outer ones. In relation to such oppositions (wrapping *vs.* wrapped and outside *vs.* inside), the components of

---

6 Both rice and nori are already "culturalized" at the beginning of the sushi preparation process, since they are dried. Moreover, it should not be forgotten that even the slightest intervention of man on any substance forces it to abandon the pole of Nature and move toward that of Culture. Here we use the adjective "natural" to strengthen the opposition between these ingredients and the results of their elaboration by cooks during the sushi preparation process.

sushi are characterized by interchangeability, since the same element could correspond either to one pole or another depending on the type of sushi. In the case of futomaki, hosomaki or temaki for instance, nori is the external element wrapping both rice—in an intermediate position, at the same time wrapped (by nori) and the wrapping (of fresh vegetables and fish)—and other ingredients placed at the centre of sushi. On the other hand, in uramaki, nori finds itself in an intermediate position, with fish and vegetables on the inside—wrapped by it—and rice on the outside—the wrapping of it. A second layer of seeds or roe then reinforces this wrapping structure, enclosing the whole piece. The only element that never changes its position or function despite the different configurations of sushi is its centre, made of raw fish and fresh vegetables.

This fact has major implications on the previously analyzed oppositions: dry *vs.* humid, on the one hand; and nature *vs.* culture, on the other. In maki, such contrasts are characterized by *gradualness*: while in futomaki, hosomaki and temaki, the "culturalized" rice mediates between the humidness of raw fish and fresh vegetables on the inside and the dryness of the seaweed on the outside, in the more elaborate structure of uramaki, the intermediation element becomes the "culturalized" nori, which, once put between the fish/vegetables and the cooked—and therefore partially humid—rice, absorbs part of their water, abandoning its dry nature to draw closer to humidness. The same gradualness characterizes the passage from nature to culture: given that even the most simple and slight intervention of man on any ingredient—be it the result of such process either raw or cooked—draws it away from the first pole only to move towards the second one, as it implies a certain degree of elaboration, we should ascribe the elements composing sushi to different positions on the continuum between these two extremes (for more details, cf. Stano 2015b). It is remarkable that in all the main types of traditional sushi, the elements closest to the pole of nature are placed either at the centre (raw fish and fresh vegetables) or on the outside (roe, seeds, or "natural" nori), with rice (the preparation practice of which places it in terms of proximity towards the "rotten" rather than to the "cooked," according to Lévi-Strauss's terminology) mediating their opposition. Finally, nori can occupy various positions: while appearing closer to the unelaborate when wrapping sushi from the outside, the seaweed draws closer to culture in uramaki, where its further "culturalization" makes it occupy a position similar to that of rice, to which it is also contiguous.

The configuration of sushi therefore seems to emphasize the importance of the so-called *tsutsumi* or "wrapping principle," which is central to the Japanese semiosphere and characterizes various spheres, from the presentation of gifts to the corporeal and temporal dimension, from the organization of space to the presentation of the self and the use of language (Hendry 1993). Definitely, sushi can be conceived as the prototype (Eco 1997) of all "wrapping objects": although its configuration changes when considering different typologies, its structure always implies more layers, with an *oku* ("centre" or "heart") representing its unchanging element. Moreover, the highlighted gradualness characterizing sushi stresses the importance of the centre, making its contrasts with the external layer—somehow "permeable" and "crossable" according to a precise order.

Such an order is even more important where *taste* is concerned: not only does the heart of the sushi host its most "natural" ingredients, but it always represents its most savoury part. This is true both in the cases of complete wrapping, as in the previously mentioned examples, and when it is partial, such as in nigirizushi or oshizushi. Notwithstanding the structural differences between these types of sushi, on the one hand, and "sushi rolls," on the other, the centre still remains its most flavoursome part and the one most difficult to access. In fact, in the case of hosomaki, futomaki, temaki and uramaki, the tastiest ingredients correspond to the raw fish and the vegetables (which are located at the centre), since wasabi—which is tastier than them—is not put into the plate itself, but can be added later by diners themselves. By contrast, in nigirizushi and oshizushi, the most savoury element—wasabi—is not visible, but is generally concealed between the different layers, in a hidden centre that reveals itself only at a later time, when it comes into contact with the tongue.

2.2. "Translated" sushi: Shinobu and Guu Izakaya in Toronto

What happens to the traditional configurations of sushi and the effects of meaning resulting from them when such a food is prepared and consumed in a different foodsphere? We intend to answer this question by comparing two relevant case studies analysed in Toronto from February to August 2013: a restaurant where the "traces" left by translation processes seem to be concealed as much as possible, resulting in one of those places usually referred to as "traditional" Japanese restaurants; and a restaurant where the translation processes are instead explicitly shown, enhancing the relationship with the context in which it is inserted.

2.2.1 Guu Izakaya

First established in Vancouver in 1993, Guu Izakaya opened a new restaurant in Toronto in 2009. Named after the common Japanese place for after-work drinking (where sake is served together with other drinks and foods), it aims to combine tradition with modernity, and washoku with local tastes. Probably because of its origin, as mentioned above, it overthrows the common predominance of sushi in Japanese restaurants abroad in favour of mainly cooked courses including meat, fish, soups, noodles and various rice-based plates. Nonetheless, different options are generally present on the menu of the day, including interesting forms of "fusion" with the local foodsphere.

Figure 1. Plates served at Guu Izakaya (from top left to bottom right: *Karaage Roll, Chirashi Don, Unagi Chirashi Udon, Karubi Don*).

In the so-called *Karaage Roll*, for instance, an external layer of rice (partially sprinkled with a few sesame seeds) encloses a strip of nori, in turn wrapping a heart of lettuce and *karaage*[7] chicken. The adaptation to local tastes is evident not only in the ingredients used—which nonetheless are assembled maintaining a certain degree of gradualness with respect to both the nature/culture and dry/humid oppositions described above—but also in the seasoning accompanying the course: mayonnaise. The presence of lemon, generally included only in *chirashi*, further enhances this aspect, recalling the common local habit of squeezing it onto fried meat or fish. The processes of "translation" are therefore exalted in this case, reflected by the position of the six rolls, allowing eaters to clearly identify the ingredients used.

---

7 *Karaage* consists in deep-frying chicken or other types of meat or fish in oil after marinating them in a mix of soy sauce, garlic and ginger, and coating them with a seasoned wheat flour of potato starch mix.

No other variety of maki or nigiri was encountered during the period of observation, but various versions of chirashizushi and donburi were present. *Chirashi Don*, presented as "special assorted sashimi on sushi rice," is generally served in a white ceramic bowl with a white ceramic spoon, and a small dish with two separate sections for soy sauce and wasabi. The first remarkable aspect concerns the denomination of the plate. Donburi (literally "bowl"), frequently abbreviated to *don*, consists of a dish including fish, meat, vegetables and other ingredients served over rice. More specifically, *kaisendon* is a bowl comprising thinly sliced sashimi on rice. One of the main differences distinguishing kaisendon from chirashizushi concerns the rice: while the former is made with plain steamed rice, the latter contains sushi rice. The denomination of the plate served at Guu Izakaya therefore reveals a sort of paradox, since its description makes the presence of sushi rice clear, therefore using the word *don* to reference only the container in which the food is served (which is itself generally referred to as a donburi). As regards the food-material, in this case fish, the variety is reduced to some slices of salmon, seabass, tuna and salmon roe. Vegetables include cucumber, white cabbage and ornamental chives. With respect to the structural configuration of the dish, it should be remarked that seaweed is not placed between the rice and the fish, as is usual in washoku, but rather sprinkled in very thin strips all over the plate, breaking the above-described "wrapping structure" and generating an effect of visual "disorder," making the course resemble a salad. Furthermore, wasabi is not included in the dish (as usual) but is placed in a different container, while *gari* (ginger), which generally accompanies this dish, is totally absent.

Unagi Chirashi Udon consists in "grilled eel and simmered salmon on rice." On the one hand, it recalls a very common Japanese course, *unadon* (sometimes spelled *unagidon*): a donburi dish with sliced eel served on rice. On the other hand, the inclusion of salmon—which is widely consumed within the local foodsphere—introduces an element of novelty, adapting it to the local taste. The chromatic and structural configuration of the plate further enhances this aspect, making it look like a salad, just like in the previously described case. Furthermore, wasabi and soy sauce are in this case substituted by thinly sliced celery, crumbled white onions and candied ginger, marking a further detachment from the Japanese "tradition."

Adaptation to local tastes also characterizes the *Karubi Don*, described as "Japanese Style BBQ Beef Ribs on Rice," where meat substitutes fish, also introducing another innovation: the use of barbecue sauce, very common in Canada. Moreover, green salad is added to the plate, preventing people from seeing the rice and thus making the plate *seem* what it *is not* (in Greimasian words, giving the *illusion/lie* of a meat course lying on salad). The three vegetables (sliced carrots, cucumber and cabbage) accompanying the dish further enhance its adaptation to the local foodsphere. Finally, as regards to the denomination of the plate, it should be noticed that the word "chirashi" disappears: this is the case of a proper donburi, including cooked meat on plain steamed rice, although altered to suit local tastes.

2.2.2. Shinobu

Shinobu presents itself as an "Authentic Japanese Restaurant," paying particular attention to the preparation and design of plates, which are cooked and served exclusively by its Japanese staff.

With respect to the supply of sushi, in addition to the most common nigiri, diners can find different types of maki (referred to as "sushi rolls" on the menu), which generally introduce remarkable variations. *California rolls*, although keeping the same denomination of the common American adaptation of Japanese maki—where avocado is used instead of or together with raw fish, especially salmon—are subject to changes in relation to the food material, including avocado, cucumber, or fish cake at their centre, as well as an external layer of tobiko wrapping them. More evident changes

Figure 2. Plates served at Shinobu (*Volcano Rainbow rolls* and—bottom right—*Spicy Salmon Don*).

affect the other rolls, which take on a spicy characterization (e.g. *spicy tuna roll*), and also a vegetarian connotation (e.g. *avocado rolls*, *cucumber rolls*, *avocado* and *tofu rolls*, and *sweet potato rolls*). Many plates, moreover, include crunchy components, such as tempura or other fried ingredients. Crispiness reaches its peak with the *Volcano Rainbow rolls*, which have no particular linguistic description in the menu, except for the fact that they are served with honey sauce. The visual dimension offers more details about the plate, introducing its practices of preparation: the rolls are brought to the table by the waiter who, after pouring honey sauce over them, caramelizes the topside with a small blowtorch. Such practice recalls the words of Roland Barthes in *Toward a Psychosociology of Contemporary Food Consumption* (1961):

> The Americans [the same could be said with respect to the Canadian foodsphere, which has been largely influenced by the American one, *NdA*] seem to oppose the

category of sweet [...] with an equally general category that is not, however, that of *salty*—understandably so, since their food is salty and sweet to begin with—but that of *crisp* or *crispy*. *Crisp* designates everything that crunches, crackles, grates, sparkles [...]. Quite obviously, such a notion goes beyond the purely physical nature of the product; *crispiness* in a food designates an almost magical quality, a certain briskness and sharpness, as opposed to the soft, soothing character of sweet foods. (ET 1997: 23).

In the case of the Volcano Rainbow Rolls, such an opposition is overcome thanks to the practices of food preparation, which meaningfully take place before the diners' eyes. The addition of fire, whose contact with the sushi is intermediated by the honey sauce, marks the passage from nature to culture not exactly in terms of raw/cooked (after caramelizing with the blowtorch, in fact, only the superficial parts of the toppings—the salmon and avocado—partially abandon their raw status because of the heat generated by the flame), but rather in terms of *smooth/crispy*. It is precisely the honey (*sweet*) sauce that, by reacting to fire, makes the transformation from the *soft, smoothing* character of the topside (i.e., avocado and salmon, along with the honey poured on them) of the rolls to a crunchy, crackling, sparkling—in other words, *crispy*—layer, "wrapping" them as much as possible. On the other hand, the smooth *vs.* crunchy contrast is partially kept by the presence of the melted sauce trickling to the bottom of the sushi, on a high/low axis. A major implication of such a transformation should be remarked upon: before the addition of fire, the slickness of the rolls—due to the presence of raw humid toppings, such as avocado and salmon, and of the sweet honey sauce poured onto them—would make them difficult to pick up using chopsticks. The transformation caused by the caramelization process (fire + intermediation of sauce) eliminates the slickness, making the sweet flavour of the sauce, along with its smooth character, slide to the bottom of each roll, therefore facilitating the action of the chopsticks. "Translation" and "tradition" are therefore presented as complementary in this case, precisely thanks to the action of the providers of the eating experience.

The case of the bowls of rice, presented as donburi (although containing sushi rice and raw fish), is partially different. The Spicy Salmon Don, for instance, is described as "spicy salmon, sesame, flying fish roe, sushi rice." The presence of nori further enhances its proximity to chirashizushi, although it becomes a sort of decoration, untidily positioned along the border of the container, in an upper position. This distances the seaweed from the pole of culture compared to its common usage in chirashi, where the humidity of the two layers enclosing it (humid raw fish, above, and semi-humid cooked rice, below) re-humidify the previously dried vegetable. Moreover, the visual configuration of the bowls suggests the idea of a salad, although in this case, the presence of wasabi and gari on the top of the fish and the absence of any particular local ingredient strengthen its relationship with Japanese "tradition." On the other hand, the spicy character of the plate, strongly underlined by its name, hankers to local tastes.

3. Eating almost the same thing

As highlighted, the traces left by translation processes emerge at different levels, from the arrangement of foods within the plate to the characteristics of food materials and the display of particular of preparation practices, and even the provision of specific consumption practices. Specifically, as regards the material level, some dishes seem particularly sensitive to the processes of adaptation to the local foodsphere, causing interesting processes of resemanticization. Chirashizushi is emblematic in this sense, since it involves not only differences in the nature of the foods contained in the dish—which come to include components typical of the local foodspheres—but also at the structural level—with nori becoming visible wrapping instead of being wrapped and concealed—and the deriving investments of meaning. Differences become even more evident in the case of other types of sushi, which, although more formalized, change in different ways. New ingredients are introduced, while others are eliminated or visually concealed. New configurations affect the wrapping/wrapped relationship, as well as the raw/cooked contrast and the related semantic oppositions. Beyond the peculiarities of each case, it is interesting to notice how the material dimension can never be conceived as separate from the symbolic and semantic level: ingredients, recipes, tools, etc. sum up and signalize specific aesthetics, practices, values and meanings.

This evidently recalls the dynamics described by Eco: even when the promise of an "authentic" experience is showcased, it is impossible to prepare, eat, look at—in other words to "experience"—the "same" sushi as that found in washoku; only similarity ("almost" the same sushi as that found in washoku) can be pursued. A negotiation process always takes place, and in the case of food becomes even more evident since it involves multiple aspects and dimensions. Ingredients change, their combinations change, the sensorial and aesthetic responses they activate change … Yet the reference to the Japanese foodsphere remains perceptible, more or less in the background, marking the success of a cuisine that has established its (culinary) identity by promoting a process of "admission" (Landowski 1997) of otherness (i.e. appreciating food products, practices and aesthetics precisely because it is "theirs" *and* "ours," to cite the terms used by Volli 2015)—instead of forms of "assimilation" simply reducing it to its internal codes. After all, as Paul Ricoeur (1990) reminds us, identity is constituted by an inextricable tie between *selfsameness* and *selfhood* or *ipseity*: while the former relies on unchangeable aspects, the latter is rather based on change and continuous "adjustments" (cf. Landowski 2005). In this sense, identity implies alterity to such an extent that it cannot be grasped without it. The cases considered show that, even more than language, food represents an easily crossable frontier, a space where the incommensurability of cultures gives way to encounter and comparison. Such an encounter, although partial, makes cultures acknowledge themselves as different and separate but not necessarily irreconcilable. The Canadian foodsphere definitely shows us that this is one of the greatest values of the "almostness" characterizing translation processes.

Works Cited

Ashkenazi, Michael and Jacob, Jeanne (2000), *The Essence of Japanese Cuisine. An Essay on Food and Culture*, Hampden Station, Baltimore: University of Pennsylvania Press.

Barber, Kimiko (2002), *Sushi. Taste and Technique*, London: DK Publishing.

Barthes, Roland. "Pour une psychosociologie de l'alimentation contemporaine," *Annales ESC*, XVI, 5 (1961): 977–986. English Translation (1997), "Toward a Psychosociology of Contemporary Food Consumption," in C. Counihan and P. Van Esteric (eds.), *Food and Culture: A Reader*, New York and London: Routledge, 20–27.

Barthes, Roland (1970), *L'Empire des signes*, Paris: Skira. English Translation (1983), *Empire of Signs*, New York: Hill and Wang.

Dekura, Hideo, Treloar, Brigid and Yoshii, Ryuichi (2004), *The Complete Book of Sushi*, Singapore: Periplus Ed.

Detrick, Mia (1981), *Sushi*, San Francisco: Chronicle Books.

Eco, Umberto (1997) *Kant e l'ornitorinco*, Milan: Bompiani. English Translation (1999), *Kant and the Platypus: Essays on language and Cognition*, Orlando: Harcourt Brace.

Eco, Umberto (2001), *Experiences in Translation*, Toronto: University of Toronto Press.

Greimas, Algirdas Julien. "Un problème de sémiotique narrative : les objets de valeur," *Langages*, 31,8 (1973): 13–35.

Hendry, Joy (1993), *Wrapping Culture: Politeness, Presentation, and Power in Japan and Other Societies*, Oxford: Clarendon Press.

Hobsbawm, Eric and Ranger, Terence (1983), *The Invention of Tradition*, Cambridge: Cambridge University Press.

Hosking. Richard (1995), *A Dictionary of Japanese Food: Ingredients &* *Culture*, Tokyo-North Clarendon-Singapore: Tuttle Publishing.

Itou, Kouji *et al.* "Changes of proximate composition and extractive components in *narezushi*, a fermented mackerel product, during processing," *Fisheries Science*, 72, 6 (2006): 1269–1276.

Landowski, Eric (1997), *Présence de l'autre. Essais de socio-sémiotique II*, Paris: PUF.

Landowski, Eric (2005), *Les interactions risquées—Nouveaux Actes Sémiotiques*, 101–103, Limoges: Presses universitaires de Limoges.

Lévi-Strauss, Claude (1964), *Mythologiques I. Le cru et le cuit*, Paris: Plon. English Translation (1969), *The Raw and the Cooked*, Chicago: The University of Chicago Press.

Lowry, Dave (2005), *The Connoisseur's Guide to Sushi: Everything You Need to Know about Sushi*, Boston: Harvard Common Press.

Marrone, Gianfranco (2016), *Semiotica del gusto. Linguaggi della cucina, del cibo, della tavola*, Milan-Udine: Mimesis.

Mintz, Corey. "How Japanese cuisine has blossomed in Toronto," *The Globe and Mail*, January 3 2020, available at https://www. theglobeandmail.com/canada/toronto/article-how-japanese-cuisine-has-blossomed-in-toronto/ (last access: April 27, 2020).

Mouritsen, Ole G. (2009), *Sushi: Food for the Eye, the Body & the Soul*, New York: Springer.

Nergaard, Siri (1995), *Teorie contemporanee della traduzione*, Milan: Bompiani.

Pandi, George, "Let's eat Canadian, but is there really a national dish?" *The Gazette (Montreal)*, April 5 2008, available at https://web. archive.org/web/20120823171831/http://www.canada.com/ montrealgazette/columnists/story.html?id=6ad83058-3f7b-4403-8aa8-dce47b16884e (last access: April 26, 2020)

Ricoeur, Paul (1990), *Soi-même comme un autre*, Paris: Seuil. English Translation (1992), *Oneself as Another*, Chicago: University of Chicago Press.

Stano, Simona. "The Invention of Tradition: The Case of Pasta, one of the Symbols of Italian Identity," *Signs & Media* 8 (2014): 136–152.

Stano, Simona (2015a), *Cibo e identità culturale / Food and Cultural Identity—Lexia*, 19–20. Rome: Aracne.

Stano, Simona (2015b), *Eating the Other. Translations of the Culinary Code*, Newcastle-upon-Tyne: Cambridge Scholars Publishing.

Stano, Simona. "Lost in translation: Food, Identity and Otherness," *Semiotica*, 211,1/4 (2016): 81–104.

Volli, Ugo (2015), "Preface," in S. Stano, *Eating the Other. Translations of the Culinary Code*, Newcastle-upon-Tyne: Cambridge Scholars Publishing, xiii–xvi.

Zschock Day (2005), *The Little Black Book of Sushi: The Essential Guide to the World of Sushi*, New York: Peter Pauper Press, Inc.

JULIA SIEPAK

Recuperating Tastes of Home: Indigenous Food Sovereignty in First Nations Women's Writing

BASED ON EXTRACTIVE ECONOMIES, SETTLER colonialism in Canada yielded a negative imprint not only on Indigenous communities but also on the environment. Through changes in ecosystems, environmental degradation and the dislocation of First Nations populations, the process of colonization disrupted Indigenous peoples' reciprocal relationships with their ancestral lands, including other-than-human species coexisting on these territories. As signaled by Kyle Powys Whyte, this irreversibly changed First Nations communities' lifestyles and diets (2017b: 209). This disruption of the connection between Indigenous people and their traditional foods resulted in Aboriginal health deterioration in Canada, observable in the alarmingly high percentage of the population suffering from diabetes (Crowshoe et al. 2018). Priscilla Sette, a Cree scholar and activist, argues that "it is a simple equation that when land is taken, the local economy suffers along with the sense of Native identity, and a people's physical and spiritual health deteriorates" (2018: 177). Furthermore, she observes that food is intrinsically linked to communal prosperity, functioning as a "focal point around community well-being, Indigenous sovereignty, land protection, community development, exercise and health" (2018: 175). Thus, by targeting and altering Indigenous diets, settler colonialism destabilized all the aforementioned spheres of life of First Nations communities. At the same time, Canada, like other settler societies, has promoted and sustained the globalized food monoculture that leads to the unhealthy imbalance of power regarding nutrition on a global scale (Smith 2012: 107; Nelson 2008: 183). The monoculture of food produce results in the Indigenous dependence on settler food, creating the situation of food injustice with its multiple and nuanced consequences for First Nations communities.

At an international level, the concept of food sovereignty entered the discussion in the context of globalized food monocultures to resist such an organization of food systems in contemporary capitalist societies. The food sovereignty movement is a thoroughly grassroots one, and its advocates often come from marginalized and underprivileged backgrounds (Schanbacher 53). Food sovereignty itself is defined by a peasant organization La Via Campesina as "the right of people and governments to choose the way food is produced and consumed in order to respect livelihoods" (La Via Campesina 2009: 57). This approach to food stresses the importance of the local production and distribution of foods, enhancing food diversity. Acknowledging the importance and legitimacy of the movement's postulates, Indigenous scholars emphasize, however, the need for the "Indigenization" of the movement's politics to incorporate Aboriginal perspectives and acknowledge the role of settler colonization in the disruption of traditional sustainable foodways (Whyte 2017a; Coté 2016). Charlotte Coté, in her understanding of Indigenous food sovereignty, bridges the concept with the decolonial and restorative efforts of Native communities. At the same time, she stresses the importance of returning to the underpinnings of Aboriginal reciprocal ecologies, namely responsibility and relationships. Hence, First Nations' recuperative food practices would lead to what she calls, after Jeff Corntassel, "sustainable self-determination," which refers to the practice of working from within to restore traditional ecosystems and community dynamics as a way of claiming sovereignty (2016: 10). Meanwhile, Kyle Powys Whyte argues that Indigenous communities will plausibly continue to depend on "mixed diets of different foods, from Indigenous and local foods to industrially produced food" (2017a: 363). On this note, the scholar recognizes that Indigenous food sovereignty departs from the notions of food self-sufficiency and cultural autonomy and frames the concept as a strategy of cultural reinvigoration against the oppression that has erased Indigenous ecologies. This, in turn, stresses that reappraising culturally salient foods not only revives certain plant or animal species within the context of their traditional ecologies, but it also—through the restoration of its complex roles within the community—strengthens collective wellbeing and identity. (2017a: 363) Both scholars thus focus on the ways food can heal communities and lead to reconciliation.

Leanne Simpson, in turn, bridges the cultural significance of traditional foods in First Nations communities within the realm of Aboriginal stories. In her concept of "land as pedagogy," the Mississauga Nishnaabeg scholar and writer encompasses both Indigenous relational ecology and the recuperative potential of storytelling. Simpson reimagines the traditional Nishnaabeg story of maple syrup production so as to mark resistance against Canadian settler colonial restrictions on the use of their ancestral lands by Indigenous peoples, as well as against the industrialized and commercialized production of traditional First Nation foods (2017: 154). What is proposed in her notion of land as pedagogy stresses Aboriginal embeddedness in place and the reciprocal relationality of Indigenous knowledge production. Being in a relationship with the land, according to Simpson, is a manifestation of connection to the history of resistance (2017: 167). The scholar thus emphasizes the potential of stories and therefore literature to disrupt settler colonialism. Asserting that Indigenous narratives and practices are embedded in and should be set on the land appropriated during the colonization process, Indigenous presence is thereby re-established and the hereditary legitimacy to these territories is reclaimed (2017: 162–163). In this way, storytelling seems to function as a decolonial practice: it addresses and disrupts settler colonial permanency. It is then endowed with a powerful transformative decolonial potential.

Following Simpson in her view that Indigenous stories embedded in the land have decolonial potential, in this chapter, I address the issues connected to Indigenous food sovereignty as represented in contemporary First Nations women's writing in English: Alicia Elliott's *A Mind Spread Out on the Ground* (2019), Eden Robinson's *Monkey Beach* (2000) and Tracey Lindberg's *Birdie* (2016). The aim is to locate these texts within the poetics of food sovereignty and decolonization in order to address Indigenous women's representation of foods and diets, their disruptions and the attempts at their restoration, as well as the ways in which they prompt healing and wellbeing both on an individual and collective level.

It seems vital to commence with Alicia Elliott's memoir as it refers to the author's first-hand experience and addresses the contemporary Indigenous condition in Canada. Elliott is a Tuscarora writer from the Six Nations of the Grand River. The title of one of her memoir chapters, namely "34 grams per dose," pertains to the weight of a serving size of Chips Ahoy! Cookies, which provides the human body with 170 calories. The title is not random since it refers to Elliott's binge-eating habits:

> It usually takes at least 102 grams [3 serving sizes] for me to feel like I've reached what I should probably call *proper dosage*, considering how and why I consume them. I've already swallowed 510 calories by the time I realize these cookies aren't the medicine I'd hoped they'd be (Elliott 2019: 91).

The industrial, mass-produced cookies emerge, therefore, as comfort food for Elliott. The term "comfort food" "… refers to those foods whose consumption provides consolation or a feeling of well-being" (Spence 2017: 105) and usually includes high-calorie snacks or else traditional and simple-recipe meals that a given person associates with positive feelings and/or periods in their life (2017: 105). While the poor economic situation in her household placed Elliott's family in the condition of food insecurity leading to their dependence on food pantries and inexpensive products available on the reserve, the occasional instances when she and her siblings could indulge in the glossy packed high-sugar snacks provided a sense of their connection to the experience of "other kids—richer kids, off-rez kids" (Elliott 2019: 94). Thus, products like Chips Ahoy! Cookies, the staple of Western monocultures, provide the positive association for Elliott as in her childhood they would create a sense of inclusion and belonging to the life-style that was out of reach for her on the reserve. Spence argues that comfort foods might alleviate experienced stress and anxiety (2017: 107–108). However, for Elliott, the process of eating high-sugar and high-calorie food is never followed by a lasting feeling of satisfaction or comfort. Although cookies initially seem to soothe her internal wounds, being delightful and indulgent, they are not the medicine she is searching for. In the long run, her reliance on comfort foods disrupted Elliott's diet and led to her binge-eating disorder. The widespread character of a variety of eating disorders affecting Aboriginal communities negatively influences their health, leading to disproportionately high levels of obesity and diabetes in Indigenous communities in Canada.

Elliott recognizes the roots of her eating disorder in the poverty that her family experienced when she was a child. She notices that this experience of the lack of access to healthy and nutritious food is not isolated but shared by other economically underprivileged families across the country:

> [...] the biggest indicator of obesity is a person's income level ... it should also come as no surprise that the biggest indicator of poverty is race. In Canada, a staggering one in five racialized families live in poverty, as opposed to one in twenty white families. This puts many poor, racialized families in the position where they have no choice *but* to rely on cheap, unhealthy food and, as a result, support the same companies that

have converted their poverty into corporate profit in the first place (2019: 97).

In addition to the poverty troubling many Indigenous households, food options on the reserves are limited, and products are usually more expensive than in big chain supermarkets in cities (2019: 93–94). Moreover, many First Nations reserves in Canada can be virtually considered food deserts. Billy-Ray Belcourt refers to the geographical isolation of Aboriginal reserves from the rest of Canada in terms of a "geography of misery," indicating the limited opportunities and precarity experienced by Aboriginal communities, delineating the potentialities of Indigenous bodies (2018: 2). In his article, Belcourt perceives the ubiquity of junk food in convenience stores on reserves and the lack of alternative healthy and organic options as one of the aspects of reserve life that renders its geography miserable (2018: 5–6). Consequently, the limited food options lead to what the scholar calls "diabetes epidemic," the reserve emerging as "an incubator of epidemics, a place where disease always-already teeters on the verge of unmanageability" (2018: 8). Therefore, the ubiquity of diabetes on First Nations reserves might be seen as deriving from the prevalent inequalities introduced by settler colonial structures and capitalist monocultures.

In the same way, Elliott ties her personal story of eating disorders to Canadian settler colonial history. She quotes a study by Mosby and Galloway that ties contemporary health problems of Indigenous peoples in Canada—such as obesity, diabetes, and insulin resistance—to the residential school system and, hence, approaches her own eating disorder as the "genetic inheritance" (2019: 111) of settler colonialism. It is clear that the numerous policies of the Canadian government that targeted Indigenous food traditions, such as the residential school system, restrictions on hunting and harvesting on ancestral territories, dispossession and displacement, defamiliarized Indigenous peoples from their traditional healthy eating habits. Elliott, however, attempts to envision Indigenous future food practices that reach beyond those structured by settler society. Thus, a sense of hope arises from her work. Elliott observes the possibility of food to once again acquire the status of medicine that she perceives in returning to the cultivation of traditional crops for her community foods, such as corn, beans and squash, and reappraising the elements of Indigenous diets (Elliott 2019: 116). In the past, Indigenous communities living within their reciprocal ecologies often made choices of which plants and animals to use as a source of nutrition and which to use as medicine (Mohawk 2008: 171). Likewise, contemporary attempts to uphold or recuperate traditional food practices are tightly bound to the healing properties of plants and animals both in the context of First Nations community cultural wellbeing, as stressed by Whyte, and physical health so deeply overshadowed by the spread of diabetes. Elliott poetically frames the salience of Indigenous food sovereignty as "an act of absolute, undiminished intergenerational love" (2019: 116), possessing the potential to transform Aboriginal futures.

In her debut novel, *Birdie*, Tracey Lindberg in turn addresses the issues of dysfunctional eating and eating disorders as emerging from childhood trauma. In *Birdie*, the protagonist, Bernice (also referred to as Birdie), as well as her cousin, Skinny Freda, are sexually abused by their uncles when they are children. Birdie's physical reaction to experienced trauma is manifested in her obesity. A study conducted by Imperatori et al. states that experiencing trauma in one's childhood may trigger the development of eating disorders, such as food addiction and binge eating in adulthood. The study notes that these dysfunctional eating habits might rely on comfort foods as a means of combating negative emotions as well as restoring emotional balance, and thus can be perceived as coping mechanisms. Therefore, the researchers suggest that eating habits in people who have experienced childhood trauma are closely tied to their emotional states and self-perception. (Imperatori et al. 2016: 187) Bernice puts on weight to cope with the traumas she has undergone as a child. She wants "to make her body unhospitable and unappetizing to others [...]. Her body becomes a "cage" (139) that keeps her safe from harm, but limits her movement and freedom"

(McGuire-Wood 219: 217). Indeed, the causal relationship between the traumatic event and Bernice's eating disorder is stressed
by Lindberg:

> Bernice took leave of her body that day of the
> Christmas pageant. Freda stopped seeing her. It was
> like Bernice's spirit was sleeping, only to awaken on
> the rarest of occasions. Bernice got fat, and then fatter
> and then fatter. She ate with an appetite that she had
> not earned. She ate like she was not going to eat again.
> Eventually, her pretty face gave in to the battle she was
> waging with her fork. Her eyes began to look tiny in
> her doughy brown face. Her cheeks lost their colour
> and her hair became lifeless. It was like she had put
> on the suit of an artist's caricature of Bernice—blown
> up and expanded. As if the flame of Bernice had con-
> sumed her like shrubs eaten by a brush fire (2015: 217).

Food emerges as loaded with negative affect and marks constant struggle with the protagonist's traumatic memories. Bernice's
family reacts towards the abuse and, consequently, the girl's eating
disorder with silence, repressing what has happened. This yields a
destructive impact on the family structure as it surfaces as "a sort
of bad medicine—it made Freda skinny, Bernice fat, and Maggie
[Birdie's mom] disappear" (Lindberg 2015: 62). Thus, in both girls,
the experience of sexual violence results in eating disorders and the
consequent transformation of their bodies to the state of "aberra-
tion"—being overly skinny or being obese.

The transformation of the protagonist's body caused by her
dysfunctional eating proves to be the initial stage of coping with
childhood trauma. Further in the novel, Bernice assumes a bird
identity in order to work through the experience of abuse. The protagonist virtually goes into hibernation and, in her bird-self, revises
memories to recollect her trauma story. During hibernation, Birdie
recreates her trauma story from pieces of memories and voices

it in the form of a traditional Indigenous oral story that constitutes the beginnings of most of the chapters in the book, entitled
pawatamowin—a dream. These fragments of the novel, replicating
stylistically traditional Aboriginal stories, constitute an important
step towards recovery from trauma. The process of recollecting
and telling one's trauma story as a way of working through it is
emphasized in contemporary psychoanalysis, for instance in Judith
Herman's theory (1992). While sleeping for extensive periods of
time, the young woman loses weight, no longer troubled by hunger.
Lola, an owner of a bakery and Birdie's host, perceives the protagonist's process of transformation as "melting" (Lindberg 2015:
234), stressing the metamorphosis Bernice's body undergoes while
losing weight. Meanwhile, the only activity that Bernice engages
in during that period is following the Frugal Gourmet's cooking
show on television—an immensely popular culinary American production (Lindberg 2015: 105–106). The compulsive consumption
of the TV show by Bernice serves as a prelude to a ceremony of
transformation.

When Bernice emerges from her hibernation-like period of
apathy and assumes of new her human form, she prepares a feast
that she will share with the three women who were near her while
she was asleep: Skinny Freda, Aunt Valene and Lola, whom she
calls her "womanfamily" (2015: 245). Then, the first thing she deals
with is cooking, as she asserts "I need to cook" (2015: 244). The
ingredients that she uses to cook are collected by Skinny Freda and
Aunt Val based on lists that Bernice has prepared:

> All sit on top of the journal that Bernice has been
> writing ingredients in for years. She thumbs through
> it, stops at the first entry and wonders how the hell she
> is going to find bison marrow in Vancouver. And. Puts
> her foot on the gas. And. Goes hunting" (2015: 221).

The process of collecting ingredients—and later cooking and
feasting—becomes a ground for mutual understanding and both

individual as well as collective transformation and rejuvenation. Food emerges as a positive rather than a negative association. Women feast and celebrate together with the spirits of ancestors near the tree. *Pimatisewin*, a tree of life, symbolizes harmony in Cree culture and is interchangeable with the concept of a "good life" (Gross 2002: 19). The condition of the tree before the feast is poor (Lindberg 2015: 236). Its illness is parallel to that of Birdie. This representation of *Pimatisewin* as diseased symbolically refers to the condition of the Cree community, troubled by intergenerational traumas, a heritage of settler colonialism. The dinner prepared by Bernice and her women helpers becomes a ceremony that transforms both individuals and the collective, strengthening community bonds and restoring Cree culture. It feeds people, spirits and the tree, which is also treated as a relative: "The earth around Pimatsewin soaks up the exotic and the sacred, taking the foods to its roots, its branches and its bark" (2015: 247). Hence, food assumes sacred and healing qualities. Lindberg's novel emphasizes, then, the recuperative potential of food and cooking in the face of personal as well as intergenerational trauma.

In her *Monkey Beach*, Eden Robinson encourages the restoration of Haisla food traditions, re-storying them in order to promote the rejuvenation of traditional elements of diet among her people. Being a Haisla-Heiltsuk writer, the author sets her novel on her ancestral coastal territories of British Columbia. The protagonist, Lisamarie, lives in her assimilated household, with the Aboriginal traditionalism of her grandmother, Ma-ma-oo, and the Indigenous activism of her uncle, Mick. In the novel, the salience of berries and fish is emphasized as they were traditionally the main sources of Haisla food prior to contact. The community's profound engagement with berry plants is evident as Ma-ma-oo can distinguish between two different types of blueberry alone: "We found the other kind, sya'k°nalh, 'the real blueberry,' shiny bluish-black berries, prettier, but not as sweet as pipxs'm" (Robinson 2001: 159). Fish also emerge as the essential part of Haisla cuisine, taking into consideration their immersion within the coastal landscape. Iba

Habermann stresses that "*Monkey Beach* emphasises the omnipres-
ence of water as well as its connectedness to land and its people"
(2016: 125). At the same time, Habermann's reading stresses the
ecocultural challenges brought by the industrialization of Haisla
territories, undermining the community's relationship with water
and its fish (2016: 137–138).

The importance of one species of fish, namely oolichans, appears
particularly significant both in the novel and in Robinson's original
Haisla culture. In *The Sasquatch at Home: Traditional Protocols and
Modern Storytelling*, Robinson describes the importance of fish for
her people:

> Oolichans spend their lives in the Pacific Ocean feed-
> ing on plankton. Weak swimmers, they rely on tidal
> flows to help return to their spawning grounds at the
> upper tidal reaches of rivers. *Thaleichthys pacificus* (rich
> fish of the Pacific), as the oolichan is known formally,
> has 15 per cent oil content. Salmon may be vital to
> the coastal nations of British Columbia, but oolichans
> arrived at the end of winter when most stored food
> supplies were depleted and, in harsh winters, peo-
> ple were facing starvation. Oolichans are eaten fresh,
> smoked and salted. Oil rendered from oolichans is
> commonly known as "grease" and was used to preserve
> food (in the days before refrigeration), as a spread like
> butter, and as a cure-all (2011: 19).

This multipurpose character of oolichans is also stressed by
Jacquie Green Kundoque, who outlines different functions of the
fish in Haisla communities: from giving light through feeding community to its medical use (2008: 15–18). As a food of sustenance,
oolichans gained an important cultural role and entered Haisla
storytelling, becoming an element of collective Haisla identity.
Kundoque stresses that the relationship with the fish constitutes
"the essence of being Haisla" (2008: 21), and in the face of the

threat of oolichans becoming extinct due to industrial fishing, its reinvigoration is indispensable for the wellbeing of the community (2008: 22–23). For the Haisla scholar and storyteller, Indigenous food sovereignty does not only address food in terms of nutrition but also in terms of collective integrity. Traditional stories emerge as a fundamental part of the process of reappraising traditional relationships with fish (Kundoque 2008: 22).

In *Monkey Beach*, Robinson re-narrates these stories to hand down the traditional ecological knowledge of her people, often abbreviated to TEK, in order to regain the fish's cultural significance, whose livelihood is becoming more and more uncertain due to environmental degradation. As a term, Traditional Ecological Knowledge (TEK) does not only pertain to the whole environmental knowledge that a given community possesses, but also to active relational engagement with different parts of their ecosystems (McGregor 2018: 111–113). The process of the transmission of TEK in the novel is twofold, as Ma-ma-oo passes down Heisla TEK to Lisamarie, and who in turn, shares bits and pieces of it with the reader through the means of the narrative. Ma-ma-oo makes her granddaughter assist her in her errands to the beach or the forest; thus, the teaching of traditional ways of obtaining food and medicine and their further preparation takes place on the land. The protocols concerning their engagement with different species are rigidly structured, based on the principle of reciprocity with the surrounding environment, and accompanied by the practice of storytelling. Thus, the passing on of TEK in the novel reinforces the sense of embeddedness in place, and thus resonates with Leanne Simpson's concept of "land as pedagogy." The protagonist gains extensive knowledge about oolichans and sounds scientific in her narration, learning not from books but from exposure to the oral tradition and interaction with the land. Lisa accurately describes the various ways oolichans can be prepared for consumption and outlines the conditions in which it can be stored (Robinson 2000: 85). Furthermore, the protagonist knows how to catch them and what the most favourable weather and environmental conditions are for their passage (2000: 92). Moreover, Lisa appreciates the cultural importance of grease (the oolichan's oil) for her people, and recognizes the geographical, historical, cultural and linguistic contexts for the significance of the fish for her community. Hence, even though the novel is not addressed solely to a Haisla reader, it assumes a recuperative potential, perpetuating traditional Haisla food practices via a work of fiction. Robinson's writing thus provides an opposition towards what Melissa K. Nelson calls "global monoculture of low-quality consumers who have lost touch with their unique food practices," embracing the local traditional cuisine based on "unique plants, animals, herbs, recipes, and tastes" (2008: 183). Thus, *Monkey Beach* may be seen as a work encouraging food sovereignty and, from a broader perspective, as a decolonial text.

To conclude, the selected literary works by First Nations women writers discussed in this paper promote food sovereignty and direct attention to the contemporary issues connected to First Nations diets, emphasizing their roots in settler colonial domination. Aboriginal writers reflect on the concept of food sovereignty voiced in activism opposing global alimentary monocultures and "Indigenize" its politics. The poetics of food sovereignty emerging from these texts demonstrates the genealogy of disruptions to ecologies, foodways and diets inflicted by settler colonialism in Canada. Nevertheless, Aboriginal women writers strive to represent the salience of reappraising traditional diets and practices that bear the potential to restore cultures and bring collective wellbeing. This multidimensional healing that permeates literary works discussed in this paper transforms settler colonial impositions and their precarious impact on the Aboriginal condition, including traumatic experiences and eating disorders. In the face of the diabetes epidemic on First Nations reserves and the spreading eating disorders in urban Canadian communities, the return to the medicinal character of food proves to be more important than ever. At the same time, the reappraisal of Indigenous food practices is inextricably inter-twined with respecting environments, engaging with and learning from them. Then, the shift towards land and its teaching becomes a central issue in the Indigenous conceptualization of food sover-eignty, as emerging from works written by Canadian Indigenous women. This understanding of the concept aligns with the theories proposed by Whyte and Simpson, determining a strong connection between Indigenous activism, research and literature. Moreover, the power of storytelling to demonstrate, undermine and reimagine settler colonial structures situates literature on the forefront of the decolonial struggle. While addressing food practices, Indigenous literature promotes healing and strengthens sovereignty. providing possibilities for new potentialities among First Nations communi-ties in Canada.

Works Cited

Belcourt, Billy-Ray, "Meditations on Reserve Life, Biosociality, and the taste of Non-Sovereignty," *Settler Colonial Studies* 8, 1. (2018): 1–15.

Coté, Charlotte, "*Indigenizing* Food Sovereignty. Revitalizing Indigenous Food Practices and Ecological Knowledges in Canada and the United States," *Humanities* 5, 57. (2016): 1–14.

Crowshoe, Lynden et al. "Type 2 Diabetes and Indigenous Peoples," *Canadian Journal of Diabetes* 42 (2018): S296–S306.

Elliott, Alicia (2019), *A Mind Spread Out on the Ground*, Doubleday Canada.

Gross, Lawrence W. "*Bimaadiziwin*, or the 'Good Life,' as a Unifying Concept of Anishinaabe Religion," *American Indian Culture and Research Journal* 26.1. (2002): 15–32.

Habermann, Ina. "*Drifting Away in the Tide*: Water Symbolism and Indigenous Environmentalism in Eden Robinson's *Monkey Beach*". *TransCanadiana: Polish Journal of Canadian Studies* 8 (2016): 123–144.

Herman, Judith (2015 [1992]) *Trauma and Recovery. The Aftermath of Violence—From Domestic Abuse to Political Terror*. New York: Basic Books. Kindle edition.

Imperatori et al. "Childhood Trauma in Obese and Overweight Women with Food Addiction and Clinical-Level of Binge · Eating," *Child Abuse & Neglect* 58 (2016): 180–190.

Kundoque, Jacquie Green. "Reclaiming Haisla Ways: Remembering Oolichan Fishing," *Canadian Journal of Native Education* 31, 1. (2008): 11–23.

La Via Campesina (2009), *La Via Campesina Policy Documents*, viacampesina.org/en/wp-content/uploads/sites/2/2010/03/BOOKLET-EN-FINAL-min.pdf. DOA: 10 Apr. 2020.

Lindberg, Tracey (2015), *Birdie*, Toronto: HarperCollins Publishers.

McGregor, Joan (2018), "Towards a Philosophical Understanding of TEK and Ecofeminism," in Melissa K. Nelson and Dan Shilling (eds.), *Traditional Ecological Knowledge: Learning from Indigenous Practices for Environmental Sustainability*, Cambridge University Press, 109–128.

McGuire-Wood (2019), "*Waiting to Be Fed:* Reading Memories of Hunger in the Tsilhqot'in Land Claim Trial Transcripts and Tracey Lindberg's *Birdie*," in Barbara Parker et al. (eds.), *Feminist Food Studies: Intersectional Perspectives*. Toronto–Vancouver: Women's Press, 205–224.

Mohawk, John (2008), "From the First to the Last Bite: Learning from the Food Knowledge of Our Ancestors," in Melissa K. Nelson (ed.), *Original Instructions: Indigenous Teachings for a Sustainable Future*, Rochester, Vermont: Bear & Company, 170–179.

Nelson, Melissa K. (2008), "Re-Indigenizing Our Bodies and Minds through Native Foods," in Melissa K. Nelson (ed.), *Original Instructions: Indigenous Teachings for a Sustainable Future*, Rochester, Vermont: Bear & Company, 180–195.

Robinson, Eden (2000), *Monkey Beach*, New York: Open Road Integrated Media, Kindle edition.

Robinson, Eden (2011), *The Sasquatch at Home: Traditional Protocols & Modern Storytelling*, Edmonton: The University of Alberta Press.

Schanbacher, Wiliam D. (2010) *The Politics of Food: The Global Conflict between Food Security and Food Sovereignty*. Santa Barbara–Denver–Oxford: Praeger.

Sette, Priscilla (2018), "Indigenous Food Sovereignty in Canada," in Melissa K. Nelson and Dan Shilling (eds.), *Traditional Ecological Knowledge: Learning from Indigenous Practices for Environmental Sustainability*, University of Cambridge Press, 175–187.

Simpson, Leanne (2017), *As We Have Always Done: Indigenous Freedom Through Radical Resistance*. Minneapolis–London: University of Minnesota Press.

Smith, Linda Tuhiwai (2012), *Decolonizing Methodologies: Research and Indigenous Peoples*, London–New York: Zed Books.

Spence, Charles. "Comfort Food: A Review," *International Journal of Gastronomy and Food Science* 9 (2017): 105–109.

Whyte, Kyle Powys (2017a), "Indigenous Food Sovereignty, Renewal, and US Settler Colonialism," in Mary C. Rawlinson and Caleb Ward (eds.), *The Routledge Handbook of Food Ethics*, London–New York: Routledge, 354–365.

Whyte, Kyle Powys (2017b), "Our Ancestors' Dystopia Now: Indigenous Conservation and the Anthropocene," in Ursula K. Heise, Jon Christensen and Michelle Niemann (eds.), *The Routledge Companion to the Environmental Humanities*, London–New York: Routledge, 206–215.

KAMELIA TALEBIAN SEDEHI

The Lack of Food and Trauma in Basil H. Johnston's Indian School Days

Introduction

MAY 27, 2021, BBC, CBC, *USA Today, New York Times*, and many other newspapers and news channels published the news of the bodily remains of 215 Indigenous children who were found at Kamloops residential school in British Columbia, Canada. The world mourned for this loss. Those who knew about residential schools were aware of the fact that they had been shut down in 1996, but why had those bodies remained at the school without the principal's acknowledgement? The current paper intends to shed light on residential schools, specifically the trauma the Indigenous students underwent by focusing on Basil H. Johnston's *Indian School Days*.

For over a century, Canada's Indigenous policy was to elim-inate the Indigenous race and they intended to reach this goal by basically ignoring Indigenous rights, and also by assimilating Indigenous Peoples into Euro-Canadian culture. They intended to erase the Indigenous: their individual cultures and religions, and the establishment of residential schools was the main policy to reach that goal. European countries claimed Indigenous lands; in some places through negotiation and treaties and in others by occupation of the land. The negotiations for lands and properties were not always honorable, but they were "often marked by fraud and coercion" (TRC 2015: v.1, 18).

The land taking was part of the policies which led to the elimination of Indigenous peoples and their assimilation into new rules and policies. While establishing residential schools, the federal government claimed that the Indigenous parents were not fit to take care of their children. One Truth and Reconciliation report mentions that "the parents often kept their children out of schools because they saw those schools, quite accurately, as dangerous and harsh institutions that sought to raise their children in alien ways" (v. 1, 20). The expansion of residential schools, one after another, could be seen through the lens of imperialism that was set long before the first residential school had been established. One of the treaties which forced Indigenous families to send their children to residential schools was the Indian Act. Hele claims that "the coercion and aggressive assimilation policies found within the Indian Act from 1884 to 1951 rested on five planks": pass laws, governmental laws, ban on cultural practices, obligatory education, and land policies (2013: 3). The Truth and Reconciliation report mentions that "the Canadian residential school experience is part of the history of imperialism of the past 500 years. In particular, it is part of the history of settler colonialism" (2015: v.1, 38).

Over 150,000 children passed through the system of 125 schools over a century in Canada (MacDonald 2007: 1001). At residential schools, Indigenous children underwent physical, sexual, and mental abuse. The training was not sufficient for those children to be prepared for white-collar jobs; it focused on manual labor and domestic work. Indigenous cultures were overlooked and belittled by the residential school system, and this attitude affected the Indigenous community for generations. The loss of cultures and languages were the consequences of those schools. As the children were taken away from their families, they were deprived of nurturing families. Indigenous students not only faced lack of food at schools, but at times they underwent scientific experiments.

In 2018, the Indigenous peoples filed a lawsuit against unconsented experiments carried out by the Canadian government. The main argument said that the Indigenous children, who were taken away by force and sent to residential schools for assimilation purposes, were subjects of nutritional experiments, mostly vitamins, and certain foods. According to an article published by *The Guardian* in 2018, entitled "Canada Sued over years of alleged experimentation on Indigenous people", "the number of those affected by the experiments could run into the thousands. 'Some people do not even know that they were the subject of experiments'" (2018: 1).

Some students were control groups while the other group of students was deprived of nutrients, and the researchers would do their study on the benefit of those nutrients. "Court documents describe the lengths researchers at times went through to protect their results: after a principal in Kenora, Ontario, asked that all the residential school's children be given iron and vitamin tablets, the researcher asked him to refrain from doing so, as it would interfere with the experiment" (2018: 1). The students suffered from ear problems, tooth, and gum issues due to the experiments. In this paper, I intend to apply Judith Herman's concept of trauma and Laub and Felman's concepts of testimony, and witnessing to Basil H. Johnston's *Indian School Days* in order to focus on the issues of food and the trauma of Indigenous students.

Trauma is the subject of various fields and disciplines, such as sociology, psychology, philosophy, and literature. Different critics from Sigmund Freud to Shoshana Felman, Dori Laub, Judith Herman, and Cathy Caruth worked on trauma from different perspectives, theoretically and clinically. Judith Herman was the first one who conceptualized complex PTSD. Herman notes that "the conflict between the will to deny horrible events and the will to proclaim them aloud is the central dialectic of psychological trauma" (1992: 1). When the atrocities occur, people banish those memories from their consciousness; moreover, some of those atrocities are too horrible to be uttered, and they remain unspeakable.

However, the atrocities return to consciousness and remind the victim of the impossibility of denial. As a result, the victim needs to remember and tell the truth about the incidents that happened. In order to be healed, the survivors of atrocities tell their experiences in a fragmented and emotional manner; therefore, the listener should listen to the stories with patience to make sense of those broken phrases. At the moment of trauma, the victims remain helpless, and they go numb. The terror and helplessness felt by the victims of traumatic experience threaten their bodily integrity. At the moment of a traumatic incident, the victims are overwhelmed by extreme fright, which leaves them with no sense of meaning and connection to the incident.

Traumatized patients experience the repercussions of traumatic moments by day and night; consequently, they are prone to use alcohol or drugs to alleviate their tension. Substance abuse is a defense mechanism that helps the traumatized patients to suppress their thoughts regarding traumatic incidents. The traumatized patients, who experienced atrocities imposed by others, can have poor communication and interaction with others. They cannot form a connection with their community as their trust was once betrayed at the moment of traumatic experience.

The testimony that Laub and Felman use in their research does not serve only as a straightforward transcript of events, but as "a point of conflation between text and life, a textual testimony which can penetrate us like an act of life" (1991: 1). Laub and Felman base their main focus on two points: the moment the trauma was inflicted, explored in minute detail, and the long-term changes affected by the traumatizing moment. To perceive the trauma among new generations of Indigenous communities, one needs to have insight into the context of the events. As the witness gives his testimony about the incidents, his speech act is not finished, but it is in process. Testimony is not a finished statement, but its language is in process. The accounts of these events are incapable of closure. They are never truly finished. Felman and Laub mention that "testimony is a discursive practice" (1991: 5)

> As a relation to events, testimony seems to be composed of bits and pieces of a memory that has been overwhelmed by occurrences that have not settled into

understanding or remembrances, acts that cannot be constructed as knowledge nor assimilated into full cognition, events over our frames of reference. (Laub and Felman, 1991: 5)

Testimony is speaking about the moments which have been left long unspoken. Too intense to be grasped at the moment of their occurrence, these incidents always evade complete recapture and full perception. Felman and Laub ask whether testimony is a simple medium of transmission or whether it can also be considered an "unsuspected medium of a healing" (1991: 9). As the survivor of traumatic incidents gives his testimony, he intends to perceive those intense moments and find words to express them. Even when the attempt appears unsuccessful, it can lead to healing. A critical step toward healing implies to grasp the reality of the wound to re-emerge from the numbness, and engage within that reality. Herman writes, "The central task of the second stage is remembrance and mourning" (Herman 2015: 155). Writing can be considered one of the ways through which the survivors can heal themselves as they remember their past and mourn the incidents.

Analysis

Basil H. Johnston's *Indian School Days* reflects the trauma of Indigenous children at residential schools. The Indigenous students witnessed the abuse by their principals. Laub and Felman believe that "the scene of witnessing is thus the scene of historical recording—and of the historical documenting—of an event" (1991: 168); however, in *Indian School Days*, the scenes of witnessing are the scenes of the non-recording and non-documenting of historical events. Events are witnessed but they are not experienced. The experience of events is missing. The seeing and hearing do not match the exact time each event takes place, which leads to the lack of perception of the incidents. In the present article, the significance of the survival, speech, silence, deafness and hearing is discussed in *Indian School Days*, in the light of Herman's concept of trauma and Laub and Felman's concepts of witnessing and testimony. In the selected reminiscence, silence is an act of avoidance of retelling which leads to the denial of acknowledgement. The transmission of witnessing to awareness was blocked as such reality was denied through a willful blindness or deafness. Silence and unacknowledgement can interrupt the process of historical documentation. The challenge is to make and rewrite history despite the presence of the censor's silence. One can always remember that for Indigenous peoples, the trauma continues and there has not been an end (Styvendale 2008: 208).

Basil H. Johnston (1929–2015) was an Anishinaabe author. He was a member of Chippewas of Nawash Unceded First Nation and he was sent to St. Peter Claver school at Spanish, Ontario. He narrates his experience at school in his novel, *Indian School Days*. He won the Stephen Leacock Memorial Medal for humour for his collection of short stories Moose Meat and Wild Rice (1978). In 1939, Basil was told by his mom that he would go on a short trip. Once the agent arrived, Basil noticed that he was going to Spanish, St. Peter Claver's Indian residential school. He was ten years old and he stayed there for 6 years. In the reminiscence he uses the first person to emphasize his presence at the residential school and what he experienced. *Indian School Days* was published in 1988, giving an account of the narrator being taken away from his parents and sent to the Jesuit school in Northern Ontario. The book was written in a humorous way, which emphasized how residential school students faced bitter incidents in their lives with a smile on their faces.

Within this reminiscence, the reader is informed of how the Indigenous students faced the lack of food and hygiene at residential school. The students worked hard and studied so much and they needed proper food not to be weak and lose their energy, but the portion of food was not enough for them. The quality of the food was so bad that the teachers did not eat the same food as students. Teachers ate better food, but when the government promised to support those schools financially, the schools should have provided proper food for students as well as the teachers. "'Hey! Father!' an anonymous voice called out. 'How come you not eating carrots like us?' to which there was no answer" (Johnston 1988: 38). Moreover, one of the students complains that "if I starve to death, it's going to be their fault; we never have enough but they have lots for themselves" (Johnston 1988: 37). The barley or pea soup was served to students while the teachers ate "roasts of beef and pork and poultry" (Johnston 1988: 137). The students questioned their teachers about this difference but the teachers ignored their questions. Milloy notes that students suffered from poor nutrition, unsafe buildings and neglect of their health (2013: 208). Canada, the land of plenty in the 1940s, becomes a nightmarish place for Indigenous students, who were used to their family hunting and fishing for food according to the seasons. At the residential schools, they were served the food that they did not hunt or they were not used to eat.

The food portions were so small that "'I'm full' was an expression alien in our world and to our experience" (Johnston 1988: 40). Edward B., 'at the Union Lake residential school remarks that "we are going to tell you how we are treated. I am always hungry. We only get two slices of bread and one plate of porridge ... We are treated like pigs, some of boys, always eat cats and wheat. I never ask anyone to give me anything to eat. Some of the boys cried because they are hungry. Once I cry too because I was very hungry" (Milloy 2013: 16), therefore, "grumbling about food was a daily exercise performed with varying degrees of bitterness and ingenuity" (Johnston 1988: 139). Milloy notes that:

> During this long period from 1879 to 1946, the Department and the churches failed to "be humane and kind," to meet their "parental" responsibilities to these children. The churches and the Department did not ensure, throughout the system, that children were well-fed and adequately clothed, safely housed,

cherished, and provided with the education that was used as the fundamental justification for removing them from their parents and communities. (2013: 15)

The students showed their discontent through their complaints, but nothing changed. The lack of action on the side of teachers led the students into psychological problems. Herman explains, "a secure sense of connection with caring people is the foundation of personality development. When this connection is shattered, the traumatized person loses her basic sense of self" (2015: 52). The students knew they were not important and that the teachers did not care about them, and this lack of care affected them in their adulthood. Even the smallest kid with a small stomach would not feel full, and those bigger-sized students would not have more food to eat. At times they stole food to survive. Milloy reports that "at St. George's it was, according to Lett, a way of life. 'Stealing was chronic and from all this was done without hesitancy because it was necessary for survival" (2013: 17). As a result of lack of enough food, they were prone to catch diseases very easily which, at times, consequently led to their deaths.

Despite all the malnourishment and hunger, the tragic news was that students' deaths were neglected even by the newspapers. "There was one terrible period in the fall of 1918 when many boys died in the dreaded flu epidemic that gripped the world. There was one pathetic entry in the newspaper, '*Personne mourit aujourd'hui* [no one died today]'" (Johnston 1988: 82). The journalists were blind and deaf to the death rate of students at residential schools, and they denied the obvious facts and the evident presence of their deaths. The journalists did not always document the fact that Indigenous children died at residential schools. The question that Laub and Felman ask is "what does it mean to *inhabit history* as crime, as the space of the annihilation of the Other" (1991: 190). The history of residential schools was denied and censored as much as the teachers could hide the information. However, the

Indigenous community was affected by it and its later repercussions and literature constitute a way to claim back the annihilation that Indigenous community faced.

Meals were so meager that "meals became rituals" (Johnston 1988: 40). The students did not talk during their meal as they intended to eat the small portion that they were given within their limited time. While male students suffered from lack of food, they thought that female students had a better life in the residential school as they looked plump and healthy. "Only a few sidelong glances at the girls gave us reason enough to 'bemoan our outcast state and trouble deaf heaven with our bootless cries'" (Johnston 1988: 58). The word 'outcast' emphasized the impression boys had about their status at the school. They felt ignored by their teachers while the female students received superior care. Despite their supplication to Heaven, nothing changed in their lives. When the boys had the chance to visit their sisters at St. Joseph's, "they got first-hand evidence of how much better the girls lived and of the vastly superior care they received from the good sisters" (Johnston 1988: 81). Their observation was biased as they were obsessed with their hardships. In reality, both boys and girls experienced traumatic incidents at residential school; only the kind of trauma differed. Capitaine and Vanthuyne note that at residential schools "people are different, but stories are basically the same" (2017: 50).

At times, the students could not tolerate their condition anymore and they attempted to escape the residential school. Gordon, one of the students, addresses his friend: "I hate this place. I wanna go home an' never come back … I'm gonna run away, Ben! I can't take it no more. Maybe I won't see you no more … waah … waah" (Johnston 1988: 108). The pauses in between his speech emphasize that he intended to gather his thoughts. Herman mentions that traumatized patients do not use ordinary language but they use "set of images" that were crystallized in their mind (Herman 2015: 38). The pauses indicate his anger and his helplessness as he has no option in his life. He suffered a lot and he did not want to stay there, but still he was not sure about escaping from the school. Once in a group, they decide to run away from school as they can think of the plights in their plan and they might gather food together. When the students stand in the line, Father Buck cannot see Benedict Shigwadja, Gordon Solomon or Russel. He asked out loud from other students where these students could be, but no one knows or they just simply do not want to inform him and keep their silence. Hunger, punishments and the death of their classmates were just a few reasons for the students to run away from school.

The students suffered from both physical hunger and emotional hunger. The teachers punished them and beat them all the time rather than caressing them and giving them love, now that they were far from their families and parents. Even though the teachers intended to show kindness to students by teaching them, their approach was wrong since it led to the students' suffering.

> Food was the one abiding complaint because the abiding condition was hunger, physical and emotional. Food, or the lack of it, was something that the boys could point to as a cause of their suffering; the other was far too abstract and therefore much too elusive to grasp. (Johnston 1988: 137)

As they were little children, they expressed their lack of food but the main reason they suffered was the lack of human compassion from the teachers. "The traumatized people feel utterly abandoned" (Herman 2015: 52), and here the students felt lonely and abandoned as a result of the indifferent, cold and harsh behaviour of the Fathers. However, the reader may notice that the narrator at the same time talks about a few kind Fathers who take care of the students and give the love and affection they need albeit only for a short while.

> There were two young men who, by disposition and temperament, were well suited to look after the little

ones. The first was Father "Barney" Mayhew, S. J., a man of tremendous compassion and understanding, who served the "natives" until his recent retirement… The other, Father Schretlin, S. J., who came some years later, was made of sterner stuff, with a strong predilection for law, order and discipline. (Johnston 1988: 61)

Though these two Fathers were examples of kind-hearted people who gave care and attention to students, the general atmosphere of schools was threatening. The students were taken away from their families with the promise that they would be in great care of the Fathers of the church and teachers, while at school they came up against all types of abuse. The paradoxical part was that when some inspectors from the main church reported the health and food condition at Spanish residential school, they gave false reports. The schools used to display healthy food when the inspectors arrived, and those inspectors did not trust the students' words about the food. Milloy remarks that "some school menus were collected, as a matter of course, during inspections, but they are mute; they say nothing about what was actually served and in what amounts" (2013: 2776). Once the inspectors visited the Spanish residential school, they mentioned that they were there "to inspect the food and to make reports on the quality" (Johnston 1988: 142) of students' meals; however, they joined the conspiracy of silence as journalists and Fathers had previously done. "What is the significance of deafness" (Laub & Felman 1991: 182): deafness is a kind of conspiracy of silence, unacknowledgement of what really happened. The inspectors did not listen to students' complaints about the quality of the food, and they were deaf to their words. The students were ready to talk to investigators and discuss "how best they might assist the investigation and provide testimony" (Johnston 1988: 142), yet the inspectors ignored them. Despite the tales of misery and hunger they heard from students who were the victims of abuse at the school, the inspectors were blind to the reality or they just did not intend to involve themselves when religious Fathers were in charge of the schools. They kept their silence towards historical incidents of hunger and lack of food at residential schools. They just gave false hopes to the students that they would reflect their words in their report; however, their report said that:

> [...] up to this point we can only report in generalities, but we do have enough information to state that it is our impression that the Indian boys are receiving as balanced a diet of protein and carbohydrates as is necessary for their growth and health. (Johnston 1988: 143)

The students suffered from a lack of food on their plates, yet the report said that their diet was suitable for their health. The hunger that the Indigenous children experienced was not recorded by the inspectors, becoming, nowadays, an historical report at Spanish residential school. Instead of supporting the Indigenous students when they needed help and care, inspectors and church supported each other. In fact, it clarified the point that they did not really care about what happened to these students at school as long as their civilized Euro-Canadian society was not threatened by these 'savage' Indians.

Conclusion

Johnston's *Indian School Days* recounts the trauma of being an Indigenous child in Euro- Canadian society. The Indigenous students underwent maltreatment, malnutrition and beatings at residential school, but at some level they "toughed it out" since they supported by each other. Various narratives such as newspapers and reports by school inspectors ignored the deaths, disease and malnourishment at the school. Basil survived those years in order to tell the world about his experience and at the same time his narrative helped him to reconcile with his past. As Herman points out, "the victim demands action, engagement and remembering" (2015: 7–8). The incidents that happened at those schools had ripple effects and caused deep harm, and they should not be forgotten. They need to be narrated within novels, stories and songs. While seeking archives to shed light on the historical incidents, one must note that some of them were neither recorded nor fairly documented, but the absence of those incidents from the documents does not guarantee their absence from history.

Works Cited

Capitaine, Brieg and Vanthuyne Karine (2017), *Power through Testimony Reframing Residential Schools in the Age of Reconciliation*, Vancouver: UBC Press

Hele, Karl. S. (2013). The Indian Act - From 1876 to Today. *Geoscope* 44 (1) (Fall), pp. 6-17.

Herman, Judith (2015), *Trauma and Recovery*, New York: Basic Books.

Johnston, Basil. H. (1988), *Indian School Days*, Oklahoma: University of Oklahoma press: Norman.

Laub, Dori and Felman Shoshana (1991), *Testimony; Crises of Witnessing in Literature, Psychoanalysis and History*, London: Routledge.

MacDonald, David. (2007). First Nations, Residential Schools, and the Americanization of the Holocaust: Rewriting Indigenous History in the United States and Canada. *Canadian Journal of Political Science* 40 (4), pp. 995- 1015.

Milloy, John (2013), "Doing Public History in Canada's Truth and Reconciliation Commission," *The Public Historian*, 35 (4): 10–19.

Mosby, Ian (2013), "Administering Colonial Science: Nutrition Research and Human Biomedical Experimentation in Aboriginal Communities and Residential Schools, 1942–1952," *Histoire sociale/Social history* (46) 91.

Mosby, Ian and Galloway Tracey (2017), "'Hunger Was Never Absent': How Residential School Diets Shaped Current

Patterns of Diabetes among Aboriginal Peoples in Canada,"
CMAJ 189 (32).

Styvendale, Nancy (2008), "The Trans/Historicity of Trauma in
Jeannette Armstrong's Slash and Sherman Alexie's Indian Killer,"
Studies in the Novel 40, pp. 203–223.

TRC Volume 1. (2015). Montreal: McGill University.

ANNA MONGIBELLO

Moosemeat & Marmalade: Analyzing Mediatized Indigenous Food Cultures on TV

Food as Discourse

IN RECENT YEARS, WE HAVE seen an increase in media discourses about food, especially in the form of television food shows, including instructional cooking shows, travel shows on culinary destinations and cooking competitions. However, these shows mostly bring culinary experiences to global attention framed so as to satisfy 'normative appetites' and teach pragmatic culinary knowledge that promotes regimes of culinary taste (De Solier 2005). Indeed, while Canadian TV screens do reflect the multicultural essence of the nation, with cooking programs focusing on Italian, French, Japanese, and other 'fancy' culinary cultures, no space is devoted to Indigenous eating traditions on mainstream TV networks. Studies have pointed out that Indigenous cooking knowledge, habits and ingredients have long been neglected and Indigenous food sovereignty violently negated as an effect of cultural and linguistic imperialism. However, since the 1990s, Indigenous cultural knowledge has undergone a process of mediatization and has been profoundly affected by the rise of mediating technologies (LaDuke 1999). The Aboriginal Peoples Television Network (APTN), for instance, broadcasts cultural contents, re-mediated for television consumption, produced by and for Indigenous peoples, including Indigenous food knowledge. However, before diving into the core of the present study, it is important to lay out the theoretical framework in order to clarify our starting point.

A theoretical assumption crucial to this work is the relationship between food, language and identity. Food is not merely central to humankind as a requirement for survival, but it also functions "as a defining element of human culture and identity" (Frye & Bruner 2012: 1), having profound socioeconomic, sociopolitical and socio-ecological motives and consequences. In this sense, food cannot but be understood as a complex, multimodal system of communication, allowing signification through codes that are continuously negotiated and shared within and among cultural communities. Such codes play a special role in the definition of communal and individual identities. As a communication system, food and its meanings shift depending on the socio-cultural contexts in which they operate as processes and practices that produce ideals and represent models. Therefore, food has an ideological potential that can be used by various actors on the basis of specific agendas when food is made into discourse or is employed as discourse in the construction and sustainment of social values and power structures as well as resistance to both. We can therefore hypothesize that food is used as a discursive device across media and genres in the form of a social practice to shape social and political realities.

In the broader field of Food Studies, an emerging area of research focusing on the complex relationships between food, culture and society, Food Discourse is seen as a discursive device and a sociolinguistic phenomenon. Food Discourse may occur in several forms, including but not limited to food shows on TV and food blogs on the internet. The term has been used by scholars like Matwick and Matwick (2019) in reference to food-related communication, either verbal or non-verbal, functional and/or ideological. Food Discourse includes texts about food preparation, presentation and consumption. In these texts, individual and collective sociocultural values about food are expressed. An analysis of Food

Discourse reveals the relationship between food and language, and sheds light on the creation, sustainment and legitimation of power relationships between agents/patients of Food Discourse. At the same time, since Food Discourse is seen as taking place in processes of socialization that create, sustain, legitimize or challenge power positions, the relationship between food and identity is also crucial. The wider relationship between food, language and identity has been explored by means of various approaches and theoretical-methodological tools, ranging from those offered by sociolinguistic studies to cultural studies. Most of the work in lexical semantics between the end of the 1960s and the beginning of the 1980s dealt with the terminology of cooking within the theoretical framework of structuralist semantics and the language of "wine talk" in English (Lehrer 1969 and 1983). Later research in the 1980s investigated the relationship between what people eat and how others perceive them or how they see themselves (Sadella & Burroughs 1981; Stein & Nameroff 1995). One fruitful field in the research on the relation between language and food is the analysis of dinner talk based on transcriptions of taped interactions in families (see for example the study by Blum-Kulka 1997; Laurier & Wiggins 2011; Larson et al. 2006). Other studies on food language have highlighted how food is a potent maker (and marker) of cultural identity. Such studies include those conducted by Beagan and Chapman (2012), to mention but one. The role of food in identification processes is explored by Bell and Valentine (1997), who provide an analysis of the social and cultural meanings of food preparation and consumption and how food can strengthen regional identity.

Food and the media—or food in the media—has recently received critical attention. Over the last twenty years, we have witnessed an increase in media discourse about food globally (Matwick and Matwick 2015). TV food shows provide insights into the construction of social values and social roles. One example is the transmission of encoded forms of knowledge about gender, class, ethnicity and national identity that perform ideological work (Matwick and Matwick 2015) in popular cooking shows,

hosted by beloved chefs and foodies such as Nigella Lawson and
Jamie Oliver (Chiaro 2013; Andrews 2003). Overall, as observed
by Murray (2013), despite the recent proliferation of food programming, there remains a sparse body of academic research on
food and television, and on food and the media in broader terms.
Two studies worth mentioning are those by Collins (2009) and
by Veri and Liberti (2013), both showing how contemporary
American cultural values are mediatized on the Food Network,
a popular American television channel owned by the Television
Food Network. A portion of food and television research has
dealt with how cooking shows perpetuate the relationship between women, domestic expertise and food, while reifying men's
professional alignment with food in public spaces (Sanders 2009;
Hollows 2007). On the other hand, not much has been said on
how food shows are raced and classed, and create taste hierarchies,
for example, reminiscent of colonial culinary imperialism. At the
same time, Food Discourse as a counter-ideological tool has still
to be addressed. The present study aims to investigate how food
is deployed counter-discursively in the television space of the
Aboriginal Peoples Television Network (APTN), a Canadian cable TV channel made for and by First Nations, Inuit and Métis
people, in light of the broader process of Indigenous cultural revitalization and Indigenous food sovereignty.

Indigenous Food Cultures and Sovereignty

Race, ethnicity, nationalism and colonialism are imbricated in
food. This is what Warnes maintains in *Savage Barbecue: Race,
Culture, and the Invention of America's First Food* (2008), a book on
how the practice of barbecuing was taken from Native Americans.
If food is a cultural marker, as already said, what cannot be ignored
is that historically—especially in places that have experienced the
trauma of colonialism—food has served as a potent identity maker
both to subjugate and erase as well as to impose and construct

subaltern identities and hierarchical power relations based on tastes. Although today attitudes towards ethnic cuisines are often ones that see persons of racial privilege approach the food of the 'ethnic' other as a resource for one's own use and adornment (as part of a passion for "authenticity"), many Indigenous food cultures are still not even listed into the category of 'ethnic cuisine.' On the contrary, they are silenced, denied and discriminated against as a result of what settler colonialism did to Indigenous cultures globally, in order to enforce control through the imposition of cultural practices. When the French and then the British stole Indigenous ancestral lands from the sixteenth century onwards, colonialism traumatically affected Indigenous food cultures. In residential schools, for instance, cultural practices were violently prohibited. There, Indigenous children were forced to eat foods that were alien to their traditional diets. For instance, they were forcibly introduced to farmed meats, cheese, wheat flour and sugar (Waziyatawin 2012) and denied traditional diets based on berries, fish and wild game (Mosby 2013). It is sadly ironic to think that the foods that were banned were the same ones that kept the first Europeans alive when they got to Canada and journeyed across the continent. At the same time, normative appetites were imposed as well as "a regime of culinary taste" (De Solier 2005) that dismantled Indigenous culinary traditions and disregarded Indigenous traditional foods. This is not an old story nor one that can be relegated to the kitchen. According to Ian Mosby (2013), between 1942 and 1952, some Canadian nutrition experts and the Department of Indian Affairs conducted secret nutritional experiments on Aboriginal communities and residential school children without the subjects' informed consent, thus confirming Canada's disregard of Indigenous lives and the exercise of biopolitical control. A crucial point in the imposition of culinary regimes was the disconnection of the land from its people, considered as "key to the process of colonization" (Waziyatawin 2012). The prohibition of Indigenous culinary traditions can in fact be seen as part of the brutal dispossession of ancestral lands, since it was meant to keep

Indigenous peoples away from their foods and, consequently, from their lands, forcing them off the land onto reserves. Moreover, it resulted in a major dietary issue in Indigenous communities, with alarming levels of malnutrition linked to increasing dependence on store-bought and processed foods that has led to a growing epidemic of diseases such as diabetes, hypertension and obesity, still visible today.[1] For many Indigenous peoples, hunting wild game and harvesting local plants provided a healthy, affordable and sacred connection to their ancestors and the land.

Food talk was also useful for constructing the 'other' as uncivilized. Think, for instance, of the word "Eskimo" used by British explorers in the eighteenth century to refer to the Inuit people. The term most certainly derives from an Algonquian language of the Atlantic Ocean Coast, recalling the word "askamiciw" that means "eater of raw meat" (Sturtevant 1978). The process of naming and interpellation has always taken the form of a fundamental misrecognition, aimed at producing class-based dominance relations. There was nothing innocent (nor new) about picking up a local custom in order to label the people of the Northwest Territories. On the contrary, there was a clear intention to subdue and confine them to a non-human level.

Proof of the colonial legacy disregarding Indigenous food traditions is provided by the vast array of food programming on television screens that mainstream networks offer today in Canada: Indigenous food cultures have long been excluded. Or when included, they have been regarded from a voyeuristic and othering

---

1 "An Overview of Aboriginal Health in Canada," *National Collaborating Centre for Aboriginal Health*, July 18, 2013. Available online: http://www.nccah-ccnsa.ca/en/publications.aspx?sortcode=2.8.10&publication=101 (accessed on November 15, 2015). Interestingly, in 2019 Health Canada published a revision of *Canada's Food Guide* specifically addressed to First Nations, Inuit and Métis (in English, Inuktitut, Ojibwe, Plains Cree and Woods Cree) on how to eat healthily according to Canadian standards (available online at https://www.canada.ca/content/dam/hc-sc/migration/hc-sc/fn-an/alt-formats/fnihb-dgspni/pdf/pubs/fnim-pnim/2007_fnim-pnim_food-guide-aliment-eng.pdf, last accessed June 28, 2020).

viewpoint, from an ethnographic perspective. Part of the problem is also due to the fact that Indigenous food traditions, especially with regard to wild game, are still treated with contempt and viewed as detrimental to models of progress. At the same time, bureaucracy and societies view the need to hunt, fish or harvest on the basis of sustainable ancestral traditions with suspicion. As a consequence, Indigenous practices have often been prohibited or obstructed. However, things are slowly changing also thanks to a renewed interest in Indigenous cuisine. In 2010, the first First Nations restaurant, Salmon n' Bannock, opened in Vancouver, followed by a handful of other diners and cafés across Canada, including the Pow Wow Café in 2016 and NishDish in 2018, owned by Anishinaabe chef Johl Whiteduck Ringuette, both Toronto-based. These restaurants serve bannock, sockeye salmon, wild rice and berries along with bison and elk, although Canada's food preparation laws have proved another barrier for Indigenous restaurants. In most provinces, meat that has been hunted cannot be served to patrons, including moose and seal: a staple in many Indigenous communities.

Interest in Indigenous cuisine has also been picked up by some food shows on mainstream TV. For instance, on February 3, 2020, Food Network Canada launched *Wall of Chefs*, a culinary competition featuring thirty-three diverse culinary powerhouses from across Canada in front of a panel of twelve judges, including two Indigenous ones: chef Christa Bruneau-Guenther (French Métis, member of the Peguis First Nation) and chef Shane Chartrand (Cree Métis).[2] While this can be read as another encouraging signal, however, it is an isolated case on mainstream TV networks. Much still has to be done. What should be pointed out, though, is that the revitalization of Indigenous food cultures is part of the broader project of de-colonization and self-determination that has been undertaken by Indigenous peoples from the 1970s onwards in response to Canada's assimilation, restriction and control policies.

---

2 "Chefs bring Indigenous flavor to Food Network Canada", available online at https://saymag.com/indigenous-chefs-canada (last accessed June 28, 2020).

This project has been translated into a number of movements for the affirmation and recognition of Indigenous rights. In 1996, the Working Group on Indigenous Food Sovereignty started to explore the concept of food sovereignty and to work towards solutions to the reaffirmation of spiritual, emotional and physical relationships with land and water. The concept of food sovereignty was then articulated in the "Nyéléni Declaration for Food Sovereignty" in 2007,[3] which states that

> Food sovereignty is the right of peoples to healthy and culturally appropriate food produced through ecologically sound and sustainable methods, and their right to define their own food and agricultural systems. It puts the aspirations and needs of those who produce, distribute and consume food at the heart of food systems and policies rather than the demands of markets and corporations.

Later on, in 2012, #idlenomore, an Indigenous mass movement crossing Canada from side to side as a protest against Bill C-45, brought issues pertaining to established Indigenous rights back to the forefront of the political debate, including land ownership, traditional fishing methods and hunting rights that the omnibus budget bill presented by the conservative government led by Stephen Harper had threatened.

A crucial role in the revitalization of Indigenous cultures has been played by APTN. APTN joined the Canadian TV panorama on September 1, 1999 as a basic cable TV channel, financed by a monthly subscriber fee, which today reaches up to eleven million Canadian households. Due to the contents of its shows and the multitude of Indigenous languages chosen in which to deliver them, APTN may be considered "a discursive site of resistance"

---

3 Mali Sélingué. "Declaration of Nyéléni." February 27, 2007. Available online at: http://nyeleni.org/spip.php? article290 (last accessed January 5, 2016).

(Mongibello 2018) and is viewed "as the only space in Canada's national mediascape where Aboriginal people are regularly visible" (Dowell 2013: 91). APTN is not just a TV network based on Indigenous stories, but it is also created by Indigenous peoples: in fact, 65% of its employees are of Indigenous ancestry (mostly First Nations, then Métis and lastly Inuit). A considerable part of APTN's programming is devoted to food shows such as *Feast*, hosted by Tiffany Wahsontiiostha Deer, a professional chef with a passion for Indigenous cuisine; *Nunavummi Mamarijavut*, which explores ways of retrieving, gathering and preserving food in the traditional Inuit way; *Niqitsiat*, which features the preparation and cooking of traditional Inuit food; and *Moosemeat & Marmalade*, a show hosted by a classically trained British chef and a bush cook of Cree ancestry, which will be analyzed in this study. These shows, in Indigenous languages and/or in English/French, bring together traditional ingredients, traditional knowledge and Indigenous languages. In fact, revitalizing Indigenous traditions and languages is one of APTN's mandates.

Research questions and methodology

In light of the theoretical premise, the present study aims to address the following research questions:

1. How are Indigenous food cultures mediatized?
2. What are the main features/strategies of mediatized Indigenous Food Discourse?

While the notion of Food Discourse has already been introduced, a definition of Indigenous Food Discourse could be advanced within this study. Indigenous Food Discourse may be conceptualized as a specialist kind of discourse revolving around food and its narration in resistance to the discrimination of Indigenous food cultures from Indigenous-centered perspectives. Such perspectives not only influence the kind of contents covered, but also the languages through which these contents are conveyed. In this study, we want to investigate how Indigenous Food Discourse works as a strategic device through specific discursive practices in contrast with the dominant Canadian discourse on Indigenous peoples, nutrition and food, which is the hegemonic discourse in Canada. In this sense, Indigenous Food Discourse may be seen as counter-hegemonic. In other words, we postulate that the representation of Indigenous food cultures filtered through Indigenous worldviews relies on multimodal, linguistic and rhetorical strategies that subvert the mainstream discourse on Indigenous peoples, interrogate the broad and complex repertoires of images and narratives created by mainstream media, and interrupt the ethnographic, voyeuristic gaze through which Indigenous food cultures have historically been framed and dismissed as unmodern and uncivilized.

The analysis will be conducted using the tools of Multimodal Critical Discourse Analysis (Machin & Mayr 2012; Bateman & Schmidt 2011; Iedema 2001 and 2003; Kress & van Leeuwen 2001, 1996; Thibault 2000) in order to shed some light on how diverse semiotic modes of expression interact to create meaning. Looking merely at discourse without considering other semiotic categories is not enough if we want to grasp the complexity of social practices in the social situations where they are produced. Since language "is just one among the many resources for making meaning," and "a partial bearer of the meaning of a textual/semiotic whole" (Kress 2011: 38), a multimodal approach allows us to see how multiple modes are interconnected as one cultural resource in a complex semiotic entity. Together with social semiotics, multimodality helps us to ask and answer questions pertaining to the process of meaning-making, the agency of those who produce the meaning, the construction of identity and meaning, the social constrains occurring in between, the production of knowledge and how and by whom knowledge is produced. To put it in another way, an analysis of visual communication "can tell us something about the contexts where it was produced, about social relations, about ideology and the kinds of motivated ideas that are being shared" (Ledin & Machin 2020: 9). A multimodal approach provides the chance to identify the narrative elements deployed, to show the meaning-making roles of the semiotic modes and to explain how their interrelations contribute to a discursive presentation of reality. We will therefore consider the semiotic material, the choices and the potential meaning of semiotic resources that shape communication and social behavior in order to reveal the discourses communicated. Attention will be paid to the characters' semiotics and embodied signifiers—such as dress code and hairstyle—as well as to language.

A case study: *Moosemeat & Marmalade*

For the purpose of the analysis, we will concentrate on *Moosemeat & Marmalade*, a popular food show airing on APTN. The show presents four seasons, for a total of fifty episodes of twenty-two minutes each. It features a peculiar couple of chefs: Art Napoleon, who is of Cree ancestry from the Saulteau First Nation Reserve in northeastern BC, and his counterpart, Dan Hayes, from Hammersmith, Central London, UK. The show is filmed in Canadian English but it is also subtitled and dubbed into Cree and French. The episodes are set in several Canadian locations including the Gulf Islands, Vancouver Island, the Northwest Territories as well as overseas in the UK. Napoleon and Hayes lead each episode alternately. One of the two chefs picks a journey and an ingredient, while the recipes work as narrative devices that activate the information exchange between the hosts and their audience. In order to answer our research questions, we will consider the show promo picture and clip and three extracts taken from episode 1 of season 3.

   As a first step in the multimodal analysis, we consider how the social actors are construed in the economy of the show. The audience is presented with a sharp dichotomy right from the beginning. In the promo video and photo (see Fig. 1), the dichotomy is set up by means of both visual and textual elements. While Napoleon is presented to the public as a bush cook, Hayes is introduced as a classically trained British chef. Clips and photos of both, recalling their 'natural' environment, support and reinforce this dichotomy. Napoleon is seen sporting a Mohawk and the typically Canadian, black and red lumberjack jacket, standing in a bush, by a fire, holding a rifle; Hayes, on the other hand, is wearing a chef's apron over formal clothes, standing outside his city restaurant and then in his professional kitchen. The bush and the kitchen appear as opposite worlds to which symbolic referents are attached. In the background of Napoleon's clip, symbols recalling his Indigenous roots are also included, such as Indigenous art works and traditional Indigenous recipes on screen. Other symbols, characterizing Hayes's culinary education and cultural influences, are visible in his clip as well, featuring cutting boards, knives and dishes on which he places sophisticated food.

The explicit dichotomy constructed in the promo is reiterated in the title of the show, *Moosemeat & Marmalade*, the former being symbolically linked to Napoleon's cultural background and the second to Hayes's. As for the first, wild moose meat and wild game in general have sustained Canada's First Nations for centuries, and indeed hunting is deeply ingrained in First Nation cultures. Therefore, the term clearly refers to a well-known culinary and cultural tradition among Indigenous nations. As a sacred activity, it is protected under Section 35 of Canada's Constitution Act, according to which Indigenous peoples have a legal right to hunt, fish and trap on their ancestral lands. The moose is also an iconic Canadian symbol. "Marmalade," on the other hand, despite its Portuguese origins from "marmelo," is rooted in Scotland and later became a must on any traditional British breakfast table, spread generously over slices of freshly made buttered toast and accompanied by a cup of tea. So much so that in 1995, National Marmalade Day was launched to celebrate the five-hundredth anniversary of the earliest port record of the arrival of Portuguese marmalade in Britain in 1495, as Anne Wilson recalls in *The Book of Marmalade* (1999).

The font chosen for the display of the show's title is also worth noticing. In Fig. 1 two different fonts are used so as to allow the audience to clearly identify the two cultural components of the show. Design (including font and color) is an important vehicle of communication and part of the message just as much as the semantic meaning of a word. According to van Leeuwen (2005), fonts can be described in terms of a limited range of qualities such as curvature versus angularity, narrow versus wide, heavy versus light, with each quality communicating ideas at a symbolic level. The font chosen for "Marmalade," for example, is formed by fine lines emphasizing lightness to suggest the elegance connected to fine dining, while the wider lines of "Moosemeat" appear short and squat. The typeface is used here to illustrate the idea of something rustic and untamed, without sophistication, an idea that is further strengthened by the large pair of moose horns framing the title, in juxtaposition with a knife and a fork. Again, the authors and producers seem to play with dichotomies and opposite meanings.

Figure 1: screenshot of *Moosemeat & Marmalade* promo picture. Napoleon on the right and Hayes on the left.

When looking at the picture, audiences can make assumptions about the content of the show. A number of connected signifiers are attached to the dichotomy and the title, including rustic vs. gourmet; authentic vs. constructed; untamed vs. classy. The two hosts perfectly embody these signifiers, as their outfits also suggest.

The audience is encouraged to align with or against the narrative, which is particularly evident in Fig. 1 where Napoleon and Hayes's direct gaze demand the viewers engage with them in some kind of interaction. Overall, the representation of the social actors seems to re-propose the colonial dichotomy between Indigenous vs. European. However, as we will see, the colonial narrative is reversed, since the perspective is informed by Indigenous worldviews.

We shall now turn to our analysis of the extracts taken from season 3, episode 1, in order to uncover the main features and strategies of mediatized Indigenous Food Discourse. In this episode, Napoleon introduces Hayes and the audience to a reclaimed First Nation's clam garden on Russell Island, located in BC's Gulf Island National Park, which hosts the Clam Garden Re-Vitalization Project. Here they meet Skye Augustine, project coordinator for Parks Canada, as well as May and Luschin, two elders from the Coast Salish Nation. The episode is divided into two parts: in the first, traditional teachings are introduced, while in the second the focus is on traditional ways of cooking clams over a fire. As one of the interviewed guests explains, "clam gardens" are Indigenous management systems for creating an optimal habitat for clams by modifying the beach. In this extract, the reference to food works as a cultural trigger to activate the narrative of Indigenous foodways and cultural habits. Food as a cultural trigger also allows for the re-contextualization of Indigenous knowledge, which is mediatized here and translated from the oral accounts of the elders to a TV show format. In the mediatization process, Napoleon is a cultural mediator in the sense that he connects two apparently opposite worlds: that of Hayes and of all non-Indigenous viewers and that of the Indigenous elders and experts they meet and interview. Humor is used by Napoleon to release the tension caused by the cultural gap. This is a typical feature of Napoleon's talk throughout the show, and it is consistent with what is known as Indigenous humor. At the beginning of the episode, Napoleon, humorously introduces Hayes as "the guy who has never heard of a clam garden before." By so doing, Hayes's role is also set up, as the ideal addressee of a narrative designed to teach him about clams as traditional Indigenous food and clam gardens as an ancestral cultural custom.

The whole episode revolves around Indigenous Food Discourse. Clam gardens are introduced as advanced resource management systems that Parks Canada aims to revive in the wider process of revitalizing Indigenous cultures. From a linguistic perspectives, Indigenous Food Discourse features words from Indigenous languages, either translated into English or in the form of borrowings with the meanings of Indigenous cultures. An example is "skw'lehy," translated into English as "littleneck clam," a young quahog suitable to being eaten raw, or "ioqiway," translated as "clam garden." As Tab 1 shows, the introduction of Hal'q'umi'num words has an educational purpose. Therefore, Indigenous Food Discourse seems to work also as a device through which to include Indigenous ancestral languages in the narration of Indigenous cultures:

Tab. 1: The "littleneck" sequence

SKYE [08:00]	How do you say the word for littleneck again?	
LUSCHIN [08:02]	skw'lehy is littleneck	

In this sequence, Luschin and May join the hosts in the clam garden. Indigenous elders have traditionally played an important role in maintaining social cohesion within their communities since they embody the cultural memory of Indigenous nations. The inclusion of Indigenous elders in this episode reinforces the Indigenous perspective of the show and pushes the viewers towards a positive understanding of Indigenous ancestral cultures and ways of being. While the elders show how to collect clams from the clam garden, Hayes's response to their teaching is loaded with tokens of positive appraisal. In fact, the clams found in the clam garden are said to be "huge" and "amazing," and the Indigenous peoples who invented the system as "knowledgeable." The traditional colonizer/colonized duo introduced in the promo is reversed here since the "knowledgeable" perspective is that of the elders who explain to Hayes and the viewers how the clam garden works. The positive representation of social actors stands in contrast with the dismissal of Indigenous traditions and ways of being during colonization as unmodern. Indigenous knowledge is re-contextualized here within a multimodal, discursive space of resistance, where a broader understanding of food and its collection, preparation and cooking is also provided, and Indigenous teachings are legitimized. According to Calsamiglia and Van Dijk (2004), knowledge dissemination is best seen as a process of re-contextualization rather than simplification. However, since the audiences receiving the message come from different backgrounds (as do the hosts themselves) an operation of mediation is needed in order to address the knowledge asymmetry (Kastberg 2011). In this sequence, for example, Luschin explains how to dig clams out of the clam garden and shares important teachings with the hosts about the clam-digging process.

Table 2: The "clam digging" sequence

ART [21:59]	How do you select the right spot to start digging?	
LUSCHIN [21:59]	We've got these rocks here. The current's going to be	
	coming in and set ... This path there,	
	the little eggs will settle here.	
	So they'll build up around here.	

In the "clam digging" sequence (Tab. 2), the dissemination of Indigenous knowledge is triggered by Napoleon's question that prompts a conversational narrative through which Luschin explains where to find the best clams. The explanation is mediated as colloquial rather than technical. However, the register may also be due to the fact that Indigenous knowledge has always been passed on orally, for instance through storytelling, which turned traditional knowledge into stories to be remembered. Interestingly, the narrative of food intertwines with that of hunting and foraging for ingredients, which is an intrinsic part of the cooking process. The clam-digging activity is not only shown visually but also explained by the elders. By so doing, Indigenous Food Discourse stretches not only to include food language but also semantics pertaining to the field of clam harvesting in an attempt to revive and restore ancient traditional protocols that date back thousands of years. Deictic expressions, such as the repetition of the spatial marker "here," refer to the extra-linguistic context to establish a focal point for the viewer's attention. In Indigenous Food Discourse, a one-on-one relationship with the ingredients is established so as to appeal to sustainability and environmental concerns. In fact, later on, Luschin and May warn the hosts that the "baby butters" are not to be taken since conservation and biodiversity are taken very seriously in the Coast Salish culture.

Another feature of Indigenous Food Discourse is the use of collective pronouns/possessive adjectives such as "we/our" in combination with Indigenous languages. For instance, in the second part of the episode, after cooking a one-pot fire-baked clam dish, Napoleon and Hayes join the local community of Indigenous peoples to eat it. Here the combination "we/our" is used as a pan-Indigenous identity marker, meant to reconstruct, while recalling, group identity as an indicator of membership and a marker of inclusion:

Table 3: The "elder" sequence

MAY [20:55]	I can remember when I was little	 Just using our fingers. I can remember when I was little
	We'd have a meal like that and we'd have our bannock	 we'd have a meal like that and we'd have our bannock
	and it just brought back memories	 and it just brought back memories.
NAPOLEON [21:06]	I think we should all say huy ch q'u	 Art >> I think we should all say huy ch q'u.

In the "elder" sequence (Tab. 3), May, who is also seen as an authority among her people, is asked to say a traditional prayer. The practice is embedded in Indigenous food consumption. The use of "we" in the recollection of food memories serves an important discursive function insofar as it signals that—in the experience of food as a social and collective matter—the speaker's identity is construed as collective self, related to and interconnected with others. This is well exemplified by the shift from "I" to "we" in the narrating of food habits. The "we" referent is inferentially retrieved by the audience as referring not only to May and the Hal'q'umi'num Nation but also to all Indigenous peoples as a pan-Indigenous collectivity reference that produces a sense of social unity. In fact, May does not make explicit reference to her own community; however, the suggestion is retrievable from the communicative context and may apply to Indigenous peoples in Canada or in an even wider context. By so doing, the audience is led to perceive group identity and solidarity. Moreover, the introduction of a Hal'q'umi'num word to say "thank you" reinforces the idea of an in-group being construed in the recollection of memories, thus advancing the representation of a collectivity that shares the same language, action and effort towards the revitalization of Indigenous food cultures, practices and knowledge in general. While the "I" used by Napoleon to introduce the Hal'q'umi'num word may sound like a change towards the speaker's subjective perspective, the discourse marker "I think" suggests that Napoleon takes full responsibility when proposing a shift from English to Hal'q'umi'num. Such a shift is quintessentially strategic since it signals another change in perspective and another subversion of the colonial hierarchy.

Conclusions

In *Moosemeat & Marmalade*, an alternative story is told from an Indigenous perspective against Canadian food hegemonies that have long silenced and excluded Indigenous culinary traditions. In our analysis, Indigenous Food Discourse emerged as a specialized discourse that brings together Indigeneity, traditional food, cultural heritage, ancestral languages and traditional knowledge. Food is therefore transformed into a cultural trigger of Indigeneity and a vehicle of Indigenous storytelling.

What the analyzed extracts show is that Indigenous Food Discourse is not merely informed by food language but also by lexicon pertaining to the semantic field of food harvesting and foraging. Its multilayered semantic quality supports the idea that Indigenous Food Discourse is not exquisitely about food but also about identity, knowledge and tradition. In this sense, it stands out as a counter-ideological space of resistance to the discrimination of Indigenous food cultures from Indigenous-centered perspectives. The counter-discursive quality of Indigenous Food Discourse is made explicit in the show promo where a dichotomic relationship is established between the two hosts, based on traditional stereotypization of the colonizer/colonized duo. Throughout the episode, the fictitious hierarchical relationship between Napoleon and Hayes is promptly subverted, since the perspective employed to narrate food is entirely Indigenous. This is confirmed by both the choice of the episode setting (a clam garden in the Coast Salish area) and the topic, and by the representation of the social actors. The elders, for instance, are seen as a repository of Indigenous knowledge and representatives of political and cultural authority. Moreover, the narration of food is extended to processes of food recollection and consumption according to Indigenous ancestral traditions that, in the show, are not only presented but also validated. Part of the validation process is the employment of ancestral languages, revitalized in a TV format that may appeal to newer generations, and the use of pan-Indigenous "we," which contrasts with the mainstream Canadian discourse on Indigenous peoples, nutrition and food.

Overall, Indigenous Food Discourse in *Moosemeat & Marmalade* works as a strategic device. Discursive practices and semiotic materials are employed to construct ways of understanding the world that comply with Indigenous worldviews and to create awareness and recommendations around issues such as food consumption, production, land rights and the rebuilding of relationships between Indigenous and non-Indigenous peoples.

Works Cited

Andrews, Maggie (2003), "Nigella Bites The Naked Chef: The Sexual and the Sensual in Television Cookery Programmes," in J. Floyd and L. Forster (eds.), *The Recipe Reader: Narratives, Contexts, Traditions*, Burlington, VT: Ashgate, 187–204.

Bateman, John A. and Karl-Heinrich Schmidt (2011), *Multimodal Film Analysis: How Films Mean*, London: Routledge.

Beagan, Brenda and Gwen Chapman (2012), "Discourses of Food and Consumption: Constructing 'Healthy Eating/Constructing Self'," in M. Koc, J. Summer and A. Winson (eds.), *Critical Perspectives in Food Studies*, London: Oxford University Press, 136–151.

Bell, David and Gill Valentine (1997), *Consuming Geographies: We Are What We Eat*, New York: Routledge.

Blum-Kulka, Shoshana (1997), *Dinner Talk: Cultural Patterns of Sociability and Socialization in Family Discourse*, Mahwah NJ: Lawrence Erlbaum Associates.

Brownlie, Douglas and Paul Hewer, "Prime Beef Cuts: Culinary Images for Thinking 'Men'," *Consumption, Markets & Culture*, 10, 3. (2007):229–50.

Calsamiglia Helena and Teun Van Dijk, "Popularization Discourse and Knowledge about the Genome," *Discourse & Society*, 15, 4. (2004):369–389.

Chiaro, Delia (2013), "Passionate about Food: Jamie and Nigella and the Performance of Food-talk," in C. Gerhardt, M. Frobenius and S. Ley (eds.), *Culinary linguistics*, Amsterdam: John Benjamins, 83–102.

Collins, Kathleen (2009), *Watching What We Eat: The Evolution of Television Cooking Shows*, New York: Continuum.

Cook, Guy, Matt Reed and Allison Twiner, "'But it's all true!': Commercialism and Commitment in the Discourse of Organic Food Promotion," *Text & Talk*, 29, 2. (2009): 151–73.

De Solier, Isabelle. "TV Dinners: Culinary Television, Education and Distinction," *Continuum: Journal of Media & Cultural Studies*, 19, 4. (2005): 465–81.

Development, 111. (2006):1–15.

Dowell, Kristin L. (2013), *Sovereign Screens: Aboriginal Media on the Canadian West Coast*, Lincoln and London: University of Nebraska Press.

Frye, Joshua J. and Michael Bruner (eds.) (2012), *The Rhetoric of Food: Discourse, Materiality, and Power*, New York and London: Routledge.

Heinz, Bettina and Ronald Lee, "Getting Down to the Meat: The Symbolic Construction of Meat Consumption," *Communication Studies*, 49. (1998): 86–99.

Hollows, Joanne (2007), "The Feminist and the Cook: Julia Child, Betty Freidan and Domestic Femininity," in E. Casey and L. Martens (eds.), *Gender and Consumption: Domestic Cultures and the Commercialisation of Everyday Life*, Hampshire: Ashgate, 33–48.

Hollows, Joanne "The Bachelor Dinner: Masculinity, Class and Cooking in Playboy, 1953–61," *Continuum: Journal of Media & Cultural Studies*, 16, 2.(2002): 143–55.

Iedema, Rick. "Multimodality, Resemioticization: Extending the Analysis of Discourse as a Multisemiotic Practice," *Visual Communication*, 2, 1. (2003):29–57.

Iedema, Rick. "Resemioticization," *Semiotica*, 137, 1. (2001):23–39.

Kastberg, Peter. "Knowledge Asymmetries—Beyond 'to have and have not'," *Fachsprache*, 24, 3–4. (2011),137–151.

Kress, Gunter, Van Leeuwen, Teun (2001), *Multimodal Discourse: The Modes and Media of Contemporary Communication Discourse*, London: Arnold.

Kress, Gunther (2011), "Multimodal Discourse Analysis," in P. J. Gee and M. Handford, *The Routledge Handbook of Discourse Analysis*, London and New York: Routledge, 35–50.

Kress, Gunther and Teun Van Leeuwen (1996), *Reading Images: The Grammar of Visual Design*, London: Routledge.

LaDuke, Winona (1999), *All Our Relations: Native Struggles for Land and Life*, Cambridge: South End Press.

Larson, Reed W., Kathryn Branscomb and Angela Wiley, "Forms and Functions of Family Mealtimes: Multidisciplinary Perspectives," *New Directions for Child and Adolescent Development*, 111. (2006): 1–15.

Laurier, Eric and Sally Wiggins, "Finishing the Family Meal: The Interactional Organisation of Satiety", *Appetite*, 56, 1.(2011): 53–64.

Ledin, Per and David Machin, (2020), *Introduction to Multimodal Analysis*, London: Bloomsbury.

Lehrer, Adrienne (1983), *Wine and Conversation.* Bloomington: Indiana University Press.

Lehrer, Adrienne. "Semantic Cuisine". *Journal of Linguistics*, 5, (1969): 39–55.

Machin, David and Andrea Mayr (2012), *How to Do Critical Discourse Analysis. A Multimodal Introduction*, London: Sage.

Matwick, Kelsi and Keri Matwick (2019), *Food Discourse of Celebrity Chefs of Food Network*, Cham: Palgrave MacMillan.

Matwick, Kelsi and Keri Matwick, "Inquiry in Television Cooking Shows," *Discourse & Communication*, (2015):313–330.

Mongibello, Anna (2018), *Indigenous Peoples in Canadian TV News: A Corpus-Based Analysis of Mainstream and Indigenous News Discourses*, Naples: Paolo Loffredo Editore.

Mosby, Ian. "Administering Colonial Science: Nutrition Research and Human Biomedical Experimentation in Aboriginal Communities and Residential Schools, 1942–1952," *Social History*, 46. (2013):145–72.

Murray, Sarah (2013), "Food and Television," in K. Albala (ed.), *The Routledge Handbook of Food Studies*, London and New York: Routledge, 187–198.

Sadella, Edward and J. Jeffrey Burroughs, "Profiles in Eating: Sexy Vegetarians and Other Diet-based Stereotypes," *Psychology Today*, (1981): 51–57.

Sanders, Lise Shapiro (2009), "Consuming Nigella," in S. Gillis and J. Hollows (eds.), *Feminism, Domesticity and Popular Culture*, New York: Routledge. 151–163.

Stein, Richard and Carol I Nemeroff, "Moral Overtones of Food: Judgments of Others Based on What They Eat," *Personality and Social Psychology Bulletin*, 21 (1995): 480–490.

Sturtevant, William (1978), *Handbook of North American Indians: Arctic*, Ottawa: Government Printing Office.

Thibault, Paul (2000), "The Multimodal Transcription of a Television Advertisement: Theory and Practice," in A. Baldry (ed.), *Multimodality and Multimediality in the Distance Learning Age*, Campo Basso: Lampo, 311–384.

Veri, Maria and Rita Liberti, "Tailgate Warriors: Exploring Constructions of Masculinity, Food, and Football," *Journal of Sport and Social Issues*, 37, 3. (2013): 227–244.

Van Leeuwen, Teun (2005), *Introduction to Social Semiotics*, London: Routledge.

Warnes, Andrew (2008), *Savage Barbecue: Race, Culture, and the Invention of America's First Food*, Athens: University of Georgia Press.

Waziyatawin. "The Paradox of Indigenous Resurgence at the End of Empire," *Decolonization: Indigeneity, Education & Society*, 1. (2012):68–85.

Wilson, Anne (1999), *The Book of Marmalade*, Philadelphia: University of Pennsylvania Press.

ESTERINO ADAMI

A Taste of Diaspora: Linguistic and Cultural Representations of Parsi Food Discourse in Canada

1. Introduction

THE PREMISE FOR THIS PAPER lies in the consideration that food represents a thematic area strictly bound up with identity, and as such constitutes a significant engine in cultural processes of migration, being and belonging, as many recent academic publications and the growth of the field of food studies demonstrate. Contemporary approaches to food in fact have been enriched not only by the traditional frames of anthropology and sociology, but also by contributions from various disciplines such as literature, linguistics and cultural studies in general (Adami 2019; Halloran 2016; Mannur 2010). Consequently, a number of critical perspectives can be applied to the meaning, representation and function of food in creative domains as well as in broader social phenomena such as mobility, settlement and cultural reinvention.

In this paper, I intend to explore the notion of food discourse as a sign of identity for the Indian diaspora in Canada—a context whose multiculturalism is reflected by the coexistence of different types of Indian cuisine such as Punjabi (Chapman, Ristovski-Slijepcevica & Beaganb 2011). Indeed, the nationality adjective "Indian" actually designates a wide range of references, given the multicultural composition of India, whilst my analysis explores a very specific segment of

Indian society, namely the Parsi community, whose presence is quite widespread in the Toronto area. Here my purpose is to investigate the linguistic and narrative representation of Parsi food culture in Canada, considering how the diaspora experience shapes and influences the broad discursive construction of cuisine and its identitary implications. In particular, my investigation looks at the Parsi community, and examines their stylistic rendition of food discourse as a strategic means for cultural mediation and a repository of values and memories. As a case study, I focus on Niloufer Mavalvala, a famous Parsi chief who lives in Canada, and who—along with other well-known chefs such as Cyrus Todiwala (based in London) and Jehangir Mehta (based in New York)—foregrounds, spreads and indexes this particular kind of Indian cuisine around the world.

My research questions address 1) the overall cultural project and multiple narrative through which Mavalvala conveys her Parsi identity and heritage against the multicultural backdrop of Canada 2) the host of stylistic and multimodal resources she employs in her food narratives. To do so, I draw data from her volume *The Art of Parsi Cooking: Reviving an Ancient Cuisine* (2017) and her recipe blog and website (http://www.nilouferskitchen.com/).[1] This research builds on ideas growing out of various fields such as food studies, critical stylistics and cultural studies (e.g. Gibbons & Whiteley 2018; Jurafsky 2014) to reach a better understanding of the ways in which the exponent of a migrant community reappraises the alchemy of taste in order to rediscover roots and origins.

2. Research Context: Parsi Culture and Niloufer Mavalvala

Before presenting the case study of Mavalvala's representation of food discourse, it is vital to provide some general background to

---

1 In-text citations from Mavalvala's cookery book and her website are respectively indicated with page number between brackets and with abbreviation NK between brackets. Quotations are reproduced verbatim, hence the variation in spelling, capitalization and standard lexis.

Parsi (also spelt Parsee) cultures and communities,[2] which is one of the two main ethnic/religious groups that migrated from Persia to the Indian subcontinent to escape religious discrimination after the spread of Islam in Iran from the seventh–eighth centuries. The Parsi people and the Iranis are two distinct groups, but they share Zoroastrianism, described by Foltz (2009: 561) as one of the oldest monotheistic religions in the world. Today, Parsi culture is often associated with a host of different domains such as the arts (e.g. Rohinton Mistry, Zubin Mehta, Freddy Mercury), education (Homi Bhabha) or industry (Jamsetji Nusserwanji Tata, founder of the Taj Mahal Palace Hotel in Mumbai). Most Parsis developed trade ties with and settled in Southern India, especially in Maharashtra, and thus they are usually tied to the city of Mumbai (formerly Bombay), somehow playing the role of cultural mediators "living between the two worlds of the East and the West" (Tindall 1992: 72), where they also worked to promote the popularization of their culinary habits.

In fact, their folklore can also be investigated through the lens of food discourse. As Collingham writes (2006: 205), "in the 1890s, the working men of Bombay were provided with tea and snacks by Parsee immigrants from Iran who set up small tea stalls on street corners, selling soda water, cups of tea and biscuits, fried eggs, omelettes." But this was simply the first step because such stalls evolved into more refined shops and restaurants, known for their "Parsee specialities such as dhansak, green chutney and patra fish" (Collingham 2006: 206) as well as other dishes adapted from the English colonial community. It can be argued, then, that the creation of Parsi communities went hand in hand with the refashioning of their cuisine, keeping some of the original Persian flavours and adding new dishes, spices and cooking methods from both the Indian context and the English colonial tradition.

---

2 I would like to thank my Mumbai-based Parsi friends for providing valuable information, details and anecdotes about their cultural background.

In more recent times, the two groups have taken part in world migration, settling in Canada too and contributing to the local cultural landscape, often coordinated by cultural associations, such as Persian language magazines, music events and of course restaurants offering their specialities. The Zoroastrian (in particular the Parsi) presence is now strong in the major cities such as Toronto and Vancouver, with communities being present since the 1970s, with some notable exceptions (the first Parsi to enter Canada is documented as arriving in 1866, while the University of Toronto admitted the first Parsi student in 1922—Foltz 2009: 561). Although Zoroastrian diasporic groups clearly are still attached to their religious heritage, it is mainly through cultural practices that they express their identity and values, and such a representation strategy naturally embraces the world of food.

To introduce Parsi food customs, I will now outline the figure of Niloufer Mavalvala, using some biographical notes I gathered from her book and her website. Mavalvala was born in Karachi (Pakistan) and started giving cookery classes at the age of seventeen. When she moved to Dubai with her family, she continued her activity, but she also organized similar activities in the UK before finally moving to Canada. With the intent of popularizing Parsi foods and dishes, she now uses a number of both traditional and participatory media such as books and a successful blog, set up in 2013. The website in particular gives visibility to her career, public events and publications, and is also a way to promote her volumes thanks to multimodal resources (texts, videos, images and other semiotic means) that cumulatively construct a certain type of persona: a real and authentic representative of the Parsi culinary tradition who tries to spread this type of cuisine in Canada, sometimes mistaken for or generalized as Indian. In this light, recipes inherited from family members and tradition become a means by which to inscribe a private performance onto a new palimpsest accessible to the general public.

3. Parsi food narratives as a site of diasporic identity

Even a cursory look at Mavalvala's printed and online materials reveals her goal to index a cultural connection mediated via the food
discourse. In actual fact, it is important to note that the overlapping
between food and culture with regard to the Parsi world implies
an ambitious reflection on the sense of mobility and diaspora of
subjects at large: Mavalvala's experience encapsulates the idea of
moving across countries (Pakistan, Arabia, Britain and Canada),
but the dishes she speaks about evoke even wider and more complex movements of people. They project images of migrations across
time and space, from ancient Persia to India and then to the world,
but they also suggest cultural flexibility in creating contacts, borrowing customs and extending traditions. In this respect, Parsi
culinary habits keep "some of the Anglo-Indian ethos" (Appadurai
1988: 14), along with Indian military food practices that date back
to the period of the Raj. Thus, the idea of Parsi food mingles a range
of influences from various contexts to form what Mavalvala on her
website defines as "a distinct cuisine that brings together Gujarati,
Maharashtrian, Persian and even British flavours" (NK), but at the
same time, it mirrors the cultural transformation of the Parsi community and implicitly their social mobility. In actual fact, any food
tradition in the world is the result of various dynamics that continuously reshape its boundaries and forms (Leong-Salobir, Ray &
Jaclyn 2018). The very notion of Indian food, for example, draws
from many histories and constantly redesigns the meaning of authenticity because what appears to be the "real" culinary identity
of the country actually is the hybridization of imported ingredients, newly developed techniques or modified practices. In Nandy's
words (2004: 12), the intertexts of Indian food heritage in fact arise
from "the management of chaos, celebrations of diversity and or-
thogenetic transformation of the exogenous." As an illustration, we
should remember that spices such as cinnamon, ginger and fen-
ugreek are not native to the Indian subcontinent; that the kebab
method was adopted and adapted to the new territory, while rice

dishes such as biryani and pulao were originally invented in the Persian world.

Built in an idiosyncratic style, Mavalvala's project consists in a partial narrativization of recipes available in various formats and typologies, in which the author points out the different layers of what constitutes a gastronomic tradition. However, at the same time, she also adds cultural and biographical elements with a view to providing details about the sociocultural and historical context of origin, as well as retaining aesthetic effects and bonds of intimacy. In a parallel manner, Mavalvala also contributes to the broad rereading and implicit empowerment of Indian women, stereotypically portrayed as silenced cooks in the traditional household.

In her book, the paratextual structure displays a short opening text entitled "Dedication. Blessed are all whose parents support their passion in life" (pp. VII–IX), which essentially contains a narrative enhanced by colourful photographs. This part is aimed at celebrating the author's parents and family by revealing and sharing sentiments of domestic affection and closeness. Although Mavalvala's father is described as a medical doctor who specialized at different hospitals in the UK and the US, the tone is not excessively formal or rhetorical, but rather tends to infuse a sense of social proximity through evaluative patterns implemented through positively connoted phrases and items ("generous of heart and mind"; "he had a heart of gold"; "Dad had good values and morals in all he did"), and the same type of treatment is extended to her entire family, including her mother ("the epitome of elegance"), husband (defined through the informal term "hubby") and siblings. The writer's inner identity is also mirrored by the concluding greeting phrase "Salamati!": a Persian term for "healthiness" used during a toast, thus the equivalent of "cheers." The insertion of a foreign lexical item, the use of punctuation and the one-word expression reinforce the entire passage and operate as attention-grabbing devices.

The subsequent text is a sort of introduction bearing the eponymous title of the book (pp. X–XI), in which the author captivatingly constructs her discourse by shifting from a cultural and historical account of Parsi culture and Zoroastrianism to a concise presentation of the most famous Parsi specialities. Therefore, from a stylistic perspective, this section is lexically rich, in particular with nouns denoting ingredients such as "saffron, jaggery, turmeric," and names of dishes borrowed from Persian/Parsi such as "Dhansak" or compound expressions ("Lagan nu custard").

4. Cooking the Parsi world: language, culture and diaspora

After the introductory biographical sections, the book then offers a selection of recipes organized under different headings, in a bilingual form, as summarized in this table:

Category	Number of recipes	Pages
Appetizers – pehli vani – first courses	4	4–10
Side dishes – beeji vani – second courses	7	14–28
Main dishes – teeji vani – third courses (rice dishes – chawal nu bhonu)	7	32–53
Rotli dishes – rotli nu bhonu	4	59–68
Desserts – mithoo mōnu	5	72–80
Tea time snacks – chai ni satheh	6	84–98
Parsi cook's spice island	2	103–106

As Notaker (2017) argues, cookbooks constitute a specific genre and have a long and complex history, and their ideal readership can be either professional or domestic. Essentially, they appear as collection of recipes, namely procedural texts of variable length, pivoting around a list of quantities and instructions, but very often integrating other elements that reinforce and extend their sociocultural value. The recipe genre, in particular, can express different forms of naming (e.g. via geographical references, personal names or metaphors) while here, instead, we immediately notice the co-textual presence of expressions in both English and Parsi as a stratagem to provide authenticity and engage with different types of reader (i.e. both inside and outside the cultural community). Recipes also abound in the author's blog, of which the catchy name, "Niloufer's Kitchen," denotes a sense of social proximity and domesticity. The website features the following categories typical of a multimodal object, namely "home / about the author / reviews / e-cookbooks / publications / chat with the author / update," and of course allows interaction through blogging with other virtual visitors.

The layout of Mavalvala's recipes follows a pattern covering title + cultural/autobiographical comment + list of ingredients + methods + tips. By exploiting all such elements, the author manages not only to explain how to make a specific dish but how to introduce a story that foregrounds an ancient origin and a diasporic dimension as well (Sarkar 2013). In other words, the stylistic makeup of recipes acquires a narrative salience that fosters the strengthening of a community and the diffusion of culinary practices. With Labov in mind, Cotter (1997: 58) states that:

> Beyond its distinctive linguistic features, a recipe is also a narrative, a story that can be shared and has been constructed by members of a community. The recipe narrative not only transforms culture-based meaning, as do more traditional narratives, it can also be viewed as sharing many aspects of the formal structure of basic narratives. The temporal structure and sequential presentation of information in a recipe link it with the more traditional narrative framework.

Mavalvala's recipes utilize the gastronomic theme to revive a story of displacement across space and time for the Parsis, celebrating their traditions and meanings. To introduce the recipe for Parsi lagan nu custard (wedding custard), for example, the author explains that "traditionally, Parsi weddings are large events where all the elders of the community are invited, and the weeklong pre-wedding ceremonies are celebrated with close family and friends" (p. 73). Thus, the text evolves from a mere set of instructions (i.e. how to make a sort of pudding) to a brief illustration of Mavalvala's cultural background. Very frequently, the narrative turn of the author's texts encourages the reader to explore Parsi culture and history, and once again brings to the fore the dialogic nature of recipes, in which the relation between author and reader is positioned as giver and receiver. From this perspective, dishes and ingredients become plot-advancing elements that map out the stratification of food discourse and sense of belonging, as shown in the following passages:

> Khichri/Khichdi/Khichuri is derived from a Sanskrit word, simply meaning rice and lentil. It has many variations and is popularly referred to as a comfort food. Generally, its texture is wet rather than dry, similar to a risotto. It is often seasoned with clarified butter or pure ghee. From the Greeks to the Persians, it was a favourite of the Mughal Emperor Akbar! Egyptians and their neighbours add vegetables to it, while the Indian subcontinent likes to serve it with yogurt and other forms of curries. Like the Parsis, other communities living on the shores of the Arabian Sea, Maharashtrians and the Sindhis tend to add shrimp to their khichri, as do the Sri Lankans and Bangladeshis that thrive on the Bay of Bengal. [...] Many cultures, including the Parsis, dedicate a meal of Khichri during their week of wedding festivities; yet it is deemed inauspicious to be served as part of the wedding feast or on the day of! (p. 43)
>
> This combination of braised meat, yogurt and nuts make a good Korma/Qorma. Generally with lots of gravy and oil or ghee, it is a dish relished in the subcontinent. Persians ad Turks have their own versions of the same. Originated in the 1600s, the Mughal Dynasty made it popular and called it the Shahi Qorma, i.e. Royal Qorma by adding saffron, cream and assorted nuts—very royal indeed! Fortunately, Korma does not

always have to be topped with oil or ghee to make it perfect. A Parsi version of this recipe omits the use of excess oil and instead uses ground almonds and yogurt for richness. Delicious in flavour, thick in texture with a beautiful caramel colour, this version of the original Persian Korma is a favourite in our home (p. 69).

Both extracts, respectively referring to Khichri (rice and lentil) and Chicken badami (almond and yogurt curry), sum up complex histories, movements of peoples and transformation of communities. The linguistic infrastructure here sketches some of the etymological difficulties of tracking down the origin of the name of a food or dish as these are cultural elements constantly subjected to circulation and transformation. Moreover, in the Indian context, which is the natural context of reference for Parsis, the philological question of food terms brings in a range of linguistic influences that over the centuries have intermingled and given rise to a multicultural world. The different spelling systems adopted to translate the original name of dishes into English testifies to the diversity of the environment and at the same time reinforces the lexis of diatopic varieties of English spoken across the Indian subcontinent. Collingham, for example, seems to prefer the term kichari, originally conceived as a "simple dish of two grains, usually rice and lentils, boiled together in a little water" (2007: 22), whereas in the case of the second recipe, she makes a reference to East India, and affirms that the people of Lucknow added cream "to perfect the Mughal dish qaurama or what we would call korma (2006: 94-95). The etymological puzzle of names and words for food, dishes and ingredients metaphorically "devours" and overlaps linguistic usage, echoes and modifications: clearly Mavalvala's idea is not to provide a scientifically sound critique of culinary terms but to hint at the power of food discourse to evoke, intertwine and revive memories and values.

The author again leads the reader (and implicitly the new enthusiast of Parsi cuisine) to ponder the historical intricacies of food vocabulary and its many adaptations across continents and times when she deals with the prototypical example of Indian food: curry, a sort of umbrella term that in actual fact covers a number of preparations but which was lexically crystallized as a symbol for the West to refer to "exotic" food. Scholars from different fields (e.g. Achaya 1994 and Collingham 2006) have discussed the broad semantic spectrum of the word and its possible origins, and Mavalvala too provides some linguistic notes when she deals with the recipe for Jhina na curry Chawal (shrimp coconut curry with rice). In particular, she sketches out the etymology and history of curry before the recipe is presented, but she also adds a closing note in which she tries to distinguish between curry as a preparation and as a blend of spices, for which it is often mistaken:

> Without a doubt, Parsis embrace Curry Chawal (literally, Curry Rice) as their own. A favourite in most Parsi homes, curry—especially the fish or prawn one—come very close to Dhansak, and is also quintessentially Parsi. "Curry" is a loose term used universally to describe a spicy sauce with meat, chicken, seafood or vegetables. […] Tamil for "sauce," the word "Kari" was anglicized in the 1770s by the British who colonized India. However, some records show the word "curry" which means cooking, to be part of the Olde English language as early as 1300s (p. 45).
>
> Note: curry powder is not to be mistakenly affiliated to any Curry. Interestingly, Curry powder was specifically mixed and boxed just for the Colonizers who were returning, allowing them to prepare their version of curry once back home. Many people use it in Mulligatawny soup for flavouring, and it is also used in Coronation Chicken (p. 46).

In these extracts, the tone is consistently descriptive, following the rules governing the recipe genre and indicating many words for ingredients, places and historical references, but a closer look reveals a certain degree of modality, i.e. a range of different devices that define the text producer's point of view and attitude (Gibbons & Whiteley 2018: 109). Here, modal markers take the form of more or less explicit appraisal patterns like phrases, adverbs and adjectives ("without a doubt," "favourite," "quintessentially," "interestingly"). The ending note is significant in ideological terms because it seems to be grounded upon a binary vision, the colonized and the colonizer, and the influence they mutually exercised one on the other: at the same time it evokes dishes of the colonial and postcolonial traditions, respectively represented by Mulligatawny, a spicy soup from the colonial time whose name is probably of Tamil origins, and Coronation chicken, a preparation invented to celebrate the new sovereign in Britain after WWII. This type of view is also reinforced by the use of negated structures ("not to be mistakenly affiliated with any curry") as well as exclusive pronouns ("them," "their version") in opposition to an implied inclusive perspective, meaning the speaker and the ideal audience or community. In this way, Mavalvala cleverly appropriates the richness of Indian food discourse to expand Parsi gastronomic traditions, thus enhancing the diasporic bridge that links territories and eras, from ancient Persia to contemporary Canada via multicultural India.

However, as previously mentioned, the most famous and prestigious preparation in the Parsi cuisine is dhansak. It is worth mentioning that the term is attested in some dictionaries, such as the *Cambridge English Dictionary* online (https://dictionary. cambridge.org/dictionary/english/dhansak) with the following definition: "an Indian meat or vegetable dish cooked with lentils." On the other hand, Burnett and Saberi (2008: 191), in reporting the recipe for dhansak followed by Camellia Panjabi, the marketing director of Taj Hotels chain, argue that "*dhan* in Gujarati means wealth, but in Parsee-Gujarati *dhaan* means rice. *Sak* means vegetables. Dhansak is a meat, vegetable and lentil curry eaten with a caramelized brown pulao." For Mavalvala, cooking dhansak is an affirmation of Parsi identity and celebration, in a sort of "culinary linkages and sensorial geographies" (Leong-Salobir, Ray & Jaclyn 2018: 13) that turn the very mundane act of cooking into an act of *commensalité*: a social practice of living in and belonging to the same community:

> Food being the number one priority for most Parsis, the famous Dhansak is a favourite dish and is best described as a speciality. Being both tedious and time-consuming to prepare, as well as heavy to digest, Dhansak is generally left for a treat and more traditionally, for a Sunday afternoon lunch. Families gather for the meal and get-together, followed by a siesta! There are many versions and stories of its origins, both in name and ingredients. But like most recipes, it has evolved over time and geography. I believe that it originates from our Persian roots, mimicking the Khoresh, a stew that was made up of lentils, spinach, plums and meat, served on a bed of rice with an array of mokhalafat or sides. Once we migrated to India, it turned into Dhansak; Dhan meaning golden/gold or wealth and Sak/sag/shak meaning greens or vegetables. [...] There is no right or wrong [sic] to cooking Dhansak and each family has its own ingredients and methods for this historic dish. Love of Dhansak just seems to endorse one's "Parsi-pannu" or Parsi-ness. Serve this with a chilled beer or shandy for the ultimate Parsi eating experience! (p. 54)

This introduction to the actual recipe activates a narrative of migration and transformation of human experience, and the effort of scattered individuals to come to terms with it, calibrating the use of both singular and plural pronouns ("I" vs "we"). The text mirrors the composite cultural heritage of the Parsis, and the anglicized image of dhansak as a "Sunday afternoon lunch" may be explained by the fact that Parsis were in contact with the East

India Company in the eighteenth and nineteenth centuries, and during the Raj they often worked as butlers in the English colonial districts, thus enriching and transforming their food habits (Collingham 2006: 121).

In anthropological terms, sharing food constitutes a building block of social processes of group (and identity) formation, so membership is also mediated via the consumption of food. Consequently, the author indexes her own and her community's identity by metaphorically juxtaposing this special dish with a time-honoured heritage, shifting between material and immaterial levels. However, she also specifies that, as often occurs in the world of food, the recipe can be subjected to changes and improvements, therefore celebrating a form of "flexible" authenticity (i.e. authentic food is not what is cooked by following strict rules, but rather what individuals and families decide and personalize). Furthermore, the inclusion of the recipe in the book testifies to a desire to speak about and discuss one's own culture, in a dialogic position between the author and the reader, who is somehow invited to explore this type of food and culture through the dissemination and popularization of recipes.

5. Concluding remarks

In this paper, I have tried to come to grips with some forms of cultural and textual representation of the Parsi diasporic experience and food discourse in the Canadian and, more generally, globalized scenario. The language of recipes utilized by Mavalvala in her book and on her website offers evidence of her approach to identity, belonging and hybridity, in which the redesigning of roles and functions (i.e. the humble and often marginalized sphere of food for migrants) allows inclusion and the creation of a new multicultural environment. The author's gastronomic storytelling brings to the fore the transgression of different kinds of boundaries—geographical, historical and cultural ones—with the scattering of the

Parsi, who moved from their native land to settle in India and who then moved again to the Western world. Yet this is a project that that goes beyond the mere dimension of nostalgia and a mythicized past because it envisages a new positive form of authenticity that promotes respect for individuals and groups.

Although Mavalvala's multimodal texts do not technically belong to the memoir genre, they nonetheless promote a biographical and personal account, which is a key element in migration, and as such they constitute a sort of cultural archive. In this respect, the author manipulates and reinvents the structure of a how-to manual as a tool to "embark upon a combined genealogical and gastronomic undertaking by celebrating specific cultural traditions through family recipes" (Halloran 2016: 110). To build up her story of Parsi food and culture, the writer employs a range of different linguistic strategies, most of which operate as appraisal patterns in the form of adjectives, phraseology and metaphor, as the following excerpt illustrates: "Sās Khichri is a favourite in most Parsi homes. Made in a variety of ways, this version is a tomato-based spicy, sweet and sour dish. This is a prime example of the perfect Parsi Cooking Trinity of Tikhu, Katu, Mithy (spicy, sour and sweet). Taste it before serving it to perfect the fine balance that your family will enjoy!" (p. 40). By means of quantification ("most"), premodifying adjectives ("prime example," "fine balance") and the use of direct verb forms (with the imperative "taste"), the passage conveys a positive and appealing voice for the Parsi community and its food tradition, also thanks to a rather unusual metaphor of sacred origin, in which the presence of three main flavours is humorously rendered in religious terms, and further enriched by onomatopoeic effects.

Given the intersecting of various factors, conditions and actions, the arena of food discourse is vast and rhizomatic (Leong-Salobir, Ray & Jaclyn, 2018) and further research is needed, for instance with an exploration of the role that food plays in the performance of gender identity and ethnicity (D'Sylva & Beagan 2011) or the pragmatic and ideological effect generated by food texts in society (Berger 2018). Ultimately, Mavalvala appropriates and refashions a discourse of nostalgia for the diasporic subject by stressing the power of narratives to uphold traditions but also to strengthen communities, foster tolerance and foreground civil values. In this light, food is an all-encompassing cultural symbol that indexes Parsi lifestyle and origins, but simultaneously human experience at large, as the author emphasizes: "Blogging is all about storytelling. Just instead of people being the centre of attention on my blog, food is the star using recipes to unfold the story it holds. We all have a story to tell, good, bad or funny to share. It unravels in many different ways. This is mine" (NK).

Works Cited

Achaya, K. T. (1994), *Indian Food. A Historical Companion*, Delhi: Oxford University Press.

Adami, Esterino, "What's in a Curry? Interdisciplinary Approaches to Indian Food Discourse," *Textus*, XXXII, 2. (2019):17–30.

Appadurai, Arjun. "How to Make a National Cuisine: Cookbooks in Contemporary India," *Comparative Studies in Society*, 30.1 (1988): 3–24.

Berger, Rachel, "Alimentary Affairs: Historicizing Food in Modern India," *History Compass* (2018): 1–10.

Burnett, David & Helen Saberi (2008), *The Road to Vindaloo. Curry Cooks and Curry Books*, Totnes, Prospect Books.

Cambridge English Dictionary online https://dictionary.cambridge.org/dictionary/english/dhansak (last visited April 15, 2020).

Chapman, Gwen, Svetlana Ristovski-Slijepcevica & Brenda Beaganb. "Meanings of Food, Eating and Health in Punjabi Families Living in Vancouver, Canada," *Health Education Journal*, 70, 1. (2011): 101–112.

Collingham, Lizzie (2006), *Curry. A Tale of Cooks and Conquerors*, London: Vintage Books.

Foltz, Richard. "Iranian Zoroastrians in Canada: Balancing Religious and Cultural Identities," *Iranian Studies*, 42, 4. (2009): 561–577.

D'Sylva, Andrea & Brenda Beagan, "'Food is Culture, but it's also Power: the Role of Food in Ethnic and Gender Identity Construction among Goan Canadian Women'," *Journal of Gender Studies*, 20, 3. (2011):279–289.

Gibbons, Alison & Sarah Whiteley (2018), *Contemporary Stylistics. Language, Cognition, Interpretation*, Edinburgh: Edinburgh University Press.

Jurafsky, Dan (2014), *The Language of Food*, New York: W. W. Norton and Company.

Halloran, Vivian Hu (2016), *The Immigrant Kitchen. Food. Ethnicity and Diaspora*, Columbus: The Ohio State University Press.

Leong-Salobir, Cecilia, Krishnendu Ray & Rohel Jaclyn, "Introducing a Special Issue on Rescuing Taste from the Nation: Oceans, Borders, and Culinary Flows," *Gastronomica: The Journal for Food Studies*, 16, 1. (2016): 9–15.

Mannur, Anita (2010), *Culinary Fictions. Food in South Asian Diasporic Culture*, Philadelphia: Temple University Press.

Mavalvala, Niloufer (2016), *The Art of Parsi Cooking. Reviving an Ancient Cuisine*, London: Austin Macauley Publishers.

Nandy, Ashis. "The Changing Popular Culture of Indian Food: Preliminary Notes," *South Asian Research*, 24, 1. (2004): 9–19.

Niloufer's Kitchen http://www.nilouferskitchen.com/ (last visited April 16, 2020).

Notaker, Herry (2017), *A History of the Cookbooks; from Kitchen to Page over Seven Centuries*, Oakland, California: University of California Press.

Sarkar, Sucharita (2013), "Stories' Digest: Narrating Identities and Cultures through Food in Blogs, Cook-books and Advertisements in India," in Shafer, S. (ed.), *Storytelling: Exploring the Art and Science of Narrative*. Leiden: Brill, pp. 97-115.

Tindall, Gillian (1992), *City of Gold. The Biography of Bombay*, Gurgaon: Penguin Random House India.

RITA CALABRESE

In a Mississauga Indian Kitchen

Motivation

STARTING FROM THE ASSUMPTION THAT Indian English is in general more oriented towards written norms even in spoken language, the present paper investigates different culinary representations in a corpus of Indian Canadian restaurant menus in the city of Mississauga. The primary focus will be on whether there are norms or shared language behaviours as well as trends towards the standardization within the same "non-native-English" variety in a certain speech community with reference to expressions of national identity and belonging in a given register.

The main question to be addressed will be therefore whether certain language features are used consistently enough to warrant their being called characteristics of a given register of Indian English (Rogers 2002). To verify these assumptions and address such empirical questions from a corpus-driven perspective, I carried out a preliminary study on a sample of written data derived from specific restaurant websites. The data collected were later automatically parsed using Visual Interactive Syntax Learning (VISL) applications and language analysis tools (http://beta.visl. sdu.dk/) which can provide both morphological and semantic information on a given structure. Following the automatic procedure generally adopted to detect and extract semantically and

grammatically annotated data, I matched corpus-based evidence
and linguistic diagnostics in order to:

a.   explore linguistic features that are functionally related
     and relevant to the menu register as identified in previous
     studies;

b.   establish the extent to which the frequency of such fea-
     tures may contribute to the identification of the genre
     with strong ethnic /cultural connotations.

Since "discourse of all types is a potent creator and enforcer of
identity" (Lakoff 2006: 144), the language of menus will be analyzed as a text form that is locally situated as a community practice
and as a text that embodies linguistic relationships underlying a
number of cultural assumptions and practices (Cotter 1997: 53).
Looking at menus as a form of informative text and viewing them
formally and structurally can serve as a guide to describe the discourse structure of menus by noting their syntactic and semantic
regularities.

The paper is organized as follows. First, a brief theoretical background will be provided pertaining to the concepts of identity, food
as ethnic heritage belonging to culturally distinguishable groupings
in a given speech community, cooking practices as communicative practices consequently conveyed in specific text genres (such
as restaurant menus). Moreover, references to the socio-linguistic
context of Mississauga—where the sources of the data analyzed
in the study originate—will be also provided. Then, the results of
a preliminary study of Indian English (IndEng) features will be
presented by sampling data from different menus / sources. The implications of the present findings for future research on the process
of language standardization of communicative practices in IndEng
in comparison with features emerging from previous studies are
discussed in the final section.

Background

The study of Indian culinary practices to restate/assert ethnic identity: In ethnic literature, food figures as a powerful symbol of ethnicity, becoming a significant arena in which identity construction, community building and social critique can take place. Descriptions of culinary practices trigger thoughts on belonging and national identity, offering affective encounters with the past. As anthropologists have long stated, food helps define group identities, and through cooking and eating, people perform rituals of cultural belonging and identity. In the field of discourse studies, Wodak et al. (2009) refer to the concept of identity that seems to possess considerable explanatory force. Formally and logically, "identity" is a relational term that defines the relationship between two or more related entities (Wodak et al. 2009: 11). Hence, one of the aims of discourse studies and of the present study is to look at the linguistic means involved in the discursive construction of national identity. Particular attention is focused primarily on lexical units and syntactic devices which serve to convey the meaning of uniqueness, origin and continuity. Traditionally, the most important of these meanings are:

1. personal reference (anthroponymic generic terms, personal pro/nouns);

2. spatial reference (toponyms/geonyms, adverbials or geographical adjectives);

3. temporal reference (by means of nouns, adjectives).

Cooking practices as communicative practices: In "Toward a Psychosociology of Contemporary Food Consumption," Barthes (1997) famously argued that food "is not only a collection of products that can be used for statistical or nutritional studies [but] also, and at the same time, a system of communication, a body of images, [...] situations and behaviour [...] One could say that an entire world (social environment) is present in and signified by food" (1997:21–23).

The importance of situational differences determining communicative practices had already been stressed by Leherer in 1972 (p. 169) when she argued that Lévi-Strauss's main error was to assume that "we can have a neutral structure of cooking concepts that will be valid for all languages." As also confirmed by the data analyzed in the present study, each world language selects some of the components in Lévi-Strauss's universal culinary triangle (Fig. 12) and Leherer's tetrahedron (Fig. 13) in different ways, before arranging them into different hierarchies and finally coming up with certain semantic structures.

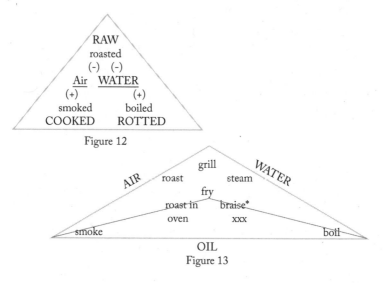

Figure 12

Figure 13

Menu as a register: This concept emerged early on, with Zwicky and Zwicky's seminal study (1980) of different restaurant menus in various regions of the US and Canada. It was one of the first studies to examine the American restaurant menu as a register "to show the conventions that govern its form" (p. 83). Their study showed that the language of American restaurant menus presented information about food in standard and clearly recognizable formats essentially as "restaurant advertising." The only difference lies in the amount of descriptive material. As a specific register, menus have a certain format which may be described as a set of statistical preferences for particular lexical items, morpho-syntactic constructions and discourse structures. As registers, menus are also situation-specific and therefore dependent on a number of relevant dimensions: one of these is the medium of communication that—in the case of the selected menus—is written visuals mediated by computers. Another important dimension is represented by the purpose ("point") of the communication, which in the case of menus is intended to inform. Like news headlines and advertisements, menu entries are intended to create or foster positive attitudes towards something offered. All these registers share the constraints imposed by their format: "they involve the compression of content to fit in a small space" leading to heaviness in compound constructions (ibid, 86).

Another important feature of such a register is the markedness of its forms with respect to ordinary conversational language, given the rule that features of an unmarked register may be imported into a marked one, but not vice versa.

The Present Study

The concepts outlined above and the related methodologies of investigation provided the rationale for the present preliminary study aiming to investigate the general features of "Indianness" across different menus, and verify whether the list of features elaborated so far in most major studies on the menu register and accounted for as typical are also to be found in the Mississauga corpus. Following similar studies in the field, I adopted a stratified approach by sampling data from different menus. This procedure should help shed light on norms or shared language behaviour as well as trends towards standardization within the same "non-native-English" variety in a certain geographical area, characterized by a high degree of multilingualism (see tables from census 2016 below). Following a procedure currently adopted in research based on the automatic detection and extraction of semantically and grammatically annotated data, corpus-based evidence and linguistic diagnostics have been matched in order to:

a. investigate the heaviness (in terms of conveyed informa-
   tivity) of noun phrase constructions;

b. explore linguistic features (including formal features such
   as list format, past participle modifiers, adjectives) that
   are functionally related and relevant to the menu register
   identified in previous studies;

c. establish the extent to which the frequency of such features
   may contribute to the "Indianness" of the genre;

d. finally, verify whether the results are consistent with the
   assumption of markedness of the menu register with
   respect to ordinary conversational language (CanEng).

Method

Materials: The study is based on data from the *Mississauga
Corpus of Indian English Menus* (hereinafter MissCor), specifically compiled for a synchronic investigation concerning written
texts from a well-established speech community of Indians in
the city of Mississauga. For the purpose of this preliminary
study, certain sections of the *Strathy Corpus of Canadian English*[1]
(https://www.english-corpora.org/can/) which features 50 million examples of spoken and written data which were selected
and normalized in order to be compared to samples from the
MissCor.[2] For the purpose of the present study, the socio-linguistic context of the speech community was carefully observed,
taking into account the multilingual Canadian context. As a
matter of fact, Canada is a linguistically diverse country, with
two official languages, dozens of Indigenous languages and

---

1 The *Strathy Corpus* was designed on the model of available corpora like the
Brown-LOB Corpora with the aim of monitoring the evolving role of English in
Canadian society over the years 1970–2010.

2 The two corpora were normalized by using the log-likelihood and effect size
calculator available at http://ucrel.lancs.ac.uk/llwizard.html

many heritage languages spoken by immigrant communities. With shifting demographics, 42.2% of the population reporting a mother tongue other than English (see Tab. 1 from the 2011 Census), increasing numbers of multilingual speakers and increasing varieties of English in Canadian society, the role of English in Canada is ever-changing.

Table 1
Population of immigrant mother tongue families, showing main languages comprising each family, Canada, 2011 [1]

▸ Description

Language family	Main languages	Number	Percentage
Niger-Congo languages	Akan, Swahili, Rundi	81,135	1.2
Cushitic languages	Somali, Oromo	45,880	0.7
Semitic languages	Arabic, Hebrew, Amharic	449,580	6.6
Turkic languages	Turkish, Azerbaijani	36,750	0.5
Armenian	Armenian	31,680	0.5
Indo-Iranian languages	Punjabi, Urdu, Persian, Gujarati, Hindi	1,179,990	17.3
Dravidian languages	Tamil, Malayalam, Telugu	175,280	2.6
Chinese languages	Chinese (n.o.s. [2]), Cantonese, Mandarin	1,112,610	16.3
Tibeto-Burman languages	Tibetan, Burmese	8,210	0.1
Korean	Korean	142,880	2.1
Japanese	Japanese	43,040	0.6
Malayo-Polynesian languages	Tagalog, Ilocano, Malay	443,750	6.5
Tai-Kadai languages	Lao, Thai	22,615	0.3
Austro-Asiatic languages	Vietnamese, Khmer	174,455	2.6
Romance languages	Spanish, Italian, Portuguese	1,196,390	17.5
Germanic languages	German, Dutch, Yiddish	611,165	8.9
Slavic languages	Polish, Russian, Ukrainian	721,605	10.6
Baltic languages	Lithuanian, Latvian	14,055	0.2
Finno-Ugric languages	Hungarian, Finnish, Estonian	96,200	1.4
Celtic languages	Welsh	3,885	0.1
Greek	Greek	117,890	1.7
Albanian	Albanian	25,010	0.4
Creole languages	Haitian Creole	75,255	1.1
Other languages	Kabyle, Georgian, Mongol	29,410	0.4
All immigrant languages		6,838,705	100

[1] Language families are listed according to major region of origin: African and Middle Eastern languages are shown first, followed by Asian languages (Indian subcontinent, East Asia and Southeast Asia), European languages and, finally, Creole languages, which come mainly from the Americas but are also found in other regions such as the Indian Ocean.

[2] n.o.s. means 'not otherwise specified.'

Source: Statistics Canada, Census of Population, 2011.

Five years later in 2016, another Census sees an increase in multilingualism and a dramatic increase of the Indian community in the city of Mississauga (Municipality of Peel, Tab. 2). In particular, Tab.

2 shows the number of South-Asian immigrants in Mississauga representing 40.54% of the immigrant population in the city.

Tab. 2 Number of visible minorities and immigrant population in the municipality of Mississauga and adjacent municipalities.

ABORIGINAL IDENTITY

Municipality	2016 Population	Aboriginal Identity	% Pop.	First Nations	% Aborig.	Métis	% Aborig.	Inuit	% Aborig.	Multiple Aboriginal identities	% Aborig.	Not included elsewhere	% Aborig.
Peel	1,372,640	9,120	0.66%	5,420	59.43%	2,950	32.35%	165	1.81%	280	3.07%	310	3.40%
Mississauga	713,470	4,175	0.58%	2,420	57.96%	1,475	35.33%	40	0.90%	100	2.40%	140	3.35%
Brampton	590,945	4,330	0.73%	7,630	60.74%	1,255	28.98%	100	2.31%	180	4.16%	160	3.70%
Caledon	66,220	615	0.93%	370	60.16%	215	34.96%	20	3.25%	0	0.00%	15	2.44%

VISIBLE MINORITIES

Municipality	2016 Population	Total Visible Minorities	% Minority	South Asian	% Minority	Chinese	% Minority	Black	% Minority	Filipino	% Minority	Latin American	% Minority	Arab	% Minority
Durham	639,495	173,330	27.10%	55,025	31.75%	12,105	6.98%	51,380	29.64%	14,530	8.38%	6,135	3.54%	5,780	3.33%
York	1,100,950	541,200	49.16%	116,695	21.56%	244,320	45.14%	27,745	5.13%	25,870	4.78%	13,630	2.52%	13,105	2.42%
Toronto	2,691,665	1,385,855	51.49%	338,965	24.46%	299,465	21.61%	299,850	17.31%	157,715	11.07%	77,165	5.57%	36,830	2.60%
Halton	540,975	138,995	25.69%	50,075	36.03%	19,980	14.37%	15,230	10.96%	11,135	8.01%	8,945	6.44%	12,515	9.00%
Peel	1,372,640	854,565	62.36%	434,105	50.80%	63,745	7.46%	131,065	15.34%	57,305	6.69%	31,060	3.63%	47,500	4.97%
Mississauga	713,475	408,930	57.16%	165,760	40.54%	54,090	13.23%	47,005	11.49%	36,570	8.94%	16,150	3.94%	34,200	8.85%
Brampton	590,950	433,200	73.31%	261,705	60.41%	8,955	2.07%	82,175	18.97%	20,100	4.64%	14,015	3.24%	6,045	1.40%
Caledon	66,215	12,410	18.74%	6,620	53.43%	695	5.60%	1,880	15.15%	535	4.31%	905	7.29%	250	2.01%
GTA	6,345,725	3,093,945	48.76%	994,865	37.16%	639,615	20.67%	465,295	15.04%	261,455	8.49%	136,955	4.43%	109,930	3.55%

Municipality	2016 Population	Total Visible Minorities	% Minority	Southeast Asian	% Minority	West Asian	% Minority	Korean	% Minority	Japanese	% Minority	Visible Minority, n.i.e.	% Minority	Multiple Visible Minorities	% Minority
Durham	639,495	173,330	27.10%	2,395	1.38%	6,565	3.79%	1,165	0.67%	1,415	0.22%	8,380	1.31%	8,475	4.89%
York	1,100,950	541,200	49.16%	14,050	2.60%	41,735	7.71%	16,955	3.13%	2,755	0.23%	7,310	0.66%	16,995	3.14%
Toronto	2,691,665	1,385,855	51.49%	41,650	3.01%	60,320	4.35%	41,640	3.00%	13,415	0.50%	36,975	1.37%	47,670	3.44%
Halton	540,975	138,995	25.69%	7,900	2.09%	4,180	3.01%	4,890	3.52%	1,625	0.31%	2,760	0.51%	4,710	3.39%
Peel	1,372,640	854,565	62.36%	23,415	2.74%	13,495	1.57%	6,630	0.78%	2,395	0.19%	23,470	1.86%	23,335	2.73%
Mississauga	713,475	408,930	57.16%	14,795	3.62%	7,910	1.93%	6,095	1.49%	1,965	0.27%	9,050	1.26%	13,370	3.27%
Brampton	590,950	433,200	73.31%	6,425	1.49%	5,275	1.22%	430	0.10%	530	0.09%	15,950	2.70%	9,585	2.21%
Caledon	66,215	12,410	18.74%	195	1.57%	215	1.97%	105	0.85%	100	0.15%	475	0.72%	380	3.06%
GTA	6,345,725	3,093,945	48.76%	84,415	2.73%	126,235	4.08%	71,285	2.30%	21,865	0.71%	80,895	2.61%	101,175	3.27%

IMMIGRANT POPULATION

Municipality	2016 Population	Immigrant Population	% Population	% Immigrants	Recent immigrants	% Recent Immigrants
Durham	639,490	150,885	23.6%	5.4%	10,315	6.8%
York	1,100,950	515,225	46.8%	18.4%	51,405	10.0%
Toronto	2,691,665	1,266,005	47.0%	45.2%	187,950	14.8%
Halton	540,980	160,165	29.6%	5.7%	20,485	12.8%
Peel	1,372,640	706,825	51.5%	25.3%	94,105	13.3%
Mississauga	713,475	381,700	53.4%	13.6%	53,410	14.0%
Brampton	590,950	308,790	52.3%	11.0%	39,915	12.9%
Caledon	66,215	16,310	24.6%	0.6%	780	4.8%
GTA	6,345,725	2,799,115	44.1%		364,260	13.0%

Figures may not add up due to rounding.
To view detailed data tables related to this bulletin, please visit www.peeldatacentre.ca

Other variables like educational background of the speakers were not considered for the purpose of the present study.

Procedure: The sample data used for the present study were gathered by copying 13 menus available from Indian restaurant websites in Mississauga. The collected data were then processed in a comparative analysis with available data from the *Strathy Corpus* in order to achieve a wide coverage of IndEng menu usage. The comparison could also indicate directions of change as well as convergence trends. The data were automatically parsed by using the language analysis tools provided by the VISL website (http:// beta.visl.sdu.dk/). The parsers available at the VISL interface are based on the theoretical framework of the "Constraint Grammar": a methodological paradigm widely adopted in Natural Language Processing (NLP) which can provide both syntactic and semantic information on a given constituent structure by assigning tags of lemmatization, inflection, derivation, syntactic function, constituent dependency, valency and semantic classification. The system also marks the dependency relation structures between parts of speech (POS), with the symbol @ placed before (>) or after (<) the head, and therefore proves to be particularly useful for investigations into lexico-grammatical and morpho-syntactic patterns in specific variety usage. Uppercase tags describe word classes as well as morphological inflection (e.g. MV= main verb, PRP= preposition, N = noun, GN= genitive). In example (1) and (2), the noun (N) is annotated as the prenominal modifier on the left (@>N) and as a compound noun <ncomp>:

> (1) lentil [lentil] <Bveg> <fruit> <comp1> <
> ncomp> N S NOM @>N #27->28 soup [soup] <food>
> < Menu 5_tagged.txt   0   9
> (2) [cottage] <build> <comp1> <comp1> <idf> <comp1>
> < ncomp> N S NOM @>N #57->58 cheese [cheese]
> <food>   Menu 5_tagged.txt   0   12

The system therefore generates not only constituents and tags, but also the representations of dependency relations.

The starting point of the analysis was the list of lexical and grammatical features identified as characteristic of the menu register to observe their occurrence also in the Indian menus under investigation in comparison with the monitor corpus represented by the *Strathy Corpus*. Drawing on the matrix proposed by Lévi-Strauss and later revised by Leherer (see above), I first completed that matrix with further cooking verbs referring to cooking procedures from my corpus and then matched the data with co-occurring collocates in the form of compounds.

In particular, the most frequent pre-modifying adjectives in the wordlists of each menu were compared to those occurring in the *Strathy Corpus of Canadian English* by calculating the log-likelihood value. The log-likelihood calculation is a method of comparing linguistically annotated corpora which uses frequency profiling to measure lexical significance in quantitatively different corpora. The comparative method can be used, for instance, to discover keywords which differentiate one corpus from another, and it is shown to have effective applications in the study of social differentiation in the use of English vocabulary. In particular, it can indicate a statistically significant difference at the 5%, 1%, or 0.1% level when critical values are registered as follows:

Tab. 3 Critical values in log-likelihood calculation

95th percentile; 5% level; $p < 0.05$; critical value = 3.84
99th percentile; 1% level; $p < 0.01$; critical value = 6.63
99.9th percentile; 0.1% level; $p < 0.001$; critical value = 10.83
99.99th percentile; 0.01% level; $p < 0.0001$; critical value = 15.13

Consequently, the comparison of the two corpora started with the identification of significant values reported in the matrix, with the aim of discovering features in the sample corpus with significantly different usage (i.e. frequency) to that found in "general" language.

To acquire a more comprehensive rather than fragmented view of the IndEng variety under investigation through a specific register, the grammatical features were observed at the level of phrase structure. The grammatical and lexical features mainly assumed as characteristics of menus as well as presumed IndEng innovations were searched for in the corpus and then mapped onto VISL tags by observing the constituent structure of the Noun Phrases in the corpus. The features examined in the study and the corresponding VISL tags are shown in Tab. 4.

Tab. 4: List of features at phrasal level examined in the study.

Grammatical Features	Type of VISL Tags used
Noun Phrase: • Type of noun modification (**Adj. + N, NN,** N's, N of N) • **compound nouns** • **pre-mod. proper nouns**	**@>N** (prenominal elements such as article, determiner, modifier) <ncomp> <proper>
Verb Phrase: • past participles	**PCP**

Once annotated, tags/instances for each feature could be automatically extracted from the corpus with the application of the *AntConc* concordancer and then manually mapped to the corresponding structural patterns selected for the study as shown in Tab. 4. In order to accurately classify and estimate all pre-modifying occurrences in the annotated corpus, I established a specific syntactic setting in my queries and I could extract all examples of pre-modifiers occurring with Ns (**@>N**) as their right collocates.

Then, to estimate the occurrence of those patterns also in Canadian English, the findings were compared to sample data taken from an interactive database, available at https://www.english-corpora.org/can/ which provides quantitative information on recurrent phrase structures in the *Strathy Corpus of Canadian English*. The queries were ordered according to specific criteria such as minimum frequency of the searched item (e.g. $n=1$), data chunk size (e.g. $n=1000$, which corresponds to the average number of tokens examined in the Mississauga Corpus) and word forms or POS (Parts of Speech) tags to match or exclude items from a given query within a specified range of *n-grams* (from 1 to 3). The analysis was carried out to test two main hypotheses:

hypothesis 1: data show a number of shared traits of convergence toward a set of localized forms or linguistic habits;

hypothesis 2: data show clear signs of divergence with respect to:

a. the target norms in Canadian English

b. the set of features identified in past literature.

In order to test hypotheses and estimate peculiarities of Indian menus as Indian-specific traits, the list of features generally accounted for—typically genre-specific—were first searched for in the corpus and then matched with the list of features identified by Zwicky et al. (Fig.s 12 and 13 above).

In particular, the sections below report on the early results stemming from a preliminary study on verb phrases and lexical features in the corpus.

Results and discussion

Though part of general changes to the English noun phrase, adjectival and nominal modifiers typically add further description, among others things denoting subtypes (hyponyms such as *green chilli, red onions*), properties (*sweet spices*) or evaluation (*delicious dried plum, rich cream*). Proper nouns (such as *Tandoori, Tandoor)* used as modifiers play a particular role in the group of pre-modifiers given their prototypical usage to identify individual people, places, etc. (Breban & Kolkman 2019:1). Used as modifiers, proper nouns retain their identifying function in contrast to common nouns in pre-modifying position, which serve to describe rather than single out the entity denoted by the NP (ib.). In theoretical models of the NP, elements with an identifying function are typically found to the left end of the phrase, which can be summed up by the sequence identifying > qualifying > classifying (Teysser 1978: 227). As for the morpho-syntactic status of proper noun modifiers, they sometimes overlap with the function of compound nouns and of determiner genitives.

Tab. 5 gives an account of the occurrences of the most frequent adjectives attested in the corpus as well as the log ratio, indicating the degree of significance of such occurrences in comparison with the *Strathy Corpus*.

Tab. 5

Pre-modifying Adjectives in NPs	Strathy Corpus of CanEng LogRatio*	Menu1	Menu3	Menu5	Menu8	Menu12	Menu13
authentic			2	24		2	
classic		20	4	4	4		
creamy			14		2		
Fresh 152	7.95	64	26	40	8	7	7
Green 141	6.82	29	32	8	16	50	6
Mild 110	9.17		6	2	6	72	24
Spicy 116	12.39	10	12	2	4	67	21
Sweet 110	8.40	4	6	2	6	70	22
Tender 66	8.33	32	14	12	2		6
Thick 25	6.23	6	2	6	2	9	
Traditional 81	5.95	22	7	26	2	18	6
Whole 74	5.49	16	2	26	4	12	14

Tab. 6 shows the most frequent past participles in the corpus referring to the basic vocabulary used to describe ways of cooking food in comparison with Levy-Strauss's and Leher's models (Fig.s 12–13).

Tab. 6 Occurrences of modifying past participles

Past Participles	Strathy Corpus of CanEng LogRatio*	Menu1	Menu3	Menu5	Menu8	Menu12	Menu13
baked	7.76	11	1	1			
boiled	7.07	2			2	2	
braised			4	1			
(char-)broiled	16.08	12	2	1			
Cooked 195	11.24	33	5	10	9	92	46
(deep-/stir-) fried 262	12.49	15	33		6	148 (30/70)	60
(char-)grilled	9.43		3	(3) 8	3	4	2
Marinated 65	13.20	23	9	8	3	11	11
Roasted 50	11.28	2	3	11	4	20	10
smoked							4
steamed		9			1		
stewed[3]	—	—	—	—			—

The higher the LogRatio value, the more significant the difference is between two frequency scores. For these tables, a LogRatio of 3.8 or higher is significant at the level of $p < 0.05$ and a LogRatio of 6.6 or higher is significant at $p < 0.01$.

The data analysis confirms the assumption that menus may be considered a register in which pre-modifying constructions and past participles expressing processes are particularly productive because of their condensed form without prepositions or other forms of additional marking. The association of these features in menus matches up therefore with the more general opinion concerning noun modifiers and written genres (Biber & Gray 2016).

---

3 The zero occurrence of this cooking practice, which was identified as lexical universal in Levy-Strauss and Lehrer's models, deserves further analysis.

In particular, as for the formal / grammatical features of menus, the use of past participles such as *fried, charbroiled, marinated* referring to completed cooking preparations / procedures are extremely common. Among participles naming ways of cooking, some are often modified:

> lightly [lightly] <ly> ADV @ADVL> buttered [butter] <v.contact> <mv> <fn:cover_ize> <fn:prepare_food> V IMPF @FS-STA #4->0

> refreshingly [refreshing] <ly> ADV @ADVL> marinated [marinate] <mv> <fn:prepare_food> V IMPF @ FS-STA in [in] PRP @<ADVL a [a] <indef> ART S @>N blend [blend] <ac-cat> <idf> <nhead> N S NOM @P< of [of] PRP @N< #9->8

Adjectives that do not refer specifically to methods of preparation are common but often uninformative. Results in Tab. 5 show that by far the most common items are descriptive adjectives such as *fresh* (confirming a steady trend also attested in Zwicky & Zwicky's data), *green, sweet* and *spicy* along with a counter-tendency regarding the decreasing use of *hot* and *tender* (following a general trend also attested in the Strathy Corpus) which all together, with the exception of *green*, represent a group of basic words generally used to describe tastes. Evaluative adjectives such as *traditional, authentic* or compounds such as *cottage cheese* directly relate to identity and offer a means by which it is possible to interpret the text and its social and historical context.

More interesting are the culture-specific examples of proper noun pre-modifiers throughout the whole corpus for their strongly identifying force:

1. Tandoori Salmon [Tandoori=Salmon] <complex> <*> <
    Proper> <asisprop> <heur> N S NOM @>N #1->3 Thick
    Menu 1_tagged.txt   0   1

2. Tandoori Snapper [Tandoori=Snapper] <complex> <*>
    <   Proper> <heur> N S NOM @SUBJ> \xA4AG \
    Menu 1_tagged.txt   0   2

3. > Shrimp Sherdil [Shrimp=Sherdil] <complex> <*> <
    Proper> <heur> <nhead> N S NOM @SUBJ> \xA4
    Menu 1_tagged.txt   0   3

4. Tandoori Drumsticks [Tandoori=Drumsticks] <complex>
    <*> <   Proper> <asisprop> <heur> <pre-long> N S NOM
    @>   Menu 1_tagged.txt   0   4

5. Murg Malai Tikka [Murg=Malai=Tikka] <complex> <*>
    <   Proper> <heur> <nhead> N S NOM @NPHR \
    xA4   Menu 1_tagged.txt   0   5

6. Nirvana Chicken Tikka [Nirvana=Chicken=Tikka]
    <complex> <*> <   Proper> <heur> <nhead> N S
    NOM @NPHR \xA4 Menu 1_tagged.txt   0   6

7. Kung Pao [Kung=Pao] <complex> <*> <Proper> <
    asisprop> <heur> <ncomp> N S NOM @>N #8->9 sauce
    MENU 3_TAGGED.txt   0   22

Conclusion

The data analysis shows rare signs of divergence throughout the
corpus. This common trait confirms the conformity to a set of
shared norms of usage within the same register as that identified
by Zwicky et al. (1980). Such homogeneity contributes to identifying menus and more specifically those of Indian restaurants in
Mississauga as a clear "identity vehicle" with specific characteristics.
Divergent trends clearly emerge, instead, when the results of the
analysis are compared with the *Strathy Corpus of Canadian English*.

As matter of fact, some evidence of "divergence" is represented by the high log ratio value representing the semantic density of certain items throughout the corpus as reported in the table. Some other forms attested only in Menu 5 (*speciality cottage cheese)* and Menu 8 *(smoky succulence,* where "smoky" is the only occurrence attested in the corpus) can be interpreted as a "breakaway" tendency toward creative diversification with respect to ordinary discourse in a highly multilingual context. Again in this context, food emerges as a discursive space able to critically interrogate the nostalgic and affective rendering of food in relation to racial / ethnic identity. The attachment of taste to place can be seen as one of the tautologies of food and identity leading to "a food-centred worldview" (Sutton 2010: 216) in which a taste is typically naturalized and associated with a specific local place and particular social practices (Trubek 2008: 216).

At this stage, definitively explanatory information cannot be provided from the available materials to establish whether the innovative elements attested in the corpus reflect an individual or an entire community of speakers' linguistic habits. Regular occurrence of the same innovation/s in other sources needs to be further investigated to provide evidence of its/their stabilization of a creative tendency, and this is the next task of the present study.

In conclusion, the results of the study are not particularly surprising but the methodology adopted provides statistical evidence to back up the intuitions and observations made in past literature.

Works Cited

Roland Barthes, (1997) "Toward a Psychosociology of Contemporary Food Consumption," in Carole Counihan and Penny Van Esterik (eds.), *Food and Culture: A Reader*, London: Routledge, 20–7.

Biber, Douglas and Gray, Bethany *(2016), Grammatical complexity in academic English*, Cambridge: Cambridge University Press.

Black, Max (1962), *Models and Metaphors*, New York: Cornell University Press, Ithaca.

Breban, Tine and Kolkman, Julia (2019), "Different perspectives on proper noun modifiers". *English Language and Linguistics*. Special issue, pp. 1–10.

Fellner, Astrid (2013), "The flavors of multi-ethnic North American literatures. Language, ethnicity and culinary nostalgia," in Gerhardt, Cornelia, Frobenius, Maximiliane and Ley, Susanne (eds.), Culinary Linguistics, Amsterdam: J. Benjamins Publishing.

Lakoff, George (2004/2006), *Don't Think of an Elephant*, Chelsea Green, USA.

Lakoff, George and Johnson, Mark (1980), *Metaphors We Live By*, Chicago: The University of Chicago Press.

Lehrer, Adrienne (1972), "Cooking Vocabularies and the Culinary Triangle of Lévi-Strauss," *Anthropological Linguistics*. Vol. 14, No. 5, pp. 155–171.

Lévi-Strauss, Claude (1966), "The culinary triangle," *Partisan Review*. Vol. 33, no. 4 (Fall 1966) p. 586–595.

Mannur, Anita (2010), *Culinary Fictions: Food in South Asian Diasporic Culture*, Philadelphia PA: Temple University Press.

Reichl, Susanne (2003), "'Like a beacon against the cold': Food and the construction of ethnic identities in Black British novels," In *Eating Culture: The Poetics and Politics of Food*, Tobias D. Ring, Markus Heide and Susanne Mühleisen (eds.), 177–193. Heidelberg: Winter.

Rogers, Chandrika K. *(2002), "Syntactic features of Indian English:* An examination of written Indian English," in *Using Corpora to Explore Linguistic Variation* [Studies in Corpus Linguistics 9], R. Reppen, S. M. Fitzmaurice and D. Biber (eds.), 187–202.

Sutton, David E. (2010), "Food and the senses," *Annual Review of Anthropology, 39*, 209–323.

Teysser, Jacques (1968), "Notes on the syntax of the adj in modern English". *Lingua* 20, 225–49.

Trubek, Amy B. (2009), *The Taste of Place. A Cultural Journey into Terroir*. University of California Press.

Zwicky, Ann D. and Zwicky, Arnold M. (1980*)*, "The American Dialect Society. *America's National Dish: The Style of Restaurant Menus," American Speech*, Vol. 55, No. 2, pp. 83–9.

Wodak, Ruth et al. (2009), *The Discursive Construction of National Identity*, Edinburgh: Edinburgh University Press.

MARINA ZITO

Pâté chinois, tourtières et autres délices de la cuisine québécoise

LA RENCONTRE INTERPERSONNELLE À TABLE est un moment de profonde et joyeuse connaissance; par conséquent, l'étude différenciée du moment convivial au Québec nous permettra de mieux nous approcher de cette culture et de la civilisation que nous avons préférée au cours de nos études des différentes francophonies.

Tout d'abord, il n'est pas inutile de rappeler que la cuisine traditionnelle québécoise n'est ni légère ni diététique car elle avait (et a encore) pour but de combattre le froid. Et … c'est sur les plats de la tradition que nous allons nous pencher, sur certains mets traditionnels—sans aucunement faire référence aux chefs à la mode qui pratiquent la "nouvelle cuisine".

Légendes et rhétorique autour du plat national

Au concours lancé par le journal *Le Devoir* sur "le plat national du Québec" en 2007, ce fut le "pâté chinois" qui remporta la victoire, suivi par la tourtière. Nous allons examiner la composition et l'histoire de ces deux plats (Lemasson 2009: 10).

Les premiers témoignages écrits du "pâté chinois" datent des années Trente du siècle dernier mais cela prouve implicitement que le plat existait bel et bien depuis longtemps.

Assiette-reine, plat national, il nous semble nécessaire d'essayer de comprendre son nom. Pourquoi et comment ce renvoi à la Chine, si renvoi il y a? Le canal Lachine ne suffisait-il pas pour remémorer aux gens le malentendu initial de la découverte? Sur le thème de l'adjectif "chinois", une bibliographie sympathique s'est établie que nous examinerons rapidement à travers quelques hypothèses.

Selon la première, la piste des travailleurs chinois, ce plat québécois serait la modification de la nourriture des immigrés chinois engagés pour construire le chemin de fer d'un océan à l'autre à la fin du XIXème siècle. Mais cette théorie peut être facilement réfutée car ces ouvriers travaillaient aux tronçons de la côte Ouest.

Deuxième hypothèse : le mérite de l'importation de ce plat reviendrait aux Américains et aux travailleurs québécois qui, au début du XXème siècle, se rendaient dans le Maine, notamment dans la localité appelée China. Là-bas, ils auraient pu connaître le *cottage pie* dans lequel, entre deux couches de purée de pommes de terre, se trouvait du bœuf en tranches. Ils auraient ensuite ramené au Québec et l'idée et la préparation de ce plat "exotique" qu'ils avaient goûté dans la ville de China dans le Maine. Le *cottage pie* se présente en effet comme un souvenir, une "idée", quoique lointaine, du pâté qui nous intéresse mais c'est quelque chose de très évanescent et de, somme toute, banal. Le pâté chinois, nous allons le voir, présente une organisation différente de ses composants—qui d'ailleurs sont plus nombreux.

Examinons ensuite la troisième hypothèse, celle du riz. À la base de cette hypothèse, il y a une recette des Sœurs du Saint Nom de Marie et de Jésus datée de 1941, selon laquelle les restes de viandes pouvaient être réutilisés entre deux couches de riz, de quelques assaisonnements et d'un œuf. La fantaisie populaire aurait vu dans la présence du riz, que les Chinois apprécient, le lien pour inventer la qualification d'un plat. Encore une fois, cette hypothèse ne convainc pas.

Il y a enfin la théorie de la passoire. En effet, selon le *Trésor de la langue française*, le "chinois" est une "passoire fine et conique rappelant la forme du chapeau des mandarins chinois". Les ménagères québécoises auraient-elles connu cet ustensile de la haute cuisine et l'auraient-elles utilisé pour avoir une purée fine? Cela semble par trop audacieux …

En conclusion, concernant le nom du plat, selon le spécialiste déjà cité, ce nom "tiendrait du pur plaisir de la métaphore, d'une ironie à l'égard de cette Chine lointaine et populeuse à laquelle parfois les Québécois ont pu se comparer à une époque de fécondité considérable" (Lemasson 2009: 90)—les nombreux grains de maïs aidant!

Si le mystère demeure entier sur l'adjectif qui compose l'appellation du plat, n'oublions pas que l'utilisation québécoise du substantif "pâté" est totalement liée à la Belle Province; en vérité, si on s'en tient à ce qu'en dit le *Trésor de la langue Française*, le nom "pâté" n'aurait que deux significations : soit de "pâte feuilletée légèrement salée enveloppant un hachis de viande … cuite au four", soit de "préparation de charcuterie cuite… dans une terrine et consommée froide"; or, un bref examen des composants du "pâté chinois" nous permettra de souligner la nouveauté de la signification au Québec—où, à l'évidence, la fantaisie populaire a inventé une troisième acception pour le substantif "pâté".

Il nous faut avant tout mentionner les trois ingrédients principaux qui sont : la viande hachée, le maïs, la purée de pommes de terre. Pour la préparation, on répartit en couches, dans une large terrine, d'abord la viande hachée—préalablement cuite une dizaine de minutes avec de l'huile et un oignon haché –, ensuite le maïs, dont une moitié doit être réduite en crème, et enfin la purée de pommes de terre. Le tout sera parsemé de paprika qui, au moment de la cuisson, donnera au plat gratiné sa caractéristique nuance rougeâtre (Bérubé 2015: 62).

Après avoir examiné les composants du plat, il est important de faire une dernière différenciation avec le "hachis Parmentier" où, évidemment, le blé d'Inde est totalement absent et pour cause, car, à l'époque de l'inventeur, l'apothicaire Antoine Parmentier, pendant la guerre de Sept Ans, les Français ne l'utilisaient pas encore pour la consommation humaine.

Il est intéressant de remarquer que le pâté chinois a sa place dans la littérature, par exemple dans les romans de Michel Tremblay, et pas seulement …

Pour conclure cette partie de notre exposé, nous pouvons définir le pâté chinois comme un plat non seulement familial (car assez bon marché) mais également social. Cela tient à deux remarques qui se complètent l'une l'autre. Par le fait que les différentes couches –viande, maïs et pommes de terre—ne se mélangent pas, le pâté chinois, selon l'expression de l'humoriste Boucar Diouf, serait l'image de la société—car "le Blanc est en haut, le Jaune est au milieu et le Noir est en bas" (Lemasson 2009: 32). Mais de plus, si on fait attention au double sens de l'adjectif "gratiné" qui, au figuré, signifie "remarquable, qui sort de l'ordinaire", on peut interpréter la couche supérieure du pâté, qui est destinée à être gratinée, comme étant l'image des classes sociales élevées.

La longue histoire de la tourtière

Accordons maintenant toute notre attention à la tourtière qui, pour moi qui parle, est liée au souvenir d'une amitié importante, d'un invité à nos conférences de "l'Orientale" qui, pour la première fois m'a parlé de ce plat comme d'un souvenir auquel il était profondément lié : "la tourtière de maman" dit-il—faisant aussi référence, au passage, au lieu d'où il était originaire, le Saguenay-Lac-Saint-Jean. Ayant besoin d'un peu de bibliographie, tournons-nous avant tout vers la Bible des littéraires, à savoir les dictionnaires. Selon le *Petit Robert,* la tourtière est "un ustensile de cuisine pour faire des tourtes", la tourte étant à son tour "une pâtisserie de forme ronde (à la viande, au poisson)". Le *Trésor de la langue Française* vient aussi à notre aide car, après la définition de tourte—"Tarte circulaire aux bords légèrement élevés, recouverte d'une abaisse, garnie notamment de viandes, de volaille, de quenelles et qui est servie comme entrée chaude"—on peut lire les mots suivants : "Synonyme au Canada : "tourtière". La figure de la synecdoque triomphe donc dans le Nouveau Monde! Or, étant donné que parmi les ingrédients de cette "tourte recouverte d'une abaisse", il y a différents types de viandes, l'histoire des civilisations anciennes prouve que rien n'est nouveau sous le soleil! On va voir comment.

Interprétant les travaux et les études des archéologues, Jean Botéro, dans *La plus vieille cuisine du monde,* donne la recette d'un plat mésopotamien où, à l'intérieur de deux abaisses, on trouvait un mélange à base de "petits oiseaux" (Botéro 2002: 52-53) : il démontre ainsi la présence à la fois des deux abaisses et d'un certain type de viande cuite à l'intérieur : des oiseaux, je le répète—d'autant que la viande de porc n'était pas encore connue et que seule la civilisation grecque commencera à utiliser cet ingrédient destiné à devenir fondamental dans la tourtière québécoise! Quant aux Romains, ils ont eux aussi leur part dans cet examen chronologique car on leur doit l'étymologie du nom "tourte", variante de "torta panis" (pain rond). On arrive au moment du triomphe de ce plat, au Moyen Âge, époque où les Hommes du Nord encouragent la consommation de la viande de porc car ces animaux sont faciles à élever : il s'ensuit que la tourte devient un plat dont la consommation traverse tout le corps social (Lemasson 2011: 423).

La tourte arrive au Canada avec les premières vagues d'émigration. Un peu de bibliographie peut nous aider, une fois de plus. Dans *Le cuisinier françois,* le sieur La Varenne décrit des innovations importantes de notre plat : non seulement quant à la manière de plier la pâte pour la feuilleter, mais aussi parce que l'utilisation de la farine de seigle pour le "pasté à la marotte" allait permettre la conservation—et, par conséquent, les longs voyages outre-Atlantique (La Varenne 2002: 143). En même temps, l'importation de porcs s'impose au Québec, facilitant ainsi la diffusion de ce plat.

Les réceptions chez les notables de la Nouvelle Colonie deviennent peu à peu ostentatoires, par exemple celles du Gouverneur Frontenac (1672-1698) à l'occasion desquelles notre tourte est toujours présente.

Après 1763, tout le monde le sait, le Régime anglais prend pied. Les marins anglais eux aussi avaient des mets qui devaient traverser l'Atlantique, en particulier une tourte aux couches superposées qu'ils appelaient *sea pie*. Elle arrive donc en Gaspésie : les francophones auraient alors imaginé que ce nom indiquait les six abaisses de pâte dont se composait cette "version" anglaise d'un mets déjà connu; de là, la francisation en "six-pâtes" qui va s'écrire "cipâte", et enfin "cipaille" (Bérubé 2015: 90).

Cipaille (ou cipâte) vs tourtière? Aujourd'hui, le *Dictionnaire nord-américain de la langue française* (Bélisle 1989: ad vocem) enregistre les deux entrées pour le premier plat et, pour ce qui est du deuxième, insiste sur l'ancienneté de la préparation. De plus, ce *Dictionnaire* mentionne la présence de pommes de terre dans la cipaille. Cela me rappelle l'exclamation de mes amies québécoises m'assurant inlassablement que dans toute la Province du Québec, la tourtière est une tourte sans pommes de terre! C'est peut-être aujourd'hui en cela que se situe la différence fondamentale.

Un saut dans le domaine littéraire est dès lors opportun pour mettre en évidence d'autres ressemblances dans la cuisine québécoise, un "pâté de Pâques" étant à l'honneur dans un célèbre roman, *Les Anciens Canadiens* de Philippe Aubert de Gaspé père, publié en 1863. La narration se déroule en 1757, deux ans avant la Conquête, et c'est presque au début de l'histoire qu'on trouve la description qui nous intéresse :

> Le menu du repas était composé d'un excellent potage ... [et] d'un pâté froid appelé pâté de Pâques ... [Celui-ci] était composé d'une dinde, de deux poulets, de deux perdrix, de deux pigeons, du râble et des cuisses de deux lièvres : le tout recouvert de bardes de lard gras. Le godiveau de viandes hachées, sur lequel reposaient, sur un lit épais et mollet, ces richesses gastronomiques, et qui en couvrait aussi la partie supérieure, était le produit de deux jambons de cet animal que le juif méprise, mais que le chrétien traite avec le plus d'égards. De gros oignons, introduits çà et là, et de fines épices, complétaient le tout. Mais un point très important en était la

cuisson, d'ailleurs assez difficile ; car, si le géant crevait, il perdait alors cinquante pour cent de son acabit. Pour prévenir un événement aussi déplorable, la croûte du dessous, qui recouvrait encore de trois pouces les flancs du monstre culinaire, n'avait pas moins d'un pouce d'épaisseur. Cette croûte même, imprégnée du jus de toutes ces viandes était une partie délicieuse de ce mets unique (Aubert de Gaspé père 2002: 107).

Il est bien évident qu'il ne s'agit pas là d'un plat pauvre! Toutefois, les ingrédients et les particularités de la cuisson autorisent le jumelage avec notre tourtière, et ce, d'autant plus que quelques années auparavant, en 1860, *La nouvelle cuisinière canadienne* affichait un chapitre intitulé "tourtières et pâtés" (Perrault 1860: 108), justifiant ainsi notre juxtaposition de la tourtière à la riche assiette du roman fondateur de la littérature québécoise!

"Les jeux sont faits!" pourrait-on s'exclamer. Juste une dernière remarque en fin d'examen, pour rappeler qu'en Languedoc, un dessert est appelé "pastis-tourtière"! Comme un joli témoignage des héritages communs de la France et du Québec.

Poutine: oui ou non?

L'histoire de la poutine est beaucoup plus récente.

Il faut se déplacer à Drummondville, ville fondée en 1815 et baptisée de ce nom en l'honneur de l'administrateur (anglais) du territoire. Avec un passé industriel remarquable, Drummondville se distingue aujourd'hui par son importance croissante due à l'enthousiasme de ses entrepreneurs.

Située sur les bords de la rivière Saint-François, entre Montréal et Québec, sur la rive sud du Saint-Laurent, elle jouit encore d'immenses espaces environnants et accueille un club de golf réputé.

Or, selon la légende—dont je suis redevable à mes amis France et Robert Gendron—un restaurateur de Drummondville, Jean-Paul (ou Jean-Guy) Roy, "inventa" en 1964 la poutine car il servait, avec des frites, le produit de la région, un fromage en grain que ses clients commencèrent à mélanger aux frites, accompagné d'une sauce (aux ingrédients encore secrets!) : de ce mélange improvisé naquit cette merveille que nous évoquons ici. Quant à son nom, il serait dû à un autre mélange, entre l'anglais "pudding" et le surnom de l'assistant cuisinier, M. Gilles Dubé : "Ti-Pout" (expression qui n'a aucune signification).

Toutefois, force est de reconnaître que malgré cette histoire fascinante, les Québécois ne sont pas fiers de ce plat—qu'ils considèrent comme trop populaire. En effet, on peut goûter des poutines partout dans les quartiers les moins élégants des principales villes. D'autre part, les multiples modes de préparation de ce plat l'ont quelque peu dénaturé—comme c'est d'ailleurs le cas de la pizza napolitaine dont les variantes qu'on peut trouver partout dans le monde risquent parfois de choquer les voyageurs napolitains …

Je prépare la poutine chez moi car j'ai transmis mon enthousiasme à ma famille. C'est très simple—même si nous n'avons pas ce fameux fromage en grains de la région de Drummondville! C'est simple parce qu'on utilise du cheddar, ou, à la rigueur, du gruyère râpé, et pour la sauce, du fond de bœuf fera l'affaire.

Un remerciement s'impose maintenant à tous et toutes mes ami(e)s québécois(es) car je leur dois une grande partie des informations que j'ai élaborées et j'adresse à mes lecteurs un chaleureux "à la prochaine" qui me donnera l'occasion de leur faire connaître quelques recettes de desserts—en particulier, les "beignes", succulente pâtisserie de Noël qui ressemble à nos "graffette" italiennes.

Works Cited

Aubert de Gaspé père, Philippe (2002), *Les Anciens Canadiens*, Montréal: Boréal.

Bélisle, Louis-Alexandre (1989), *Dictionnaire nord-américain de la langue française*, Chomedey, Laval (Québec): Beauchemin.

Bérubé, Caty (2015), *Cuisine québécoise*, Québec: Pratico-Pratique.

Botéro, Jean (2002), *La plus vieille cuisine du monde*, Paris: Audiberti.

La Varenne (2002), *Le cuisinier françois*, d'après l'édition de 1651, Houilles: Éditions Manucius.

Lemasson, Jean-Pierre (2009), *Le mystère insondable du pâté chinois*, Verdun (Québec): Amérik-Média.

Lemasson, Jean-Pierre (2011), *L'incroyable odyssée de la tourtière*, Version numérique coéditée par Numériklivres Éditions et Del Busso éditeur.

Perrault, Louis (1860), *La nouvelle cuisinière canadienne*, Montréal: Louis Perrault.

TLFi : Trésor de la langue Française informatisé, http://www.atilf.fr/tlfi, ATILF - CNRS & Université de Lorraine.

MIRKO CASAGRANDA

"Poutine is not Canadian":
Food and National Identity in Canada

Introduction

IT IS QUITE LIKELY THAT poutine was the last thing Justin Trudeau
expected to eat at a White House state dinner held in his honour
in March 2016. One may consider Barack Obama's menu choice
as the perfect example of "gastrodiplomacy", a term coined by *The
Economist* in 2002 to describe how diplomatic relations are often
established not only over meals but also through national cuisines.
The concept "can be roughly defined as the construction and reproduction of national food brands and images by the nation-state
for political, diplomatic and commercial reasons" (Ichijo and Ranta
2016: 13), and is but one of the multifaceted perspectives that can
be adopted to analyze how food contributes to the discursive construction of national identity.

Poutine had been represented as the national dish of Canada in
public discourse across the country way before it appeared on the
White House dinner table, which is considered by many a Quebecer
as a form of appropriation or Canadianization of Quebecois culture
(Fabien-Ouellet 2019), a debate that has been echoing on the media and social networks for quite a few years now. This paper aims
to assess how poutine has been discursively construed as a marker
of national identity by applying the framework of banal nationalism theorised by Ichijo and Ranta (2016) to a selection of tweets

in English collected in November 2019, where social media users discuss poutine and Canadianness.

Food, national identities and … poutine

Even though in Canadian English "poutine" is attested as a borrowing with a distinctive Anglophone pronunciation, the term is usually associated with the French language by most Canadians. According to *The Canadian Encyclopedia* online, it is "a Québécois dish made of fresh-cut French fries topped with cheese curds and gravy [which] first appeared in 1950s rural Quebec snack bars [and] was widely popularized across Canada and beyond in the 1990s. […] It has become an iconic symbol of Québécois cuisine and culture."[1] As the anecdote about Trudeau and Obama exemplifies, however, poutine has been recently re-branded as an "iconic symbol" of Canadian cuisine and culture at the detriment of Quebec's claim of ownership over the authentic dish.

For over forty years its working-class background and caloric ingredients were used by Anglo-Canadians to stereotypically mock Quebecois culture and dismiss poutine as comfort junk food to be consumed late at night, especially after large intakes of alcohol (Théorêt 2007). The stigma was internalized by Quebecois culture to such an extent that it took the uproar over its Canadianization to re-appropriate it, especially within urban youth culture, and reclaim it as a symbol of Quebecois "national" identity.

For these reasons, poutine is a good case in point of the complex relationship between food and identity, both in terms of how individuals perceive themselves and the way their identities are shaped and regulated in relation to food and food production and consumption. Over the last twenty years, such a multifarious topic has been tackled from theoretical perspectives that focus both on culture (Ashley, Hollows, Jones and Taylor 2004; Cooke 2009; Montanari

---

1 thecanadianencyclopedia.ca

2004) and the contested concepts of territory and nationhood (Edensor 2002; Ferguson 2010; Monterescu 2017; Wilson 2006). Several case studies have been devoted to food in multicultural and diasporic contexts (Imilan 2015; Mintz 2008; Rabikowska 2010; Reddy and van Dam 2020; Vallianatos and Raine 2008), food and national identity (Bell and Neill 2014; Caldwell 2002; Cwiertka 2006; Hiroko 2008; Metro-Roland 2013; Raviv 2015; Rozin 2003), cookbook discourse (Snell 2014; Wilmherst 2013), and food policies (Guy 2003; Nowak, Jones and Ascione 2020).

Most approaches to food studies share the assumption that food is an arbitrary semiotic system to which social, cultural and political beliefs and values become attached (Ashley, Hollows, Jones and Taylor 2004: 5). Barthes considered this process as a form of "national symbolism" (1972: 64) and stated that, from a structuralist point of view, food is more nationalized than socialized. Consequently, it comes as no surprise that most cultural representations of food contain political or social meaning (Barter 2013) that need to be interpreted and contextualized. In the case of Canada, a few studies have been published on Indigenous foodways (Bodirsky and Johnson 2008), gender and multiculturalism (D'Sylva and Beagan 2011), Newfoundland and Labrador (Everett 2011) and Quebec (Desjardins 2011), while the topic of poutine has been investigated in terms of food science (Rioux, Perrault and Turgeon 2020) and cultural-political dynamics (Fabien-Ouellet 2016).

In their investigation of food discourse and national identity, Ichijo and Ranta (2016) use the framework of banal nationalism, a term that covers "the ideological habits which enable the established nations of the West to be reproduced" (Billig 1995: 6), and apply it to a selection of texts that are analyzed from a top-down, bottom-up and global perspective:

> Food culture, through routine and mundane activities, such as the procurement and consumption of food, also helps construct and reproduce the nation. [...] food culture 'institutionalises' our lives and identities

by providing common structuring and normalising patterns of 'how things are' and 'how we do things', and [...] how we talk about things (Ichijo and Ranta 2016: 7).

In order to evaluate how poutine serves as a discourse resource for the process of meaning-making and to index and negotiate identity (Tovares and Gordon 2020), a selection of 25 poutine-related interactions on Twitter, one of the most powerful digital tools to create affiliation online (Zappavigna 2012), has been collected on November 13, 2019, using the term "poutine" as search word. The tweets were subsequently analyzed from Ichijo and Ranta's above-mentioned perspectives.

Top-down perspectives: shaping national identity

In their need to exert control over their geographical boundaries and citizens, nation-states actively contribute to the creation of nationalism by turning cultural items into symbols of national identity: the stronger the identification with the symbol, the tighter the association with the nation-state. Food culture is often exploited by institutional discourse in order to establish such direct connection:

> The construction of a national food culture can thus be seen as part of the process of constructing, establishing or reifying nations. [...] Constructing, reifying, asserting and at times inventing a common food culture is a useful method through which national entrepreneurs and movements try to bring different groups of people together; this process is made easier if it taps into existing or imagined shared food practices and traditions (Ichijo and Ranta 2016: 10-11).

The invention of a common food culture in multicultural contexts like Canada may also envisage the extension of a regional culinary tradition to the whole nation-state. The dissemination of institutional discourse via its official social media accounts allows the government to reach social media users on a regular basis. In so doing, new digital media become powerful tools of banal nationalism as they allow institutional discourse to enter the private sphere directly, with no other form of mediation.

When Canada celebrated 150 years since confederation in 2017, the promotional material issued by government agencies often relied on cultural and historical symbols like the maple leaf or the moose. The following tweet, for instance, was posted on Global Affairs Canada's official account as a sort of entry of an ideal list of everything distinctively and uniquely Canadian:

1. Its origin is up for debate but many say the poutine (fries with cheese curds & gravy) was invented in 1957 in Warwick, Quebec #Canada 150. [Canada @Canada, May 20, 2017]

Even though the Quebecois origin of the dish is fully acknowledged, the use of the hashtag #Canada 150 immediately binds poutine with Canadian culture and creates a sense of national tradition that is deceivingly rooted in the foundation of the country.

The importance of poutine in Canadian institutional discourse is emphasized also when it is not directly associated with nationhood. At the beginning of November 2019, a tweet caused quite a stir nationwide because of its endorsement of the Toronto-based Enchanted Poutinerie and its rainbow version of the traditional recipe:

2. If you didn't think poutine was magical enough, Toronto's Enchanted Poutinerie has got you covered! Looking like mystical delight, their Unicorn Poutine is made

with fresh rainbow Quebec cheese curds & multi-co-
lour gravy—don't mind if we do [emoticons] [Canada @
Canada, Nov 3, 2019]

Notwithstanding the unusual choice of publicly supporting a
private business, the government organization seems to combine
some features of poutine—its "magical" and "mystical" qualities—
with LGBTQ+ symbolism, i.e. the rainbow colours and the unicorn,
an enchanted animal which is displayed also on the logo of the
Torontonian poutinerie. Even though to my knowledge there is no
official statement about the reasons why such tweet was posted, it is
quite likely that it intended to benefit from the popularity of poutine especially among foreigners—the account aims at "showcasing
Canada to the world"—and turn it into a symbol of Canadian diversity and the country's policies to support and preserve it.

Both private citizens and the media, particularly in Quebec,
fiercely criticized the tweet by posting comments based on the
"us" versus "them" dichotomy that is extremely common in the
discursive construction of national identity (De Cillia, Reisigl and
Wodak 1999):

3. Canada promoted 'unicorn poutine' on Twitter, and now
    we may be separatists? [Montreal Gazette @mtlgazette,
    Nov 4, 2019]

4. This justifies the destruction of the Confederation. Wexit,
    Québec secession, Maritimes secession, this is where it all
    starts [David Beck-Mac Neil #beckbat, Nov 5, 2019]

5. People are really mad at Toronto right now over unicorn
    poutine [blogTO @blogTO, Nov 5, 2019]

6. I'm so sad for our national meal … [Frédéric Harper @
    fharper, Nov 7, 2019]

7. Toronto has committed a crime against Quebec with this
    "Unicorn Poutine" [emoticons] Would you try this …?!
    [C100FM @C100FM, Nov 8, 2019]

8. Quebec is not here for Toronto's "unicorn poutine" (Via @ EaterMontreal) [Eater @Eater, Nov 10, 2019]

The opposition is described above all in terms of geography, like in examples (7) and (8), where Toronto and Quebec are personified and placed one against the other, which in examples (3) and (4) leads to a shift towards politics and nationalism. Indeed, while the *Montreal Gazette* seizes the opportunity to ironically hint at Quebec separatism in the headline of an article that was shared on Twitter as well, a private user becomes extremely angry and wishes for the collapse of the federal government and the secession of Quebec, Maritime Canada and Western Canada.[2] The juxtaposition between Anglophone Canada, embodied by Toronto like in example (5), and Francophone Quebec is further stressed by the *Montreal Gazette* in the subheading of the above-mentioned article: "The offending—and offensive—poutine shared on the government account was from Toronto, because of course it was". By employing the terms "offending" and "offensive" and the clause "because of course it was", the Montreal-based newspaper stresses the political and ideological gap between Quebec and the rest of Canada and implicitly reclaims cultural ownership over poutine.

Other media followed a similar line and based such dichotomous relationship on linguistic devices representing the distinctive qualities of multicoloured poutine. In the headline "Canada calls unicorn poutine 'magical'; Quebecers have other words for it", for instance, CTV News introduces the euphemism "other words for it" to allude to the outcry against the government and the audacity to call something unauthentic "magical". While the politicization of poutine is here only implied, example (6) identifies the dish as overtly national and describes it as a meal—another evidence of the social upgrade of what was previously considered merely as a rural

---

2 Adopting the same linguistic pattern as Brexit, Wexit is a blend of "west" and "exit" and promotes the independence of Western Canada, namely the provinces of British Columbia, Alberta, Saskatchewan and Manitoba.

snack. By using the adjective "national" in this context, the user is explicitly making a statement about their political opinion about Quebec as a nation distinct from the other provinces and territories of Canada.

Bottom-up perspectives: individual and collective identities

The reaction of Canadians to unicorn poutine is a good example of the way food is embedded in individuals' life and their social interactions, both privately and publicly. They are forms of participation in the discursive representations of the nation, which "is created, given meaning and maintained by everyday/banal acts of cooking, talking about and consuming food" (Ichijo and Ranta 2016: 21). The analysis of online interactions on Twitter allows to assess whether poutine is perceived as the contemporary Canadian national dish notwithstanding its Quebecois origin and whether this is considered as an act of cultural appropriation, as claimed by Fabien-Ouellet (2016).

Even though it does not offer the statistical knowledge provided by a quantitative approach, the qualitative analysis of tweets about poutine gives evidence of the shaping of national identity and belonging through food discourse in Canada. In the following tweets, for instance, poutine is indexed as primarily Quebecois:

9. The Montreal poutine is calling to you @torygillis! I feel very Québécois suddenly. [Ted Deller @TDellerCBC, Aug 14, 2014]

10. Friday mean [sic] pizza poutine time! [emoticons] Only a true Quebecois/Quebecoise know [sic] what I mean [emoticons] [Émily Bélensky @MimiMaibe, Sep 21, 2018]

11. Une tradition du Quebec… a Quebecois tradition in foods class today [Laurier Heights School @LHSEPSB, Oct 15, 2018]

12. Dear Twitter, Day 96 in America: I have ordered poutine at a restaurant in Oakland. French fries covered in ground beef was what was delivered to me. Today is a sad day for Canada and Québécois around the world. I hope tomorrow is a brighter day. With love, Umi [umiscar @umisacr, Apr 7, 2019]

13. Happy #fryyay! [emoticon] If you are looking for a #lunch suggestion, try #La_Poutine_! It is a cozy little spot on the edge of the #UofA campus serving up faithful Quebecois #poutine, as well as countless variations. I had the The Big Mack, #vegetarian style. [YEGTweetUp, @YEGTweetup, Jul 5, 2019]

14. Really? Arkansas serves something they claim is poutine… a dish that cannot be perfected outside of Québec. Anything else is a poor knockoff calling itself poutine. Delete your account and renounce your statehood. [Dial H for How's That Workin' For Ya? @TheUnrealJTH, Nov 13, 2019]

Poutine is associated with Montreal (9) and traditional Quebecois culture (11). In this case, authenticity is geographically bound (14) and any other version made outside *la belle province* is pejoratively labelled as a "poor knockoff". The bond with Quebecois identity is strengthened by the use of modifiers such as "very" (9), "true" (10) and "faithful" (13). From a linguistic point of view, example (11) alternates a phrase in French with its English translation, one of the typologies of code-switching that are very frequent in bilingual communication and that may serve here to authenticate the statement about tradition. On the other hand, tweets (9) and (12) opt for the French diacritics in the spelling of the adjective "Québécois", while tweet (10) includes its French masculine and feminine forms, "Quebecois" and "Quebecoise". Even though they are all attested as borrowings in Canadian English, such linguistic choices may be seen as instances of awareness of the morpho-syntactic features of the French language and a way to acknowledge the Francophone origin of the dish.

In most tweets selected for this paper, however, poutine is identified as Canadian, rather than Quebecois, by foreigners:

15. My first Canadian poutine. #CSIKraken [Cherise Lakeside @CheriseLakeside, Nov 9, 2019]

16. Canada is wonderful so far. Just look at this poutine. [theMadz @MadzTheSmol, Nov 10, 2019]

17. In Canada for the first time, so naturally I bought many Kinder chocolate eggs & poutine! [emoticons] [Emperatriz @mprtrzng, Nov 10, 2019]

18. Oh Canada, I've missed you. It's been too long. Nothing like some poutine and timmies to say welcome back to Canada [Canadian flag] [Erin (FireBall1725) @ FireBall1725, Nov 11, 2019]

19. Homemade poutine to fill the poutine filled void in my heart that Canada left [Fyrus @FyrusYT, Nov 12, 2019]

20. There's two things that are important to me in this picture: the opportunity to do #scipol and poutine (Not pictured is the third important thing: the ketchup chips I had for breakfast) Cant wait for @sciencepolicy's Canadian Science Policy Conference to start tomorrow [Alessandra Zimmermann @alesszimm, Nov 12, 2019]

Visitors to Canada tend to identify their travel experience with national foods and construe poutine as quintessentially Canadian. In (17), for instance, the adverb "naturally" points to the fact that for the user poutine is the obvious choice for a first-time tourist— something that is only implied in (15) where the user's first poutine is presumably linked to their first visit to the country. In (16) the pleasantness of Canada is exemplified by a picture of poutine, a correlation made by inserting the adverb "just" between the first and the second sentence. A similar strategy is used in (20) to emphasize how food and important events are related for a scholar who is attending the 2019 Canadian Science Policy Conference in Ottawa and who expresses her enthusiasm by posting a picture of poutine taken in front of Parliament Buildings, another symbol of Canadianness. The association between food and the nation is even stronger in tweets like (18), where the user addresses Canada directly and presents poutine and Tim Horton's coffee as paragons of Canadian hospitality rather than successful examples of national branding (Cormac 2008). The entanglement between food and national identity discourse is almost bodily conveyed in tweet (19), where nostalgia for Canada is replaced by a homemade version of the recipe which rhetorically replaces the country in the user's heart.

The bond between national identity and poutine is even stronger among Canadians:

21. @lizrenzetti Welcome to Berlin! There are many Canadians living in the city. On 15/11/2019 there is a Canadian Meetup at the Poutine Kitchen. Come out! [Tara C. Taylor @TaraCTaylor, Nov 6, 2019]

22. And so today, after 12 years in Canada, my wife and I took our oath of citizenship—we get to call this beautiful country home. And by chance it was at our kids school, in front of them and their classmates. Time for some maple doughnuts and poutine… eh! [Satvinder Flore @satflore, Nov 13, 2019]

23. Delicious things that could not exist without Canadian multiculturalism: Witness the butter chicken poutine [Dr Matthew Scarborough @mattitiahu, Nov 13, 2019]

24. Doesn't get anymore Canadian than this! Poutine and the @GFRapidshockey game [Jess @JessicaBurgoyn, Nov 13, 2019]

For those living or temporarily staying abroad, poutine becomes a taste of home and poutineries turn into a place of aggregation for fellow citizens, like in example (21). In other tweets, poutine is discursively paired with other symbols of Canada, e.g. multiculturalism in (23) and hockey in (24). In the first case, the user picks the plurality of Canadian cultures and flavours—the sentence is linguistically marked by the adjective "delicious" in initial position—over a traditional representation based on an authentic, and possibly Quebecois-only, recipe.[3] In the second case, the expression "doesn't get any more Canadian than this!" activates the correlation between food, sport and national identity discourse. It is in (22), however, that poutine is overtly associated with being and becoming "truly" Canadian. The user, as a matter of fact, is celebrating his and his wife's newly granted Canadian citizenship by showing a picture of his family with one of their children waving a small maple leaf flag and suggesting they eat some maple doughnuts and poutine. National identity and sense of belonging, moreover, are linguistically strengthened by the insertion of the typically Canadian tag "eh" at the end of the sentence (Denis 2020).

Alongside individuals, also social groups participate in the construction and performance of national identity through food and a series of events where collective identity is defined by the product(s) on display and momentarily shared by attendees:

> [T]he nation consists of diverse ethnic and cultural
> groups who are in constant competition in their claim
> to nationhood. In other words, we take the view that

---

3 The "multiculturization" of poutine is one of the strategies adopted in October 2019 by Air Canada to promote their eleven-day pop-up store at Boston Logan International Airport, where recipes inspired by other cuisines were presented to travelers: "Poutinerie by Air Canada is a pop-up that gives travelers from the Boston area the chance to explore flavors from some of our favorite destinations around the globe. In addition to classic Canadian poutine (French fries, cheese curds, gravy), the Poutinerie will serve up ten unique poutine dishes inspired by destinations like Casablanca, Toronto, Sao Paulo, London and Seoul" (aircanada.com).

the nation is a 'zone of conflict' […], a dynamic space where a variety of identities interact in the daily act of formation, revision and maintenance of the nation-ness (Ichijo and Ranta 2016: 43).

In this respect, food festivals are powerful triggers of identity as the Ottawa Poutine Fest and the Quebec City Hackfest testify to, especially when "dynamic space" is transferred online and becomes virtual. On their websites, as a matter of fact, poutine is presented as typically Canadian and authentically Quebecois respectively. For the 2017 edition, the Ottawa Poutine Fest created the following slogan:

WE ARE POUTINE!
Home of the Canadian Salad

WHY WE DO IT …

Simply … we love poutine. As Canada celebrates its 150th Birthday, PoutineFest is celebrating the Canadian Salad.

In the text there are several linguistic devices that contribute to the Canadianization of poutine: on the one hand, it is labelled as "Canadian salad", a shift in food category obliterating the association with junk food that stigmatized Quebecois poutine until the 2000s (Fabien-Ouellet 2016). On the contrary, as a salad, poutine sounds healthier and trendier, especially among young consumers. Moreover, besides the adjective "Canadian", the repetition of the personal pronoun "we" reinforces the connection between poutine and social group: the attendees of the Ottawa Poutine Fest are discursively asked to identify with the organizers who "love poutine" so as both, in turn, identify with the dish in a circular movement linking food, national identity, festival promoters and general public. Finally, the reference to the 150th "birthday" of the country and the parallel syntactic structure of the last two clauses explicitly associate poutine with nationhood and Canadianness.

As a bilingual hacking event taking place each November in Quebec City, Hackfest, on the other hand, is not directly about food or poutine. However, it used to organize an underground poutine party, which was turned into a poutine village for its 2019 edition. The dedicated page on the festival website, as a matter of fact, states that:

> Nothing says Quebec quite like poutine, and the mysterious poutine party at Hackfest has been an underground tradition for the past 3 years. This year, we are bringing it mainstream with an official Hackfest Poutine Village. Details of this village are shrouded in mystery, but rumour has it there may be a token for free poutine somewhere on the village floor? (hackfest.ca)

As in the examples discussed above, also in this case poutine is geographically bound and exclusively linked to Quebec by the insertion of the phrase "nothing says Quebec quite like" at the beginning of the short text. The same discursive representation, moreover, is disseminated on other social media. On Twitter, for instance, the association is linguistically realized through the phrasal verb "go together", which justified the creation of the "poutine village":

25. Because Quebec and Poutine goes [sic] together—Our secret poutine village is now official! Find your free poutine tokens in the event!!! [Hackfest.ca @hackfest_ca, Oct 23, 2019]

Conclusion

The online debate over poutine displays the tensions within the discourse of Canadian nationhood since Anglophone Canada and Francophone Quebec have historically interpreted and appropriated the term in different ways, i.e. Quebec as a nation within a nation and Canada as a confederation. The above-mentioned headline chosen by the *Montreal Gazette* to report on Toronto's unicorn poutine is quite telling as it addresses Canada as if Quebec were not part of it. From the point of view of an independent Quebec, as a matter of fact, the (Anglophone) Canadianization of poutine has to be read in terms of Ichijo and Ranta's global perspective, according to which "actions are taken [by nation-states] against attempts to appropriate what are seen as national food brands and or images and are viewed as direct attacks on the nation's heritage and culture (2016: 13). Anglophone Canada is thus represented as a foreign opposing national influence, a legacy of the British conquest of New France:

> The construction of a national food culture often takes place in opposition to the spread of what are perceived to be foreign, or in some cases opposing national, influences. This is especially true with regard to postcolonial states, where the construction and reproduction of a common food culture enforce and instil the idea of the nation in relation to the colonial power (Ichijo and Ranta 2016: 11).

A more reconciling interpretation can be added to the picture instead, since the growing popularity of poutine outside Quebec may be considered as a sign that Quebecois culture is getting recognition nationwide (Fabien-Ouellet 2016). The re-appropriation of poutine by Quebecois youth could be another element suggesting that it is about time Anglophone Canada and Francophone Quebec shared a common "national" dish besides maple syrup or decided that as a truly multicultural country they need none. The slogan in the picture[4] closing this paper may not be only an advertising strategy by Kraft Dinner, but a form of national belonging for all Canadians regardless the province they come from or the language they speak.

_____

4 I wish to thank Oriana Palusci, who took the picture in Toronto in August 2019, for sharing it with me and allowing me to use it for this paper.

Figure 1: Kraft Dinner's ad "Poutine Canada's National Dish"

Works Cited

AirCanada,"JoinusatPoutinerieby AirCanada"https://www.aircanada.com/us/en/aco/home/book/special-offers/aircanadafliestherepoutinerie.html (last accessed 13 November 2019).

Ashley, Bob, Hollows, Joanne, Jones, Steve and Taylor, Ben (2004) *Food and Cultural Studies*, London and New York: Routledge.

Barter, Judith A. (2013) *Art and Appetite: American Painting, Culture, and Cuisine*, Chicago, The Art Institute of Chicago.

Barthes, Roland (1972) [1957] *Mythologies*, New York: The Noonday Press (translated by Annette Lavers).

Bell, Claudia and Neill, Lindsay (2014) "A vernacular food tradition and national identity in New Zealand", *Food, Culture & Society*, 17.1, 49-64.

Billig, Michael (1995) *Banal Nationalism*, London: Sage.

Bodirsky, Monica and Johnson, Jon (2008) "Decolonizing diet: Healing by reclaiming traditional Indigenous foodways", *Cuizine: The Journal of Canadian Food Cultures / Cuizine: Revue des cultures culinaires au Canada*, 1.1, https://www.erudit.org/fr/revues/cuizine/2008-v1-n1-cuizine2503/019373ar/.

Caldwell, Mellisa (2002) "The taste of nationalism: Food politics in postsocialist Moscow", *Ethnos: Journal of Anthropology*, 67.3, 295-319.

Canadian Encyclopedia, "Poutine", https://www.thecanadianencyclopedia.ca/en/article/history-of-poutine, last accessed 13 November 2019.

Cooke, Nathalie (ed.) (2009) *What's to Eat? Entrées in Canadian Food History*, Montreal: McGill-Queen's University Press.

Cormack, Patricia (2008) "'True stories' of Canada: Tim Hortons and the branding of national identity", *Cultural Sociology*, 2.3, 369-384.

Cwiertka, Katarzyna J. (2006) *Modern Japanese Cuisine: Food, Power and National Identity*, London: Reaktion Books.

De Cillia, Rudolf, Reisigl, Martin and Wodak, Ruth (1999) "The discursive construction of national identities", *Discourse and Society*, 10.2, 149-173.

Denis, Derek (2020) "How Canadian was eh? A baseline investigation of usage and ideology", *Canadian Journal of Linguistics/Revue canadienne de linguistique*, 64.4, 583-592.

Desjardins, Renée (2011) "L'étude de menu comme representation de l'identité culinaire québécoise: Le cas des menus au Château Frontenac", *Cuizine: The Journal of Canadian Food Cultures / Cuizine: Revue des cultures culinaires au Canada*, 3.1, https://www.erudit.org/fr/revues/cuizine/2011-v3-n1-cuizine1807820/1004729ar/.

D'Sylva, Andrea and Beagan, Brenda L. (2011) "'Food is culture, but it's also power': The role of food in ethnic and gender identity construction among Goan women", *Journal of Gender Studies*, 20.3, 279-289.

Edensor, Tim (2002) *National Identity, Popular Culture and Everyday Life*, Oxford: Berg.

Everett, Holly (2011) "Newfoundland and Labrador on a plate: Bed, breakfast, and regional identity", *Cuizine: The Journal of Canadian Food Cultures / Cuizine: Revue des cultures culinaires au Canada*, 3.1, https://www.erudit.org/fr/revues/cuizine/2011-v3-n1-cuizine1807820/1004728ar/.

Fabien-Ouellet, Nicolas (2016) "Poutine dynamics", *Cuizine: The Journal of Canadian Food Cultures / Cuizine: Revue des cultures culinaires au Canada*, 7.2, https://www.erudit.org/fr/revues/cuizine/2016-v7-n2-cuizine02881/1038479ar/.

Fabien-Ouellet, Nicolas (2019) "The Canadian cuisine fallacy", in Ichijo, Atsuko, Johannes, Venetia and Ranta, Ronald (eds.) *The Emergence of National Food: The Dynamics of Food and Nationalism*, London: Bloomsbury Academic, 151-163.

Ferguson, Priscilla Parkhurst (2010) "Culinary nationalism", *Gastronomica. The Journal for Food Studies*, 10.1, 102-109.

Guy, Kolleen (2003) *When Champagne Became French: Wine and the Making of a National Identity*, Baltimore: Johns Hopkins University Press.

HackFest, "Poutine Village", https://hackfest.ca/en/villages/poutine/ (last accessed 13 November 2019).

Hiroko, Takeda (2008) "Delicious food in a beautiful country: Nationhood and nationalism in discourses on food in contemporary Japan", *Studies in Ethnicity and Nationalism*, 8.1, 5-30.

Ichijo, Atsuko and Ranta, Ronald (2016) *Food, National Identity and Nationalism: From Everyday to Global Politics*, Basingstoke: Palgrave Macmillan.

Imilan, Walter (2015) "Performing national identity through Peruvian food migration in Santiago de Chile", *Fennia—International Journal of Geography*, 193.2, 227-241.

Metro-Roland, Michelle Marie (2013) "Goulash nationalism: The culinary identity of a nation", *Journal of Heritage Tourism*, 8.2-3, 172-181.

Mitz, Sidney (2008) "Food and diaspora", *Food, Culture & Society. An International Journal of Multidisciplinary Research*, 11.4, 509-523.

Montanari, Massimo (2004) *Il cibo come cultura*, Bari: Laterza.

Monterescu, Daniel (2017) "Border wines: Terroir across contested territory", *Gastronomica. The Journal for Food Studies*, 17.4, 127-140.

Montreal Gazette, (2019) "Canada promoted 'unicorn poutine' on Twitter, and now we may be separatists?", https://montrealgazette.com/news/local-news/canada-promoted-unicorn-poutine-on-twitter-and-now-we-may-be-separatists (last accessed 13 November 2019).

Nowak, Zachary, Jones, Bradley M. and Ascione, Elisa (2020) "Disciplining polenta: A parody on the politics of saving food", *Gastronomica. The Journal for Food Studies*, 20.2, 1-11.

Rabikowska, Marta (2010) "The ritualisation of food, home and national identity among Polish migrants in London"; *Social Identities: Journal for the Study of Race, Nation and Culture*, 16.3, 377-398.

Raviv, Yael (2015) *Falafel Nation: Cuisine and the Making of National Identity in Israel*, Lincoln: University of Nebraska Press.

Reddy, Geeta and van Dam, Rob M. (2020) "Food, culture, and identity in multicultural societies: Insights from Singapore", *Appetite*, 149, 1-12.

Rioux, Laurie-Eve, Perrault, Véronique and Turgeon, Sylvie L. (2020) "Textural characteristics of Canadian foods: Influences and properties of poutine cheese and maple products", in Nishinari, Katsuyoshi (ed.) *Textural Characteristics of World Foods*, New York: Wiley, 37-51.

Rozin, Paul and Siegal, Michael (2003) "Vegemite as a marker of national identity", *Gastronomica. The Journal for Food Studies*, 3.4, 63-67.

Snell, Rachel A. (2014) "As North American as pumpkin pie: Cookbooks and the development of national cuisine in North America, 1796-1854", *Cuizine: The Journal of Canadian Food Cultures / Cuizine:*

Revue des cultures culinaires au Canada, 5.2, https://www.erudit.org/fr/revues/cuizine/2014-v5-n2-cuizine01533/1026771ar/.

Théorêt, Charles-Alexandre (2007) *Maudite poutine! L'histoire approximative d'un plat populaire*, Montréal: Éditions Héliotrope.

Tovares, Alla and Gordon, Cynthia (eds.) (2020) *Ideology in Digital Food Discourse: Social Media Interactions Across Cultural Contexts*, London, Bloomsbury Academic.

Vallianatos, Helen and Raine, Kim (2008) "Consuming food and constructing identities among Arabic and South Asian immigrant women", *Food, Culture & Society. An International Journal of Multidisciplinary Research*, 11.3, 355-373.

Wilmsherst, Sara (2013) "How to eat like a Canadian: Centennial cookbooks and visions of culinary identity", *Cuizine: The Journal of Canadian Food Cultures / Cuizine: Revue des cultures culinaires au Canada*, 4.2, https://www.erudit.org/fr/revues/cuizine/2013-v4-n2-cuizine0888/1019317ar/.

Wilson, Thomas M. (ed.) (2006) *Food, Drink and Identity in Europe*, Amsterdam: Rodopi.

Zappavigna, Michele (2012) *Discourse of Twitter: How We Use Language to Create Affiliation on the Web*, London: Bloomsbury.

RENÉ GEORGES MAURY

Un goût du vin affirmé au Canada— fortes croissances de la consommation vinicole et de la production viticole

À la mémoire de Louis-Edmond HAMELIN (1923-2020),
Maître de la Géographie canadienne
("L'âme de la terre", 2006)

Introduction

DANS L'IMAGE GÉNÉRALE QU'ON SE fait du Canada, la présence de la vigne et du vin pourraient surprendre nombre de personnes. Pourtant quel touriste curieux, travailleur ou chercheur parcourant cet immense pays, ne manquera pas de s'étonner en apercevant çà et là des vignes parmi les cultures agricoles variées du sud canadien, et en ayant la possibilité de déguster, à une table de restaurant ou à celle d'amis ou collègues, un vin d'importation ou, plus étonnant encore, de production locale. Le cas du Canada est en effet fort intéressant à cet égard: l'augmentation de la consommation vinicole mais aussi de la production viticole du pays sont-elles le résultat du changement climatique et/ou d'une nouvelle mode de consommation?

Les fortes croissances de la consommation et de la production des vins au Canada, au Québec

S'il semble que des vignes sauvages aient été aperçues, au Xème siècle déjà, par l'explorateur viking Leif Erikson, non loin des côtes de l'actuelle Nouvelle Écosse (Vinland), puis bien plus tard, non sans surprise, par les colonisateurs français Jacques Cartier (en 1535) et Samuel de Champlain (en 1603), qui découvrent une sorte de vigne au Québec—probablement s'agit-il de lambrusques ou peut-être confondent-ils des variétés de baies ou myrtilles pour des raisins[1]—ce n'est qu'au XIXème siècle, après quelques modestes tentatives qui furent surtout le fait de communautés religieuses, que de courageux colons entreprirent de planter des vignes de manière plus rationnelle au Canada, dans le cadre d'une diversification de cultures agricoles modernes, sous l'impulsion d'un marché urbain demandeur et avec le soutien de capitaux et cavistes européens. D'abord dans l'extrême sud de l'Ontario (la Péninsule du Niagara), au climat favorable, à des latitudes méditerranéennes, au beau milieu d'autres cultures irriguées, fruitières et maraîchères, y compris le tabac, d'un bon rendement, durant les relativement chaudes saisons printanière et estivale (Rougier, 1987). Le premier essai, jugé moderne et rationnel, date de 1866 dans l'Île Pelée **(FIG. 1 : vigna Colio)**. Le développement successif intéressa non seulement l'ensemble de la partie méridionale de la riche province, dans le courant du XXème siècle, et plus tard, dans les années 1970 et 1980, des vallées et bassins encaissés de la Colombie britannique (Okanagan, Fraser), puis se répandit rapidement, au cours de ces deux dernières décennies, dans les provinces orientales (surtout au Québec, également dans l'Île du Prince Edward, au Nouveau-Brunswick et en Nouvelle-Écosse) si l'on en juge par le nombre de vignobles et

---

1 Du *Journal* de Jacques Cartier (1535): "… y treuvasme force vignes, ce que n'avyons veu, par cy-devant à toute la terre; et pour ce, la nommasmes L'ISLE DE BASCUS [l'actuelle Île d'Orléans]".

caves, par la quantité de production de vins de relative bonne qualité, le tout accompagné d'une politique de soutien à la sélection de meilleurs cépages et à la qualité des vins, et d'une commercialisation plus rationnelle et diversifiée.[2]

Longtemps considéré comme pays importateur de vins, le Canada figure désormais parmi les pays producteurs viticoles, en 19ème position, bien loin des grands pays producteurs (Italie, France, Espagne, USA, Argentine, Chine, Chili) et de beaucoup d'autres pays dans le monde. Avec 548 000 hl, ce pays d'Amérique du Nord ne représente que 0,24% de la production mondiale (évaluée à 260 M d'hl).

Au Canada, la superficie plantée en vigne est de 11 195 ha (7,4 M d'ha dans le monde).[3] On relèvera toutefois la forte augmentation de ces toutes dernières décennies, une véritable explosion de 550% entre 2003 et 2016, et la grosse activité commerciale, liée à une demande croissante, concernant aussi bien des importations massives, que des exportations, quoique rares, de qualité.

Sur une superficie cultivée en vignes de 12 627 hectares au Canada en 2019, la production est évaluée à 70 millions de litres de vin. Si l'Ontario reste de loin la première province, en plus d'être la pionnière dans le secteur viti-vinicole (62% de la production totale), et que la Colombie britannique confirme un bonne seconde place (33%, avec l'extension du vignoble, soit 10 zones déclarées; Pélouas, 2019), c'est bien le Québec qui affiche le plus

---

2 Comme exemple d'une winery moyenne de l'Ontario: la *Colio Estate Wines*, sur 240 acres (0.97km²) de vignoble et cave renommée, située à Harrow (à la latitude de la Toscane), créée en 1980 par l'immigré italien Carlo Negri, produit des vins blancs et rouges et du vin de glace.

3 Selon l'OIV-Organisation Internationale de la vigne et du vin (Paris). L'OIV est une organisation intergouvernementale à caractère scientifique et technique dont la compétence est reconnue dans le domaine de la vigne, du vin, des boissons à base de vin, des raisins de table, des raisins secs et autres produits issus de la vigne, qui rassemble 47 États membres, de pays producteurs et pays consommateurs, et publie des statistiques mondiales et divers documents, comme référence du monde des vignes et vins.

vif dynamisme durant ces toutes dernières années pour atteindre, en 2017, 808 ha plantés sur 138 vignobles (11 en 1990), ce qui montre, par là même, l'euphorie du secteur de production viti-vini-cole (Lasserre & Dorval, 2019).

Un engouement, ce nouveau goût du vin illustrant certains phénomènes au Canada, au Québec: un nouveau mode de consommation et la diffusion de l'œno-tourisme dans un contexte de changement climatique

Le goût des Canadiens pour les vins canadiens, qui représentent 40 % du marché, a stimulé la multiplication de nouveaux vignobles et caves, ainsi que du tourisme rural, dans l'ensemble du pays, non seulement dans les trois grandes provinces viticoles du pays, mais aussi ailleurs, notamment dans les provinces atlantiques. On peut facilement relever ce véritable engouement collectif (producteurs, consommateurs), qui se manifeste lors de fêtes de vendanges ou autres occasions, dans les caves, souvent de belles résidences de particuliers ou bien acquises à des fins de production, transformées en petites entreprises viti-vinicoles, mais aussi en agréables struc-tures agro-touristiques, qui génèrent des emplois familiaux ou non, (techniciens et œnologues), mais aussi dans le secteur commercial. L'œno-tourisme est désormais pratiqué dans tous les pays viticoles, nouveaux et anciens, des USA au Chili, en passant par l'Australie, l'Afrique du sud et la Chine, qui s'affiche désormais comme un nouveau grand pays viticole. Au Canada, on organise des fêtes de vin, une Cuvée Grand Tasting en Ontario et des week-end Wine Experience, des Routes du vin, etc. (Hope-Ross, 2006).

Si l'on s'en tient seulement au Québec—et aux Québécois, qui sont les plus gros consommateurs de vins au Canada (18,2 litres/adulte/an; moyenne du Canada: 16,5 l; 80,3 l de bière; 7,4 l d'al-cools supérieurs)—la courbe ascendante est aussi bien relevée dans la consommation générale que dans la production locale. Ce n'est qu'à partir du début des années 1980 que deux vignobles, *l'Orpailleur* et les *Côtes d'Ardoise*, décidèrent de relever le défi de la culture commerciale de la vigne malgré les rigueurs du climat. Ensuite, on assiste récemment à la multiplication de petites maisons aux noms caractéristiques ou imaginatifs, soit 224 exploitations (630 ha), présentes surtout en Montérégie (la moitié des viticulteurs) et dans les autres régions agricoles moins froides du Québec, la plupart de quelques hectares, mais qui dynamisent d'une certaine façon le milieu rural et le rapport villes-campagnes dans la Belle Province (Zerouala, 2010).[4]

Les Canadiens, comme, du reste, aux États-Unis et ailleurs, s'orientent de plus en plus vers un modèle de consommation mondialisé euro-méditerranéen (fruits et légumes, pâtes et pizzas, huile d'olive, vin …), et non plus seulement le modèle anglais (viandes, laitages et matières grasses, thé, bière …), comme l'illustrent la place donnée au vin parmi les boissons considérées comme faiblement alcoolisées et la nette diminution de la bière.[5]

Par ailleurs, d'autres boissons alcoolisées sont caractéristiques du Canada, parmi lesquelles figure le cidre, très prisé (obtenu à partir de la fermentation des pommes), comme dans la plupart des pays atlantiques européens et dans le New England, et la plus célèbre qui est l'icewine (ou vin de glace), primé et exporté. Bien souvent, c'est ainsi que ces maisons, qu'elles soient grandes ou petites, diversifient les produits de la vigne et des vergers et autres

---

4 Quelques domaines viticoles au Québec: *Vignoble de l'Orpailleur* (34 ha), *Les 1001 vignes, Domaine des Trois-Moulins, Le Cep d'Argent, Le Chat-Botté, Saint-Rémi* (9 ha), *Isle de Bacchus* (12 ha), *Vignoble de la Source à Marguerite* (3 ha de vigne, cave et cidrerie), *Domaine des Trois-fûts, Les Vents d'Ange, Coteau Rougemont* (vignoble et cidrerie).

5 Selon un entretien avec le grand géographe canadien Louis-Edmond Hamelin (1926-2020). Selon Mathieu Perreault (La Presse.Ca): Le vin continue de gagner du terrain au Québec, alors que le déclin de la bière progresse peu à peu. Une nouvelle étude de *Statistique Canada* montre que la bière est passée de 64% à 55% du total des ventes depuis 2000, alors que le vin grimpait de 24% à 33%.

dérivés dans leurs offres commerciales au public.[6] Signalons aussi la production croissante de vins issus de la fermentation de fruits et légumes (pêches, tomates, miel, rhubarbe; sirop d'érable, etc.), étiquetés comme tels, au Canada comme désormais dans beaucoup de pays de par le monde, répandus dans les Prairies et autres zones plus froides du pays, mais aussi produits par les caves viticoles et cidreries, qui cherchent ainsi à diversifier leurs produits, en les destinant aussi à des clients abstèmes. (**FIG. 2**)

Cependant, un développement si rapide de vignes et vins au Canada n'est pas sans être relié au réchauffement climatique de la Planète, très sensible dans les hautes latitudes boréales et australes, donc en Amérique du nord - l'ouverture estivale du Passage au Nord-Ouest arctique n'en est qu'un exemple (Lasserre, 2010; Maury, 2010; Maury, 2011). Comme dans le sud austral (Argentine, Chili, Nouvelle-Zélande), les vignes gagnent en latitude: au Canada, plus au nord du Québec, de l'Ontario et de la Colombie britannique, non sans un effort particulier du viticulteur, qui s'astreint à un labeur agricole harassant et incertain - ne parle-t-on pas, en québécois, de renchaussage et débuttage (couvrir et déchausser) ainsi que d'autres moyens pour protéger les ceps de vigne de grands froids prolongés (Lasserre and Dorval, 2019).

Ce double aspect de la situation évolutive des vignes et vins au Canada représente dans son suivi une approche utile pour mesurer le rapport homme-nature, qualité de la vie et culture, dans un double contexte continental américain et mondial (Hamelin, 1980; Manzagol, 2006).

---

6 L'icewine (vin de glace) est une boisson alcoolisée résultant d'une fermentation de jus de raisins en surmaturité glacés, vendangés en plein hiver. Inventée en Allemagne à la fin du XVIIIème siècle à la suite d'un gel imprévu, cette méthode fut plus ou moins pratiquée dans quelques pays (elle s'apparente vaguement au *vin santo* italien), mais remporta un vif succès au Canada dès 1978 (Colombie britannique, Ontario, Québec) qui l'a rendue célèbre et commercialisée aussi à l'étranger. On y produit aussi un cidre de glace (fermentation de jus de pommes gelées). *Sortilège* est le nom commercial d'une liqueur originale à base de whisky canadien et de sirop d'érable, "produit du terroir québécois", de la *Maison des Futailles* (1922).

Conclusion

Si le vin est à la fois culture (agricole) et culture (culturelle), soit un savoir-faire, un esprit—ici au Canada, une passion et une fermeté, un courage, un travail harassant, pour reprendre une idée là-bas très répandue, un tel engouement pour les vins exprime à la fois une évolution d'esprit dans un cadre naturel et géopolitique, comportemental que le Canada exprime par son originalité, dans un contexte mondial général. Le goût très prononcé pour le vin au Canada, au Québec en particulier, en est un exemple.[7]

Works Cited

Hamelin, Louis-Edmond (1980), *Nordicité canadienne*, Québec: Hurtubise HMH.

Hamelin, Louis-Edmond (2006), *L'âme de la Terre. Parcours d'un géographe*, Québec: MultiMondes.

Hope-Ross, Penny (2006), *De la vigne à la coupe: la production de raisins et du vin au Canada*. Ottawa: Statistiques Canada.

Lasserre, Frédéric (2010), *Passages et mers arctiques. Géopolitique d'une région en mutation*, Québec: Presses de l'Université du Québec.

Lasserre, Frédéric and Dorval, Guy (2019), *Le développement des vignobles canadiens et l'impact des changements climatiques*, conférence "Les rencontres du Clos-Vougeot, Québec, 3,4,5 octobre 2019 ".

Manzagol, Claude (2003), *La mondialisation*, Paris: Armand Colin, 2003.

Maury, René Georges (2018), "Northern american atmosphere (Canada, Alaska, Greenland): ecumene and nordicity in Canada, climate change and geostrategies in the far and extreme north", in AA.VV, *Atmosphere/Atmospheres*, Mimesis International, 99-110.

---

7 Ce texte est une mise à jour d'études et recherches au Canada et d'un texte en cours de publication à la suite d'une conférence auprès du Centre d'Études du Québec et des Francophonies d'Amérique du Nord à Paris. Remerciements à Frédéric Lasserre et Anna Romei pour la collaboration à ce travail.

Maury, René Georges (2010), "De la Méditerranée au Canada: questions d'eau, de climat et d'environnement", in Buono A. and Zito M. (eds), *Ambiente e società canadesi, Environnement et sociétés canadiennes, Environment and Canadian Societies*, Napoli: Università degli Studi "L'Orientale", 323-351.

Maury, René Georges. "Geostrategia artica", *Bollettino della Società Geografica Italiana*, 3, 2011: 615-616.

Pélouas, Anne (2019), "Le Canada, terroir d'avenir - Du sable, du vin et des ours, bienvenue dans l'Okanagan", in *Le Monde des vins*, 05-09-2019.

Rougier, Henri (1987), *Espaces et régions du Canada*, Paris: Ellipses.

Zerouala, Larbi (2010), *Portrait de la viticulture au Québec* (texte de la conférence présentée à Agri-réseau), Québec: MAPAQ.

Fig. 1: Vignes *Colio Estate Wines* (Harrow, Ontario) (Ph.: RgM)

Fig. 2: Vignoble et cidrerie *Domaine de la Source à Marguerite*
(Île d'Orléans, Québec) (Ph.: RgM)

NOTES ON CONTRIBUTORS

Esterino Adami is associate professor of English language and translation at the University of Turin (Italy). His main research areas include critical stylistics, postcolonial writing and sociolinguistics. He has published articles and book chapters on various linguistic, literary and cultural aspects on food ("What's in a Curry? Interdisciplinary Approaches to Indian Food Discourse", 2019, and "Pragmatics and the Aesthetics of Food Discourse: *Jamie's Italy*", 2017), naming and ideology in the postcolonial Indian world, and the narrative rendition of specialised discourse (botany, food, the railways). He has authored *Railway Discourse. Linguistic and Stylistic Representations of the Train in the Anglophone World* (2018) and co-edited *Other Worlds and the Narrative Construction of Otherness* (2017, with F. Bellino and A. Mengozzi).

Angela Buono enseigne les littératures francophones à l'Université de Naples "L'Orientale" (Italy). Spécialiste de la littérature franco-canadienne et québécoise, elle fait partie du Conseil de Direction de l'Association Italienne d'Études Canadiennes. Elle a écrit plusieurs articles et prononcé de nombreuses communications sur l'œuvre de Hédi Bouraoui, de Marie-Claire Blais et sur les écritures migrantes. Ses intérêts de recherche portent actuellement sur les littératures autochtones du Québec et sur les nouvelles approches critiques des littératures émergentes.

Rita Calabrese (PhD) is professor in English Language and Linguistics at the University of Salerno (Italy), where she teaches. She is the author of several monographs, including *Insights into the Lexicon-Syntax Interface in Italian Learners* (2008) and essays on the use of corpora for teaching purposes (*Corpus Linguistics and English as a foreign language*, 2004). In 2015 she co-edited *Variation and Change in Postcolonial Contexts* (with J. Chambers and G. Leitner). She is currently working on a diachronic corpus of Indian English including data from the years between 1839 and 2011.

Licia Canton, PhD (Université de Montréal), is the author of *The Pink House and Other Stories* (2018) and *Almond Wine and Fertility* (2008), published in Italy as *Vino alla mandorla e fertilità* (2015). Her writing deals with women and the sandwich generation, cultural and culinary heritage, and overcoming trauma and depression. A literary translator and self-translator, her writing has been anthologized internationally in English, French, Chinese, Italian and Venetian dialect. The co-founder and editor-in-chief of *Accenti Magazine*, she is also the (co)editor of ten volumes, including two on the internment of Italian Canadians during WWII. She received the 2018 Premio Italia nel Mondo for her work in culture. In June 2019, she was Visiting Professor and Writer-in-Residence at the University of Calabria.

Mirko Casagranda (PhD) is associate professor of English Linguistics and Translation Studies at the University of Calabria (Italy). His areas of interest include onomastics, variational sociolinguistics, critical discourse analysis, gender studies, postcolonial studies, and translation studies. He has published articles on gender and translation, ecocritical discourse analysis, multiculturalism and multilingualism in Canada, place and trade names. He has edited the volume *Names and Naming in the Postcolonial English-Speaking World* (2018) and authored the books *Traduzione e codeswitching come strategie discorsive del plurlinguismo canadese* (2010) and *Strategie di naming nel paesaggio linguistico canadese* (2013).

Carmen Concilio is professor of English and postcolonial literature at the University of Turin (Italy). She is recipient of *Canada-Italy Innovation Award 2021*. Since 1999 she has been a member of

AISC and former recipient of Faculty Enrichment Programme Awards. Since 2016 she has been president of AISCLI. In the field of Canadian Studies, she translated short stories by Nino Ricci and published on various novelists, including H. O'Haggan, M. Ondaatje, A. Michaels, A. Munro, A. York, M. Thien, poets R. Bringhurst and M. Dumont, and artists E. Carr and M. Creates. Her most recent contribution is "The Mark on the Floor": Alice Munro on Ageing and Alzheimer's Disease in *The Bear Came Over the Mountain* and Sarah Polley's *Away From Her.*

Nathalie Cooke is professor of English and associate dean of the Library at McGill University in Montréal. Her publications focus on Canadian literature and foodways. She is founding editor of the journal *CuiZine: the Journal of Canadian Food Cultures* (2009-), editor of *What's to Eat? Entrées into Canadian Food History* (2009), and co-editor of *Catharine Parr Traill's* Female Emigrant's Guide, *Cooking with a Canadian Classic* (2017). Cooke is currently working with colleagues on *Canadian Literary Fare,* a book that looks to what Canadian authors serve their characters in their poetry, fiction and drama—and what stories such choices can tell.

Ylenia De Luca est professeur agrégé de littérature française à l'Université Aldo Moro de Bari (Italie). Elle est directeur de la Revue: "Echo" et Président du Cours en Sciences de la Communication. Elle s'intéresse à la poésie canadienne de langue française entre le XX et le XXI siècle, à la poésie française du XX siècle ainsi qu'à la littérature francophone contemporaine et à la littérature de voyage et de genre. Elle a déjà publié quatre volumes sur ces thèmes et de nombreux essais dans des revues nationales et internationales.

Daniela Fargione is former Fulbright scholar at the University of Massachusetts, Amherst, where she earned her Ph.D. in Comparative Literature. Currently, she teaches American Literatures at the University of Turin (Italy). Her main research interests include: environmental humanities (food and migrations), the interconnections of modern and contemporary American literatures and the other arts, translation studies. Among her recent publications: *Antroposcenari. Storie, paesaggi, ecologie* (2018), co-edited with Carmen Concilio, and *ContaminAzioni ecologiche: cibi, nature e culture* (2015), co-edited with Serenella Iovino. She is one of the two current translators of Julian Barnes's works (Einaudi).

Alessandra Ferraro est Professeure de Littérature française et Littératures francophones à l'Université d'Udine. Co-fondatrice du Centro di Cultura Canadese et du Centro Internazionale di Ricerca sulle Letterature Migranti, elle co-dirige la revue *Oltreoceano. Rivista sulle migrazioni* (Udine), fait partie du Comité éditorial d'*Italian Canadiana* (Toronto) et du Comité Scientifique de *Ponti. Ponts. Langues, littératures, civilisations des Pays francophones* (Milan). Auteure du volume *Écriture migrante et translinguisme au Québec* (2014), elle a édité plusieurs collectifs sur les littératures et les cultures du Canada. Parmi ses ouvrages: *L'autotraduction littéraire: perspectives théoriques* (avec Rainier Grutman 2016) et *Marie de l'Incarnation, la Relation de 1654. Postface, chronologie et bibliographie* (2016). Elle dirige avec É. Nardout-Lafarge la collection "Littérature québécoise" (Bibliothèque francophone) aux éditions Classiques Garnier (Paris).

Eva Gruber is associate professor of American Studies at the University of Konstanz, Germany. Her research interests include Indigenous North American literatures and film, conceptualizations of race in 20th- and 21st-century American literature, and the fields of Critical Race Narratology and literature and food. She is the author of *Humor in Native North American Literature: Reimagining Nativeness* (2008) and the editor of *Thomas King: Works and Impact* (2011), *Literature and Terrorism: Comparative Perspectives* (with Michael Frank. 2011) as well as *Gained Ground: Perspectives on Canadian and Comparative North American Studies* (with Caroline Rosenthal, 2018). She has also published on space in Caribbean-Canadian writing and on the politics of translation.

Roberta La Peruta is a Ph.D. candidate at the University of Naples "L'Orientale". Her thesis focuses on *Post-diasporic English in Canada: Language, Identity and Migration*. She specialized in cognitive and functional linguistics at KU Leuven (Belgium), with a thesis on complementizer choice in several varieties of English. Her research interests include World Englishes, variationist sociolinguistics, corpus linguistics, and cultural linguistic representations. She recently authored papers on linguistic epicentral constellations, diasporic language and belonging, cultural commodification through the language of food, gender issues and pronominality, and future tense patterns.

René Georges Maury est professeur retraité de Géographie humain à l'Université de Naples "L'Orientale" (Italy), chargé du cours de Géographie régionale de l'Amérique, titulaire de bourses de recherche au Canada, membre du Centro di Studi Canadesi—Società e Territori (Université "L'Orientale"). Parmi ses publications sur le Canada: "De la Méditerranée au Canada: questions d'eau, de climat et d'environnement" (2010) et "Northern American Atmosphere (Canada, Alaska, Greenland): Ecumene and Nordicity in Canada, Climate Change and Geostrategies in the Far and Extreme North" (2018).

Marco Modenesi (Milan, 1960) est professeur de Littérature française et de Littératures francophones à l'Università degli Studi de Milan. Dans le domaine de la Littérature française, ses recherches et ses publications portent sur le roman et sur la poésie fin-de-siècle et sur la première moitié du XXe siècle. Dans ces domaines, il a publié de nombreux essais (Huysmans, Baudelaire, Mallarmé, Rimbaud, Rachilde, Rodenbach, Max Jacob, Apollinaire, Green). Dans le domaine des Littératures francophones, il s'intéresse en particulier aux littératures extra-européennes, notamment du Canada (Québec, Acadie), de l'Afrique subsaharienne (Mali, Burkina-Faso, Bénin, Sénégal, Togo) et des Caraïbes. Il est l'auteur de plusieurs essais, et, avec Liana Nissim et Silvia Riva, d'une histoire de la littérature du

Mali (*L'incanto del fiume, il tormento della savana. Storia della lettera-tura del Mali*, 1993). Il est directeur de la revue *Ponti/Ponts. Langues littératures civilisations des pays francophones* depuis 2014. Il dirige, avec Liana Nissim, la collection d'études françaises et francophones "Multiples" aux Editions MIMESIS.

Anna Mongibello, PhD, is Tenure-track Researcher in English Language at the University of Naples "L'Orientale". Her research interests range from the intersections of language, ideology, power and identity to news discourse and translation in the Canadian context, explored through the lens of Critical Discourse Analysis and the tools of Corpus Linguistics. She has been a member of the board of the Italian Association for Canadian Studies (AISC) since 2017. She has authored *Indigenous Peoples in Canadian TV News: a Corpus-based Analysis of Mainstream and Indigenous News Discourses* (2018) and *Geografie alternative: scrittrici indigene contemporanee del Canada anglofono (2013)*.

Oriana Palusci is a professor of English at the University of Naples 'L'Orientale' (Italy). She has published extensively on con-temporary Women writers, Gender Studies, Utopia and Science Fiction, Travel Writing, Postcolonial Studies, Translation Studies, Canadian Linguistics and Cultures, the Languages of Tourism, Critical Toponymy, and Environmental issues. She has recently ed-ited: *Wastelands. Eco-narratives in Contemporary Cultures in English* (2015, with H. Ventura), *Green Canada* (2016), *Alice Munro and the Anatomy of the Short Story* (2017), *Miss Man? Languaging Gendered Bodies* (2018, with G. Balirano). She is the current President of the Italian Association for Canadian Studies and President of the Centre for Canadian Studies at the University of Naples 'L'Orientale'.

Julia Siepak graduated with both a BA and an MA degree in English Studies from Nicolaus Copernicus University in Toruń (Poland), as well as with a BA degree in Interdisciplinary Studies (English and

Native American studies) from Southern Oregon University. She is currently a PhD student in Interdisciplinary Studies at NCU. Her research focuses on the poetics of space emphasizing intersections between the feminine and the environmental in contemporary North American Indigenous fiction in English. Julia is a member of the Polish Association for Canadian Studies.

Kamelia Talebian Sedehi was born in Iran in 1987. She received her B.A. (2009) and M.A. (2011) in English Literature from the University of Isfahan. She received her PhD (2016) in English Literature from University Putra Malaysia. Currently, she is doing her second PhD at Sapienza University, Rome and her thesis is on trauma and witnessing in Canadian residential schools. Her publications include: *The Melancholic Subject and The Bluest Eye, Beloved and Kristevan Melancholic Subject*, and *Natural Selection and The Cage* and some other titles. Her research interests are trauma, melancholia, identity crisis, comparative studies and interdisciplinary topics. She has presented at various national and international conferences.

Simona Stano is Tenure-Track Assistant Professor at the University of Turin and vice-Director of the Centre for Interdisciplinary Research on Communication (CIRCe). Her work focuses mainly on the semiotics of culture, food, corporeality and media communication. She has published several papers on these topics, edited volumes (including special issues of top semiotic journals such as *Semiotica* and *Lexia*), and monographs (*I sensi del cibo*, 2018; *Eating the Other. Translations of the Culinary Code*, 2015). She was awarded a Marie Curie Global Fellowship for a research project (COMFECTION, 2019-2021) on the semiotic analysis of food communication.

Marina Zito a été professeure de Littérature Française auprès de l'Université de Naples "L'Orientale" où elle a proposé la fondation du Centre d'Etudes Canadiennes "Sociétés et Territoires"—dont elle a été la Présidente pendant une décennie. Ses intérêts envers la francophonie nordaméricaine datent de la rencontre avec la poésie d'Hector de Saint-Denys Garneau dont Raïssa Maritain avait écrit un témoignage lors de son séjour en Amérique. Ensuite Marina Zito a bénéficié de plusieurs bourses d'étude du Gouvernement Canadien qui ont abouti à une série d'articles : sur Gabrielle Roy, Laure Conan, Anne Hébert naturellement, Jacques Brault, Hubert Aquin, Benoît Lacroix, Robert Lalonde, Cécile Cloütier, Rita Mestokosho. Elle a promu la traduction italienne de *Agonie* de Jacques Brault et de *Où vont les sizerins flammés en été?* de Robert Lalonde. Livre : *Itinéraires littéraires et spirituels : Raïssa Maritain, de Saint-Denys Garneau, Anne Hébert* (2004).

Silvia Domenica Zollo est *Doctor Europaeus* en "Eurolinguaggi scientifici, tecnologici e letterari" (Université de Naples Parthenope) et enseignant-chercheur en linguistique française auprès du Département de Langues et littératures étrangères de l'Université de Vérone. Ses principaux axes de recherches sont la lexicologie historique, les langues de spécialité et la didactique du FLE (*Français Langue Étrangère*). Parallèlement, elle s'intéresse aux mécanismes de construction morpho-lexicale et sémantico-discursive de nouveaux phénomènes langagiers dans les médias numériques français et francophones. Elle est membre du secrétariat de REALITER (Réseau panlatin de terminologie) et de nombreux projets de recherche nationaux et internationaux, tels que *Néoveille, Termorfèvre* et *Corsi MOOCs per un percorso sperimentale di didattica delle lingue straniere*.

Valeria Zotti est professeure associée de langue et traduction française à l'Université de Bologne. Lexicologue de formation, ses recherches portent principalement sur la lexicographie, la linguistique de corpus et le traitement automatique des langues. Elle s'est consacrée à l'étude de la traduction du lexique québécois et, récemment, de l'apport de l'intelligence artificielle dans l'industrie des langues. Elle est membre et secrétaire du CISQ (Centre

Interuniversitaire d'Etudes Québécoises) depuis 2007. Elle a coordonné le travail de création de la base de données numériques de traductions littéraires QU.IT Québec-Italie (2013). Parmi ses publications: la monographie *Dictionnaire bilingue et francophonie. Le français québécois* (2007) et les ouvrages *La variation des français. Dictionnaires, bases de données, corpus* (avec A. Farina, 2014), *Informatica umanistica: risorse e strumenti per lo studio del lessico dei beni culturali* (avec A. Pano Alaman, 2017), *The Language of Art and Cultural Heritage: a Pluringual and Digital Perspective* (avec A. Pano Alaman, 2020).

Éva Zsizsmann completed the English and American Literatures and Cultures PhD Programme at the University of Szeged, Hungary. Her field of research covers Postcolonial studies, Canadian literature as well as place and memory in contemporary Canadian fiction, with a special focus on Alice Munro's short stories. In 2012 and 2013 she was a doctoral research fellow at the Wirth Institute, University of Alberta, Edmonton, Canada. She currently teaches ESP (English for Special Purposes) and translation at Szent István University and the Károli Gáspár University of the Reformed Church, both in Budapest.

Printed in September 2022
by Gauvin Press,
Gatineau, Québec